PANZER
OPERATIONS

The Eastern Front Memoir of
General Raus, 1941–1945

ERHARD RAUS

Compiled and Translated by
STEVEN H. NEWTON

DA CAPO PRESS
A Member of the Perseus Books Group

Library of Congress Cataloging-in-Publication Data

Raus, Erhard, 1889-1956.
  Panzer operations : the Eastern Front memoir of General Raus,
1941-1945 / Erhard Raus ; compiled and translated by Steven H. Newton.
      p. cm.
Reconstruction of a lost original manuscript by General Raus through the use of other writings by him, both published and unpublished.
  ISBN 0-306-81247-9
  1. Raus, Erhard, 1889–1956. 2. Generals—Germany—Biography. 3. World War, 1939-1945—Tank warfare. 4. World War, 1939–1945—Campaigns—Eastern Front. I. Newton, Steven H. II. Title.
  D764.R337A3 2003
  940.54'1343'092—dc22

                                                                              2003017612

Set in Sabon MT by the Perseus Books Group

First Da Capo Press edition 2003
Published by Da Capo Press
A Member of the Perseus Books Group
http://www.dacapopress.com

Da Capo Press books are available at special discounts for bulk purchases in the U.S. by corporations, institutions, and other organizations. For more information, please contact the Special Markets Department at the Perseus Books Group, 11 Cambridge Center, Cambridge, MA 02142, or call (800) 255-1514 or (617) 252-5298, or email j.mccrary@perseusbooks.com

1 2 3 4 5 6 7 8 9–07 06 05 04 03

TO LIN THOMPSON,
*Who taught me to be very careful about
handling other people's words*

CONTENTS

MAPS

ACKNOWLEDGMENTS

This narrative never would have been recovered without the assistance of Andrew Heilmann and Jonathon Scott, who located and copied several key fragments of Raus's work at the National Archives. Lieutenant Colonel David Wrenn, Executive Officer, 1st Brigade, 29th Infantry Division (Light), deserves much of the credit for teaching me how to read battle narratives critically, and how to make even the most complex tactical situations more clear to the reader. I received constant encouragement (and the occasional free lunch) from Dr. Yohuru Williams of Delaware State University, and considerable dispensations for travel and writing time from my department chair, Dr. Samuel Hoff. Both of these individuals I value highly as friends, colleagues, and critics. My wife, Faith; my children, Marie, Alexis, and Michael; and our recently arrived grandson (Shane Michael Adams) as always have contributed to any publishing success by putting up with my strange writing schedule and—in Shane's case—by not throwing rice cereal onto the keyboard.

INTRODUCTION BY STEVEN H. NEWTON

ON JUNE 22, 1941, COLONEL ERHARD RAUS entered the German campaign against Russia as an unknown quantity to both his soldiers and superiors. An Austrian by birth, his last combat experience had been as acting commander of the Bicycle Light-Infantry Battalion 1 in the Austro-Hungarian army for five months in 1918 during World War I. Raus spent the interwar years in staff and training posts, and when he was absorbed into the German army in the 1938 *Anschluss* (the German annexation of Austria), he continued in staff assignments (most notably as chief of staff, XVII Corps, during the French campaign) for the next two years, with the sole exception of a two-month stint commanding a training regiment. Following the practice of transferring General Staff officers between staff and line positions, Raus took over Infantry Regiment 243 in June 1940, transferring to Motorized Infantry Regiment 4 one month later. In May 1941 he advanced to command of the 6th Motorized Infantry Brigade, 6th Panzer Division, without having led his regiment in even a skirmish. At that time there would have been little reason to expect that the bespectacled, forty-two-year-old Austrian would rise to army command.

"Untested" may well have been the description of Raus in the mind of division commander Franz Landgraf. Aside from having no recent battlefield experience, Raus lacked any prior association with the panzer troops, a particularly disquieting circumstance for the 6th Panzer Division's second-ranking officer. Landgraf would have learned that the modest Austrian was a meticulous planner, an indefatigable trainer, and an officer whose command persona depended less on bravado than upon ensuring that every subordinate understood his mission as completely as possible. Those were valuable traits—but not necessarily any guide regarding Raus's reaction under the fast-paced, unforgiving conditions of mechanized combat.

Within days of his taking command, however, Raus had proven himself as imperturbable on the battlefield as he was at a staff briefing, and by the time 6th Panzer Division reached the outskirts of Leningrad, in northern Russia, the troops assigned to fight under him were already prone to comment in tough spots that "Raus will get us through." The Austrian's keen eye for terrain, his innate understanding of combined-arms warfare, and his flair for unorthodox tactics made him Landgraf's natural successor at division command. When the onset of winter, long supply lines, and sheer exhaustion of men and machines left the 6th Panzer Division little more than a shadow unit outside Moscow in January 1942, Colonel General Walter Model (newly promoted commander of the Ninth Army) showed remarkable prescience in turning over control of his entire rear area and line of supply to Raus's headquarters. In the freezing weather Raus assembled a motley force of construction units, Luftwaffe ground crews, and other flotsam to hold the critical railroad line leading through Sychevka to the front lines. Had Raus not been able to defend Model's communications, Ninth Army would probably have lost the entire XXIII Corps, which had been encircled northwest of the town. By mid-February, Raus had collected enough strength to initiate his so-called snail offensive strategy to push the Soviets out of key villages and create a security zone several miles wide along the length of the railroad.

His performance during the Soviet winter counteroffensive earned Raus the sobriquet *Der Nochdenker* (the Far-sighted One), and cemented his working relationship with Model, under whom he would serve as an army commander in Galicia two years later. The 6th Panzer Division had earned a hiatus of several months in France for reorganization, but it returned to Russia in December 1942 to spearhead Fourth Panzer Army's ill-fated attempt to relieve the Sixth Army at Stalingrad. Despite the makeshift offensive's failure, Raus abruptly found himself elevated to corps command in early 1943, where—in succession—he: played a supporting role in Field Marshal Erich von Manstein's "backhand blow"; held the extreme right flank of *Armeeabteilung* Kempf during the battle of Kursk; supervised Army Group South's grudging defense of Kharkov; and conducted a fighting withdrawal across the Dnepr River against overwhelming odds.

Hitler rewarded Raus with command of the Fourth Panzer Army, which he led during von Manstein's counterattack at Kiev in December 1943. He would remain an army commander until Hitler finally relieved him in March 1945, heading in succession the Fourth, First, and Third Panzer Armies in Poland, the Baltic States, East Prussia, and finally Pomerania. Despite the names associated with his headquarters, these armies more often contained poorly trained volksgrenadier outfits than panzer divisions, but on occasion—at Kiev, Lvov, and in the Baltic—Raus had the chance to prove that he could handle large-scale armored operations with the same aplomb that he had displayed in division command. Heinz Guderian, then Chief of the Army General Staff, considered him "one of our best panzer generals" and habitually inserted Raus into critical situations.

Because he reached army command at a time when Germany had irrevocably been forced to undertake the strategic defensive, Raus found himself forced to become a defensive specialist. What made him especially unusual, however, was that despite having worked his way up as a panzer division commander the Austrian generally eschewed the better-known "mobile" or "elastic" defensive concepts in favor of what he later called "zone defensive tactics." Where generals like Hermann Balck or Hasso von Manteuffel favored dealing with Soviet penetrations by initiating fluid mobile operations that temporarily surrendered ground with the aim of eviscerating enemy tank spearheads and recovering any lost territory, Raus preferred to repulse such breakthroughs and hold his position. He did not blindly advocate anything resembling Hitler's infamous "stand fast" orders, but he did believe that the relative immobility of German infantry divisions and the shortage of panzer divisions combined to make large-scale mobile operations (like von Manstein's "backhand blow") too dangerous to risk after mid-1943.

Raus's operational preferences combined to make him a favorite of both Hitler and Model, since he was one of the few officers genuinely willing to attempt to defend territory rather than call for its abandonment. Unfortunately for the Austrian's postwar reputation, this made him nearly an invisible man. As David Glantz and other historians have repeatedly observed, between the late 1940s and 1980s the Western understanding of the war in Russia has been unduly shaped by the memoirs of German officers like Heinz Guderian, Erich von Manstein, and Friedrich-Wilhelm von Mellenthin. In none of those pivotal works does Raus make more than a token appearance. Guderian defended Raus at the moment Hitler sacked him, but he failed to recount the fact that the Austrian's relatively successful defensive operations in East Prussia had been conducted along lines with which "Fast Heinz" vehemently disagreed. Raus received respectful treatment from von Manstein in passing, but nothing more, primarily because Raus became the beneficiary when Hitler fired Hermann Hoth as commander of the Fourth Panzer Army. In von Mellenthin's famous *Panzer Battles*, Raus comes in for heavy criticism (though not always by name) for his refusal to conduct the Kiev counteroffensive or the Lvov defensive in the same manner that the author and his idol, Hermann Balck, would have preferred. When von Mellenthin penned his follow-up volume on influential German generals, he omitted Raus entirely.

Yet the U.S. Army Historical Program has valued Raus highly and made his writings the focal point of several well-known topical studies on the war against the Soviet Union. Raus is listed as the primary author of works on military improvisations, climate, small-unit tactics, and other issues. These studies have enjoyed a long and influential life, first in the slender *DA* (Department of the Army) pamphlet series, then in a limited edition reprint series, and most recently in a full-scale set of reproductions edited by Peter Tsouras. The preservation of these works, as originally published, has been critical both to keeping alive the German view of the conflict and to providing a modern audience with access to key Cold War documents, but exactly how much of the writing actually stemmed from Raus himself has remained problematic. What escaped even Raus's biographers is that the underlying material was clipped out of a complete narrative memoir covering Raus's war in Russia.

The original manuscript remains lost and may no longer exist, but by taking the longer segments that lay behind the already published material, combining them with unpublished studies, and supplementing these with the text from several articles that Raus published in *Allgemaine Schweizerische Militarzeitschrifte*, nearly the entire document can be reconstructed. Careful readers will notice differences in syntax and translation between this memoir and previously published segments. The young officers who provided the first translations were—to be charitable—blissfully unaware of professional canons of translation, surprisingly unfamiliar with Wehrmacht technical terminology, and often completely lost in the nuances of the grammar and syntax of a foreign language. Comparisons of their translations to the original German often yields surprising results, including entire sentences or paragraphs whose meanings have been unintentionally (one hopes) reversed. Moreover, later editors, condensing and revising the material from these translations for a more polished publication, took additional liberties with the narratives, often truncating entire sections or carving up longer narratives into illustrative fragments to be sprinkled throughout several pamphlets.

Where possible, the translation provided in the chapters that follow returns to the German manuscript materials and tries to recapture the original style and feel of Raus's writing. In addition, wherever possible I have included the specific unit designations and names of commanders, rendered place-names consistently, and resequenced several parts of his account of the war's final days for easier reading. That portion of the original work thus far unrecoverable appears primarily to be framing or transition material, wherein Raus could be expected to place the operations he commanded into the greater perspective of the war. The only substantive gap in this memoir is extensive coverage of the 6th Panzer Division's role in the final German drive on Moscow in November-December 1941. The small amount of narrative recovered has been supplemented by material from the 6th Panzer Division's War Diary. When the 6th Panzer Division left Russia for six months of reorganization in France during mid-1942 there is another gap, but it does not noticeably impair the overall flow of the document.

In its scope and value as a historical source, the Raus memoir rivals and potentially eclipses those of Guderian, von Manstein, and von Mellenthin. Erhard Raus was an entertaining writer with a keen tactical eye—his narrative is easily more readable and less self-serving than Guderian's. His work is very much a Cold War period piece, in which the Germans fought hard but honorably against the malevolent Soviet hordes. (However, Raus does admit that the Germans shot commissars and implies the controversial order to do so, in fact, penetrated down to divisional level at least.) He is occasionally inaccurate in his chronology, and his anecdotes occasionally confuse similar events, people, and units, but these minor discrepancies do little to harm the historical importance of his recollections.

The primary limitation—and greatest strength—of the Raus memoir is its nearly exclusive focus on tactical warfare. Readers will not find character sketches or extended analyses of von Manstein or Model, or extended summaries of the "big picture" of the war in other sectors. Many junior officers fighting their small, intense battles for nameless Russian villages remain anonymous themselves—knowable only through their actions. Yet the unrelenting concentration on small-unit combat (even when Raus was an army commander) provides greater insight into the combined-arms tactics of the German army than almost any other account available in English or German. As such, the memoir is an invaluable historical source, as well as an excellent read by any standard.

Chapter 1

THE INVASION OF THE SOVIET UNION

Failures of German Planning and Preparation

THE PREREQUISITE FOR A SUCCESSFUL WAR against the Soviet Union was a systematic preparation for the undertaking. One could not provoke such a conflict and expect to carry it through in a spirit of adventure. Unfortunately, due to the lack of vision and the fundamental blunders of Germany's leadership, it is no exaggeration to state that the entire Russian campaign will go down in history as one gigantic improvisation. Prior to the invasion of the Soviet Union, the *Oberkommando der Wehrmacht* [OKW—German Armed Forces High Command] and OKH [*Oberkommando der Heer*—Army High Command] did not think far enough ahead. Senior commanders in the armed forces and military specialists in all important fields must acquire firsthand knowledge of the climate and terrain, as well as the social, economic, political, and military conditions in any potential theater of war, or at least in those neutral or friendly countries that possess similar characteristics. Both OKW and OKH were in a good position to learn the general, as well as the climactic, conditions of European Russia and the far north. If the officers involved actually acquired this knowledge, they certainly failed to draw the proper conclusions with respect to strategy and military policy. If they did not get that information in the first place, they were obviously guilty of neglect.

The problem may have been that German planners were too deeply entrenched in Central European military traditions and not sufficiently familiar with foreign lands and particularly with countries whose climatic conditions differed from the German. As a result, they lacked a personal understanding of what was to be expected and probably took matters too lightly at the outset. Especially in the fields of tactics and logistics in European Russia and the arctic, better preparations should have been made before military operations began.

Any observer who looks at the Russian campaign in retrospect will come to the conclusion that the multitude of tactical and logistical improvisations that had to be employed to compensate for this lack of planning far exceeded what Field Marshal Helmuth von Moltke once designated as a "system of expedients" in a tactical sense. In reality, our troops found themselves forced to introduce their first improvisations as soon as they crossed the Russian border. The farther they penetrated into the Soviet Union, the more expedients they had to devise, and the number rose by leaps and bounds when operations began to be hampered first by mud and swamps and later by snow and ice. German soldiers had been neither trained nor equipped to withstand the raging elements of nature because OKH had been under the impression that the Red Army could be destroyed west of the Dnepr and that there would be no need for conducting operations in cold, snow, and mud.

Russia as a Theater of Operations

The German soldiers who crossed into Russian territory felt that they had entered a different world, opposed not only by the forces of the enemy but also by the forces of nature. Nature was the ally of the Red Army, and the struggle against this alliance was to be a severe test for the Wehrmacht. The influence of climate was felt in every effort of the German military establishment, whether on land, over water, or in the air. Climate was not only a dynamic force in the Russian expanse; it was the key to military success. Our troops had to become thoroughly familiar with Russian land and climate—new enemy weapons to them—in order to deal with them or—at least—to neutralize their restrictive efforts. Their qualities altered tactical procedures formerly in common use, forcing the adoption of local expedients and improvisations suited to military operations in a particular area and climate.

Summer, the season in which Operation Barbarossa began, was the most favorable period for operations in European Russia. Days were warm, nights cool, and only in the southern regions was the heat intense. Moors and swamps dried up, and swampy lowlands that were otherwise impassable during the muddy season could be used by peasant carts and—to a limited degree—by wheeled and tracked vehicles. All roads were passable during the summer, and even driving in open terrain was possible, despite numerous fissures and cracks in the ground. Summer not only dried out roads but reduced the level of rivers and streams as well; rivers could be forded, and smaller streams represented only minor obstacles, even though swampy terrain remained a serious barrier. All arms, therefore, enjoyed optimum mobility.

Even in summer, however, weather and terrain created severe challenges for the troops to overcome. Sudden thunderstorms could almost instantly change passable dirt roads and open terrain into mud traps. Once the rain ended and the sun returned, dirt roads dried out rapidly and could again be used by normal traffic, provided that undisciplined, overeager drivers had not plowed them up while the roads were still soft. During dry periods, on the other hand, dust wreaked havoc on our motor vehicles. Even our panzers sustained severe damage from the clouds of dust they stirred up while crossing vast sandy regions because many of them had no dust filters, and those so equipped soon became thoroughly clogged. The huge dust clouds raised by our convoys frequently provoked air attacks that resulted in serious losses of vehicles and horses.

Swampy and sandy terrain repeatedly had a decisive effect upon movement and combat. Likewise, the great forests of northern and central Russia often forced all movement into narrow, unpaved lanes. It proved impossible to estimate the time required for a march through such areas; careful ground and air reconnaissance had to be conducted to compare our maps with the actual terrain conditions. Provision had to be made for supplementary gasoline, extra engineer troops, portable bridging equipment, and wreckers.

As our panzer and motorized units plunged across the dusty Russian plains during that first summer, nobody paid much attention to the insignificant little peasant horses of the steppes. The tankers and truck drivers could not fail to notice the industrious little animals pulling heavily loaded peasant wagons cross-country whenever they were pushed off the road by the modern mechanical giants. Our troops viewed them sympathetically, but what was their performance compared to that of the steel colossi and multi-ton carriers? Any comparison obviously was out of the question. Many a man dismissed them with a disdainful gesture and the words: "A hundred years behind the times." Even next to the heavy, cold-blooded draft horses and the tall mounts of the infantry divisions their dwarfish cousins seemed slightly ridiculous. A few months later the *panje* horse would be judged quite differently.

The Russians favored forests for their approach marches and as assembly areas for attacks. They appeared and disappeared invisibly and noiselessly through the woods. Narrow strips of woodland leading to the outskirts of villages were utilized as concealed approaches by reconnaissance patrols. The woods also indicated the logical course to be followed for the forward assembly prior to an attack, as well as for infiltrating into German positions. Outskirts of woods were a preferred jump-off position for Soviet mass attacks. Wave upon wave could surge out of the forests. Even the smallest clearing found use as artillery firing positions; when necessary the Russians created such clearings by rapidly felling trees. They quickly and cleverly constructed positions for heavy weapons and observation posts in the trees, which thus situated provided effective support to advancing infantry. In contrast to our own difficulties, bringing up even medium artillery and tanks through almost impenetrable forests presented no problem to the Russians.

The Soviets also proved exceptionally adept at preparing towns and villages for defense, converting them into virtual fortresses very quickly. Wooden houses sported well-camouflaged gun ports almost flush with the floor, their interiors reinforced with dirt or sandbags, and observation slots cut into the roofs. Bunkers were excavated into the floors and connected with adjacent houses or exterior defenses by narrow trenches. Although almost all inhabited places were crammed with Red Army troops, they appeared deserted to German reconnaissance units, since even water and food details were allowed to leave their shelters only after dark. The Russians blocked approach routes with well-camouflaged antitank guns or dug-in tanks, especially favoring the use of knocked-out tanks as observation posts or heavy weapon emplacements. When the front line neared a village, the inhabitants carried their possessions into the outlying woods or bunkers for safekeeping. They did not take part in the fighting of the regular troops but served as auxiliaries, building earthworks and passing on information.

The utmost caution had to be exercised when passing through unknown terrain. Even long and searching observation often failed to reveal excellently camouflaged Russians. Frequently our patrols passed by the immediate vicinity of Russian positions or individual riflemen without noticing them, only to be taken under fire from behind. Caution had to be doubled in wooded areas, where the Russians often had to be driven out individually, Indian-fashion. There, sniping from trees was particularly favored.

The water supply in European Russia varied greatly from region to region, the quality and quantity generally deteriorating toward the south. During summer it was uniformly poor. In the Baltic region nearly every inhabited place had an adequate number of wells that furnished potable water; between Leningrad and the Luga River we found many wells sunk as deep as eighty feet. These wells provided water that was cold and of excellent quality. Villages in central and southern Russia each had one or two wells, but during the summer their water was scant and warm; many wells and cisterns in southern Russia nearly dried up in summer droughts, and such water as they furnished had to be boiled before drinking. Drinking water often had to be taken from brooks and rivers.

The Red Army in 1941

Military history should have provided a source of valuable information about Russian capabilities. It is never too late to determine the reasons for the success or failure of past operations. Many of the decisive factors retain their validity across the years and exert the same effect on military operations in the present. In 1807 it was the Russian soldier who for the first time made a stand against Napoleon after his victorious march through Europe— a stand that may be called almost epic. The underestimation of the Russian soldier and the Red Army was a serious error by the German command, even though neither the man nor the organization quite fit the pattern of modern warfare and the educated fighting man.

The difference between the Imperial Russian Army in World War I and the Red Army, even at the outset of the German invasion, was considerable. Whereas in the earlier war the Russian army fought as a more or less amorphous mass, immovable and without individuality, the spiritual awakening through communism had already begun to show itself in 1941. In contrast to the situation between 1914 and 1917, the number of illiterates was small; the Russian masses were well on the way to acquiring individuality, though the number of good noncommissioned officers [NCOs] was still not large, and the great mass of soldiers had not yet overcome their sluggishness. The force bringing about this change was communism or—more precisely—a spiritual awakening of the people directed by a rigidly centralized state. The Russian was fundamentally nonpolitical; at least that was true for the rural population, which supplied most of the soldiers. He was not an active Communist, not a political zealot. But he was—and here should have been noted a decisive change—a conscious Russian who fought only in rare instances for political ideals, but always for his Motherland.

The industrialization of the country, carried out in a comparatively short period of time, made available to the Red Army a larger number of workers with full command of technical skills. Soldiers trained in technical subjects were carefully distributed through the ranks, where they taught the necessary rudiments to their duller urban comrades and to those who came from rural areas. Whereas in World War I the telephone was still magic to the average Russian, in World War II he regarded the complicated radio as an amusing toy.

In line with this awakening, another determining factor had been introduced into the Red Army by the political commissar: unqualified obedience. Systematic training, drill, disregard for one's own life, the natural inclination of the Russian soldier to uncompromising compliance, and, not least of all, the real disciplinary powers available to the commissar were the foundations of this iron obedience. The commissar was probably the most controversial man in the Red Army; even in the Soviet Union opinion varied concerning his usefulness, his position, and his duties. He was the driving force of the army, ruling with cunning and cold-bloodedness.

It is not true, however, that the Russian soldier fought well only because of fear of the commissars. A soldier who is motivated solely through fear can never have the fighting qualities displayed by Russian soldiers. Instead, the attitude of the common soldier toward the commissar was conditioned not only by fear of his power but also by his personal exemplification of the soldier and fighter. His concern for the welfare of the troops also determined to a large extent his relationship with his men. Thus the example set by the commissar was largely responsible for the tenacious resistance of the Russian soldier, even in hopeless situations. It is not wholly true that the German "Commissar Order," directing that upon capture commissars be turned over to the SD [*Sicherungsdienst*—Security Service] for "special treatment," that is, execution, was solely responsible for inciting the commissars to bitter last-ditch resistance. The impetus much rather was fanaticism together with soldierly qualities and probably also a genuine feeling of responsibility for the victory of the Soviet Union.

The higher command echelon of the Red Army proved capable from the very beginning: flexible, full of initiative, and energetic. However, they were unable to inspire the mass of Russian soldiers. Most commanders had advanced in peacetime to high positions at a very early age, although there were some older men among them. All social levels were represented, from the common laborer to the university professor of Mongolian languages and cultures. Of course, merit in the Revolution played a part, but a good choice was made with respect to character, military understanding, and intelligence. Purely party generals apparently received positions carrying little more than prestige.

During the various political purges, an appreciable portion of the high command strata disappeared. But it is a mistake to assume that a deterioration of the higher command levels necessarily resulted. Such great progress had been made in military education that even the higher commanders available at the beginning of the war were of a stature commensurate with their duties. The many developments in the sphere of strategy, which now and then gave rise to doubts about the ability of these leaders, require an examination of their background before they can be properly judged. The alleged failure during the Finnish winter campaign of 1939–1940 is well known, but nevertheless the conjecture cannot be dismissed that there was some bluffing involved. The timing of the operation was correct and produced results as soon as the will of the immeasurably superior attacker desired them.

Nor was the immediate tactical and operational success of the German surprise attack at the outset of the campaign against Russia any proof to the contrary. Along the central front, and also in the Baltic region, it appeared as though the Soviets did not consider the actual war to have begun until our troops had reached the Dnepr and Luga Rivers. One of Marshal Timoshenko's strategic war games, which was captured by our soldiers, as well as the course of events during the first weeks of the campaign, tended to substantiate this assumption. Especially in front of Army Group Center along the Bug River, only customs and frontier guards were encountered initially; very weak enemy forces appeared after a few days. Finally, we had a big battle in the Dnepr-Berezina triangle, and thus began the Russian campaign in earnest. Again and again reports gave the impression that large-scale enemy movements did not get under way until after the opening of the campaign and that they took place beyond the Dnepr. From the point of view of Soviet grand strategy, this was undoubtedly an expedient solution. Nevertheless, *Fremde Heer Ost* [Foreign Armies East—the German military intelligence service] maintained its belief that it had identified continuous troop movements to the Russo-German frontier, supposedly involving 130 divisions, as early as the spring of 1940.

The flexibility demonstrated by the commanders of armies and fronts was not evident at the lower levels. Command echelons below division level in the Red Army, and for the most part the intermediate echelons (generally division level), entered the conflict inflexible and indecisive, avoiding all personal responsibility. The rigid pattern of training and a too-strict discipline so narrowly confined the lower command within a framework of existing regulations that the result was lethargy. Spirited application to a task, born of the decision of an individual, was a rarity. Russian elements that broke through our lines could remain for days behind the front without recognizing their favorable position and taking advantage of it. The Soviet small-unit commander's fear of doing something wrong and being called to account for it was greater than the urge to take advantage of a situation.

The commanders of tank and mechanized units were often well trained along tactical lines, but to some extent they had not grasped the essence of tactical doctrines and therefore often acted according to set patterns, not according to circumstances. Also, there was a pronounced spirit of blind obedience that had perhaps carried over from the regimented civilian life into the military field. This lethargy and reluctance to assume responsibility was a serious drawback to the Red Army, completely neutralizing a great many good points of the Russian soldier at the outset of the campaign.

The German Army on the Eve of the Invasion

Insufficiently prepared for the campaign in the East, as the pillar of Germany's military might the army nonetheless had to bear the brunt of the fighting. The heartbeat of the army was at the front, where deficiencies and shortages of any kind were immediately felt.

From the very first days of the campaign, the vastness of European Russia and the peculiarities of Russian warfare led to the repeated isolation of individual units and combat teams. All-around defenses and security measures were the only possible remedy, but far from being stressed, these defensive tactics were frequently not even mentioned in the field service regulations. The field forces had to improvise them. With regard to our artillery, wire and radio communications could be lost between gun positions and their observation posts for extended periods, a complication not previously encountered. As substitutes, field expedients had to be used to maintain communications, including signals transmitted by discs, inscriptions on blackboards read with the help of field glasses, mounted messengers, runner, and relayed messages. Much time had to be devoted to training in Morse code transmission by signal lamps.

The clothing issued to our soldiers proved too heavy for summer wear. As a result, the men perspired too easily, became very thirsty, and were soon caked with dirt. Only the mountain trousers and field jackets that were worn by the mountain and jaeger divisions turned out to be practical for year-round usage. For protection against the dust, masks for mouth and nose and goggles should have been issued; individual equipment should have included mosquito head nets. Hard-packed dirt roads cut like glass into shoe leather, and boot soles quickly went to pieces; spare boots should have been available to every soldier.

The German army was not modern enough to overcome these difficulties easily; our supply and transportation systems in Russia were especially dependent on improvisations because of the peculiarities of terrain and climate. From the outset of the campaign, supply columns had to be improvised from motor vehicles of every type that had been requisitioned from private owners. Many of these vehicles were in poor condition and therefore of little service, and the problem of replacing spare parts for so many different types of trucks caused incessant difficulties.

With respect to the draft horses that transported the bulk of the supplies for our infantry divisions, the light and medium breeds of Western European countries proved generally satisfactory for summer duty. Heavier breeds were less hardy and needed excessive amounts of forage. It would have been better not to have used heavy breeds in Russia.

The 6th Panzer Division Prepares for the Campaign

The 6th Panzer Division entered the Soviet Union under control of XLI Panzer Corps, which itself belonged to Panzer Group 4. Panzer Group 4, itself subordinated to Army Group North, was organized as follows:

Panzer Group 4
> Colonel General Erich Hoepner
> Chief of Staff: Colonel Walter Chales de Beaulieu
> Operations Officer: Major von Schoen-Angerer

LVI Panzer Corps
> General of Infantry Erich von Manstein
> Chief of Staff: Lieutenant Colonel Harald Freiherr von Elverfeldt
> Operations Officer: Major Erich Dethleffsen
> 3rd Motorized Infantry Division
> Lieutenant General Curt Jahn

8th Panzer Division
> Major General Erich Brandenberger

290th Infantry Division
> Lieutenant General Theodor Freiherr von Wrede

Corps Troops
> Artillery Commander 125
> II/Artillery Regiment 61 (105mm howitzers)
> Engineer Regiment Staff (motorized) 678
> Engineer Battalion (motorized) 48
> Commander of Construction Troops 4
> Construction Battalions 44, 55, 87
> Panzerjaeger Battalion 559 (47mm self-propelled guns)
> Light Flak Battalion 92 (20mm flak; Luftwaffe)
> II/Flak Regiment 23 (mixed) (20mm and 88mm flak; Luftwaffe)

XLI Panzer Corps
> General of Panzer Troops George-Hans Reinhardt
> Chief of Staff: Colonel Carl Roettiger
> Operations Officer: Major Klostermann

6th Panzer Division
Major General Franz Landgraf
Operations Officer: Major Joachim A. G. Graf von Kielmansegg

1st Panzer Division
Lieutenant General Friedrich Kirchner
Operations Officer: Lieutenant Colonel Walter Wenck

36th Motorized Division
Lieutenant General Otto Ottenbacher

269th Infantry Division
Major General Ernst von Leyser

Corps Troops
Artillery Commander 30
Artillery Regimental Staff 618
Artillery Battalion 611 (100mm cannon)
II/Artillery Regiment 59 (150mm howitzers)
II/Artillery Regiment 67 (150mm howitzers)
Mortar Battalion 615 (210mm mortars)
Engineer Regimental Staff (motorized) 628
Engineer Battalion (motorized) 52
Commander of Construction Troops 71
Construction Battalions 62, 254
Nebelwerfer Regiment 52 (multiple rocket launchers)
Army Light Flak Battalion 601 (20mm flak)
Light Flak Battalion 83 (20mm flak; Luftwaffe)
II/Flak Regiment 411 (20mm flak; Luftwaffe)
I/Flak Regiment 3 (20mm and 88mm flak; Luftwaffe)

Army Troops
SS *Totenkopf* Motorized Infantry Division
Gruppenfuehrer Theodor Eicke

Senior Artillery Commander 312
Engineer Battalion (motorized) 62
Senior Construction Staff 32
Panzerjaeger Battalion 616 (47mm self-propelled guns)
Flak Regiment Staff 133 (Luftwaffe)
Flak Regiment Staff 164 (Luftwaffe)
Flak Battalions (mixed) II/36, I/51, I/111 (20mm and 88mm flak; Luftwaffe)

The most noteworthy characteristic of the 6th Panzer Division at the outset of the Russian campaign was the fact that the entire division contained the equivalent of only a single heavy panzer company. Panzer Regiment 11 consisted of three battalions of four companies each. The predominant panzer model was the light PzKw 35t, an older vehicle of Czech manufacture that was no longer in production and whose frontal armor had a maximum thickness of only 25mm. Only the 4th Company of each battalion was provided with some PzKw IVs and a few PzKw IIIs. By contrast, the 1st Panzer Division boasted an entire battalion of heavy panzers. The higher numerical strength of Panzer Regiment 11 could not compensate for its technical deficiencies. From the outset, his awareness of this weakness all but forced Major General Franz Landgraf, the division commander, to forbid the commitment of all panzers en masse and instead to employ them in conjunction with our infantry battalions. Alone our PzKw 35ts would have been grossly inferior even to the Russian tanks and antitank weapons about which we were already aware.

These facts require special mention because they entailed different combat methods on our part from those utilized by other panzer divisions, as the 6th Panzer Division was the only one in the German army still equipped with those obsolete tanks. Moreover, because production of the PzKw 35t had been discontinued for some time, providing for spare parts became increasingly difficult. Thus the number of serviceable tanks in the division sank steadily despite only small losses due to enemy activity. By contrast, it should be admitted that the PzKw 35t did possess certain advantages for operating in Russian terrain, including light weight, good maneuverability, and the ability to cross bridges with a load capacity of only 8.5 tons.

Our antitank weapons were also generally inferior. In Panzerjaeger Battalion 41 only one platoon in each of the three companies had been issued 50mm antitank guns. The other platoons, as well as the antitank elements of our motorized infantry regiments, were equipped only with towed, 37mm antitank guns. The division did have at its disposal one 20mm flak battery and one antitank rifle company. For the initial attack of the campaign, XLI Panzer Corps had also attached II Battalion, Artillery Regiment 59 (150mm howitzers), and II Battalion, Luftwaffe Flak Regiment 411 (20mm and 88mm flak).

In Panzer Reconnaissance Battalion 57 the division possessed an organic reconnaissance unit that functioned extremely well and whose result proved to be of the utmost importance to our conduct of operations. Unfortunately, shortly before we reached Leningrad, higher headquarters detached this battalion from 6th Panzer Division, a measure that proved to be very detrimental.

Our knowledge of the Red Army in our sector was confined to reports from higher headquarters. General Landgraf ordered reconnaissance by eyewitnesses and agents during the last four days of our assembly, which revealed Russian field fortifications in our sector and discovered enemy forces of unknown strength on both sides of the Siline-Kangailai road. We also discovered that the terrain in the Tauroggen area was extremely unsuitable for the attack of a panzer division. The dense, swampy forest offered only one practicable road. This meant that full deployment of the division could not be contemplated before reaching Ervilkas, thirty-five kilometers east of the border.

Just prior to the beginning of Operation Barbarossa, the 6th Panzer Division, which had originally occupied the area around Deutsch Eylau and Torun, assembled in the area around Osterode, Riesenburg, and Deutsch Eylau. From this point the buildup for the attack proceeded in a succession of four night marches. The assembly movements proved very difficult because of the sheer mass of troops in Army Group North that were approaching the border and their often-conflicting routes of march. Crossing the Memel River turned out to be particularly difficult. Our lighter vehicles crossed at Schreitlauken on an auxiliary bridge over which a test run had only been driven at the last moment. Tanks and heavier vehicles moved across the Memel bridge at Tilsit, which also had to be used by 1st Panzer Division, so that two parallel columns converged at a single point. Nevertheless, the entire assembly succeeded without any major stoppages, with all movements restricted to the hours of darkness and never allowed to extend into the daytime.

The division had to organize a double-echeloned order of battle for the final buildup and approach to the Lithuanian border. Advance elements took up defensive positions through 21 June. We were permitted to occupy the actual positions for the attack only during the night of 21–22 June. Because of these factors, General Landgraf organized the lead elements of the division into two *Kampfgruppen* of different strength. On the right, the weaker of the two—*Kampfgruppe* von Seckendorff—received the mission of leading the assault and opening the road to Kangailai. The more powerful *Kampfgruppe* Raus on the left was to attack later, breaking through the Russian border fortifications as quickly as possible and proceeding then as ordered by division. In the evening of 21 June, division headquarters located itself at Szugken.

The initial tactical organization of 6th Panzer Division for the attack on 22 June 1941 was:

Kamofgruppe von Seckendorff (Headquarters, Motorized Infantry Regiment 114)
  Lieutenant Colonel Erich Freiherr von Seckendorff
  Motorized Infantry Regiment 114
  Panzer Reconnaissance Battalion 57
  one company, Panzerjaeger Battalion 41
  Motorcycle Battalion 6 (morning only)

Kampfgruppe Raus (Headquarters, Motorized Brigade 6)
  Colonel Erhard Raus
  Panzer Regiment 11
  I/Motorized Infantry Regiment 4
  II/Artillery Regiment 76
  one company, Panzer Engineer Battalion 57
  one company, Panzerjaeger Battalion 41
  one battery, II/Flak Regiment 411
  Motorcycle Battalion 6 (afternoon)

Division Main Body
  Major General Franz Landgraf
  Staff, II and III/Motorized Infantry Regiment 4
  Staff, I and III/Panzer Artillery Regiment 76
  Panzer Engineer Battalion 57 (minus one company)
  Panzerjaeger Battalion 41 (minus two companies)

Attached
  II/Artillery Regiment 59
  II/Flak Regiment 411 (minus one battery)

(Note that while the division continued to operate using the same two *Kampfgruppen*, their composition changed often on a daily basis.)

Chapter 2

RASEINAI

The Campaign Opens

FOLLOWING AN ARTILLERY PREPARATION that began at 0305, 22 June 1941, a Fieseler "Storch" liaison plane saw to it that a wooden machine-gun tower outside of Siline was neutralized, after which 6th Panzer Division crossed the Soviet border south of Tauroggen. *Kampfgruppe* von Seckendorff, assaulting through the village of Siline, succeeded relatively quickly in clearing the road to Kangailai, though in the woods east of that town two Russian companies put up a defense more tenacious than any so far seen in the war. Our infantry eliminated the last of this resistance toward 1600 after heavy fighting in the woods.

This obstacle notwithstanding, *Kampfgruppe* Raus launched and sustained the division's main attack during the morning hours. The bridge across the Sesuvis River at Kangailai fell into our hands, and we rapidly broke isolated resistance in the open terrain around Meskai. Expected Russian counterattacks from the northern bank of the Sesuvis did not materialize, and my leading units reached Erzvilkas toward evening.

Increasing terrain difficulties delayed the advance of the division's main body, especially holding back *Kampfgruppe* von Seckendorff on the left wing, which was moving via Kuisiai. By nightfall our troops had been widely scattered along the Siline-Meskai-Gaure-Erzvilkas road, but during the night the Russians in the Sakaline area to the south showed little activity. General Franz Landgraf moved division headquarters up to Meskai.

Ambush at Paislinis

On the second day of combat after the deep breakthrough at the frontier, both *Kampfgruppen* quickly pushed east in order to prevent the enemy from taking up positions along the Raseinai heights and to reach the important

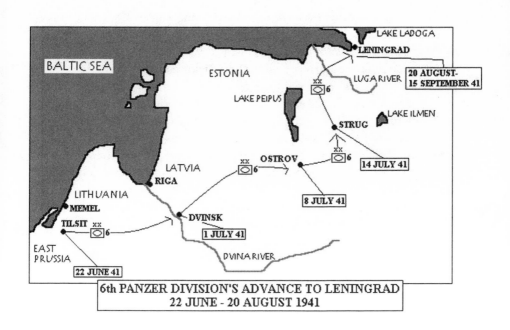

6th PANZER DIVISION'S ADVANCE TO LENINGRAD
22 JUNE - 20 AUGUST 1941

Dubyssa sector. The 6th Panzer Division received the assignment of occupying the Lithuanian town of Raseinai, after which the division was to press on to the east in order to seize the two vehicular bridges across the Dubyssa River beyond the towns at Betygala and Kybaryteliai. Proceeding in the direction of Raseinai, we found that the Russian infantry, which we had overtaken the day before, had now apparently disappeared.

Our troops drove at speed along all available roads and highways, the panzer and artillery columns rolling relentlessly ahead, prepared to crush everything opposing them. Far to the front, clouds of dust finally appeared on the horizon. "The enemy after all," many a man thought, as the speed of the advance picked up. Up to this point no shots had been fired. Fighter planes circled peacefully in the sky by themselves; not a single Soviet aircraft had risen to challenge them. The beauties of the landscape still spread before us in the soft light of the morning sun. Rather than the second day of a great war, the large-scale forward movement of the 6th Panzer Division resembled a peaceful march to the starting position of a field maneuver.

Suddenly a heavy barrage tore through the air. From the dust clouds still visible on the horizon, black earth now spouted into the air. Machine guns began to chatter, and their fire penetrated the sound of the increasing barrage. The *landser* [enlisted soldier], now covered with dust, wondered what could be happening up front. The column commanders already knew the answer. Much earlier, our advance detachment (the cause of the dust clouds the troops had been watching) had radioed that strong Russian forces had been found occupying the heights south of Raseinai. These enemy elements lay near the route of advance for *Kampfgruppe* von Seckendorff and spread in front of the town like a protective bulwark.

In the distance, our troops could already discern the chapel spire that represented the highest point in Raseinai. All echelons advanced steadily and without hesitation, as they had been assigned to support the advance detachment in overcoming enemy resistance as rapidly as possible. In this case the advance detachment had already attacked the Russians from the march but had been too weak to defeat them. Major Linbrunn's Reconnaissance Battalion 57, which had been subordinated to Major Schliekmann's Motorcycle Battalion 6, had quickly reconnoitered the local situation. Shortly thereafter, the bulk of *Kampfgruppe* von Seckendorff, which was ahead of *Kampfgruppe* Raus, entered the engagement. Under the protection of friendly artillery fire, Motorized Infantry Regiment 114 and the panzer battalion attached to it moved to attack across ground that had already been thoroughly plowed up by our own shells.

After a severe struggle Colonel von Seckendorff's troops seized an advance ridge against strong opposition, but the Russians—having built their main battle line on the reverse slope—had no intentions of relinquishing the key point in their defense. The fight for this position lasted more than two hours, primarily because the completely open nature of the terrain made attacking difficult. In addition, our artillery lacked sufficient ammunition, and the panzers had to pick their way through swamps and forests in order to take the enemy in his flanks and rear.

The protracted length of this struggle made it even more important for my command (which had started out on the same road as *Kampfgruppe* Seckendorff but had left the road at Erzvilkas in order to reach Raseinai by the shortest route) to arrive before Raseinai in time to seize the town with a co-ordinated attack by both groups. The final segment of this route followed a narrow dirt trail leading along Blyna Brook through a somewhat marshy forested area in which visibility was severely limited. East of Paislinis, the terrain changed into open meadowland covered with large fruit trees.

To this point *Kampfgruppe* Raus had not met any enemy resistance, but no sooner had our leading company moved into the open country than its left flank came under rifle and machine-gun fire delivered from very close range. The first victim of the ambush was the company commander, who was driving at the head of his column. Before he even had time to shout an order, he was shot through the forehead by a Russian sniper from a distance of at least 100 meters. Even without his direction, the company dismounted at lightning speed and returned fire, while the panzers assigned to the lead company rolled ahead quickly, firing into the thickets and holding the enemy. Unfortunately, the lead tank soon received a direct hit from an antitank gun and dropped out. Shortly thereafter the two following companies of the advance guard penetrated the forest and attacked the Russians in their flank and rear with small arms. The enemy's destruction seemed certain, but the troops storming into the attack could make little headway through the densest part of the thicket of the young forest and thus were unable to cut off the Russians' retreat to the north.

Although only a company, beset by a force outnumbering itself three-to-one, the enemy managed to escape. Moreover, since the Soviets operated with full cover, their losses were small. We captured several weapons, among them a 37mm antitank gun of German origin. This appeared to be the weapon that damaged our tank at a distance of about fifty meters; the crew had apparently been killed by the fire of our other tanks while attempting to flee.

Though the predicament of our leading elements, caught by an ambush in open terrain, had looked critical at first, our casualties turned out to be light, consisting only of a few wounded and the very capable company commander who had been killed. Fire from the thicket, which was unsteady and whizzed harmlessly over our heads, did not account for our casualties. These resulted almost exclusively from snipers, concealed in the tops of the fruit trees and aiming at their targets from close quarters. These snipers remained in their hiding places even after the main body of the enemy withdrew, looking for worthwhile victims—primarily officers. Some of these men held to their positions even after our panzers stopped directly beneath their trees and began to fire into the fringes of the forest.

As long as the snipers fired during the height of the battle, they remained unnoticed, and it was not until they continued firing after the noise had died away that we discovered them and brought them down with machine-gun fire. The last of them tried vainly to flee, but immediately spotted in the open, they were killed by the fire of the nearest machine gun before they managed to reach the cover of the forest. Snipers in the trees of a forest were no novelty to our troops, but here, for the first time, they had been found in fruit trees in the open, where no one expected them. Though doomed, they had executed their mission. They had carried it out regardless of the fact that their lives were being forfeited. That willingness to die was one of the new experiences in the ambush at Paislinis.

Unmistakably, the Russians had employed a systematically planned ambush to delay the rapid advance of the strong *Kampfgruppe* Raus, since our appearance at Raseinai would not only threaten the town but also the rear of the strong forces fighting in the hills to the south. The Soviet commander had skillfully chosen his ambush site: It was immediately adjacent to our line of march, at a point where all of his weapons would be able to dominate our flank. The location allowed him to place his snipers in the fruit trees, offered full protection against early discovery, made a quick envelopment difficult, and enabled his forces to withdraw from the attack unobserved. The plan to have his snipers concentrate on eliminating our officers was especially clever. The commander and his numerically weak unit could take pride in the success of the ambush. It had forced our advance elements to interrupt their rapid motorized progress and caused a delay of more than one half hour, as well as inflicting the casualties enumerated above.

On the other hand, given the tactical situation outside Raseinai, *Kampf-gruppe* Raus was justified in trying to use its vehicles as long as possible, in order to bring about a quick decision in the battle outside the town. The risk of a minor ambush had to be accepted. Dismounting and expending the time to comb through the strips of woods for small enemy units or stragglers would have led to a loss of time far out of proportion to any success we might have hoped to gain. The actual loss of time in the ambush did not turn out to be critical, however, as our leading elements reached the assembly area for the planned attack on Raseinai on time, and the bulk of the troops followed without delay.

The danger that several commanders might have simultaneously fallen victim to such an ambush was prevented by previous training and repeated orders that officers should not form groups. As usual, our officers had endeavored to be as far to the front as possible, in order to orient themselves quickly at the outset of any engagement, enabling them to receive or issue orders instantly. Including the fallen company commander, they had nearly all joined the advance column but had dispersed themselves in such a manner that they could take matters in hand immediately without presenting a large target.

The ambush at Paislinis involved only a small unit and had no psychological repercussions on our troops. All eyes remained focused on Raseinai, which lay on the ridge in the bright noonday sun like a fortress dominating the surrounding country. There, as well as in the countryside in front of the town, the Russians had dug in so as to halt our panzers (which were already approaching) and Motorized Infantry Regiment 114 (echeloned in depth and following closely behind). The batteries of Colonel Grundherr's Panzer Artillery Regiment 76 had already begun hammering those enemy positions that our observers had located, battering the reserves that were hurrying to reinforce his line.

Simultaneously, *Kampfgruppe* von Seckendorff, which had been engaged throughout in the hard fight on the height south of town, prepared to strike a decisive blow. Its panzers had penetrated the Russian position and joined those of *Kampfgruppe* Raus at Raseinai. Soon after, our combined groups cleaned out the town and the surrounding ridges. Enemy resistance collapsed very rapidly in the face of concentric attacks by all the forces of 6th Panzer Division. Some courageous Red Army battalions still offered resistance to *Kampfgruppe* Raus as we immediately thrust toward the bridge on the road to Siluva. Our panzers overran them, however, after which our infantry dispersed them, storming individual pockets of resistance. Only a brief struggle sufficed to eliminate them.

By early afternoon both *Kampfgruppen* had reached the objective for the day: the two bridges across the Dubyssa, which we occupied after overcoming minor resistance. Somewhat beyond Raseinai, these bridges lay fifty meters below the level of the surrounding countryside. Our panzers traversed the river first, by the aid of a derelict bridge, and cleared the area around Kybaryteliai. I then sent elements of Motorized Infantry Regiment 4 across the northern bridge to form a bridgehead on the heights beyond, which was supported by several panzers which remained on the eastern bank of the river as a reserve. A few hours later, Colonel von Seckendorff also had dislodged the Soviet rear guards and occupied the eastern bank of the Dubyssa at Betygala with Motorcycle Battalion 6. After having covered fifty-five kilometers and spent several hours in combat, 6th Panzer Division by evening had achieved and consolidated the day's objectives. The setting sun cast a rosy glow, and quiet prevailed even before twilight fell. Steaming field kitchens and everyone not occupied with guard duty assembled around them to enjoy a well-deserved hot meal, bringing a successful day to a happy conclusion.

The officers discussed the actions of the day and made preparations for the following morning. But we also reflected upon the accomplishments of the Russians as well, and many verbally expressed their astonishment that the same infantry that had faced them the day before, south of Tauroggen where they had been overrun at noon and left far behind, could have covered seventy-five kilometers on foot within twenty-four hours. These Red Army soldiers had not only conducted a grueling forced march in the absence of proper roads but had again immediately prepared defensive positions and fought stubbornly for several hours without any rest. This fact put a damper on their joy in the day's victory, for it had instantly become apparent that Germany had engaged a stubborn opponent who might well lose ground but never accept defeat. The next day only confirmed the accuracy of these observations. During the night, our troops widened and improved both bridge-heads without incident in order to facilitate continuation of the offensive.

The arrival of the division's main body was considerably delayed because the 269th Infantry Division, which XLI Panzer Corps was moving north by way of Erzvilkas, continually crossed 6th Panzer Division's route of march. Meanwhile, Luftwaffe reconnaissance flights revealed strong Soviet armored forces (exceeding 200 tanks) arriving from the Jonava-Kadainiai area, and pivoting west toward Kroki. Such movements could obviously be directed only against 6th Panzer Division's spearhead elements, which had advanced farthest in the direction of the critical town of Siauliai, since the success of LVI Panzer Corps's attack to the south was not yet known. The same reconnaissance flights also reported general troop withdrawals from the border areas toward the northeast. It could therefore be assumed that those Russian tanks had the assignment of halting XLI Panzer Corps's advance in order to facilitate an unhampered withdrawal by the enemy's main forces. Division headquarters received continuous information from aerial reconnaissance about the relatively rapid progress of the Russian tanks. He knew by the morning of 24 June that the enemy armored force, upon reaching Kroki, had split into two columns, obviously directed against Kybaryteliai and Betygala.

General Landgraf tried to move substantial reinforcements from the division's main body toward Raseinai as quickly as possible to reinforce the two forward *Kampfgruppen* and prevent the Soviets from crossing the Dubyssa. This plan could not be carried out as intended because of the continuing congestion in Erzvilkas, where the advance of 6th Panzer Division was now entangled not only with the 269th Infantry Division but elements of the 1st Panzer Division as well. Not only did this mean that Colonel von Seckendorff and I would not be immediately reinforced, but also that we would not have timely support available on our flanks. General Landgraf was particularly worried about the right flank of the advance at Betygala, where the 269th Infantry was to have been employed. Instead, the 269th Infantry was still northeast of Erzvilkas and the 1st Panzer Division apparently advancing in the highway toward Kelme. Obviously the spearhead elements of 6th Panzer Division would have to bear at least the initial brunt of the enemy attack alone.

Unfortunately, it proved impossible to get word of this enemy maneuver forward to the spearhead *Kampfgruppen* in a timely manner. Thus, when dawn arrived, I received no orders to continue the advance, though I knew it might arrive at any time, for it was only necessary to press a button and the war machinery would starting running again within a few minutes. We wondered if our high command had become aware of Russian movements or intentions that had upset our own plans. Perhaps, but to all appearances such an occurrence seemed unlikely.

First Attack of Russian Heavy Tanks

No sooner had the sun begun to send forth its first rays, however, than suddenly the roar of artillery became audible from the south. The intensity of this fire increased, volley after volley of shells bursting in the southern bridgehead held by *Kampfgruppe* von Seckendorff. Even the houses in Raseinai trembled as windowpanes rattled in their frames. The sound of the barrage and the explosion of the shells made it clear that the Russians were preparing to attack in force. Regrettably, the area east of Raseinai was too flat and too overgrown for our observers to determine what was happening in the adjacent bridgehead, six kilometers distant, but we soon heard the artillery supporting Colonel Seckendorff's troops commence firing in response to the Soviet barrage. These sounds of battle had lasted approximately twenty minutes when the heavy sounds of guns and machine-gun fire added themselves to the crescendo. The trained ear of the veteran panzer soldier immediately recognized that tank-to-tank fighting had begun.

The sound of the fighting slowly shifted to the west, not at all a good sign. An inquiry to division headquarters confirmed our fear that *Kampfgruppe* Seckendorff was under heavy attack. We later discovered that our troops in the southern bridgehead faced the 2nd Tank Division of the III Mechanized Corps, whose objective was to recapture Raseinai and dislodge 6th Panzer Division from the plateau. What placed Colonel Seckendorff and his men in such a precarious position was not so much the numerical superiority of the enemy but the totally unexpected appearance of colossal tanks against which German panzers and antitank guns seemed to have no effect. These tanks were the super-heavy Russian model KV-1, the most dangerous heavy tank they possessed until the very end of the war (later improved and designated the KV-2).

Soon after the beginning of the heavy artillery exchange, these tanks attacked and pierced the positions of Motorcycle Battalion 6 in the extended bridgehead. Major Schliekmann fell in this fighting. The KV-1s ran over and crushed not just motorcycles but even some of our seriously wounded soldiers, forcing the battalion to withdraw under heavy pressure to the western bank of the Dubyssa. We later discovered that all of the wounded and captured soldiers left behind on the eastern bank of the river were murdered and mutilated.

Now covered by the main body of *Kampfgruppe* von Seckendorff, the motorcycle battalion turned and prepared to offer stubborn resistance. At this point Colonel von Seckendorff still hoped to hold the western bank, until the giant tanks traversed the river without apparent difficulty and began rumbling up the bank. Even the concentrated fire of the artillery and all other heavy weapons his troops possessed did not deter the steel pachyderms. Though enveloped in fire and smoke, they immediately lumbered to attack, crushing everything in their paths. Untroubled by the shower of heavy howitzer shells and debris raining down upon them, they attacked a roadblock, shrugged off the flanking fire of our antitank guns in the woods, turned and overran those positions, and then broke into the artillery area.

About 100 tanks from Colonel Richard Koll's Panzer Regiment 11, one-third of which were PzKw IVs, now assembled for a counterattack. Some of them faced the Russian behemoths from the front, but the bulk made their assault from the flanks. From three sides their shells hammered against the steel giants, but the effort to destroy them was made in vain. On the other hand, our own panzers very soon began taking casualties, and after a long, futile struggle against the Russian giants, Colonel Koll's vehicles had to withdraw into covering terrain to escape destruction.

To make matters worse, II Battalion, Motorized Infantry Regiment 114, which had been defending the woods west of the Dubyssa against the Soviet infantry following in the wake of the KV-1s (a few of which had broken off to support them), had by now suffered heavy casualties, particularly from artillery fire. As it became clear that no weapon possessed by *Kampfgruppe*

Seckendorff, not even our own panzers, was a match for the Russian monster tanks, the danger of a general panic became imminent. Captain Quentin, the battalion commander, reached the extraordinary decision to systematically withdraw the bulk of his vacillating troops. Along with his company commanders and senior NCOs, Captain Quentin took over the machine guns and held the battalion's defensive line against repeated Russian infantry attacks. Despite the surprise achieved by the heavy tanks and withdrawal of the bulk of the battalion, the enemy proved unable to force a penetration and follow his armor forward toward Raseinai.

New Soviet tanks now entered the fray from the east, while the bulk of the super-heavy tanks continued driving relentlessly forward despite the steady fire of German artillery and panzers. The only tactical solution to this dilemma was for Captain Quentin to let the second group of Russian tanks overrun his defensive line, after which his detachment of officers and NCOs would be able to escape toward the flanks if necessary and make contact with the main body of Motorized Infantry Regiment 114—if it was still there.

Squatting in small trench positions, under road bridges and culverts, or in grain fields, German soldiers awaited the approach of the second wave of heavy tanks. Waiting became hell, as the long arm of our own artillery now targeted these tanks, unaware that it was wounding our own troops as well. Envied were those comrades who had succeeded in hiding underneath bridges and in passageways, and therefore able to observe these events at close range without being noticed by the enemy. Nearer and nearer rolled the giant tanks, echeloned in width and depth. One of them encountered a marshy pool in which a PzKw 35t had become mired. Without hesitating, the black monster rolled over the helpless panzer. The same fate befell a German 150mm howitzer, which had not been able to escape in time. When the KV-1s approached, the howitzer fired at them over open sights without causing any damage at all. One of the tanks drove straight for the howitzer, which now delivered a direct hit to its frontal armor. A glare of fire and simultaneously a thunderclap of the bursting shell followed, and the tank stopped as if hit by lightning. "That's the end of that," the gunners thought as they took a collective deep breath. "Yes, that fellow's had enough," observed the section chief. Abruptly, their faces dropped in disbelief when someone exclaimed, "It's moving again!" Indeed, the tank advanced again, chains rattling loudly, and crashed into the heavy gun as if it were nothing more than a toy, pressing it into the ground and crushing it with ease as if this were an everyday affair. The heavy howitzer was finished, though the crew fortuitously escaped without harm.

Since the beginning of this action, Colonel von Seckendorff had been beseeching division headquarters for aid, but General Landgraf had no further means to send him after our panzers had proven ineffective. The message came back that everything depended on holding the line until XLI Panzer Corps could take steps to provide additional support, which Colonel von Seckendorff was initially told could not be expected until the following day (25 June). He then raised the question as to whether the moral strength of his officers and men would hold out that long and avoid a panicky disintegration under the impact of this apparently unstoppable tank attack. The problem was that 6th Panzer Division's reports of the fighting had met initially with considerable skepticism at XLI Panzer Corps headquarters, where the impression seemed to prevail that General Landgraf and Major Joachim von Kielmansegg had lost their nerve. Following a visit to the front by General Georg-Hans Reinhardt, however, during which he quickly concluded that a genuine crisis had arisen, he promised the immediate attachment of several batteries of 88mm flak, which had thus far been committed in an antiaircraft role around Tauroggen. At this point everyone supposed that only the 88mm flak guns would prove equal to the challenges of these fifty-two-ton tanks.

The Russian tanks had scarcely suffered any damage from Panzer Regiment 11's brief counterattack, but they had been forced to stop and disperse to repel it, thus losing the impetus of attack. Some of the KV-1s seemed uncomfortable in their isolation from supporting infantry and began to pull back. This momentary grace period allowed Colonel von Seckendorff to pull his own troops, including Captain Quentin's detachment, back into a new defensive position around Hill 106 and to begin reorganizing his shaken battalions. He pressed all branches of the combat arms into service for his antitank defense. His sole advantage at this point was the fact that the apparent invulnerability of the KV-1 had been disproved by the direct fire of a 100mm battery, which had finally succeeded in finishing off some of the monsters at point-blank range. At about the same time, Lieutenant Eckhardt, of the 6th Company of Captain Quentin's battalion, immobilized another KV-1 with a concentrated charge of five antitank mines. Like wildfire the word now spread through the ranks that these tanks could be destroyed; not only did our troops take heart, but the Russian tanks became more cautious (and correspondingly less dangerous), which greatly aided our defense.

Around 1500 the commander of the most advanced 88mm flak battery reported to division headquarters, where he was greeted with great relief. General Landgraf personally led this unit forward to be committed against the Soviet tanks.

Eventually the Russians assembled their entire force in the wooded areas and grain fields, then began a decisive tank drive against Hill 106, employing a mass formation of super-heavy tanks. No sooner had the steel giants left their shelter than our 88mm flak and the 100mm battery met them with volleys of armor-piercing shells. Well camouflaged and sited in staggered positions, these weapons quickly destroyed a number of Soviet tanks and brought their attack to a standstill. Rising columns of smoke from the burning tanks spread the word of our defensive victory far and wide. Later disjointed attempts by the remaining Russians to pierce or outflank Colonel von Seckendorff's defensive positions met the same fate; nor could the local attacks by cooperating Soviet infantry turn the tide. Now thoroughly exhausted by three days of forced marches and heavy fighting, the Russian infantry no longer possessed the ability to effect a breakthrough. This was, it should be remembered, the same infantry that had faced 6th Panzer Division on the first day of the war, and it had not received any special training for work in conjunction with tank formations.

Motorcycle Battalion 6 and Motorized Infantry Regiment 114 were particularly severely tested in this engagement. To be attacked by surprise by unusually heavy tanks, to have their defenses twice penetrated and overrun without having any weapons able to halt or destroy the enemy, demands more than can reasonably be expected of even battle-tested veterans. The cool behavior of the troops must be prized even higher when one realizes that they had never before been overrun by enemy tanks. In the later stages of the Russian campaign, rifle formations integral to the panzer divisions no longer faced the problem of being run over in shelter holes by Soviet tanks.

As always in critical situations, so in this case the iron discipline of the troops, the spirit and morale of battle-tested, well-trained commanders and subordinate officers, decided the issue. These men did not depend on outmoded rules and instructions but knew how to act decisively in situations not covered in the regulations or beyond their personal experience. Their success confirmed the suitability of the measures taken. The troops who survived this experience with unbroken courage and few losses would again and again prove their excellent spirit in the engagements that followed.

The period of 6th Panzer Division's isolation at Raseinai had also passed, since the 269th Infantry Division had arrived to take up position on Colonel von Seckendorff's right flank, and next to it the 290th Infantry Division of LVI Panzer Corps had also been moved up. The 1st Panzer Division had been diverted from its advance on Kelme and had seized a bridgehead over the Dubyssa at Lydavenai to the north, and the 36th Motorized Division was also approaching from the general direction of Kelme. As Russian attacks against Colonel von Seckendorff's front east of Raseinai ceased toward evening, General Reinhardt had succeeded in placing the elements of the XLI Panzer Corps in position to encircle and annihilate the Soviet III Mechanized Corps.

Isolated by a Single Tank!

The reader . . . must naturally wonder what *Kampfgruppe* Raus was doing during the tank battle at Raseinai. Why did we not come to the aid of Colonel Seckendorff's hard-pressed troops?

Nothing of any great importance occurred in our sector. The troops improved their positions, reconnoitered in the direction of Siluva and on the eastern bank of the Dubyssa in both directions, and chiefly attempted to find out what was happening in the area south of the bridge. We encountered only scattered enemy units and individual stragglers. In the course of these efforts we made contact with the outlying elements of both *Kampfgruppe* von Seckendorff and the 1st Panzer Division at Lydavenai. Upon cleaning out the wooded area west of the friendly bridgehead, some of our infantry encountered a stronger Russian infantry force, still holding out in two places on the western bank of the Dubyssa.

Contrary to procedure, some prisoners captured during these local operations, among them a Red Army lieutenant, had been transported to the rear by motor vehicle in a group, under the guard of a single NCO. Halfway back to Raseinai the driver suddenly saw an enemy tank in the road and stopped. At that moment the Russian prisoners—about twenty of them— unexpectedly attacked the driver and the NCO. The NCO had been standing next to the driver, facing the prisoners, when they attempted to seize both men's weapons. The Soviet lieutenant had already reached for the NCO's submachine gun when the latter managed to free one arm and strike him such a heavy blow that he staggered back, dragging with him the closest prisoners. Before the prisoners on either side were able to tackle the NCO again, he had—with the power of an athlete—torn free his left arm from the three men who held him, so that he momentarily had both arms free. With lightning speed he braced his submachine gun against his hip and fired into the mutinous crowd. The effect of this burst was horrendous: Only a few prisoners besides the wounded officer succeeded in leaping out of the vehicle to escape into the forest. The rest had been mowed down in seconds. The vehicle, now emptied of living prisoners, wheeled around and reached the bridgehead safely, in spite of having been fired on by the tank during the fight.

This little drama was my first indication that our bridgehead's only supply route had been blocked by a super-heavy KV-1, which had also somehow managed to sever our telephone connection with division headquarters. Although enemy intentions were as yet unclear, we had to expect an attack against the rear of our position. I immediately ordered Lieutenant Wengenroth's 3rd Battery, Panzerjaeger Battalion 41, brought into position near a flat hilltop in the vicinity of 6th Motorized Brigade's command post, which also served as headquarters for the entire *Kampfgruppe*. In order to reinforce our antitank defense, I also had a field howitzer battery stationed in the area turn its gun tubes 180 degrees to the south. Lieutenant Gebhardt's 3rd Company, Panzer Engineer Battalion 57, was directed to block the road and the immediately surrounding countryside with mines if necessary. Our attached panzers, half of Major Schenk's Panzer Battalion 65, which had been stationed in the forest, were told to organize and be prepared to launch a counterattack on a moment's notice.

Hours passed, but the enemy tank blocking the road hardly moved, though it sporadically fired in the direction of Raseinai. At noon on 24 June the scouts I had dispatched to reconnoiter the vicinity of the giant tank reported that they could not locate any nearby concentrations of Red Army troops or vehicles that might suggest an impending attack. The officer commanding this detachment concluded that the most logical explanation was that the unit to which the single tank belong was probably engaged in the fight against *Kampfgruppe* von Seckendorff.

Even though there thus appeared to be no danger of immediate attack, steps had to be taken at once to destroy this annoying tank, or at least to drive it away. Its fire had already set ablaze twelve trucks on their way from Raseinai with much-needed supplies. Nor was it possible to evacuate the soldiers wounded in fighting around the bridgehead to the medical aid stations, the consequence of which was that several severely wounded men (among them a young lieutenant who had received a point-blank shot in the abdomen) died in their ambulances because an operation to save their lives could not be carried out in time. All attempts to drive around the tank proved futile; either the vehicles became mired in the mud or, in making a wider detour, ran afoul of the scattered Russian units still lurking in the woods.

I therefore ordered Lieutenant Wengenroth's battery (newly equipped with 50mm antitank guns) to work its way through the woods to effective range of the tank and to destroy it. The battery commander and his brave soldiers had beamed with joy at this honorable mission and had set to work full of confidence that they would quickly be able to carry it out. From the command post atop the hill we followed their progress as they slipped from hollow to hollow through the woods. (Nor were we alone. Dozens of soldiers clambered onto roofs, climbed to the tops of trees, or perched on piles of wood, waiting with rapt attention for the outcome of this adventure.) Everyone saw the first gun approach to within 1,000 meters of the tank, which stood plainly visible in the middle of the road but did not seem to have noticed the threat. A second gun, which had been out of sight for some time, suddenly emerged from the last hollow in front of the tank and took up a well-camouflaged firing position. Within another thirty minutes the remaining two guns had been manhandled into similar positions.

As we watched from the crest of the hill, someone suggested that perhaps the tank had been damaged and subsequently deserted by its crew, since little else could account for it simply squatting motionless in the road, a perfect target. (The ridicule to be received from one's fellows, after having spent hours jockeying into position to finish off a dead tank, can be imagined.) Suddenly the first round flashed forth from one of the antitank guns, tracing a trajectory like a silver ray dead into the target. In no time the armor-piercing shell had covered the intervening 600 meters. A glare of fire appeared, followed by the sound of a violent impact. A direct hit! A second and then a third shot followed.

Officers and troops alike cheered and shouted as if spectators at a shooting match. "A hit! Bravo! The tank's been polished off!" The tank did not move until it had been pelted by at least eight direct hits. Then its turret rotated, it took careful aim, and methodically silenced our antitank battery with a few 80mm shells. Two of our 50mm guns were shot to pieces, and the remaining two seriously damaged. The battery suffered dead and wounded; Lieutenant Wengenroth had to withdraw the balance of his personnel into safe cover in order to avoid further losses. Only after night fell did he manage to recover his guns. The Russian tank still commanded the road, undamaged, our operation having failed disastrously. Deeply depressed, Lieutenant Wengenroth returned to the bridgehead with his soldiers. His newly introduced weapon, in which he had felt absolute confidence, had proven completely inadequate against the monster tank. A general sense of disappointment fell over the entire *Kampfgruppe*.

A new way to master the situation would have to be found.

Among the weapons available to us, it was now clear that only an 88mm flak gun, with its heavy armor-piercing shells, would be up to the task of destroying the behemoth. That afternoon, one 88mm gun was withdrawn from the fighting near Raseinai and cautiously advanced south toward the tank. The KV-1 still faced north, the direction from which it had been previously attacked. The long-barrel flak gun approached to within 2,000 meters of the beast, a range from which satisfactory results should be guaranteed. Unfortunately, some burned-out trucks, earlier victims of the monster tank, still lay at the side of the road, obstructing the gun crew's line of sight. On the other hand, these smoking wrecks offered camouflage behind which the gun could be maneuvered closer to the target. Having been prepared with numerous tree branches fastened to its exterior, the gun was manhandled cautiously forward, in order not to warn the stationary tank.

Eventually the gun crew reached the fringe of the forest, which offered the best visibility for a firing position, the distance to the tank having now been reduced to 800 meters. The first shot, we thought, was therefore bound to be a direct hit and would certainly destroy the offending tank. The crew began setting up their piece to fire.

Though the tank had not moved since its encounter with the antitank battery, its crew was alert and its commander possessed of cool nerves. He had observed the approaching gun without interfering, because as long as the flak gun was in motion it could not endanger his tank. The closer it approached, the more readily it could be destroyed. The critical moment for both adversaries in this small-scale duel arrived when the gun crew began final preparations to take up a firing position. Immediate action by the tank crew had now become imperative. As the gunners, under extreme mental strain, struggled to ready their weapon for firing, the tank swung its turret around, opening fire first. Every shot hit the mark. Heavily damaged, the flak gun was knocked into a ditch, where the crew had to abandon it. Again, the gun crew took casualties. Machine-gun fire from the tank now prevented the recovery of either the gun or the dead gunners.

The failure of this second attempt, which had begun with such high hopes, was bad news. The optimism of the troops had been lost along with the 88mm gun. Our soldiers spent a dismal day consuming canned food, as no supplies could reach us.

A much greater anxiety, however, had been at least temporarily removed. The Russian attack on Raseinai had by now been repelled by *Kampfgruppe* von Seckendorff, which had made a successful stand at Hill 106. Thus the danger that the bulk of the Soviet 2nd Tank Division might wheel around into our rear, surrounding us, had been averted. Only the smaller but extremely annoying matter of driving off the monster tank from our supply route remained. What could not be done by day, we thought, would have to be accomplished at night. The brigade staff spent several hours discussing every possibility for destroying the tank, and preparations commenced for several different solutions.

The third solution involved having our combat engineers blow up the tank during the night of 24–25 June. It must be admitted that our engineers had inwardly relished the fact that the crew-served weapons had failed to destroy the tank, for now they had the chance to upstage their comrades. When Lieutenant Gebhardt asked for twelve volunteers to raise their hands, all 120 men put their hands in the air. In order not to offend anyone, every tenth man was chosen. The twelve lucky ones waited impatiently for night to fall. Explosives and all necessary equipment had already been prepared. Lieutenant Gebhardt, who intended to lead the mission personally, oriented every man in detail with respect to the general mission, the plan of action, and his individual role. At the head of this confident column, their lieutenant marched off just after dark. The road led east past Hill 123 on a little-used sandy path to a projecting tip of the strip of woods in which the tank was located, then through a sparsely wooded region to the old assembly area.

The pale light of the stars twinkling in the sky was sufficient to reveal the contours of the nearest trees, the road, and the tank. Avoiding any noise that might give them away, barefoot scouts crept to the edge of the road and examined the tank from close quarters to select the best avenue of approach. The Russian giant stood placidly at the same spot, its turret shut. Complete calm reigned far and wide, interrupted only occasionally by a short flash of light cutting through the air, a dull thundering close behind. At times random enemy shells whizzed past, bursting in the area near the fork of the road north of Raseinai. These were the last rumblings from a day of hard fighting to the south, and around midnight the harassing fire on both sides ceased completely.

Suddenly, a crashing and snapping sounded in the forest on the other side of the road. Whispering, ghostlike figures moved toward the tank. Had the crew gotten out? There followed knocks against the turret, whereupon the hatch lifted, and something was passed upward. Judging from the soft clicking noise, it must have been bowls of food. The scouts immediately passed the word back to Lieutenant Gebhardt, who was besieged by whispered questions: "Shall we rush them and capture them? They seem to be civilians." The temptation was great, for this probably would have been easily accomplished. Yet the tank crew remained in the turret, obviously awake, and such an attack would have alarmed them, risking ruin for the entire enterprise. Regretfully, Lieutenant Gebhardt decided that it was out of the question. As a result of this unanticipated episode, another hour of waiting had to pass until the civilians (partisans?) had departed.

In the meantime, the tank and its surroundings were even more carefully reconnoitered. At 0100 hours the engineers got down to work, as the crew of the tank slept in their turret with no idea of what was happening. After an explosive charge had been attached to the caterpillar track and the tank's thick side-armor, the patrol withdrew and lit the fuse. Seconds later, a loud explosion tore the night air. The mission had been carried out, and their success appeared decisive. Yet no sooner had the echoes of the explosion died out than the machine gun of the tank burst into action, its fire sweeping the near vicinity over and over again. The tank itself did not move. Presumably its caterpillar track had been destroyed, but no direct examination was possible while the machine gun continued firing wildly in every direction. Lieutenant Gebhardt and his patrol, therefore, returned to the bridgehead quite dejectedly, none too sure of their success and also forced to report one man missing. Attempts to find him in the darkness would have proven useless.

Shortly before dawn a second, though smaller, explosion was heard from the area of the tank, for which no one could think of an explanation. The vehicle's machine gun again swept the surrounding terrain for several minutes. Then everything became calm again.

Shortly thereafter, as the day began to dawn, the rays of the golden morning sun bathed the forests and fields in light. Thousands of dewdrops glittered on flowers and grass, and the first birds began to sing. The soldiers stretched their limbs inside their tents and rubbed the sleep from their eyes. A new day had come.

The sun had not risen too high in the sky when a barefoot soldier, his boots hanging over his arm, walked past the brigade command post. It was his apparent misfortune that I, the brigade commander, first spotted him and summoned him over sharply. As the anxious wanderer stood before me, I asked in clear language for an explanation of his morning walk in such strange attire. Was he a passionate follower of Father Kneip? If so, such an enthusiasm was surely out of place here. (Father Kneip had been the nineteenth-century founder of a "back to nature" movement for physical health, icy baths, sleep under the stars, etc.)

Very embarrassed, the solitary walker confessed the reason for his guilt. Every word from this taciturn delinquent had to be extracted through severe questioning. As each answer was given, however, my face brightened. After some ten minutes of such questioning, I offered this lonely adventurer a morning cigarette, which he accepted with great embarrassment. Finally, with a smile, I patted him on the shoulder and shook his hand in parting. A strange turn, thought the curious onlookers, who had only been able to observe our conversation from a distance, without hearing what had been said. What could the barefoot boy have possibly done to find favor so quickly? It certainly could not have been anything trivial. I did not satisfy their curiosity until the brigade order of the day published an extract of the report that the young engineer had given me:

I was the listening sentry and lay in a ditch close to the Russian tank. When everything was ready, I and the company commander attached a demolition charge that was twice as strong as the regulations provided to the caterpillar track of the tank, returned to the ditch, and lit the fuse. Since the ditch was deep enough to offer protection against splinters, I waited there to see the effect of the explosion. The tank, however, repeatedly covered the fringe of the forest and the ditch with its fire after the explosion, and more than an hour passed before things calmed down again. I then crept to the tank and examined its caterpillar track at the place where I had attached the charge. Hardly half of its width had been destroyed. I could not find any other damage to the tank.

When I returned to the assembly point of the combat patrol, it had departed already. While looking for my shoes, which I had left there, I found another demolition charge that had been left behind. I took it, returned to the tank, climbed on it barefooted, and fastened the charge to the gun barrel in the hopes of at least destroying this. It was not large enough to do any greater damage. I crept under the tank and detonated the charge.

Upon this explosion, the tank immediately covered the forest fringe and ditches with its fire again. The fire did not cease until dawn, and not until then could I crawl out from underneath the tank. Inspecting the effect of this demolition, I saw to my regret that the charge I had found had been too small. The gun barrel was only slightly damaged. On arrival at the assembly point, I tried to put on the boots but discovered that they were too small and did not belong to me. One of my comrades must have changed boots by mistake. That is why I returned barefoot and too late.

This was truly the tale of a brave man.

Despite his efforts, however, the tank still blocked the road, firing and moving about as if nothing had happened. The fourth solution, set for the morning of 25 June, was to request Ju87 "Stuka" dive-bombers to attack the tank. This could not be executed because the aircraft were urgently needed elsewhere, and—even if available—whether they would have succeeded in destroying the tank by a direct hit remains an open question. We could be sure that the stubborn occupants of the steel giant would never have been chased away by near-misses.

Now the tank had to be eliminated by any means possible. The fighting power of the bridgehead garrison would become seriously endangered if the road remained blocked. Nor would the division be able to carry out its assigned missions. I therefore decided to put into effect our plan of last resort, a scheme that involved the potential loss of men, tanks, and other weapons to an extent that could not be accurately forecast. My intention, however, was to mislead the enemy and thus keep our own losses to a minimum. We planned to divert the attention of Russian KV-1 through a feint attack by Major Schenk's panzers while bringing up another 88mm flak gun to the destroy the monster. The terrain around the tank suited this purpose well, making possible a close approach to the tank and providing observation positions from the higher wooded area to the east of the road. Since the forest was sparse, consisting only of small trees, our mobile PzKw 38ts could move about quickly in all directions.

Panzer Battalion 65 soon arrived and started hammering at the tank from three sides. The crew of the KV-1 was visibly nervous. The turret repeatedly swung around to catch one or another of the pesky, smaller German tanks with its gun as they slipped past, firing at it through narrow gaps in the woods. But the Russians were always too late; no sooner had a German tank been located than it had already disappeared. The KV-1's crew knew that their tank's thick armor, which resembled elephant hide, would shrug off our shells, but the crew had ambitions of destroying the annoying tormentors without leaving the road unguarded.

Fortunately for us, in their eagerness the Russian crewmen overlooked the security of their rear, from which direction disaster was approaching. The flak gun had already taken up a position beside the one that had been knocked into the ditch on the preceding afternoon. Its powerful tube pointed at the tank, and the first shot thundered away. Wounded, the KV-1 still tried to swing its turret to the rear, but the gunners managed to get off two more shots in the meantime. The turret stopped moving, but the tank had not been set afire as we confidently expected. Though the vehicle no longer reacted to our fire, after nearly two days it seemed too early to be certain of success. Four additional armor-piercing shells from the 88mm flak gun tore into the beast. Its gun, which had been hit seven or eight times, now rose into the air, yet the tank itself stood motionless in the road, as if it meant—even now— not to give up the blockade.

The witnesses to this exciting duel were now eager to ascertain the effect of their fire. Great was their surprise when they found that only two shots had pierced the armor, and five other shots of our 88mm flak gun had only made deep dents. We further discovered eight blue spots made by the new 50mm antitank guns. The result of the attack of the engineer patrol consisted of damage to the caterpillar track and a slight dent in the gun barrel. No traces of fire from the 37mm guns of our PzKw 38ts could be found. Driven by curiosity, the small "Davids," climbing up on the fallen "Goliath," in vain tried to open the hatch of the turret. In spite of drawing, pushing, and hammering, they did not succeed.

Suddenly the gun barrel started to move again, and our soldiers dispersed in amazement. Quickly, the engineers took hand grenades and pushed them into the hole produced by the hit at the lower part of the turret. A dull explosion sounded, and the hatch lid flew open. In the interior of the tank lay the bodies of the brave crewmen, who before had apparently only fainted. Deeply moved by such heroism, we buried the dead with all honors. Their fight to the last breath was a small heroic drama on the part of the enemy.

After having been blockaded for nearly two days by a single heavy tank, the road was now open, and trucks began shuttling to the bridgehead with ample supplies for further operations. The troops had full freedom of movement again and could participate in XLI Panzer Corps's concentric attack on the Soviet III Mechanized Corps. While our own supply route was interdicted it would have been a mistake to have intervened with insufficient means in von Seckendorff's battle without being able to bring about a decision, unless such a desperate act had been absolutely necessary. We could not run the risk of expending all the ammunition on hand and being forced to face additional Russian attacks completely defenseless.

The fact that division headquarters kept its nerves and that *Kampfgruppe* von Seckendorff held out bravely during the most critical hours was now rewarded. The 1st Panzer Division from Livadenai on the far left and the 269th Infantry Division on the far right had commenced their concentric attacks that morning. Events had developed well enough that neither the 290th Infantry nor the 36th Motorized Divisions were to be needed. The forward attack by 6th Panzer Division was intentionally delayed, lest the enemy be prematurely squeezed out of the pocket. Thus, by the time the offending tank had been destroyed, *Kampfgruppe* Raus, by then reinforced by elements of the 1st Panzer Division, broke out from its bridgehead and pushed south in a spirited attack along the eastern bank of the Dubyssa River, cutting off the retreat of the Soviet 2nd Tank Division. In 6th Panzer Division's sector alone, 125 Russian tanks were put out of action, including twelve or fourteen KV-1s. Only a precipitous retreat with large equipment losses extricated the entire III Mechanized Corps from destruction.

By early evening, the two-day battle with all of its surprises had come to an end: a crowning German victory. The division regrouped that night, and the forward elements prepared to continue the drive eastward on 26 June.

The blitzkrieg rolled on.

Chapter 3

TO THE RUSSIAN BORDER

Pursuit through the Baltic States

AFTER THE DEFEAT OF THE RUSSIAN armored reserves near Raseinai, the armored units of the XLI Panzer Corps (of which the 6th Panzer Division was a part) launched a thrust on 26 June through Lithuania, Latvia, and Estonia toward Leningrad. The Soviets having sacrificed their tanks to safeguard the withdrawal of the bulk of their armies on the frontier toward the Dvina River, our advance was delayed only by terrain difficulties, heat, and enormous clouds of dust. Even so, the troops, while passing through this heavily forested region, still managed to find roads on which our seemingly endless motor transport columns were able to travel at a more or less swift pace. During the day our spearhead elements reached the Nevezis sector near Raguva, while the division main body entered Ramygala by way of Kroki-Surviliskis. Our leap forward on 27 June extended not quite so far, in order to give the division main body a chance to close up, since the movement of our supply and service units out of the Raseinai battlefield area had been delayed. Forward elements reached the Sventoji River crossings at Svedasai and Teraldziai, while the bulk of the division entered the Veinsintos area. General Landgraf moved division headquarters up to Svedasai.

The enemy appeared to be in full flight. Typically, when the Russians had been defeated on a broad front, they reestablished their lines only after they had retreated a considerable distance. They marched very quickly, even when retreating in extremely large numbers. Precisely at such times it was important to pursue them energetically and to give them no opportunity for renewed resistance. The German conduct of delaying actions, with leapfrog commitment of forces in successive positions, was apparently not known to them, possibly because this method of fighting required great mobility and competent leadership. The Soviets always sought only simple and complete solutions. When they decided to withdraw, they did so in one jump and then

immediately began an active defense again. When our panzer division, which
had torn through their lines, chased them off the roads, the Russians disappeared into the terrain with remarkable skill. In retreating, retiring from
sight, and rapidly reassembling, therefore, the Russians were already past
masters. Large forces covered long distances over terrain devoid of roads or
even paths. For example, south of Leningrad the 6th Panzer Division would
take prisoners from some of the same regiments of the 125th Rifle Division
that had first opposed us when we crossed the border at Tauroggen, having
withdrawn 500 miles to fight again.

Though no organized, large-scale enemy resistance existed, we learned
quite thoroughly that all-around defenses and security measures were an absolute necessity, even during offensive operations. Dispersed Red Army forces
were continuously reassembling; our *Kampfgruppen* began forming the first
"hedgehog" defenses as protection against Russian surprise attacks at night.
Several houses or hay barns in a major clearing would be selected as the location for the command post. Covered by thick underbrush, our tanks would
be placed in a wide circle around these buildings, with their guns ready to fire
at the edge of the woods. Immediately in front of the tanks was an outer ring
of infantry in foxholes and ditches or behind embankments that enabled the
tanks to fire over their heads. Security patrols and outposts formed the outer
cordon. The Russians recognized the strength of these protective measures
and did not dare carry out any surprise attacks they might have otherwise
planned. They resigned themselves to harassing the hedgehog area with tank
and machine-gun fire, sometimes accompanied by a few rounds of artillery.

Panzer Group 4 had originally forecast the Dvina River as our objective
for 28 June, but it was not yet clear whether 6th Panzer Division was to move
into the LVI Panzer Corps bridgehead at Daugapavils or reach a point on the
Dvina between Daugapavils and Jekabpils, which was 1st Panzer Division's
objective. The issue probably depended on whether or not 1st Panzer Division would succeed in capturing the Dvina bridge at Jekabpils in a condition
as equally undamaged as 8th Panzer Division had seized the bridge at Daugapavils. This was critical because the construction materials available to
XLI Panzer Corps would suffice to build only one bridge.

As a result of this situation and the nature of the road net leading toward
the Dvina, very much against General Landgraf's will the 6th Panzer Division had to be deployed across an abnormally wide front. *Kampfgruppe* von
Seckendorff, on the right wing, was supposed to reach a ford (or possibly a
Russian military bridge) thought to exist northeast of Ilukste, just northwest
of Daugapavils. *Kampfgruppe* Raus, on the left wing, had the assignment of
attaining the river at Livani; thus the division's spearhead elements were separated by roughly sixty-five kilometers. The gap between them could be con-

trolled only by patrols from Major Linnbrunn's Panzer Reconnaissance Battalion 57. General Landgraf accepted this risk because he wanted to avoid having the division squeezed into the Daugapavils bridgehead, and he thus oriented the main body toward Livani. Due to recurring contact with weak Russian forces (probably stragglers) in the Obeliai-Subbat area and to necessary stoppages among the march columns, only advance reconnaissance patrols actually reached the Dvina in accordance with our orders. They reported that our side of the river was free of Soviet forces and that the opposite bank seemed occupied only by local defenses.

Thus the Dvina River, the first major objective of the offensive, had been reached on the seventh day of the attack. Except for the tank battle at Raseinai—which had required unusual courage and endurance by the division—no heavy fighting had occurred. The relatively large quantities of booty seized were as noteworthy as the small number of prisoners taken. Contrary to losses suffered by the Red Army, 6th Panzer Division's own losses had so far been small. The loss of tanks and motor vehicles through enemy action was also low—in fact, it was considerably smaller than losses through mechnical defects. Even these losses, however, remained within normal proportions.

Faced only with weak enemy resistance, on 29 June *Kampfgruppe* Raus established a Dvina River bridgehead ten kilometers deep at Livani, south of the Dubna. The bridge over the Dubna at Livani had been destroyed, and our scant supplies of bridging materials were needed elsewhere. This circumstance forced General Landgraf to waive the idea of seizing a second bridgehead north of the Dubna, and he therefore limited *Kampfgruppe* von Seckendorff to mopping up the last Russian resistance west of the river around Livani. Colonel von Seckendorff quickly captured the dominant Hill 104 east of the town.

It became clear during the course of the day the XLI Panzer Corps would be unable to supply the additional bridging materials that division headquarters had requested. General Reinhardt therefore ordered General Landgraf to have those elements of the 6th Panzer Division that presumably could not be ferried across the Dvina into the Livani bridgehead by the evening of 30 June to cross behind the 1st Panzer Division over the military bridge at Jekabpils, which was currently under construction. Such a procedure would have amounted to considerable loss of time; General Landgraf and Major Joachim von Kielmansegg therefore decided to try improvising a bridge from the available means in order to get the division's main body rapidly across the rather fast-flowing river of at least 150 meters' width.

The bridge construction, organized by Lieutenant Colonel Erich Lehnert's Panzer Engineer Battalion 57, was remarkable because the river was being spanned by a makeshift combination of four different construction systems. All that the division possessed with which to work was one pontoon trestle bridge, one box girder bridge supported on pontoons and trestles, one trestle bridge, and an auxiliary bridge built with captured barges. Construction was slowed down but not decisively hindered by repeated Russian bombing raids, though only the division's own light 20mm flak guns were available to defend against them. By late afternoon on 30 June the entire division, except for our PzKw IIIs and IVs and the 150mm artillery battalion, for which the load capacity did not suffice, had crossed over this bridge. Lieutenant Colonel Lehnert's engineers had thus performed an outstanding feat.

Our Livani bridgehead meanwhile was being systematically enlarged toward Rudzeti and south of the town, so that the entire division could be assembled on the northeast bank of the Dvina for the next thrust toward the Latvian-Russian border. Weaker elements that had heretofore remained northeast of Ilukste were now moved up. General Landgraf's decision to advance the bulk of the division to the Dvina at Livani had proven to be the right choice.

As noted above, it was during the Dvina River crossings that the Russian air force began to make a reappearance. Concentrations of bomber units with escort fighters made their presence felt. Skillfully maneuvering, they hit the bridges and crossing sites in surprise attacks. Coming in from the flanks or from the rear, they harassed our troops crossing the river and were responsible for some losses. Overall, however, the XLI Panzer Corps's crossing of the Dvina was neither stopped nor even delayed.

Even though time was of the essence as the Red Army pulled back toward Leningrad, the Russians succeeded in carrying off large numbers of cattle, as well as a substantial amount of equipment and supplies. In withdrawing they did not hesitate to burn cities and towns to the ground, if it seemed that any advantage was to be gained (this was Joseph Stalin's heralded "scorched-earth" policy). All that remained as our troops marched in were ashes and ruins; for that reason it even became difficult in many sectors to quarter our larger headquarters organizations in locations that would ensure their ability to function. They also shot thousands of "undesirable" persons in the Baltic countries before retreating and took other tens of thousands with them.

During the first period of the war the Russians apparently sought to impress the German troops and lower their morale by committing numerous atrocities upon them. The great number of such crimes, committed on all sectors of the front, tends to support that presumption. For example, on 25 June 1941, two batteries of the 267th Infantry Division near Melniki (Army

Group Center) were overrun in the course of a Russian night breakthrough and bayoneted to the last man. Individual dead bore up to seventeen bayonet wounds, among them even holes through the eyes. Several weeks later, while combing a forest for enemy forces, a battalion of Infantry Regiment 465 was attacked from all sides by Russian tree snipers and lost seventy-five dead and twenty-five missing. When a follow-up attack secured the area, all of the missing men were found to have been shot through the neck.

In the morning of 1 July, some elements of 6th Panzer Division were again put in march, since our reconnaissance efforts had not thus far detected any Russian forces along our axis of advance. Against only weak Soviet resistance, our open right flank elements reached Varakiani. It was my understanding that General Landgraf made this decision on his own in order to exploit our favorable tactical situation, or at the very least the movement was approved by higher headquarters upon his suggestion. Panzer Group 4 had not actually intended to resume the general advance until 2 July, as many elements were still crossing the river. The 8th Panzer Division (LVI Panzer Corps) was lagging far behind on the Daugapavils-Ostrov highway, but the 1st Panzer Division also put some strong advance detachments forward.

During 2–3 July our movements were much hampered because of the continuous threat to our deep right flank and the inadequacies of the roads, especially northeast of Lake Luban. The 8th Panzer Division continued to advance but slowly along the highway toward Ostrov, having to deal with stronger Russian remnant forces than the Panzer Group's other divisions and, in consequence, always lagging forty to fifty kilometers behind 6th Panzer Division's spearheads. This meant that we had to provide our own flank protection along that highway in order to guard both our own supply line and that of the 1st Panzer Division as it pushed north of Lake Luban. By the end of 2 July, having attained an approximate forward line from Zoblewa to Birzi, 6th Panzer Division had not been forced to overcome any organized resistance but continually had to cope with small, local collisions with fragments of Red Army units. These enemy elements, in turn, attacked our forces employed for flank security. It was obvious that the Russian command was attempting to keep the highway for its own use.

On 3 July General Landgraf's orders required 6th Panzer Division to reach the highway at Gauri after detouring around the Karsava area, which was still held by significant Russian forces. Panzer Group 4 then expected the division to advance along that highway in order to assist the 8th Panzer Division (which time and again got stuck), while simultaneously maintaining contact with the 1st Panzer Division as it advanced west of the highway toward Ostrov against negligible resistance. General Landgraf, who would much rather have pushed forward via Karsava despite the Soviet forces in that sector, found himself forced to send *Kampfgruppen* Raus and von Seckendorff to find their way through the swamps around Tizla, which offered even greater difficulties than usual due to rain. Contrary to our rapid advances of the past, our spearhead units now had to pick their way through marshy terrain. Even so, by evening our forward elements reached the highway at Gauri, where we assumed flank protection against Karsava and reconnoitered in the direction of Augspils. Unfortunately, this awkward deployment left the bulk of the division scattered far and wide.

The consequences of this dispersion made themselves felt on 4 July. Our forward elements, still threatened from the rear, approached stiffening Soviet resistance along the Russian border as they maneuvered to gain assembly areas for our offensive against the Stalin Line as the remainder of the division gradually closed up. One of our march columns was hit by a surprise attack, supported by tanks, just east of Baltinava. While detouring around German-occupied Gauri, this Russian force had launched its ambush from south to north. (This attack element was probably the same force that had tried, under pressure from 8th Panzer Division, to break out in a northern direction in order to avoid being pushed into the swamps east of Gauri.) Advanced enemy detachments succeeded in crossing the Baltinava-Gauri road from south to north as they exploited the element of surprise. A dangerous situation for the entire 6th Panzer Division thus arose, because the division had been torn apart, with its major combat elements tied down at the front while the main body had to deal with the possibility of more attacks along the line of communications at any moment.

At first it was impossible to shift any combat elements back to Baltinava in order to deal with this threat. Division did, however, manage to free the road through a counterattack from Baltinava by Motorcycle Battalion 6, which had just arrived. The bulk of the Russian force, which had not yet broken out to the north, seemed—at least partly—to withdraw south again. Some enemy elements, however, remained in the stretches of woods just south of the highway, from which they kept the road under constant tank fire. Motorcycle Battalion 6 had to be committed again, this time attacking directly south. In support of this attack, Panzer Engineer Battalion 57 for the first time employed the heavy projectiles over which they disposed, with stupendous success. Not only was the forest quickly taken, but we also found twenty undamaged Soviet tanks, whose crews, impressed by the blast of these projectiles, must have abandoned their vehicles and fled. Having mastered the crisis, 6th Panzer Division continued its advance toward the Latvian-Russian border.

Cracking the Stalin Line

Directly behind the Russian frontier lay the Stalin Line, the quality of which was something of an unknown. This defensive belt consisted of concrete pillbox emplacements extending over three kilometers in depth, but we assumed that the quality of its construction varied, since 1st Panzer Division had already reached the road near the Branchanikovo railroad station by early afternoon on 4 July, thus penetrating the defenses on the far side of the line. In 6th Panzer Division's sector, after Jaunlatgale and Augspils were captured, careful reconnaissance revealed the existence of a considerable number of concrete bunkers on both sides of the road. These bunkers were occupied, especially on the heights to the southeast on the far side of the Lja River. General Landgraf decided to conduct a well-planned breakthrough assault on 5 July rather than to attack from the march that day. Major factors that entered into this decision included the need to concentrate the troops who had been drawn apart during the difficult and rapid advances of the past two days and through the fighting at Baltinava, as well as the lateness of the hour and our growing appreciation of Russian tenacity on the defensive. These considerations led General Landgraf to conclude that a thrust against such a bunker line during the advance hardly promised any success, while he also realized that terrain conditions and the extent of the southern extension of the Stalin Line precluded the possibility of detouring for a flank attack. Closing up the formations of the division required the rest of the day and much of the night of 4–5 July. Fortunately, the fall of Karsava and the establishment of contact with 8th Panzer Division finally relieved us of our preoccupation with the flanks and rear. The deliberate assembly for this assault took place despite the objections of General Reinhardt, whose insistence on the necessity of securing and expanding 1st Panzer Division's surprise success was understandable enough. By this time, 1st Panzer Division's advance elements had already driven forward to enter the southern part of Ostrov, capturing two undamaged bridges across the Vyelikaya River.

This assault was as difficult to prepare as it was to carry out, because the attack had to be squeezed into the narrow strip of land between the Lja and Udraja Rivers. The Russians offered stiff resistance and defended each position to the last. The initial assault bogged down in front of the bunker line, and the bunkers then had to be taken, one by one, in tough close combat, employing storm-troop tactics, engineer support, and antitank weapons. The breakthrough succeeded only in the late hours of the afternoon of 6 July, after the capture of more than twenty bunkers in the course of fifteen hours of fighting. On no other day since the beginning of the campaign had so lit-

tle terrain been won, yet the battle was the fiercest by far. This was where 6th
Panzer Division acquired its first combat experience against Russian bunker
fortifications, experience that would prove useful in the immediate future.
We doubted that it was sheer accident that XLI Panzer Corps would later
commit 6th Panzer Division time and time again against the best-improved
of the different Russian positions that still had to be overcome on the road to
Leningrad.

Breaking through the Stalin Line in a single day had great tactical importance, for only by doing so was it possible to bring urgently needed relief to
the 1st Panzer Division, which was being heavily attacked by greatly superior
Soviet forces in its small Ostrov bridgehead. As soon as we entered Russian
territory, we left behind the few passable roads, and conditions unmistakably
changed for the worse. Thus, during our exploitation toward Ostrov, we
found it expedient to mount infantrymen on our tanks, an improvisation effective primarily against a defeated enemy. Both *Kampfgruppen* organized
spearhead panzer units, composed of about fifty tanks with infantry
mounted on them, which pursued the fleeing Russians relentlessly. Meeting
with negligible resistance, we pressed on, reaching the city of Ostrov well before noon on 6 July. It should be noted that this expedient worked only because the enemy was vanquished and shattered, with the mere appearance of
German tanks setting off a panic in the Russian ranks. But whenever the Russians were firmly entrenched, such a venture inevitably proved both dangerous and costly. During the later years of the war this improvisation was generally discontinued because of heavy casualties caused by antitank weapons
and air attacks; the introduction of larger quantities of armored personnel
carriers [APCs], moreover, had essentially eliminated the need for it.

The main task on 6 July was for the division to move into the eastern part
of the Ostrov bridgehead, which was to be enlarged to the extent of permitting usage of the Ostrov-Novoryin highway by 3rd Motorized Division. This
division of the LVI Panzer Corps was to move across the Ostrov bridge in
order to circumvent the incredibly difficult swamps around the railroad line
running from Rezekne to Pustoshka. With this purpose in mind we attacked
against determined Soviet resistance on both sides of the Ostrov-Porkhov
road and managed to gain about ten kilometers. Constant Russian bombing
raids against the Ostrov bridges were unsuccessful, but traffic difficulties
were considerable.

On 7 July the attack continued, gaining another ten to fifteen kilometers
toward the northeast before grinding to a halt. The stalling of this attack
could be partly attributed to the exhaustion of the troops after two days of
heavy combat and forced marches. Moreover, the Russians continually
launched violent counterattacks that, though all were repelled, took their

toll. *Kampfgruppe* Raus, on the division's left wing, was finally able to resume the attack that evening. The fighting between Ostrov and the Luga River was characterized by uninterrupted combat (even at night), the fierceness of an enemy who fought a delaying action, increasing terrain difficulties (deep mud and swamps), and—not least of all—sudden changes in the direction of our attacks mandated by higher headquarters. Our orders for 8 July called for only a limited gain of territory toward Porkhov and a subsequent pivoting of our main effort to the north. General Reinhardt probably selected the latter maneuver in order to move 6th Panzer Division closer to 1st Panzer Division, and because LVI Panzer Corps was to be shifted toward Porkhov.

Carrying out these orders required a concentric commitment of the division. On the right, *Kampfgruppe* Raus encountered only weak resistance until our lead elements approached Slavkovitsi. Expected relief of units left behind on flank security by the 269th Infantry Division did not occur on time, and we therefore had to change over to the defensive against violent counterattacks by strong Russian tank forces. Despite this pressure, we held the territory we had attained. In the meantime, on the left, *Kampfgruppe* von Seckendorff fought its way north and formed a bridgehead across the Cherekha River north of Osipovets. During the night of 8–9 July *Kampfgruppe* Raus moved up into this bridgehead.

After crossing the rail line that connected Pskov to Porkhov, 6th Panzer Division again pivoted to the east and continued its attack with the same two spearhead *Kampfgruppen*. *Kampfgruppe* Raus, the northern group, quickly gained ground and the reached Zagoska by turning east through Lopatovo, while in the south *Kampfgruppe* von Seckendorff—passing across Elevation 148—had to face local Soviet resistance throughout most of the morning. The division's advance bogged down again toward evening in the face of strengthened Russian forces, now supported by tanks. The Soviets had established themselves to defend the so-called road triangle at Jamkino. General Landgraf realized that it would again be necessary to prepare a deliberate attack.

Generally speaking, on 10 July the 6th Panzer Division suffered its first tactical failure since crossing the border when the attack against the Jamkino road triangle did not lead to success. There the enemy offered stubborn and skillful resistance in the woods and thickets, time and again launching counterblows supported by tanks. Yet the main reason for the division's hesitant advance was the reappearance of Soviet heavy tanks, which had not been encountered since Raseinai. These tanks now began to appear frequently, as the plant that produced them was located near Leningrad. Near Jamkino the KV-1s were cleverly employed as "roving bunkers." Each fifty-two-ton tank was surrounded by two or three smaller tanks and about one infantry platoon, all of whom had as their primary mission the security of the heavy tank. It was therefore impossible for our assault troops to get close to the tanks, forcing us to fight them from a distance.

At Jamkino the 6th Panzer Division had no 88mm flak, because—over General Landgraf's protests—XLI Panzer Corps had taken away our attached batteries the day before. This made it necessary to experiment, under fire, with other makeshift arrangements for destroying these well-camouflaged "fifty-two-ton bunkers." Panzer Artillery Regiment 76 employed 100mm guns in a direct fire role, though they were difficult to move into position. Our engineers unsuccessfully attempted to repeat their success at Baltinava with heavy rocket launchers. Major Roemhild's Panzerjaeger Battalion 41 even engaged the KV-1s with our 50mm antitank guns. (We had determined immediately after Raseinai that, under favorable conditions, these guns actually could penetrate the side of the fifty-two-ton tanks at close range. The penetration had the approximate width of a pencil.) Through these expedients we managed several times to force the heavy tanks to change position but were unable to put any of them out of commission.

General Landgraf's eventual decision to halt the attack and bypass Jamkino could not be implemented that day. This proved fortunate in some respects, as night and morning reconnaissance on 11 July revealed that 6th Panzer Division's pressure, and perhaps LVI Panzer Corps's thrust against Porkhov, had caused the Russians at Jamkino to withdraw toward Borovichi. Still spearheading 6th Panzer Division's advance, *Kampfgruppe* Raus now pushed northeast from Ostrov toward Porkhov and Dno.

On entering into Russia proper, the current organization of *Kampfgruppe* Raus consisted of the following:

Headquarters, 6th Motorized Brigade
Motorized Infantry Regiment 4 (two battalions)
6th Company, Motorized Infantry Regiment 114 (APCs)
II/Panzer Regiment 11
II and III/Panzer Artillery Regiment 76
3rd Company, Panzer Engineer Battalion 57
One antitank company, Panzerjaeger Battalion 41
Flak Battalion 601
One ambulance column
One supply echelon

This made a total of:
1,500 riflemen

230 machine guns
Twelve 105mm Infantry Howitzers
Sixty panzers (primarily PzKw IIs and PzKw 35ts)
Twelve 105mm field artillery pieces
Twelve 150mm field artillery pieces
Nine 50mm antitank guns
Twelve 88mm flak guns
Thirty-six 20mm flak guns

We would, however, be unable to exploit this success, because Panzer Generals Erich Hoepner and Reinhardt abruptly issued new orders.

Chapter 4

THE GATEWAY TO LENINGRAD

A Battle Against Nature

ON 11 JULY, THE 6TH PANZER DIVISION received General Rein-hardt's orders diverting it from its eastward advance toward Porkhov and Dno in order to assist the 1st Panzer Division, whose drive via the Leningrad-Pskov highway toward Luga had run into stiff Russian resistance near Novoselye. This march was to become an incredibly difficult task for *Kampf-gruppe* Raus, for it required us to discontinue our current movement and abruptly wheel ninety degrees, continuing in a straight line in the general direction of Panzer Group 4's advance, over sandy and swampy roads that, from time immemorial, had never been used by motor vehicles. Hardly had *Kampfgruppe* Raus, then the division lead echelon, started for the trouble spot than the road shown on the map as leading directly through a swamp to Novoselye came to an end.

The occupants of the wretched huts, which we came across here and there, appeared equally bewildered when we requested them to make a circle around the swampy area and lead us to a village that was marked on our ob-solete maps as being located on our line of march. These people were not fa-miliar with the name with which the village was labeled on our maps, be-cause the name had been changed decades earlier. Often we were left relying solely on our compasses and our instincts. With guides and engineers to the front, we took up a zigzag course, from village to village, over the best wagon roads that could be found. At the first swampy hole (about ten meters wide), an apparently sturdy bridge collapsed under the weight of one of our light PzKw 35ts, delaying the entire movement for five hours until Lieutenant Geb-hardt's engineers could improvise a new bridge.

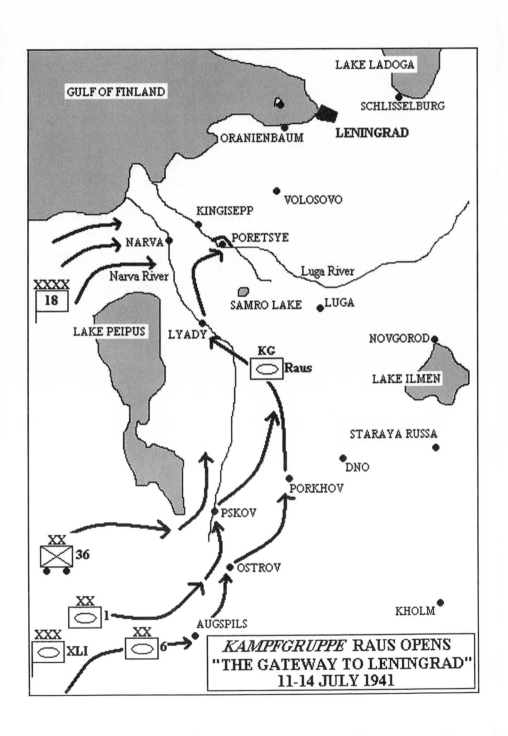

LAKE LADOGA

GULF OF FINLAND

SCHLISSELBURG

ORANIENBAUM

LENINGRAD

VOLOSOVO

KINGISEPP

PORETSYE

NARVA

Narva River

Luga River

XXXX
18

SAMRO LAKE

LUGA

LAKE PEIPUS

LYADY

NOVGOROD

KG
Raus

LAKE ILMEN

STARAYA RUSSA

DNO

PORKHOV

PSKOV

XX
36

OSTROV

XX
1

KHOLM

XXX
XLI

XX
6

AUGSPILS

KAMPFGRUPPE RAUS OPENS
"THE GATEWAY TO LENINGRAD"
11-14 JULY 1941

Whenever possible, driving in the tracks of the preceding vehicles had to be avoided, otherwise wheels sank deeper and deeper until they became completely stuck. The column had to cross twelve swampy brooks, and at each one a long delay ensued while the engineers strengthened rotted bridges with girders or rebuilt them entirely. Detouring around such swampy parts was futile, as vehicles and tanks broke through the crusted top layer of ground and became so mired that they had to be towed out by other tanks. Often the towing vehicle sank in beside the one it was attempting to assist. Sometimes vehicles roped together to help each other became so badly stuck that they had to be extricated one by one by our most powerful wreckers—a twenty-ton prime mover with super-size tracks. To maneuver these huge wreckers to the points at which they were needed was an entirely separate problem. The cart roads were so narrow and clogged that there was little opportunity to turn out or edge around other vehicles. Commanders could not exercise effective leadership because emergencies developed everywhere at the same time, and bottlenecks could be reached only on foot.

To keep the *Kampfgruppe* from becoming scattered, I ordered halts at regular intervals, whenever the terrain permitted, so that vehicles could close up. One such halt was made sixteen kilometers south of Novoselye to let the troops assemble and recover their strength for the impending attack. The first vehicles reached the halt point at 2000, after a day in which the only enemy they had fought was the swamp. The last truck did not pull in until 0400 the next morning. The rate of march averaged about 1.5 kilometers per hour. Men and motors had run out of water, and the troops were exhausted from the burning summer heat. By radio I notified division headquarters of the conditions encountered, which allowed *Kampfgruppe* von Seckendorff to follow another route. The day-long struggle against the swamp, caused by the inaccuracy of the available maps and the lack of engineer equipment, prevented us from attacking near Novoselye on 11 July.

Next morning, our advance detachment attacked the flank of the Russian forces guarding the highway, whose presence south of a small, swampy stream had been reported the day before. After a short, sharp engagement, including a tank fight, we threw the flank guard back across the river. American amphibious tanks made their first appearance on the Russian front in this action. Six of them fell victim to our antitank and panzer fire at close range from a wooded area—three knocked out on land and three while crossing the small stream. The first German troops to gain the northern bank seized two of them that were still serviceable.

The six-foot-deep, swampy stream was not fordable, so our engineers again had to construct a bridge for the *Kampfgruppe*'s main body. By 1000 the entire column had crossed, and—after destroying more Russian light tanks—drove the Soviets to a point just south of Novoselye. That afternoon we launched an all-out assault against the Russian flank, while other forces (including a panzer battalion) hit the enemy rear. After a bitter fight, the main attack caved in the enemy's flank, and when the panzer thrust crashed into the rear, the entire Russian defense collapsed. While we began reorganizing, the 1st Panzer Division took up the pursuit.

Hardly had *Kampfgruppe* Raus reorganized than we received orders to march north to seize the bridge over the Plyussa River at Lyady and establish a bridgehead on the far bank. This order ruined all chances for a night's sleep, and early on 13 July, after just three hours of rest, the march began. As before, our route led through many swampy places, and we crept forward slowly. Time and again vehicles—or even whole sections of the convoy—became stuck in swamps or intermediate sandy areas. Motors ran hot as they were forced under the strain; numerous halts had to be called to add water to radiators, consuming precious time. At several steep banks all of our trucks had to be towed over by tanks or wreckers.

After these extremely difficult and time-consuming marches and battles, our advance detachment managed, by launching a sudden attack, to capture the bridge over the Plyussa River and occupy a bridgehead position at Lyady. This surprise raid was executed by a lieutenant of the advance detachment without waiting for orders. After he and his advance party had routed a Russian engineer unit in a fierce battle a few kilometers south of the river, he leaped into his cross-country command vehicle, shouting at his troops nothing but the brief order, "Follow me!" Driving rapidly over sand roads and through brushwood, he rushed toward the bridge in order to reach it before the retreating enemy engineers. His platoon followed, recklessly unmindful of the fact that the Russians had resumed firing. Running this gauntlet, they succeeded in capturing the Soviet bridge guards, who had been taken completely by surprise, before they could be alerted and reinforced. Through this decisive action the bridge, which was 150 meters long and ten meters high, fell into our hands without a fight. We established our bridgehead after clearing out the last pockets of Soviet resistance in Lyady. The objective had been attained after a march of fifty-nine kilometers in nine hours, a rate of slightly better than 6.5 kilometers per hour.

The troops had just finished a meal and completed their first-echelon maintenance preparatory to taking a well-earned rest when we were alerted for a new mission. General Reinhardt appeared in person, ordering an immediate thrust to seize and hold the two large wooden bridges over the Luga River near Porechye, the so-called Gateway to Leningrad. Elements of 1st Panzer Division would be conducting a parallel advance directed toward Ssabsk. As the general gave his instructions, I immediately understood the importance of the mission. Up to that time no German unit had been able to penetrate the Luga River line, which was protected by defensive fortifications and an extensive swamp. Eighteenth Army had stalled in front of Narva to the north, and the rest of Panzer Group 4 had been held up before the city of Luga to the south.

Prior to receiving General Reinhardt's orders, we had been but vaguely informed about the situation of the adjoining units that composed Army Group North. Within Panzer Group 4, we knew that the four divisions of XLI Panzer Corps were spread across an air distance of over 130 kilometers and that LVI Panzer Corps was engaged in heavy fighting in the Soltsy-Utorgozii area, another sixty kilometers southeast of 6th Panzer Division. The stiffening resistance reported along the front indicated that the Red Army had obviously succeeded for the first time in establishing an essentially uniform and coordinated line of battle in front of the entire army group, a circumstance that was bound to slow down our advance from Ostrov onward. Notwithstanding the trail-blasting and rapid success of Panzer Group 4, the Sixteenth and Eighteenth Armies had advanced very slowly.

General Landgraf was laboring under the impression that higher command (Panzer Group 4 and Army Group North) was not quite sure of itself and was overreaching its objective, at least as far as the time elements were concerned. He deduced that the actual purpose in pivoting the two panzer divisions to the northwest was to bypass increasingly fierce Soviet resistance on the highway to Luga. Given the fact that Russian resistance could be expected only to increase as we approached Leningrad and the extended swamps south of the Luga River that were barely passable for mechanized units, General Landgraf wondered whether the new start would prove expedient.

Everyone faced the next several days with apprehension, because we had to expect the enemy to endeavor to throw all available forces against our spearheads and flanks. This would certainly occur as soon as the Russian command recognized that the thrust of 1st and 6th Panzer Divisions posed equal dangers for Leningrad and its remaining forces in Estonia, forward of Lake Peipus. General Landgraf knew that 6th Panzer Division could find itself in a precarious situation if its combat elements were still within the swamps when hit by the expected counterattack. Moreover, the division's main body would necessarily lag far behind *Kampfgruppe* Raus, for pulling out of the Lake Radilovskoye region would be complicated by the necessity of 1st and 6th Panzer Divisions crossing each other's march routes.

My immediate concerns revolved around the advance to Porechye. Without delay I dispatched the motorcycle messengers, who had been left at headquarters by my subordinate units, to summon their respective commanders, and I passed these orders on to them, giving them the necessary information regarding the point of departure and the route and organization of march. Some of the commanders made notes of certain particulars and asked questions, while others discussed ways of rendering mutual assistance—how to make the assigned engineers, tanks, radio trucks, artillery, and other heavy weapons an integral part of the organization. We also discussed problems of supply. All these instructions, too, including the most minute details, were issued only by word of mouth.

Throughout the march I remained with the battalion in the lead, at times as far ahead as the advance detachment, or with those elements of the column bogged down in the rear, and with whom radio contact was maintained. General Reinhardt's rallying cry "Open the gates to Leningrad!" like an electric spark kindled a flame in the hearts of the soldiers. All weariness was immediately forgotten. Dusk had not yet fallen when the engines that had only just stopped began to hum again.

The region we initially entered consisted of sand dunes that were in part sparsely overgrown with coniferous trees. The march unit, now using the method of following in the tracks of the preceding vehicle, was able in spite of all difficulties to traverse this area at the rate of ten kilometers per hour. Unit after unit rolled smoothly along, in duly protected march formation. We were beginning to hope that it would prove possible to reach the objective, which was still 100 kilometers distant, in a few hours.

As soon as we reached the swampy region south and west of Lake Samro the road suddenly changed into marshland of the worst kind. Tanks and guns bogged down, and here even the prime movers and other emergency vehicles suffered the same fate. Progress became increasingly difficult, and before dusk tanks that had tried to skirt especially bad spots, as well as those that attempted to drive through swampy ponds by main force, had become stuck fast. The first moor could only be traversed after hours of backbreaking work by every officer and man, tormented by swarms of mosquitoes as they employed tree trunks, boughs, planks, and the last available fascine mats to create a barely passable route. It was only after a night-long struggle against the sand and mud that we finally reached a passable road.

We regained our momentum once beyond the swamp, but this relief was short-lived, as a burned-out bridge loomed up to the front, its timbers still glowing. Our scouts quickly marked out a diversionary route through a neighboring village. As the leading elements approached the village, explosions sounded on all sides, followed by fires, which rapidly engulfed the narrow road through the settlement. For the next two hours this fire made movement impossible. As the flames died, the *Kampfgruppe* edged slowly through the smoldering embers and falling boards. By then it was midnight, and a great distance still remained to be covered. Time and again I received radio messages from corps and division urging speed because of the importance of the mission. With great difficulty our vehicles tried to find their way in the dim light, and for a few kilometers the column moved jerkily forward. Then real trouble started. Swamp hole after swamp hole appeared, and bridge after bridge broke under the weight of tanks, disappearing into the mud. We had neither the time nor the materials to rebuild these bridges; our engineers gathered tree trunks and threw them over the collapsed structures until a sufficient, though precarious, load-bearing surface was built up. We followed this method in numerous places until reaching the hard-surfaced road near Zaruchye some eight hours later.

On good roads we could achieve speeds exceeding thirty kilometers per hour, but in a short time there was another halt—the bridge across a deep lake was on fire. This time it was the commander of the engineer platoon of 3rd Company, Panzer Engineer Battalion 57, attached to the advance who, without orders, dashed at utmost speed across the burning Dolgaya bridge, so as to be able to begin extinguishing the blaze at the other side of the river where the fire had first broken out. The engineers succeeded in putting the fire out so rapidly with sand and water that the load-bearing capacity of the charred bridge remained sufficient even for the weight of our tanks and prime movers. The loss of this bridge would have been a critical blow, because it was neither possible to ford the deep river nor cross the adjacent swampy terrain. If we had been delayed for any length of time at this point, which was under Russian aerial observation, the operation might well have ended in failure. Thanks to the initiative of another young lieutenant, this danger was dispelled.

Suddenly the cry "Enemy aircraft!" went up, but the planes made no attack and our march continued. Again the planes appeared, signaled with lights, and dropped pamphlets. "Identify yourselves or we will fire," is what my interpreter told me these slips said in Russian. I gave orders to resume the movement and did not allow the column to halt as the pamphlets rained down on us again. Eventually the planes flew away. Their doubt was understandable. *Kampfgruppe* Raus, a motorized column, had advanced through a large swampy area deep into enemy territory with significant concentrations of Russian troops on either side. Our position must have given the pilots cause for suspicion, but the fact that we continued to march without otherwise responding apparently convinced them that we were a Red Army unit.

Shortly before reaching the Verza bridge, I ordered the entire column to halt in a high forest in which it could be completely hidden from the view of the enemy. I did so in order to provide the opportunity to close up from the rear and to issue instructions concerning the capture of the Luga River crossings and the establishment of the bridgehead. I gave the order by word of mouth, based on an obsolete 1:300,000 map:

> The enemy in all probability has not yet recognized us as a German unit. It is of paramount importance to seize the Luga bridges quickly and intact. To this end the advance detachment will make a surprise attack on the enemy bridge guards and eliminate them. Following this, the accompanying engineer company will immediately remove all mines and take charge of securing the bridges. The main body of the *Kampfgruppe* will follow close behind, advancing without delay across the bridges toward Ivanovskoye, where it will occupy the road fork there and conduct reconnaissance by way of Yurky and Srednoye. The artillery will provide fire support from a position on the southern shore of the Luga River. Distribution of heavy weapons remains the same as before. The 6th (Armored Personnel Carrier) Company of Motorized Infantry Regiment 114 will place itself at my disposal and hold itself in readiness in the forest area south of the bridges. That is the same point where the troops will park all supply vehicles and repair to the auxiliary station. Each unit will be responsible for its own security. The flak battalion will provide air raid protection in the area south of the bridges. My command post will be established close to the southern end of the new bridge. I expect the attack to be carried out with determination and vigor, and I look forward to a complete victory.

There were no further questions, and no regroupings necessary, and so only ten minutes later the column again continued to roll, organized as heretofore. If our assumption was correct—that we had not yet been recognized by the Russians—any attempt to reconnoiter the bridge area had to be avoided because this might have seriously jeopardized the operation, whose success depended almost completely on the element of surprise. I therefore decided to effect a quasi-"peacetime" march. Spearheaded by a panzer company, the advance detachment arrived at Muravina. Advancing through the forest and the village located in front of the bridge approaches, our column reached the river crossings without being seen. Not until that moment did the Russian guards on the bridges realize their mistake. Since they possessed neither antitank guns nor other tank-killing weapons, they fled, panic-stricken, to their bunkers. Lieutenant Gebhardt's pursuing engineers drove them out without a fight and captured them en masse. Our panzers, in the meantime, had been rolling across the two bridges, after which they made short work of the large log bunkers on the northern bank of the river.

Thirty minutes later, in accordance with our original orders, we had seized without a fight not only the two Luga River bridges but also the road fork at Ivanovskoye as well. The security guards had been taken completely by surprise and fell easily into our hands. *Kampfgruppe* Raus, after three days and nights of incessant struggle with the hardships of nature, penetrated 200 kilometers, culminating at 1000, 14 July, with the seizure of the "Gateway to Leningrad," just 105 kilometers from the city.

The previous challenge from the Soviet planes—"Identify yourself!"—was finally answered in an unmistakable manner when five panzers attacked the nearby Russian airfield at Yastrebina. This again was a secondary operation undertaken at the initiative of a junior officer. The officer in question was a lieutenant in II Battalion, Panzer Regiment 11, who had captured an enemy aircraft observer in the church tower at Ivanovskoye; the man apparently had not even witnessed the action that led to our seizure of the bridges. From his interrogation of this prisoner, the lieutenant learned about the Yastrebina airfield, which was barely ten kilometers away and occupied by strong forces. Making a quick decision, the lieutenant requested permission to pay the Russian aviators a visit with the five PzKw 35ts of his platoon. This request was all the more remarkable for the fact that neither the lieutenant nor his men had been able to rest during the past three days and teetered on the brink of exhaustion. Even though I knew that the Soviets would not be long in responding to such an action, there was only one answer I could possibly give such an intrepid young officer: "Permission granted, but make sure you come back soon!"

Meanwhile it was necessary to report our safe arrival and the establishment of the bridgehead to division and corps headquarters. Our radio transmitters, unfortunately, were hampered by the extensive swampy forests and unable to overcome the immense distances involved. The only manner in which we could send a message to XLI Panzer Corps over the airwaves was to dispatch a radio truck sixty kilometers to the rear, a procedure that consumed several hours. The brief message said only, "Bridges captured intact at 1000 and secured through bridgehead. 14 July. Raus." The radio truck had just returned when a Russian regiment blocked the road behind us.

The young lieutenant's five panzers also returned from their raid about this time, completely gratified with their success. Driving through the hangars and over the planes standing about on the ground had been a rare treat for them. The operation of these five PzKw 35ts had proven more effective than any bombing attack the Luftwaffe might have made. The field, across which they left heaps of ruined aircraft and vehicles, was ablaze. Flames and dark clouds of smoke shot up into the sky and could be seen from afar. All airfields in the Leningrad area—and there were quite a number of them—were instantly alerted. Hardly an hour had passed before our completely worn-out troops, who had only just arrived in their assigned defensive sectors, were roughly jolted out of sleep. Out of a clear sky the villages, farms, roads, and adjacent fringes of forest were subjected to a veritable downpour of bombs. A particularly large share was meted out to the villages of Muravina and Porechye, situated on both sides of the bridges. My headquarters, located in Muravina, was deprived of shelter and had to take refuge in the nearby forest, suffering the same fate as the troop units.

This attack was enough of a signal to galvanize even our exhausted troops into action. Without delay, foxholes for protection against tanks and air raids were dug everywhere and provided with a thick overhead covering. These individual positions were then interconnected until they formed a narrow zigzag trench system. Waves of enemy aircraft continued to attack in succession until the day drew to a close. Unfortunately, so far to the north, darkness fell very late. Once our flak had organized the antiaircraft defense, we began to inflict serious losses on them, forcing the Russians to abandon their practice of conducting low-level flights. We knew quite well that we were on our own in combating enemy aircraft; the Luftwaffe was unlikely to appear very soon because its ground organizations could not keep pace with the rapid advances of our panzer units.

The first short night passed uneventfully, but no one doubted that the Russians would do their utmost to eliminate immediately the danger threatening Leningrad. Infantry forces in large numbers, supported by artillery and tanks, were moving up on all railroads and highways. We would learn that the Russians had committed three People's Volunteer Rifle Divisions and one tank brigade, with the mission of annihilating the presumptuous *Kampfgruppe* that had dashed across the Luga River. I was determined, despite the odds, to resist the Russians until reinforcements arrived. My subordinate commanders were well aware that extremely critical situations would arise before help could reach us—we all knew that the main body of the division was far behind, faced the same swamps we had endured, and would be unable even to contact us by radio for possibly as long as two days.

Kampfgruppe Raus had seized the "Gateway to Leningrad," but could we hold it?

Planning the Defense of the Luga River Bridgehead

The establishment and defense of bridgeheads was one of the most critical tasks throughout the Russian campaign, and this duty frequently fell to the panzer and motorized units. During four years of war, I, myself, together with the troops under my command, fought in various sectors and secured more than sixty bridgeheads, no two of which were alike in character. Each constituted an individual structure, conditioned by its mission, the terrain,

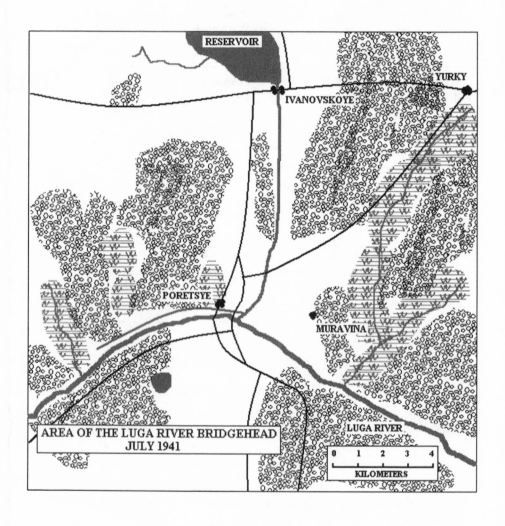

RESERVOIR

YURKY

IVANOVSKOYE

PORETSYE

MURAVINA

LUGA RIVER

AREA OF THE LUGA RIVER BRIDGEHEAD
JULY 1941

0   1   2   3   4
KILOMETERS

the forces holding it, and their equipment. Not one of these bridgeheads even remotely resembled the one at the Luga River, which even my subordinate commanders initially considered untenable. The units that subsequently arrived as reinforcements regarded my tactical setup of this bridgehead as absurd and were quite astonished that we had managed to hold it under such difficult circumstances. Yet no one, after being appraised of preceding events and given time for careful reflection, was ever able to suggest how the measures taken might have been improved. The victory gained justified the advisability of the tactics applied. It would have been impossible for infantry alone to hold the bridgehead, even in much greater strength than we possessed, but it would have been even more difficult for merely panzer units without infantry. An organized, harmonious teamwork of all arms, combining both rigid and elastic defense techniques, was the only possible procedure under the circumstances.

The tactics applied within this restricted area were particularly characterized by the necessity to grant my subordinate commanders—down to company and platoon level—much more freedom to act on their own initiative than was usually the case. This could not have occurred had not our officers been taught and trained in this manner during peacetime. My unit commanders and their subordinates of all ranks had fortunately been so trained to a high degree, and the victory we achieved must ultimately be ascribed to that fact.

I knew that our armored strength roughly equaled that of the Soviets, but I also realized that they possessed a twelve-fold numerical superiority in infantry. Bearing this factor in mind, it was imperative for us to achieve the closest possible concentration of our forces and make the most advantageous use of terrain. It was obvious from the outset that our strength was insufficient to enable us to set up an unbroken defensive ring around the bridges as well as the equally important road junction at Ivanovskoye. At the same time, I knew that these two strategic areas, as well as the intermediate terrain, had to remain in our hands if—as General Reinhardt expected—the bridgehead was to become the "Gateway to Leningrad."

Had I decided to establish just a small bridgehead, abandoning Ivanovskoye to the Russians, then holding the two bridges would have been a hollow victory. Without securing sufficient area for XLI Panzer Corps later to concentrate strong forces within our lines, the bridgehead would lose its strategic importance. Consequently, in order to defend a five-kilometer-long corridor that was not more than several hundred meters wide, I had to employ the kind of tactics whereby the bridges and the road junction remained securely under our control at any price and it would be possible for us repeatedly to mop up penetrations into the intermediate terrain. The

Ivanovskoye road junction obviously constituted the decisive point, because its possession was also of critical importance to retaining control of the bridges.

Moreover, the terrain and vegetation favored such a tactical conception. To the north the bridgehead was protected by a reservoir fifteen meters deep, and to the east by a six- to ten-meter-deep ditch with steep banks. Both reservoir and ditch functioned as perfect antitank obstacles, which Russian infantry would also find difficult to cross. To the west a swampy forest region reached nearly to the road. Although it was impossible for tanks to drive along this road, several sections of it were passable for infantry forces. South of the bridgehead there were extensive swampy forest areas, which at certain spots were passable for smaller units and light weapons; here it would be sufficient to deploy a single security detachment and small tactical reserves. Major Russian units of all types, which might have most seriously endangered the bridgehead, found themselves forced to use the supply route, where we could fight them with our panzers. In other words, owing to the peculiarities of the terrain, Soviet armored attacks would everywhere be confined to the roads. Only at the western outskirts of Ivanovskoye and within the central spine of the bridgehead itself was it possible for tanks to move along a narrow terrain corridor on both sides of the road.

The bridgehead also possessed the distinct advantage that it was not open to enemy view from any side. This meant that Soviet artillery would be able to fire only according to the map or with the assistance of aerial observation. At that point in the war, the Russians had not as yet become familiar with co-ordinated air-ground operations, and they had barely had any opportunity to plan fire missions based on map coordinates. Taken together, these factors meant that our forces occupying the bridgehead could be seriously endangered only if the Soviets employed their vast numerical superiority in infantry to launch simultaneous, coordinated attacks from all sides, or if *Kampfgruppe* Raus had to go without supplies for more than a week. We had to hope that neither of these contingencies would occur.

With the foregoing analysis constituting the psychological precept upon which I based the defense, the Ivanovskoye road junction became the focal point. There I committed the main body of Colonel Rudolf von Waldenfels's Motorized Infantry Regiment 4, with one battalion each facing east and west, respectively. This regiment had to block the two approach roads and protect the adjacent open flanks. For defense against the Soviet super-heavy KV-1 tanks, the regiment received some 88mm flak and 100mm high-velocity guns. As a tactical reserve the infantry regiment held back one infantry company, to which was added a panzer company. Responsibility for the immediate protection of the bridges devolved on Lieutenant Gebhardt's 3rd Company, Panzer Engineer Battalion 57, augmented with a number of the smaller 20mm flak guns. Lieutenant Beschke's 6th (APC) Company, Motorized Infantry Regiment 114, took charge of guarding and securing the area south of the Luga River. In case of emergency, Lieutenant Beschke could use the personnel of all supply trains stationed in this area, which had been organized as *Alarmeinheiten* [Alarm Units] and committed quickly. Every headquarters element assumed responsibility for its own safety. All artillery, flak, and antitank elements had to be ready at all times to repulse the Russians in close combat with their respective weapons, or to be committed as infantry for launching counterattacks. I kept the two artillery battalions and two panzer companies under my immediate control. The panzers had the standing mission of attacking—without waiting for orders—any and all Soviet troops trying to pass the road and to rout them. Several panzers, attached to headquarters, were detailed to remain south of the Luga and, in case of need, to come to the immediate assistance of Lieutenant Beschke's company. I intended to concentrate our artillery fire primarily on the area on both sides of the strongpoint of the road. Consequently, our artillery commander, Lieutenant Colonel Graf, depended on direct cooperation with Motorized Infantry Regiment 4. The consistent, personal contact maintained between my headquarters and both units assured coordinated action of all weapons and eliminated all possibility for misunderstanding.

Before these orders were issued, the unit commanders and I conducted a joint reconnaissance and evaluation of the terrain, which conveyed a picture at variance with our only map. We had the opportunity to do so because all the security detachments had been captured and the partisans had fled as soon as our first units had arrived, leaving only the Russian air force to trouble us. Fortunately, the nearby forest offered protection against its worst effects. This state of affairs was not only advantageous in facilitating our reconnaissance operations but also provided us with critical time to prepare the position in every respect.

Our troops made excellent use of this time. First, it was possible to inspect the construction of every position from all sides, including the angle from which an attacking enemy would view them. Above all, this gave us the opportunity to emplace our antitank weapons to the best advantage and camouflage them to perfection. Almost equally important, our infantry thoroughly reconnoitered the forest regions that extended closest to the road, allowing them to ascertain the location of several narrow trails leading across the swamps. We guarded these paths constantly so that we could not be taken by surprise by Soviet troops attacking from the forest. Such a detailed examination of the ground was crucial, because it would not be until much later that we would be able to replace our inaccurate maps with aerial photographs and prints of captured Russian 1:100,000 maps, which were up to date enough to be utilized for map firing.

Everywhere the terrain allowed the commitment of our panzers, the telephone lines connecting the troop units were installed on tall, sturdy trees or—if there were no trees—buried in shallow, dry ditches that we covered with sand or earth and camouflaged with grass. Thus the lines could be hidden from enemy view and remain intact even while tanks rolled across them. This procedure proved quite effective. The planning of this measure and similar details was neither my task nor that of the battalion commanders as tactical commanders but fell within the province of properly trained special units. Tactical commanders merely had to make sure the measures taken by these units were expedient and took action themselves only if this was not the case or something had been overlooked.

The Fight for the Bridgehead

The next morning [15 July] Russian aircraft, as expected, appeared on the scene very early. They were amazed at the completely changed picture: No evidence appeared beneath them of any German soldier, weapons, or vehicles, nor of any defensive positions. Everything had been buried in the ground or camouflaged. The familiar landscape lay peaceful and serene before them. Was it possible (they probably wondered) that the Germans had withdrawn after destroying the Yastrebina airfield? Any such hope was crushed the moment their leading bomber wing approached the Luga bridges, at which point the planes were scattered by a shower of large and small caliber shells fired by Flak Battalion 601. Not only did the Soviet bombs miss their target; two trails of smoke in the blue sky testified that our flak gunners had hit their mark. During their low-level flight the Russian fighter plane escorts also suffered losses due to the machine-gun fire that struck them from several angles. Nevertheless, it must be admitted that the Russians tenaciously returned at short intervals to attack the bridges and suspected troop concentrations, which they wanted to crush before the first Red Army infantry and tank units arrived.

The 1st Peoples' Volunteer Rifle Division, supported by tanks, made its appearance during the course of the morning, briskly advancing on Ivanovskoye on both sides of the road leading into the village from the west, its assignment to recapture both Luga bridges that same day. Suddenly the concentrated fire of concealed German batteries forced the Russian infantry to take cover. Although the enemy tanks initially stopped in confusion, they soon continued to roll forward by fits and starts. The raw Russian infantry followed in small groups in brief spurts, pushed forward by the officers and commissars with pistols in hand. The tanks, setting the pace and advancing in wedge formation, had already approached the German line to attempt a breakthrough when our 88mm flak and 100mm guns attacked them from ambush gun emplacements at a distance of barely 500 meters. A cloud of smoke signifying a hit followed every burst of fire. Meanwhile, our artillery and machine-gun fire was steadily thinning the ranks of the Russian infantry.

The attack ground toward a standstill. More Soviet infantry units were thrown into battle to provide the attack new impetus, but these units had already been hit hard in their assembly areas by the heavy 150mm batteries of III Battalion, Panzer Artillery Regiment 76. For troops who had never been engaged in combat before, this was a disastrous baptism of fire. Their irresolute rushing about in all directions and the withdrawal of their tanks (a dozen of which had already been put out of action) were unmistakable signs of a crisis. At that moment thirty panzers from Lieutenant Colonel Johann Siebert's II Battalion, Panzer Regiment 11, firing all guns, burst forth with a roar and launched a counterattack, disabling several additional Russian tanks and scattering their hapless infantry. The enemy assault, during which the Russians had suffered heavy casualties, collapsed in utter failure. After a brief pursuit, our panzers were recalled. The troops of the 1st Peoples' Volunteer Rifle Division, struck to their very marrow, subsequently moved with much more caution. It proved impossible for their officers and commissars to spur them into making a repeat attack on the same day, which as a rule the Red Army was wont to try several times.

The commander of the panzer company attached to Motorized Infantry Regiment 4 had launched the armored counterattack on his own initiative. Observing the battle from the Ivanovskoye church tower, he had been the first to recognize the crisis that had arisen in the enemy's ranks. He rushed to the nearby regimental command post and recommended the counterthrust to Colonel von Waldenfels. This action was also approved by Lieutenant Colonel Graf and, with the effective support of our guns, ended the fight with a German victory.

In the meantime, the 3rd Peoples' Volunteer Rifle Division, advancing through Yurky, had assembled for action at the fringes of the thick forest of saplings east of Ivanovskoye. This attack, launched without fire support, occurred during the early afternoon in several closely spaced waves, the Russians advancing on both sides of the road and moving toward the dam across completely open ground. Our artillery, which had earlier been blanketing the Soviet assembly areas with fire, now laid down a barrage from flanking positions on the brown-clad masses. Machine guns, tanks, and other heavy weapons also broke loose, covering the area with lethal effect. The attack disintegrated within a few minutes, a field of human carnage the only result of this senseless action. Even so, the attack was repeated three more times that day, ending in failure each time. Our infantrymen, who fought from foxholes and embrasures established along the embankment of the brook flowing from the reservoir, suffered only minor losses.

The next two days [16–17 July] were characterized by heavy artillery fire, which always commenced at 0600 in the form of an intense bombardment and which the enemy repeated prior to every attack. These attacks followed the same lines, alternating between the sectors where the fighting had raged the previous day. In these attacks, the Russians suffered heavy losses without gaining even one inch of ground. Although the concentrated fire of the Russian artillery and the constant air raids did cause disagreeable breakdowns and losses, they did not by themselves have the power to impair the overall structure of our defense.

Not until 18 July did the Soviet commanders finally realize the futility of their previous endeavors and try to gain a victory by changing tactics. They began constructing defensive positions on both sides of Ivanovskoye for the purpose of concentrating the forces necessary to carry out their new design. To this end they withdrew their western front somewhat and began entrenching. In the eastern sector they came to a standstill immediately in front of the sapling forest, with their troops remaining in the open. As cover, they used the dead bodies of their comrades, whose corpses filled the air with a pestilential smell, piling them up at night by the hundred and covering them with sand and earth.

The enemy's primary objective now appeared to be the capture of the two 200-meter-long Luga bridges, which thus far had been damaged only slightly and which could be quickly repaired. The Russians attempted to seize the bridges with attacks converging from all directions, but here, too, their coordination failed. The plan had been sound—though hazardous—but its only chance for successful execution was frittered away in isolated actions that were uncoordinated with regard to time and space.

Initially, the Russians tried to seize the bridges by a surprise raid. During the night of 17–18 July one company of the 2nd Peoples' Volunteer Rifle Division infiltrated across the brook north of the old bridge. At dawn these troops suddenly fell upon our weak security detachment, occupied the bridge, and then pushed on toward Muravina in a bid to capture the new bridge as well. At this point the raiders encountered machine-gun units that had been committed to secure the southern banks of the river. Almost immediately, Lieutenant Beschke's company, which had been standing by, appeared on the scene. This company, in its armored personnel carriers, attacked the Russian company at precisely the moment when the enemy, prompted by the noise of our approaching panzers, was attempting to make its escape across the old bridge. We wiped out the company to the last man; the Russians' audacious action had miscarried so completely that not even they had the stomach for a repeat attempt. A thrust against Muravina, launched immediately afterward by a single Soviet company on the opposite shore, had probably been intended to aid the company that had met with disaster. This attack, however, came too late, and our machine-gun detachment easily repulsed it.

Despite its ultimate failure, this surprise night attack had been prepared and executed with considerable skill and had seriously endangered the bridges. Lieutenant Gebhardt had required no special orders to defeat the Russians, since it was his assigned task to come to the aid of the bridge guards in the event these crossings were threatened. Even if this had not been his mission, he would have been expected to act in the same manner, since his engineers were stationed in the immediate vicinity of the spot where the raid occurred. In accordance with the situation and my orders, he was duty-bound to render assistance on his own initiative, without waiting for orders. Nonetheless, I credited his exemplary action in attacking so rapidly and vigorously that he promptly eliminated the danger.

During the morning some of our soldiers sighted a fighter squadron flying low over the forest at the very spot that the Russian "Rata" planes were wont to approach Muravina. As usual, our machine guns opened fire. This time, unfortunately, the planes were German—the first Luftwaffe elements to reach us. Our well-trained gunners immediately shot down the lead aircraft, which, however, managed to make an emergency landing in friendly territory. The squadron commander who had been flying this plane was only slightly wounded. Staying as my guest at brigade headquarters, he soon recuperated but found life in the encircled bridgehead highly disagreeable.

Throughout the day, several Russian battalions in succession, coming from west and east, advanced out of the swampy forests toward the road. Security detachments from Captain Dr. Boecher's II Battalion, Motorized Infantry Regiment 4, stationed along the shore and supported by our panzers, handily repulsed the attacks from the east. The Soviet infantry attacking from the west succeeded repeatedly in breaking through as far as the road. Each time this happened, they were simultaneously enveloped by our panzer companies coming from the north and south, respectively, and driven back into the forest. We were so successful in keeping the road open that, at night, our field kitchens and maintenance vehicles routinely rolled without interference across the bridges to support the troops.

The operations of our panzer companies also had to be carried out by local commanders, in conformity with the overall plan but without waiting for orders. Any order that either the sector commander or I could have issued would always have come too late in view of the rapidity with which the Russians achieved their penetrations and the short distances they had to cover. Lieutenant Colonel Siebert conducted the coordinated actions of his dispersed companies over the voice radio transmitters with which each tank was equipped. During combat it would have been suicidal—either by day or night—for troops or nonarmored vehicles to move on or near the road; this made it impossible to dispatch messengers to the units engaged in combat. Our infantry reserves, therefore, had to stand by, constantly organized for battle, so as to be able to launch a prompt counterthrust. The only orders they ever received were brief instructions issued by word of mouth, by field telephone, or over the radio.

Around Ivanovskoye only a few isolated local actions took place. We easily repelled a weak Russian attack from the north along the reservoir toward the bridge at the lock. Another surprise attack, launched from the forest by a Russian infantry unit supported by a single super-heavy KV-1, created more problems. This attack aimed at paralyzing our operational control, which was centered—precisely as the enemy presumed—near the church. Although a counterthrust by our reserve infantry company threw back the Soviet troops who had broken through our security line, the KV-1 emerged from the forest and drove with such speed, and so close, past a well-camouflaged 100mm gun that the crew had no opportunity to fire at it. The tank circled the church, crushing everything that appeared suspicious, including Colonel von Waldenfels's regimental headquarters. Our PzKw 35ts were powerless—as at Raseinai their fire had no effect on the monster. At long last one particularly plucky NCO put an end to this critical situation. He jumped on the tank and kept firing his pistol into the driver's vision slot. The latter, wounded by bullet spatter and his vision obstructed, was compelled to turn back. He obviously hoped that in crossing the Russian lines he would force his troublesome passenger to abandon his ingeniously chosen position. The smallest weapon in our arsenal had put to flight the enemy's heaviest tank. Shouting and swearing, the tank driver again steered past the 100mm gun. Only seconds before the tank crossed out of our lines the NCO leaped off, leaving the giant vehicle to its fate. Just as the offending tank reached no-man's land, it burst into flames, struck in the rear by a direct hit of the 100mm gun.

That same morning a single Russian company, moving along swampy roads, made its way to the rear of the bridgehead for the purpose of attacking our artillery positions. Simultaneously, small assault detachments slipped along the river to eliminate my brigade headquarters. Both operations failed because of the vigilance of our security detachments, which spotted the enemy in time and repelled him with local reserves.

Around noon a single Soviet battalion carried out a more menacing assault, launched from the swampy forest along the southern bank of the Luga and aimed at our supply trains, which had been parked in a pine forest. This attack—which caught us somewhat off-guard—began with some wild and aimless firing, which succeeded in creating great confusion among the service troops. Taking advantage of this momentary disorganization, the Russians crossed the road and managed to pillage a number of trucks. The enemy assault finally broke down in front of an ordnance repair ship that contained several new machine guns and a large amount of ammunition. As the Russians were attempting to regroup for a second effort, Lieutenant Beschke's company appeared on the scene (without waiting for orders) and joined the forest battle raging in its rear. Launching its attack along the road, this company sliced into the rear of the Russian battalion, firing from their vehicles and causing the utmost confusion. The remnants of the intruding battalion scattered in headlong flight, discarding all their loot. Soon thereafter our troops marked the site of this engagement with a grave on which the cross carried the inscription: "Here lie 157 Russians who died in battle."

It goes without saying that in every instance where time allowed I was notified in advance so that, in case of need, I would be able to take action and issue additional orders. In cases such as the company- and battalion-scale raids on the bridgehead, this was obviously impossible. Nonetheless, company and battalion commanders advised me as quickly as possible at the start of any action or immediately thereafter.

Enemy artillery also changed its method of firing on 18 July. The Red Army artillerymen discontinued their ineffectual firing on the bridgehead and began concentrating on bombarding the bridges themselves. After that, more than 1,000 shells droned across the woods toward these targets each day. Fortunately, owing to the fact that observation was impossible for the Russians, they never succeeded in hitting the mark with any telling effects.

Soviet aircraft also struck like swarms of hornets at our batteries and any other target they identified. Russian pilots quickly realized that, due to the increasing shortage of ammunition, our antiaircraft fire became progressively weaker. By that afternoon our flak guns had to cease firing completely, reserving the few shells remaining to them for antitank defense. Even our machine guns had to confine themselves to attacking only the most particularly troublesome of the low-flying planes. Even the *Kampfgruppe* field artillery had to curtail its rate of fire considerably, in order to maintain a reserve to intervene in critical situations.

This ammunition shortage understandably became more and more my chief source of anxiety. As long as the infantry and tanks had sufficient ammunition at their disposal, our possession of the bridgehead was in no serious danger. Yet I knew that these quantities also were apt to be depleted rapidly if we had to repel a series of large-scale attacks. Fortunately, the Russians in our front, owing to their costly attacks, had become worn out to such an extent that they could not for the moment summon sufficient strength for major operations. Nevertheless, in just a few more days they might again be able to bring their depleted units up to full strength and pandemonium would break loose again. I seriously doubted that the *Kampfgruppe* would be able to resist such assaults if faced with a shortage of panzer or small-arms ammunition. Worse, there was still no sign of life from the main body of XLI Panzer Corps. Had the troops been held up or even committed elsewhere? These were the questions that everyone discussed anxiously.

A night action closed the fighting on 18 July. Shortly before midnight our security detachments that were guarding the embankment of the reservoir reported hearing sounds made by the oars of rowboats slowing moving toward the floodgate. Owing to the prevailing dead silence, these sounds were clearly audible to our sentries. My subordinates and I, however, had been expecting a Russian attempt to destroy this strategic installation and had taken the necessary precautions to prevent such a catastrophe. The floodgate was protected by wire nets and floating minefields, which were meant to stop the Soviets from reaching the target and designed to alert the machine-gun nests. The machine-gun positions had been equipped with searchlights in case the approach of enemy troops could not be heard or observed at a distance. In this case the Russians had failed to ensure that the sound of their oars had been drowned out by the noise of battle (though we had expected them to do so). Consequently, our troops awaiting them in front of the floodgate with machine guns ready to fire. As they arrived, each boatload of unlucky Russians was illuminated by the searchlights and annihilated. This operation therefore failed miserably, and we escaped the very real danger of being swept away by roaring floods.

At daybreak on 19 July we finally heard the long-awaited boom of guns from the south. Soon thereafter we received word that III Battalion, Motorized Infantry Regiment 118 (36th Motorized Division), was approaching. This unit had taken so long to reach us because it had been turned off at Ssabsk, where the 1st Panzer Division had established its own bridgehead, and assigned as a reinforcement there. Finally it had begun pushing its way up the southern bank of the Luga toward *Kampfgruppe* Raus. The battalion had strict orders from XLI Panzer Corps to rest in the forest south of Muravina throughout the day and to wait until darkness before reinforcing the western front of our bridgehead. This delay was absolutely essential to avoid exposing the troops to the danger of being attacked by Russian planes and heavy artillery while crossing the bridges, which might have resulted in their annihilation. Throughout yet another day, therefore, the weary occupants of the bridgehead had to keep on fighting alone, holding out at all costs. Unfortunately, the battalion commander of the reinforcements, devoted to his duty, attempted a daylight reconnaissance of the front sector that would soon be assigned to him; he and the personnel with him were all killed en route. The battalion itself, without incurring any other losses, reached its sector during the night. Supported by one panzer company, it proceeded to hold its lines against all subsequent attacks.

As much as I welcomed this increase in strength, it did not alter our now-critical ammunition shortage. The battalion from the 36th Motorized Division had been compelled to travel on foot through the swampy forests along the road from Ssabsk, and the troops had therefore only been able to take along as much ammunition as could be carried or loaded in a few *panje* wagons. I now learned that the main body of XLI Panzer Corps (including the rest of 6th Panzer Division) had been stranded for days on the road that my *Kampfgruppe* had so completely destroyed during its advance. In order to get out of the swamps, it had been necessary to construct a corduroy road many kilometers long, parallel to the original march route. The good news was that their arrival could now be expected in the near future. On the whole, the sixth day of our encirclement passed relatively peacefully, except for lively air and artillery activity.

During the night of 19–20 July audible sounds of towing alerted us to the fact that the Russians had busied themselves removing the wrecked tanks. This indicated to me that they were planning new assaults, and soon after sunrise on 20 July this supposition was proven correct. Super-heavy KV-1 tanks attacked Ivanovskoye from both sides and rolled over our foremost lines, as well as some supporting machine-gun positions, before they could be put out of commission by our 100mm guns. Driven by civilian mechanics, these new tanks had come straight from the factory. A furious firefight broke out between the flock of smaller tanks following in their wake and our PzKw 35ts. This battle resulted in losses on both sides and was only brought to a successful conclusion when our panzers thrust through the gap made when the Russian engineers cleared away the wrecked tanks.

As a follow-up, the Russians attempted to accomplish what the tanks could not by committing newly arrived infantry forces that had been trained but briefly before large numbers of commissars ruthlessly pushed them into battle. Initially these troops tried to storm the dam, but their attack collapsed under concentrated automatic weapons fire. These unfortunate Red Army soldiers suffered the same fate of previous attackers, across whose piled-up bodies they had been driven. After this engagement their own bodies found use as building material to construct new Russian positions. A subsequent attack from the west was just as unsuccessful: Even before the Russians approached their goal, our tanks rushed into the battle, overran them, and scattered them. A final attempt to seize the bridges with a mass attack also failed.

Although these victories were very gratifying, the cold fact was that the fighting had expended all the ammunition dropped for us by the Luftwaffe into our artillery positions during the last two days, as well as nearly exhausting our entire supply of small-arms ammunition. Everyone realized that we had reached the critical moment, for additional aerial deliveries could only bring temporary relief, not end the shortage.

Just then a Luftwaffe single-engine fighter dropped the following message: "Enemy regiment with artillery advancing on Muravina; has started out at 0900 at Dolgaya bridge." This was very bad news, because it meant that within three hours a large Russian force might be in the rear of the bridgehead. I knew that if the Soviets launched simultaneous attacks at this point and both flanks, then our last hours had struck, for without ammunition even the bravest unit is doomed. Yet as the proverb says, "God is nearest when the need is greatest."

It was imperative to take quick action, but the question was how. Should I throw all our panzers into battle against the approaching regiment? That could mean losing the bridgehead if the Russians launched their attacks with the same fury as those made earlier in the day, for only the panzers retained a good stock of ammunition, and this made them the backbone of our defense. Hazarding such a step might amount to suicide for the *Kampfgruppe*. I therefore decided that I did not dare weaken the bridgehead by depriving it of any men or weapons whatsoever. That being the case, nothing else remained but to have the troops on the southern shore of the Luga carry out defensive measures, yet a passive defense would result in confining us to such a narrow space that we might simply be crushed by the enemy's superior numbers. Only a bold decision would make it possible to dispel all danger, and I therefore made the decision to attack.

Without delay I had the 6th Company (APC), Motorized Infantry Regiment 114, alerted and reinforced by three tanks taken from my own headquarters. My orders were issued orally and did not take long. I gave Lieutenant Beschke a brief orientation concerning the gravity of the situation and his mission. He repeated these instructions back to me and then explained in a few words how, on the whole, he intended to carry it out. Since he had already repeatedly proven his mettle, it would have been inadvisable to lay down any rules or prescribe his method of procedure, since everything would have to depend on the local situation, which could not be observed from the bridgehead. I also addressed the troops of the company before their departure, saying a few words in appreciation of their previous achievements. Their eyes radiated absolute confidence. I had not even finished giving the spirited Lieutenant Beschke his instructions when suddenly we heard the thunder of guns and furious machine-gun fire coming from the south. Everyone knew that this meant elements of the XLI Panzer Corps must have already engaged the Russian regiment, which could only improve our chances. "Very well, hurry and get going!" were the words with which I dismissed the energetic young officer.

No sooner had the lieutenant departed than I received a radio message from Motorcycle Battalion 6 informing me that while advancing toward the bridgehead along with a supply column it had become engaged in bitter fighting at the Dolgaya River against vastly superior forces. Captain Knaust, the acting battalion commander, requested my assistance. My brief radio reply, "Reinforcements are on the way," was promptly acknowledged. The 6th Company (APC), Motorized Infantry Regiment 114, had also listened in on both transmissions.

Barely twenty minutes later we heard the muffled sounds of tank and raging machine-gun fire. The company had assaulted the Russian regiment in the rear with its armored personnel carriers and three panzers at the moment when the enemy was already engaged in combat against the attacking motorcycle battalion. Our attack struck directly against the Soviet's field artillery batteries and other heavy weapons, then pushed forward on the road, firing all guns, until linking up with the motorcycle battalion. The Russian regiment, panic-stricken by this surprise attack on its rear, suffered heavy casualties and lost all of its heavy equipment. By noon both the APC company and Motorcycle Battalion 6 were already arriving south of Muravina, after winning a total victory. The route of march had been cleared, thus eliminating the danger threatening the bridgehead.

Several days later the remainder of the 6th Panzer Division also arrived, to be followed by the 1st Infantry Division and other units. They rolled up the Russian position along both flanks. Our isolation at the bridgehead, with all its hardships and distress, had come to an end. The numerous sacrifices I had been forced to demand of the troops were vividly evidenced by the battlefield, which looked like a huge cemetery. Graves of German soldiers, decorated with crosses made of birchwood, lined each side of the road. Behind these lay mass graves in which we had buried Red Army soldiers numbering fifteen times our own fallen. Surrounding us were the wrecks of seventy-eight tanks that had tried and failed to storm our stronghold on the Luga.

The "Gateway to Leningrad" was open.

The Fatal Delay

It is important to understand the difficulties General Landgraf faced in closing the main body of 6th Panzer Division to the Luga River. *Kampfgruppe*
Raus had left in its wake a road absolutely impassable for the division's tanks
and vehicles, since so many of our own vehicles had churned up the mud. On
13 July the division reached the area of Lyady only after extreme difficulties
and was widely scattered. Just to the east of Lyady, 1st Panzer Division had
also begun to get stuck in the bog.

On 14 July, as *Kampfgruppe* Raus seized the Porechye bridgehead, the
main body of 6th Panzer Division could not advance at all. The stretch of
about twenty kilometers between Maryinsko and the western tip of Lake
Dolgaya had to be transformed into a corduroy road to become passable.
Lieutenant Colonel Lehnert's engineers had to be satisfied with makeshift repairs, which in every instance the passage of our columns quickly destroyed.
Then additional repair teams would have to be dispatched by division headquarters, later aided by a few contingents of construction troops from XLI
Panzer Corps. Operations were further hampered by dense Russian mine-
fields.

Equally critical, on this day 1st Panzer Division gave up on the idea of
pushing forward on its stipulated route of advance. Elements of that division
began trying to press from the side onto 6th Panzer Division's only road.
General Reinhardt ruled that 6th Panzer Division's interests were to be disre-
garded in view of the importance of establishing a bridgehead at Ssabsk as
well as Porechye, and some units of 1st Panzer Division were passed through
until they turned northeast again near Maryinsko. It could soon be noticed,
however, that the entire 1st Panzer Division intended to choose this itinerary.
An unholy mess was the result. General Landgraf was forced to order a complete stop at the Sayanye bridge for all vehicles except ambulances and messengers. Finally, Major Walter Wenck and the operations staff of 1st Panzer
Division arrived, and through direct cooperation between the two commands
order gradually emerged from confusion, and the movement slowly resumed.
It became nevertheless necessary not to allow anybody to pass the bridge at
Sayanye unless a written order issued by 6th Panzer Division (after agreement
with 1st Panzer Division) was presented. This episode had enormous tactical
importance, as it prevented both weak bridgeheads from being reinforced
and supplied quickly enough.

The bulk of 6th Panzer Division spent the next day [15 July] still occupied
with building roads and consolidating its forces. Flank protection against the
west, where our understanding of the Russian situation remained obscure,
could only be loosely provided just west of the Loshogodva-Malatyevka

area. Our nearest "neighbor" to the left, 36th Motorized Division, was still advancing on Gdov, fifty kilometers away. News also arrived that LVI Panzer Corps had experienced a setback, raising speculations about the possibility of the division's having to interrupt the general advance to defend the Porechye bridgehead for an extended period without relief.

As noted above, the first reinforcement that succeeded in reaching *Kampfgruppe* Raus was not from 6th Panzer Division but was a reinforced battalion of the 36th Motorized Division. As this battalion was attached to 6th Panzer Division, other elements of General Otto Ottenbacher's division were attached to 1st Panzer Division at Ssabsk, and XLI Panzer Corps took direct control of additional 36th Motorized units as a general reserve. This was the first time, at least in this theater, that an organized division had been split up as an emergency measure, a practice that later became the rule in Russia, especially in certain sectors. The momentary advantage of such a measure was almost always offset by many long-lasting disadvantages, but the lack of reserves nonetheless required such measures. Despite this concern, General Landgraf and I both welcomed the reinforcement, which, apart from its other advantages, finally made some relief possible for the soldiers of *Kampfgruppe* Raus who had been in combat, day and night, for an extended period.

The next three weeks brought 6th Panzer Division's first long standstill, as well as difficult and costly position warfare under unfavorable conditions. The general cause of this delay in Army Group North's advance was the very slow progress of Sixteenth and Eighteenth Armies, which made it impossible for the narrow, small wedge that XLI Panzer Corps had driven into the steadily stiffening outer defenses of Leningrad to be pushed any farther. Yet almost equal causes of this stagnation were the exhaustion of the troops, an immediate shortage of ammunition due to as yet unresolved road difficulties (supply by air became necessary), and the Soviets' ability to improve their defenses much quicker than we could reinforce our bridgehead. Heavy attacks against the Porechye bridgehead were often the consequence, because 6th Panzer Division did not have sufficient troops to hold the bridgehead and cover the long eastern flank behind which our tenuous line of communications ran.

We concluded from unusually heavy air raids (especially on 18 July), from new reinforcements, and from the appearance of Russian railroad artillery at the Weimarn station east of Kingisepp that the Soviets were planning a major offensive against our Luga River bridgeheads. After an artillery preparation, this offensive started with great vehemence on 20 July, supported by tanks. All attacks were again repelled in heavy fighting, which proved costly for both sides. More than twenty enemy tanks were knocked out, but a local crisis arose when it became evident that the Russians, to everyone's surprise, combined their assault against the bridgehead with a flank attack our of the Monastyrek swamps against Arinovka. We succeeded, however, in recovering Arinovka with a counterthrust. In order to stabilize the situation more firmly, General Landgraf scheduled a counterattack for 21 July. This began in the small hours of the day and threw the Russians back as far as Monastyrek. Once this had been accomplished, the attacking force returned to Arinovka after reconnoitering the railroad tracks (which had not been marked on our maps). General Landgraf reject the idea of holding the region around Monastyrek because it would have required too many forces.

Thereafter, when the Russians resumed attacks on the bridgehead, they did so on a smaller scale. On 23 July the Soviets tried in vain to cross the Luga southeast of Porechye in order to encircle the bridgehead. Weak elements that reached our bank of the river were wiped out in a counterattack. Also on 23 July the 1st Infantry Division began to arrive in the division area. The 1st Infantry Division had been earmarked to relieve 6th Panzer Division so that we would later be free to lead the breakout attack from the bridgehead. At General Landgraf's suggestion, only the left half of the bridgehead was turned over to the 1st Infantry Division in order to make a simultaneous attack by both divisions possible at a later date. The necessary movements involved in this hand-over, which had to be executed very cautiously and only during the night, required several days. On 24 July, 1st Infantry Division launched a new local thrust against Monastyrek and established contact with XXXVIII Corps, finally approaching by way of Gdov.

The same day, Panzer Regiment 11 was reorganized from three to two battalions. The continuation of three battalions became pointless in view of the repair situation and the many losses. It is safe to say that the advance from the German border to the Luga River had cost the division an entire panzer battalion. The losses attributable to technical failure continued to far outweigh combat losses.

Advance elements of XXXVIII Corps reached the Luga on 27 July, just southeast of Kingisepp. This development was a noticeable relief for 6th Panzer Division, which no longer had to be concerned about the long, open flank to its left. From this point, Russian attacks against the bridgehead slowly died away. The Soviets limited themselves to attacking Porechye with artillery and from the air. Due to the smallness of the bridgehead, this constituted a considerable harassment, which eased only a little after the Luftwaffe transferred a fighter squadron into the area.

The pause gave the division a chance to catch its breath, to get rehabilitated to a certain degree, and to prepare tactics and supply for the planned breakout attack. Neither General Landgraf nor his officers had any illusions about the difficulties of this forthcoming attack. The Russians constantly improved their positions, and an all-out assault would have to be made by infantry alone, because the terrain permitted at the most the employment of a few panzers for local infantry support. Nevertheless, officers and men alike were anxious for the offensive to start, since the defense of the bridgehead had become a real meat grinder. The division suffered more casualties during three weeks of position warfare than had been the case throughout the entire advance from East Prussia to the Porechye bridgehead.

Once the general situation permitted, XLI Panzer Corps scheduled the attack for 8 August. The reinforced 1st Panzer Division (employing elements of 36th Motorized Division) would set off from Ssabsk, while the 6th Panzer and 1st Infantry Divisions attacked simultaneously from Porechye. These were not particularly strong forces, in view of the energy with which the Russians had improved their defenses and the close proximity to Leningrad. Moreover, one of the four divisions involved in the breakout attack—1st Infantry Division—was not expected to participate in the thrust once it left the bridgehead but had orders to pivot toward Kingisepp in order to assist Eighteenth Army's advance. After having passed the swamps, the three divisions of XLI Panzer Corps were supposed to reach the railroad between Smerdovitsy and Pustomersha. Finally, after a cloudburst and thunderstorm during the night of 7–8 August, it would rain throughout the following day.

Breakout!

In our attack out of the Luga River bridgehead the terrain now worked against us. The bridgehead was completely surrounded by woods, and the sector to be attacked lay in a medium-growth, partly marshy forest with thick underbrush. Elements of the 2nd and 3rd Peoples' Volunteer Rifle Divisions held the line, their most advanced positions about 300–400 meters ahead of our front. Their trenches were narrow and deep and had no parapets. Excavated earth had been scattered in the surrounding rank swamp grass, and the defensive positions were so thoroughly camouflaged with branches that neither our reconnaissance patrols nor Luftwaffe aerial photography had been able to spot them over the course of nearly four weeks. The Soviets had deployed wire entanglements no higher than the dense growth of grass hiding them. The effect was to create a set of defenses incomparably stronger than the Stalin Line.

A single-lane road from Ivanovskoye and a dirt track from the vicinity of the Luga bridges both cut through the woods to the village of Yurky, which was our immediate objective. Both avenues of approach had been blocked by heavily wired abatis and minefields. On the far edge of the woods the Russians had constructed a second position atop a sand dune. Behind this, a third defensive line ran through Yurky itself, and a fourth had been prepared northeast of the village. The second position had been constructed with special care: It consisted of a deep antitank ditch (in the front wall of which Red Army infantry had entrenched itself), supported by heavy weapons firing from bunkers.

The 6th Panzer Division attacked along both of these routes—*Kampfgruppe* Raus along the track from the bridges, and *Kampfgruppe* von Seckendorff along the road from Ivanovskoye. Both *Kampfgruppen* received strong artillery support, and each had a battalion of *Nebelwerfer* [Multiple Mortar] Regiment 52 attached. I dispatched individual tanks to support the engineer in removing the road blocks. In spite of extremely heavy fire concentrations on our projected points of penetration, we could not budge the Russians from their narrow, invisible zigzag trenches. To be sure, our panzers managed to reach the barriers, but heavy, unabated defensive fire prevented the dismounted engineers from removing the roadblocks. Infantry from Motorized Infantry Regiment 4 were committed in a fruitless effort to locate other weak spots in order to effect a breakthrough. Repulsed everywhere by murderous defensive fire from an invisible enemy, our troops finally stopped, knee-deep in swampland, stranded in front of the wire entanglements covering still unknown Soviet positions.

We later realized that the Russians had intended to launch a heavy attack against 6th Panzer Division on the afternoon of 8 August, and that was a primary cause of our tactical failure. In their own preparations, the Soviets had concentrated particularly strong infantry and artillery forces during the night of 7–8 August. Naturally, such changes were unknown to us on the morning of 8 August, and as a result the start of our attack no longer fully corresponded to the prevailing situation. Initiating our main-effort attack in the teeth of the enemy's main effort caused decidedly unfavorable results.

The shock caused by this reverse and our considerable losses made itself felt. Substantial regrouping of our infantry units became necessary and proved very difficult in the narrow bridgehead where the two lines in some spots were separated only by a few meters. General Landgraf therefore believed that the attack could not be resumed until 11 August. He had a difficult time convincing General Reinhardt of this point of view. The corps commander, naturally, wanted to exploit the successes scored by his other divisions. The combined 1st Panzer/36th Motorized Division attack at Ssabsk, as well as the 1st Infantry Division's thrust at Leininski, had been able to break through the first Soviet positions and advance approximately three kilometers.

General Landgraf agreed to continue the attack on 10 August, and 9 August passed with preparations and regrouping. Meanwhile, both 1st Panzer Division and 36th Motorized Division advanced well. The 1st Panzer Division reached Isvos, while the 36th Motorized Division was employed to mop up three wooded regions and then pivoted northwest to support 6th Panzer Division. In the course of this movement, General Ottenbacher's troops took Pustoshka.

In the late afternoon of 10 August, having reorganized for a new, tightly concentrated attack along the Porechye-Yurky road, 6th Panzer Division resumed the attack, but not until after dark did we manage to penetrate these defenses. A single company succeeded in crawling forward, man by man, through the deep-cut bed of a small stream that was overgrown with grass and bushes, and thereby infiltrated through the wire obstacle. That particular point had not been attacked during the day, and I immediately ordered up strong reinforcements. These widened the point of penetration and cleared the trenches and strongpoints along our immediate front, though only after hours of bitter, hand-to-hand fighting. Despite the loss of their forward position on this line, the Russians continued to hold their front line against *Kampfgruppe* von Seckendorff. Neither local detours nor wider turning movements could induce the defenders to evacuate positions not under immediate attack. Every single trench and bunker had to be taken individually. The mop-up operations continued for a full twenty-four hours.

On the next morning of 12 August our general attack continued, thrusting toward Yurky and rolling up the Soviets' second defensive line. Again, fierce combat at close quarters was required before we scattered the defenders and cleared the road to Ivanovskoye for *Kampfgruppe* von Seckendorff. Thus it had required a two-day battle, exacting a heavy toll of losses from both sides, before this invisible defensive system in the swampy forest could be surmounted.

On the same day, 1st Panzer Division fought its way into open terrain and reached the Syrkovtisi-Morosov area, where it encountered strong Russian tank forces, but no more substantial defensive positions outside of the woods. The 36th Motorized Division established contact with 6th Panzer Division via Krutye Rughi. The 1st Infantry Division meanwhile advanced painstakingly up to the area south of Khoroshevo, where it had to go over to the defensive against violent Red Army counterattacks.

In Yurky I took the time to inspect several Russian tanks that had been knocked out a few hours earlier near a church. A larger number of troops was looking on. Suddenly, the turret of one of the knocked-out tanks began to revolve and fire. The tank had to be blown up. We discovered that among the crew, which had been presumed dead, there was a commissar who had merely been knocked unconscious. When he revived and saw so many German soldiers around him, he had opened fire.

By 12 August we believed that we had passed the most critical part of the battle after having broken through the main enemy positions in the woods, a belief borne out by the results in the 1st Panzer Division's sector. Luftwaffe reconnaissance revealed several permanent field fortifications on the heights south of Vypolsova. Taking this into consideration, General Landgraf ordered the attack to continue on foot until reaching Vypolsova; after that, the troops would mount their vehicles to continue the advance. This was the plan, but the day took an unexpected turn. The Vypolsova heights proved to be a greatly improved fortress rather than a field fortification. Antitank ditches, concrete bunkers with armored cupolas, concrete gun positions, successive defensive lines, barbed wire, and mines had been developed into a fortification system of such density as was not even encountered directly in front of Leningrad. It is noteworthy that the Luftwaffe had not recognized the extent of this system of fortifications. Though local in nature, these fortifications could not be flanked, because they blocked our exit from the woods.

Substantial elements of the division were still tied down by mop-up operations in the woods around Yurky, but General Landgraf nonetheless committed *Kampfgruppe* von Waldenfels (the reinforced Motorized Infantry Regiment 4) against Vypolsova. Against defenders who had been much battered in the preceding engagements, Colonel von Waldenfels's determined troops succeeded in taking this fortress on the mountain, an achievement that noticeably imparted new élan to our battalions. After four weeks they had finally gotten out of that green hell of a hated forest, and the terrain gradually became more passable.

The fighting during the next three weeks (13 August–7 September) was characterized by a gradual slowing down of the advance on Leningrad, with the offensive finally bogging down in front of the city's fortifications. This was followed by a transition from a mechanized advance to position warfare of limited duration. The reasons for this change were to be found less in Russian resistance than in the circumstances of our own forces. First, the XLI Panzer Corps's advance was entirely too weak (deploying only 1st and 6th Panzer Divisions and 36th Motorized Division). Thus, as we advanced, our northern and southern flanks steadily lengthened. The northern flank was more decisive, since Eighteenth Army had been unable—even after the fall of Narva and Kingisepp—to straighten out its affairs (leading to the development of the Oranienbaum pocket). Moreover, the follow-up infantry forces advancing against the Luga River or along the Luga-Krasnogvardeysk highway made only slow progress. Taken together, these circumstances accounted for the wasting away of XLI Panzer Corps's attack.

In the exploitation of our success at Vypolsova, 6th Panzer Division finally gained both freedom of movement and considerable terrain on the afternoon of 13 August. Our spearheads crossed the Kingisepp-Leningrad railroad and reached the vicinity of Bolshoi and Malesosnitsi, while 1st Panzer Division pivoted east toward Volosovo. That was the same day that the troops of 6th Panzer Division, to their surprise, had their initial encounter with Russian rocket launchers (the Katyusha rocket projectors later to become known to the soldiers as the "Stalin Organ"). At first we thought they were German *Nebelwerfer* that had been captured by the Soviets in LVI Panzer Corps's reverse at Soltsy.

On 14 August the division pivoted east-northeast and reached the Konochovitsi-Tuchovo area, crossing the highway about halfway between Volosovo and Gomontovo the following day. At that point fighting had to be resumed on foot, even though 36th Motorized Division had been moved up behind 6th Panzer Division to protect the lengthening northern flank. Neither the 36th Motorized nor our own detached elements proved fully able to remove the constant enemy thrust from the region northwest of Moloskovitsi against our supply lines. This meant that during 16 and 17 August only slow advances of a few kilometers in the face of heavy fighting were possible. On 16 August, for example, more than 2,000 mines had to be removed in our zone of attack, not counting hundreds of mines that presumably went undetected. We noticed that the Russian use of mines increased steadily as we approached Leningrad. The same day, 1st Panzer Division's advance ground to a complete halt.

Losses in our combat units made themselves felt more and more, especially among the officers, because a replacement crisis had arisen for the first time since the beginning of the Russian campaign. No replacements were arriving. A partial explanation for this state of affairs might have been found in the fact that the replacement and supply transports for the entire XLI Panzer Corps had to make a big detour through the old Luga bridgeheads, causing considerable delays due to distance and the miserable condition of the roads. Conditions in this regard would improve only toward the end of August, after the main Soviet Luga defenses were thoroughly pierced (19 August) and the highway from Luga to Krasnogvardeysk could subsequently be taken.

On 18 August a sweeping thrust of about twenty kilometers into the region east of Volosovo succeeded as the result of heavy fighting the previous day. More than 1,000 Red Army soldiers were captured—the biggest number at one time since the outset of the campaign. Up to that point the number of

Russians killed had usually exceeded that captured, at least as far as 6th Panzer Division's sector was concerned. Despite this success, little terrain was gained on 19 August, and the following day the division changed over to defensive operations. Only 1st Panzer Division continued a limited eastward advance in order to block the highway south of Krasnogvardeysk and cut off the retreat of the enemy forces retreating from the Luga River defenses.

In the attempt to occupy the position as ordered, 6th Panzer Division shifted to the east, relieving elements of 1st Panzer Division, while 36th Motorized Division in turn relieved our western flank positions. We now occupied a defensive line about twenty-five kilometers long, facing almost directly north along its entire length. This assignment could be carried out only by organizing a mobile defense anchored to a few important points of resistance. The days that followed, to 7 September, were characterized by position warfare with much local "see-saw" activity. In the course of constant reliefs and changes, 6th Panzer Division gradually moved southeast along the Krasnogvardeysk front and then partially back again. Our farthest southeast extension was reached east of Lyadino and the railroad running from Luga to Krasnogvardeysk. On 7 September, 6th Panzer Division, supported by a reinforced regiment from the SS *Polizei* [Police] Infantry Division on the right wing, was prepared for the decisive attack along the Sigonemi-Nedlino line, west of Krasnogvardeysk. This was also the day on which I assumed acting command of the division.

The enemy opposite 6th Panzer Division had been relatively quiet for some time. Russian reserves appeared to be available only in limited numbers, and the enemy attempted to compensate for this weakness with the extensive use of mines. The Soviets were far more active against the deep left flank in the area held by the 36th Motorized Division, where Russian artillery and local forces along our flanks tried to block the road to Leningrad between Kingisepp and Begunizy. This general situation delayed the start of the attack, which was intended to be the decisive offensive toward Leningrad, by twenty-four hours, and then again to 9 September. When the assault began, the SS *Polizei* Infantry Division was committed to move directly against Krasnogvardeysk on 6th Panzer Division's right, while the 1st Panzer Division (having just been moved up) and the 36th Motorized Division attacked on our left. The Duderhof Heights, about ten kilometers north of Krasnogvardeysk, was the first common objective.

Breaching the Leningrad Line

The Russians had transformed the outpost area before Leningrad into a dense defensive system. In particular, the defenses at Krasnogvardeysk had been prepared long in advance and consisted of an outer belt of concrete and earth bunkers, with numerous intermediate installations, all interconnected by easily defensible trench systems. Tank-proof watercourses or swamps ran along nearly the entire front of the outer defenses. At the few points this natural protection was lacking, wide antitank ditches had been dug.

At a distance of 1,000–3,000 meters behind the outer defenses, there was an inner belt consisting of a heavily fortified position encircling the periphery of the town. Just north of Krasnogvardeysk ran the continuous Leningrad Line, into which the town's defenses were integrated. This line constituted, simultaneously, the rear protection for Krasnogvardeysk and a covering position in case the town had to be evacuated. Beyond the open, elevated terrain immediately west of Krasnogvardeysk lay an extensive forest zone. Within that area—a few hundred meters from its eastern fringe—ran the western front of the outer defensive belt. At that point the defenses consisted of wood-and-earth bunkers, trenches, and individual strongpoints, with all approaches barricades by minefields, abatis, and multiple rows of barbed wire. Located one or two kilometers in front of these obstacles were mobile security detachments, attached to which were engineers prepared to scatter additional mines.

The cornerstone of this entire defensive complex was the heavily mined and fortified village of Salyzy, located at the southern end of the forest zone. This village covered a road leading to Krasnogvardeysk from the west; the road forked in the middle of town with a branch heading north. The northern branch served as the Russian supply route for all the troops deployed to the west in the forest; it crossed the dammed-up Ishora River via a bridge located just in front of the Leningrad Line, traversing the line in a northwesterly direction. At that point the Leningrad Line consisted of four successive trench systems, bristling with numerous machine-gun, antitank-gun, and artillery bunkers.

On September 9, the 6th Panzer Division advanced toward Krasnogvardeysk from the west, its first assignment to break through the Leningrad Line in the vicinity of Salyzy to open up Krasnogvardeysk for an attack from the rear. I based my plan of attack on precise aerial reconnaissance photographs provided by the Luftwaffe, deciding to push with concentrated force through the outer defense belt at Salyzy, follow through with a thrust north to break through the Leningrad Line, and then roll it up toward the east. The division's main body attacked on the road and then along the edge of the forest that ran parallel to it, seizing the antitank ditch after a brief engagement. By noon we had also captured Salyzy, which required storming a large number of bunkers. One particular bunker at the edge of the forest continued to offer resistance until late afternoon.

Immediately after breaking into the village, *Kampfgruppe* Koll (Colonel Richard Koll's Panzer Regiment 11, supported by an artillery battalion and a company of engineers) drove through the rear of the Russian-occupied forest position and against the Leningrad Line. Covered by the fire of the panzers, the engineers seized the undamaged bridge by a coup de main and removed the Soviet demolition charges placed there. About six kilometers north of Salyzy, *Kampfgruppe* von Seckendorff, in the wake of the panzers, penetrated the enemy antitank ditch (which began at the bridge and ran at a right angle to the front) and established a bridgehead. Later in the afternoon, a Soviet counterattack managed to isolate our units across the river. That evening the division's main body cleared the surrounding forest of Russian forces and—with a front turned ninety degrees—assembled in the woods for a northeast thrust to regain contact with the troops in the bridgehead. Also that evening, *Kampfgruppe* Eckinger (I/Motorized Infantry Regiment 113, 6/Panzer Regiment 1, and II/Panzer Artillery Regiment 73) of the 1st Panzer Division forced a breakthrough of the inner defensive ring east of Salyzy behind a river arm. This success came in the sector of the SS *Polizei* Infantry Division, which had been stalled along its entire front. The bridgehead established by the 1st Panzer Division opened a gateway to Krasnogvardeysk for the SS *Polizei* Infantry Division.

On 10 September the bulk of the 6th Panzer Division advanced along the road toward the northern bridgehead. I detached some elements to mop up the remaining Russian forces on the plateau west of Krasnogvardeysk, while others finished rolling up the enemy's forest position that had forced us to keep a strong flank guard the previous day. In this manner the entire assault sector south of the Leningrad Line was cleared of the enemy before noon. Along the northern edge of the forest area alone, 40,000 Soviet mines had to be disarmed and removed.

Once these tasks had been accomplished, I began to push battalion after battalion through the bridgehead into the three-kilometer-long antitank ditch that ran into the forest area. These battalions managed to infiltrate so far to the north that they completely penetrated all four defensive positions in the Leningrad Line, and I was able to position four battalions (plus tanks) to roll up all the lines simultaneously. The Soviets launched a desperate attempt to repel this attack with cavalry, which we easily foiled. The antitank ditch was about four meters wide and deep, and possession of it made it feasible to change the attack front of the entire division again by ninety degrees at a single stroke. Bunker after bunker and strongpoint after strongpoint now received the attention of Stukas, medium artillery, antitank guns, and flak while being attacked by infantry in the flank and rear. All of my divisional artillery had remained in position south of the Leningrad Line, perfectly positioned so that its fire formed a complete flanking curtain in front of the attacking battalions. Step by step the trenches and final nests of resistance were cleaned out.

We reached the railroad running through the attack area that afternoon and the Krasnogvardeysk-Leningrad highway on 11 September. There we captured a group of artillery pillboxes that were equipped with disappearing armored cupolas. At that point, 6th Panzer Division stood directly in the rear of Krasnogvardeysk. Forced to retreat in a hurry, the Russians had only one side road available for their withdrawal, and that road lay under the effective artillery fire of Panzer Artillery Regiment 76. As the Soviets poured back over this road and the adjoining terrain, Lieutenant Colonel Grundherr's batteries inflicted serious losses on them. The first Red Army forces to attempt a disengagement—their motorized medium artillery—tried to escape on the wide asphalt road through Pushkin. Colonel Koll's panzers, however, had already blocked the road, with the result that the Russian artillery and all other motor vehicles were set afire by our tanks as they tried to break through. During the night of 11–12 September, the bulk of the Russian infantry—though badly mauled—managed to evacuate Krasnogvardeysk and escape, reestablishing itself with strong rear guards on the high ground between Krasnogvardeysk and Pushkin.

On 12 September the pursuing infantry divisions of L Corps (SS *Polizei* and 269th Infantry Divisions) bogged down before the heavily fortified positions. Here the Soviets had employed the most modern system of field fortifications that we ever encountered in four years of war. All of the fortified installations were underground. The defense was carried out in subterranean passages that had been established along terrain steps and equipped with well-camouflaged firing embrasures. They had likewise concealed their heavy weapons in underground emplacements that were invisible from the outside. These emplacements included subterranean rooms, capable of quartering ten to twenty men each, along with ammunition dumps, supply installations, and medical facilities. Tunnels connected virtually all of these positions, and their entrances had been situated several hundred meters to the rear, completely concealed by shrubbery and groups of trees. These entrance passages were also protected by open trenches and several standard bunkers, which could not be discerned until an attacker reached close range. Neither ground reconnaissance nor the Luftwaffe spotted this fortification system; even after the Russian heavy weapons opened fire, the infantry divisions of L Corps could not determine their locations. This made it impossible to neutralize the enemy artillery, and all frontal assaults by the infantry failed as well.

Not until 13 September was it possible to clarify the situation and capture the position. By that time 6th Panzer Division, which had been committed as an encircling force maneuvering via Posyolok Taytsy, had begun pivoting into the rear of the Russian fortifications. An odd coincidence now played into our hands. The previous evening [12 September], I had sent strong reconnaissance patrols into the high ground. Suddenly encountering the rearmost outlying bunker of the whole defensive system, the young officers in command seized the bunker by a storm, without waiting for orders. Among the captured garrison was the Red Army engineer who had supervised the construction of the defenses. With him, the plans to all installations fell into our hands, and it was easy to plan the attack for the next day.

However, the attack by Lieutenant Colonel von Waldenfels's Motorized Infantry Regiment 4 had barely gotten started when a new difficulty arose. Recognizing the danger to their frontally impregnable position, the Russians launched an attack out of Pushkin into our rear. Except for a single battery of 88mm flak, the only support available to the infantry battalion that constituted our rear guard was Lieutenant Colonel Siebert's II Battalion, Panzer Regiment 11, equipped only with PzKw 35ts. A long column of tanks, the end of which could not even be surmised in the dust, rolled into our rear-guard elements. The first of the enemy tanks—a vanguard of more than fifty of the super-heavy KV-1s—quickly passed the narrow strip of firm ground between the swamps and turned against the defended positions.

The heavy flak guns were already thundering. Flames from tanks that had sustained direct hits rose straight into the sky. The KV-1s at the head of the Russian formation spread out but kept moving forward. Suddenly the enemy's lead element came under a hail of fire at close range from Panzerjaeger Battalion 616, which had just arrived with twenty-seven heavy antitank guns. Fourteen columns of black smoke announced to the Soviet main body that its vanguard was being destroyed. Thereupon the bulk of the Russian armor abruptly halted, no longer daring to try the narrow passage through the swamp; its rear elements fanned out and disappeared into the adjoining terrain.

The remainder of Panzer Regiment 11, which had been summoned by radio, now went into action. From division headquarters we heard the unmistakable sounds of heavy tank fighting. Soon the din increased, as the panzer regiments of the neighboring 1st and 8th Panzer Divisions, which had also responded to the summons, attacked the Russian flank and rear. Realizing his position had become quite precarious, the Soviet commander no longer felt himself equal to the task. Even his KV-1s, only fourteen of which had our flak and heavy antitank guns been able to destroy, turned and fled. Withdrawing the bulk of his force, the enemy commander had avoided a decisive showdown, but the threat to the division's rear had thus been eliminated.

In the meantime, however, Colonel Waldenfels's attack, supported by Colonel Siebert's panzers, continued according to plan. In heavy fighting the bunkers and squad trenches protecting the enemy's rear fell one by one, and we reached the entrances to the subterranean defensive system. During the fighting for the first entrance, the crew resisted from an inner compartment with small arms and hand grenades. In this action three Red Army medical corps women in uniform, who defended the entrance with hand grenades, were killed. As their bodies were being removed, several more hand grenades were found on them.

Mopping up the underground passages was time-consuming and difficult. Colonel von Waldenfels had to accomplish this by using specially trained shock troops with hand grenades and machine-pistols. His attempts to clear out the strong bunker crews led to bitter hand-to-hand fighting with heavy losses on both sides, as the Russian soldiers defended themselves to the utmost. The attack stalled. Only after engineer demolition teams had managed to determine the location of the remaining bunkers, by noting the sparser growth of grass above them, could these bunkers be blown open by demolition charges from above and then captured. Even so, the closer that our shock troops came to the front-line positions of the defensive system, the more serious became the losses. Both our engineer demolition teams and infantry were advancing above the Russian defenses, which necessitated walking directly into the heavy artillery fire supporting the frontal assaults of L Corps's infantry divisions. Only when my signal troops managed to establish roundabout telephone communications with L Corps headquarters was it possible finally to complete the conquest of the subterranean defensive system. A junction was then effected with the infantry advancing from the other side. At almost the same time, advancing in the wake of the retreat of the Russian armor, we also succeeded in occupying Pushkin. That afternoon, Colonel von Waldenfels's troops captured the entrenched headquarters of the Russian Forty-second Army, which had been entrusted with the defense of Leningrad.

That the soldiers of the Red Army continued to resist with dogged perseverance even under hopeless conditions could in large measure be credited to the soldierly conduct of the commissars. For example, long after the castle at Posyolok Taytsy had been taken, and we had drawn up strong units in the castle park, tanks from Panzer Regiment 11 passing near the park wall with open hatches reported drawing single rounds of rifle fire from close range. The shots were aimed at the unprotected tank commanders as they looked out of the turrets. Not until three of our men had been killed by bullets through the head did the company's officers realize that the shots were coming from a narrow trench close under the park wall, about ten meters away.

The tanks immediately returned fire, whereupon all thirteen occupants of the trench met death. They were officers of a Russian regimental headquarters, grouped about their commissar, who fell with his rifle cocked and aimed.

Leningrad was now within sight.

Our troops were convinced that Soviet resistance outside Leningrad had been broken and that a continuation of the attack—at least in 6th Panzer Division's sector—would have led directly into the city. Abruptly, however, on 14 September we received orders from above to discontinue the offensive. Nobody understood this measure. The following day, 6th Panzer Division was ordered out of the line, except for the division's artillery. The movements necessary to withdraw from the battle were completed on 16 September. In the morning of 17 September the division received orders to begin moving that evening in the direction of Luga-Pskov, followed after several days by marches through Nevel and into the area of Army Group Center.

With that fight the most tenacious Russian defensive battles of 1941, between Krasnogvardeysk and Leningrad, came to an end. Within a week, 6th Panzer Division had managed to break through and roll up twelve positions, repulsed several counterattacks, and captured 248 bunkers (among which were more than twenty-five concrete and steel bunkers with armored cupolas).

In true blitzkrieg manner, 6th Panzer Division had rolled across Lithuania and Latvia within a few days, overrun every enemy position in its way, broken through the Stalin Line, crossed the Dvina River, and opened the gateway to Leningrad on the Luga River—all within three weeks of its day of departure. This 800-kilometer trip led through dust and sand, woods and swamps, and across river and antitank ditches. The flexible leadership at the regimental and battalion levels in a battle-tested division, and the élan with which our veteran troops attacked, made it possible to overcome every obstacle during our eighty-six-day advance from East Prussia to a point just short of Leningrad.

MOSCOW

Vyazma

AT THE VERY TIME THAT THE capture of Leningrad appeared inevitable, 6th Panzer Division was called to assume a leading part in the attack toward Moscow. Once again the division moved with lightning speed and covered nearly 1,000 kilometers to join Panzer Group 3 in Army Group Center.

Committed as the spearhead of General of Panzer Troops Ferdinand Schaal's LVI Panzer Corps on the first day of the offensive [2 October], we thrust over thirty kilometers, quickly reached the upper Dnepr, and captured two bridges there by coup de main. That movement cut off Russian forces that were still west of the river and ensured that Panzer Group 3 could continue its thrust to the east.

That night I ordered the renewed employment, by the entire division, of the defensive hedgehog tactics that *Kampfgruppe* Raus had routinely utilized in its drive through the Baltic countries. The troops deployed into an elaborate system of hedgehog positions just east of the river. I knew that in our rear and along our flanks the bypassed and defeated Red Army divisions would be withdrawing under cover of darkness. At one point a retreating Russian rifle corps staff sought refuge in the small, isolated village in the forest wherein we had established division headquarters. Enemy troop units were moving all around the entire system of panzer hedgehogs as soon as darkness fell. As long as the tanks of Panzer Regiment 11 were on their own, the intermittent firing of flares and machine guns indicated their uneasiness with this situation. This changed a few hours later as Motorized Infantry Regiments 4 and 114, along with Motorcycle Battalion 6, arrived at the bridgehead. By the time that the divisional artillery and engineers had arrived to be integrated into the defensive system, a restful night was had by all. Early the next morning, however, the Russian units in the area departed very quietly: They had been unable to find any rest in the immediate vicinity of a German panzer division.

On 3 October, as 6th Panzer Division resumed its eastward march toward Kholm, the Russians attempted to parry the German offensive by means of an armored flank attack. One hundred tanks drove from the south against the road hub at Kholm. For the most part these were only medium tanks, against which I initially dispatched a single battalion of PzKw 35ts and the 6th Company (APC) of Motorized Infantry Regiment 114. This weak force proved sufficient to contain the potentially dangerous thrust until flak and antitank guns could be organized into an adequate antitank security line between Kholm and the southern Dnepr bridge.

Their tanks split up into small groups by the forest, the Russians never succeeded in organizing a powerful, unified armored thrust. Their lead elements were eliminated piecemeal as they encountered the antitank front. As a result, the Soviet commander became even more timid and scattered his vehicles across the breadth and depth of the battlefield in such a manner that all subsequent tank thrusts, carried out in detail and by small groups, could be met by our antitank weapons and smashed. Kholm and the Dnepr bridge, as well as their connecting road (which the Russians had already taken under intermittent tank fire), remained in our hands. After eighty Russian tanks had been put out of action, the division's main body broke through the last line of strong fortifications on the eastern bank of the Dnepr, which had been occupied by the last Soviet reserves, and we were able to continue the drive to the east without concern for the remaining Russian tanks. Thus the flank attack by 100 Soviet tanks near Kholm had succeeded in delaying 6th Panzer Division's advance only for a matter of hours.

From Kholm the 6th and 7th Panzer Divisions rolled along parallel roads toward Vyazma (6th Panzer Division to the south through Khmelita, and 7th Panzer Division to the north through Dernova). Hastily assembled Russian tank and rifle units, supported by several batteries of medium artillery, attempted to stop our advance by attacking 6th Panzer Division's open right flank, which soon stretched over forty kilometers. Many of the Soviet batteries that had been emplaced to defend the Dnepr front remained in position and merely turned their guns around, while others rushed up at full speed and assumed firing positions in the open. Infantry and tanks advanced in a widespread chain against our march columns, and the artillery immediately opened fire as each battery managed to shift its front.

This attack also turned out badly for the Russians, as both 6th and 7th Panzer Divisions instantly responded with a barrage of all weapons. The divisions resembled a mighty battleship, smashing all targets within reach with the heavy caliber of its broadsides. Artillery and mortar shells from 300 throats of fire hailed down on the Soviet batteries and tanks. Soon the Russian tanks were in flames, the batteries transformed into smoking heaps of rubble, and the lines of skirmishers swept away by a swath of fire from hundreds of machine guns. This work of destruction consumed no more than twenty minutes. Hardly pausing, the two panzer divisions continued their advance, reaching Vyazma the same day [10 October]. There, linking up with the 10th Panzer Division of Panzer Group 4, which had fought its way up from the south, we completed the encirclement of 400,000 Russians.

During these operations the Red Army employed so-called mine dogs for destroying our tanks. In the manner of pack animals, medium-sized dogs carried demolition charges that were connected to a spindle fastened to the dog's back. The dogs had been trained to hide under approaching tanks. In so doing, the animal would inadvertently bring the upright spindle (about fifteen centimeters long) into contact with the belly of the tank and set off the charge.

News of this insidious tactic caused some alarm among our panzer units and made them fire at all approaching dogs on sight. There is no evidence of any case where a German tank was destroyed by a mine dog. On the other hand, it has been reported that several times mine dogs fleeing from the fire of our panzers sought protection underneath Russian tanks, which promptly blew up. One thing is certain: The specter of the mine dogs ceased just as abruptly as it had begun.

Mud on the Road to Moscow

The German army had no conception of mud as it exists in European Russia. Soon after the victory at Vyazma, when our front-line troops were already stuck fast, Hitler and OKH still believed that the mud could be conquered by main force, an idea that led to serious losses of vehicles and equipment. Large-scale operations quickly became impossible. The muddy season of autumn 1941 was more severe than any other muddy season experienced during World War I or World War II. Even during the first stages, cart and dirt roads became impassable, and major roads soon became mud-choked. Supply trucks broke through the gravel-topped roads and churned up traffic lanes until even courier service had to be carried out with tracked vehicles. By the height of the muddy season, tractors and wreckers normally capable of traversing difficult terrain had become helpless, and attempts to plow through the muddy mass made the roads even more impassable. Tanks, heavy wreckers, and even vehicles with good ground clearance simply pushed an ever-growing wall of mud before them until they finally ground to a halt, half-buried by their own motion. Eventually, only horse-drawn vehicles could move; all other transport and the bulk of the tanks and artillery were stopped dead.

Pursuit of the beaten Russians was impossible, and only divisions that had gained the all-weather Bryansk-Orel-Tula road could move. Units became separated and intermingled, with only scattered elements in contact with the enemy. The bulk of Army Group Center's forces stuck fast or could move only fitfully forward in short marches. Motor vehicles broke down with clutch or motor trouble. Horses became exhausted and collapsed. Roads were littered with dead draft animals. Few tanks were serviceable. Trucks and horse-drawn wagons bogged down.

German losses in tanks and motorized equipment of all types were extraordinarily high. Panzer Group 2, operating in the Orel area, lost 60 percent of its remaining tanks in the mud. The 10th Panzer Division of Panzer Group 4, operating north of Gzhatsk, lost fifty tanks without a shot being fired, thirty-five of them within three days. A sudden frost in late October cemented one of 6th Panzer Division's crippled, buried panzer columns into a state of complete uselessness, and it never moved again. Because we could not reach it any other way, gasoline, towropes, and food supplies had to be air-dropped along this line of stranded armor, but all attempts to move proved futile. These losses proved especially serious since no replacements were being received. Often in situations like this, when drivers found themselves bogged down far from any habitation, they abandoned their vehicles and set out on foot to contact friendly troops in the nearest village, or sought food and shelter from local civilians in order to remain alive until the worst of the muddy season had passed. At that time Germany was only producing eighty-five tanks and forty assault guns each month.

Concerning the state of 6th Panzer Division's armor, I reported on 31 October:

> The average distance driven by our Panzers was 11,500 kilometers for PzKw II, 12,500 for PzKw 35t, 11,000 for PzKw IV, and 3,200 for command tanks. The special situation in regard to repair of the PzKw 35t is well known. It is indeed deemed necessary to point out that repairs can be accomplished only by cannibalizing other Panzers because there are no longer any spare parts for the PzKw 35t. This means that after retrieval of the Panzers that are scattered around the terrain, a maximum of ten can actually be repaired out of the forty-one PzKw 35ts reported as needing repair. The PzKw 35ts can no longer be rebuilt. All of the components are worn out. To be practical, perhaps the armored hulls are still salvageable.

The few railroads of European Russia are the only means of long-distance transportation during the muddy season, and the overburdening of their facilities was inevitable. Operating schedules were disrupted because muddy highways prevented access to the railheads. Repairs to damaged track consumes endless time, because labor and materials had to be transported by rail to the damaged places. The right of ways had to be restored step by step, as simultaneous work on several sections of track was out of the question. Supply shipments suffered serious delays: In some areas in Army Group Center the supply flow became so constricted that operations came to a complete halt. Many units found themselves without bread for days and to live off the land and such local food supplies as the Red Army had not already destroyed. Requisitioning of food in unoccupied territory was possible only with strong parties, because such areas were infested with partisans and scattered Russian soldiers.

In early December the divisional war diary recorded the following:

The combination of the heavy battle casualties over the past few days with the falling temperatures (at noon averaging 25°F; at night averaging −32°F) have caused a severe decline in the division's combat strength. The current combat strength follows:

Motorized Infantry Regiment 4: 12 officers and 556 men
Motorized Infantry Regiment 114: 9 officers and 332 men
Motorcycle Battalion 6: 3 officers and 149 men
Total infantry strength: 19 officers and 784 men
Average infantry company: 1 officer and 30 men

We recorded the daily mean temperature during the first part of December as follows:

1 December:	19°F
2 December:	22°F
3 December:	16°F
4 December:	−32°F
5 December:	−34°F
6 December:	−35°F
7 December:	−36°F
8 December:	22°F
9 December:	18°F

Retreat from Moscow

The winter of 1941–1942 was the most severe in European Russia in 100 years. In the area northwest of Moscow the mean temperature during January 1942 was −32°F, with the lowest recorded temperature (−63°F) during the entire Russian campaign occurring in the same area on 26 January. Our troops, if they had any winter clothing at all, carried only the regular issue overcoat, sweater, bellyband, and hood designed for winter wear in Germany. The bulk of the winter garments donated by the German populace did not reach the soldiers at the front until the end of January, after the cold had done its worst damage. Commanders at all levels attempted to meet the emergency through improvisation. Several divisions helped themselves by organizing large sewing workrooms in nearby Russian cities and towns. From used blankets and old clothing, local workers produced flannel waistbands, earmuffs, waistcoats, footcloths, and mittens with separate thumbs and index fingers. We also managed to requisition fur garments and felt boots from local inhabitants for a small number of men, while also acquiring some winter clothing from dead Red Army soldiers. Any of the troops possessing extra underwear wore one set on top of the other; division and army supply dumps immediately issued all supplies of underclothing. Eventually, most men were able to protect their heads and ears, at least partially, by using rags and waistbands. Nonetheless, during that first crucial winter outside Moscow, the available supply of winter clothing proved sufficient for only a small percentage of our forces. Needless to say, the severe cold drastically reduced the efficiency of our soldiers and their weapons.

At the beginning of December, 6th Panzer Division stood but fourteen kilometers from Moscow and twenty-four kilometers from the Kremlin. At that moment a sudden drop in the temperature to −30°F, coupled with a surprise attack by Siberian troops, smashed Third Panzer Army's drive on Stalin's capital. By building 6th Panzer Division's defense around Colonel Koll's last five panzers, we held off the initial attack by the Siberians, who presented prime targets in their brown uniforms as they trudged forward through the deep snow. This local success facilitated the division's disengagement and provided time for the destruction of our last 88mm flak guns. (This became necessary because no prime movers were left; we lost twenty-five to the autumn mud, and in November the last seven fell victim to cold and snow.)

Elements of Army Group Center, including Third Panzer Army, held out to the northwest of Moscow until 5 December; the following day OKH issued the first retreat order of the war. In the months of the offensive, our battalions and companies had dwindled to a handful of men, while Russian mud and winter wreaked havoc on their weapons and equipment. Neither the leadership of the officers nor the personal bravery of the soldiers could compensate for the diminished firepower of our divisions. Thus the numerical superiority of the Red Army, aided by the climactic conditions, saved Moscow and turned the tide of the battle. Hitler had neither expected nor planned for a winter war.

Sixth Panzer Division's withdrawal began smoothly enough on 6 December, but the next day, while moving over hilly terrain, our vehicles skidded helplessly on the icy roads. Trucks that had been abandoned in the final attack toward Moscow now blocked the roads for our retreat, adding to the difficulties. Apprehensive that the pursuing Russians would overtake and destroy our rear guards if time were wasted in extricating each vehicle, I ordered as much equipment as possible loaded on the few surviving trucks and had the remainder put to the torch. At the same time, I reinforced the rear guard with nearly all of our available infantry and deliberately slowed the pace of the retirement. We now fell back in brief delaying actions based on villages. Inhabited places had become critical to the survival of our soldiers, who lacked winter clothing, and were attractive to the Russians as well, because they preferred permanent-type shelter for their assault troops. In a very real sense, the retreat devolved into a race from village to village.

In a few days the retreat reached Klin, a vital road junction northwest of Moscow. Unfortunately, 6th Panzer Division could not use the town to house the division overnight, as it was on the main route of other divisions streaming west and the centerpiece of LVI Panzer Corps's defensive effort. We were, however, lucky enough to find a large quantity of explosives in Klin, and our engineers used these to blast temporary shelters in the ground outside the city. Attempts to obtain dirt from the blasted shelters to sand the roads proved futile, because the explosions loosed great chunks of solidly frozen earth that could not be pulverized. The 6th Panzer Division held before Klin for twenty-four hours, then completed its withdrawal across the four-lane Smolensk-Moscow highway.

Though numerically superior, the enemy never succeeded in enveloping and annihilating our rear guards, because he could not employ his heavy weapons in frontal attacks through deep snow without suffering prohibitive losses. This meant that for attempted envelopments the Russians had to rely on cavalry, ski troops, and infantry mounted on sleighs who were unable to take their heavy weapons with them. The striking power that the Soviets were thus able to bring forward was insufficient to overwhelm our defenses.

Contributing to the Russian failure to destroy Army Group Center in the initial onslaught was the fact that Soviet air activity during the withdrawal was ineffective, being limited to scattered sorties of a few planes, which strafed columns or dropped small fragmentation bombs. During air alerts our troops burrowed into the snow at least 100 meters from the road. Some casualties resulted from delayed-action bombs when soldiers failed to remain down long enough after the missiles had been dropped. If the Russians had used strong bomber forces, the results could have been disastrous. As it was, our losses to enemy air attacks were inconsequential compared to casualties from cold weather and insufficient clothing.

By mid-December, when this phase of the withdrawal ended, 6th Panzer Division was located in Shakovskaya to refit and receive reinforcements. On Christmas Eve, Motorized Infantry Regiment 4, which had received the first replacements, was alerted to counterattack Russian forces that had broken through the 106th Infantry Division on the Lama River, west of Voloko-lamsk. Colonel Waldenfels's men moved out in a snowstorm on 26 December over roads already covered with deep drifts. Because his infantry was in-adequately clothed, lengthy warming halts had to be made in every village, and the regiment required two days to cover the nineteen kilometers to the line of departure for the attack.

After a hot meal and a night's rest, Motorized Infantry Regiment 4 at-tacked on 28 December, in conjunction with local reserves. Well supported by artillery and heavy weapons, Colonel Waldenfels made steady progress throughout the day; by evening he had made contact with the neighboring 23rd Infantry Division to the north, thus closing the gap. The troops located shelter in nearby villages and farmhouses. As they settled in for the evening, strong security detachments were posted and relieved every half-hour be-cause of the extreme cold.

The plan for 29 December called for regaining the 106th Infantry Divi-sion's original positions on the Lama River by enveloping the Russian forces that had penetrated the defenses. Colonel von Waldenfels's regiment at-tacked eastward, while Motorcycle Battalion 6 advanced from the south to-ward Vladychino. By noon the Soviet breakthrough force had been sur-rounded. Night temperatures dropped to between −30°F and −40°F, and no shelter was available to the troops holding the perimeter. Nearby villages had been destroyed in the fighting, and the entrenchments of the old German po-sitions on the Lama were buried deep in the snow. To remain exposed would have meant certain death for troops lacking winter clothing, and Colonel von Waldenfels reluctantly ordered a withdrawal to a more distant village. When the Russians observed that the encirclement had been abandoned, they con-centrated for a new breakthrough that eventually forced a retirement of the entire German front in that sector. Success had turned into failure because we were not equipped to withstand extreme cold.

The ultimate result of this failure was that, during the final days of December, 6th Panzer Division found itself dislodged from the chain of villages around Shakovskaya and forced back into a large wooded region. I now faced two equally bad alternatives. If I ordered a withdrawal through the woods to the next group of villages, the division risked envelopment and defeat in detail. On the other hand, attempting to establish a defensive line in the woods or between the indefensible villages, without winter clothing and in temperatures now averaging −49°F, promised certain death from exposure. During Colonel von Waldenfels's brief battle near the Lama River, which had of necessity taken place in open terrain, the daily casualties from frostbite had increased at an alarming rate: By 3 January 1942 our clearing stations reported that moderate and severe frostbite cases were arriving at the rate of 800 per day. At that rate the division would cease to exist in a week.

If we were to survive, much less hold our line, shelters and bunkers (with whatever heating facilities could be installed) had to be constructed immediately. Such defensive works could not be constructed, however, because the single corps and two divisional engineer battalions available contained no more than forty to sixty men each and had lost all their heavy equipment. On the other hand, a large quantity of explosives had just arrived. In view of the critical situation, I ordered the engineer battalion commanders to disregard the frost and to blast enough craters into the solidly frozen ground along the tentative main battle line to provide shelter for all the combat troops, including tactical reserves. These craters were to be echeloned in width and depth and were to be large enough to hold three to five soldiers. Any accessible lumber was utilized to cover the craters. I also instructed the engineers to mine certain areas and place tank obstacles along three key routes. The reserves, as well as all divisional service troops, were required to pack down paths between the craters, as well as paths leading back to the rear.

The blasting along the entire line commenced early the next morning [4 January]. The noise of the 10,000-pound explosive charges somehow gave the impression of a heavy artillery barrage. Fountains of earth rose all around, and dense smoke filled the air. The Russians watched with surprise, not at all sure what was happening, and therefore remained quiet. By noon the blasting had been completed, and by nightfall the combat units had occupied the now-covered craters. Soon afterward smoke rose from the craters where the gun crews kept warm at open fires. The craters formed an uninterrupted string of positions in front of which we established security outposts. A maze of abatis lay in front of these, guns had been emplaced along the roads behind the tank obstacles, and in one stroke the entire division

front had been made ready for defense within twelve hours of the first detonation. The engineers who prepared these positions in the fiercest cold and
thereby suffered 40 percent frostbite casualties had saved the combat units
and restored the situation through their sacrifice. By 5 January the overall divisional casualties from frostbite dropped from 800 to four cases and subsequently ceased for all practical purposes. This position subsequently withstood all Soviet attacks and was not abandoned until ten days later, in milder
weather, when the adjacent units on both flanks found themselves forced to
withdraw after Russian tanks penetrated their lines.

This improvisation was ordered at a time when 6th Panzer Division had
lost all of its tanks during the preceding withdrawal. Before blasting these
positions, fighting had centered on the possession of the villages that alone
offered shelter from the extreme cold. Groups of villages had formed natural phase lines for both attackers and defenders, who found themselves forced
to ignore almost every other tactical consideration. Whenever the Russians
failed to capture a village by day, they withdrew to the last friendly village for
the night. Not even the best-equipped Siberian troops attempted to continue
an attack on a village after dark. Blasting positions in the open terrain therefore represented an innovation that served the double purpose of stabilizing
the front line and maintaining the combat efficiency of the remnants of the
division.

Chapter 6

WINTER WAR

Crisis Behind Ninth Army

ON 17 JANUARY 1942 AT KARMONOVO, exactly where the division had once freed itself from the shackles of the mud and had begun to thrust toward Moscow, its remnants now regrouped, worn out from fighting the cold and the snow. The enormous losses in men and equipment, from which the German army was never quite able to recover again, is evidence of how hard the fighting for Moscow was. The 6th Panzer Division, which had fought under particularly difficult conditions, lost 80 percent of its infantrymen and cannons, 100 percent of its tanks and heavy weapons, and the bulk of its motor vehicles. All that remained of the combat troops, collected together in *Kampfgruppe* Zollenkopf, were the following:

Motorized Infantry Regiment 4: two consolidated companies
Motorized Infantry Regiment 114: two consolidated companies
Panzer Artillery Regiment 76: four consolidated companies (fighting as infantry under II/76 headquarters)

Neither Motorcycle Battalion 6, Engineer Battalion 57, Panzer Reconnaissance Battalion 57, nor Panzer Regiment 11 could be fielded as separate combat units due to excessive losses. The remainder of Panzer Artillery Regiment 76 had been consolidated under its I (Light) and III (Heavy) Battalions into batteries manning the division's surviving twenty-four pieces of field artillery. After the terrible hemorrhage of the December fighting, the remaining staffs and the supply and rear elements assembled sixty-five kilometers behind the front line for the purpose or reorganizing the division. Every day a few tankers, artillerymen, and others who had escaped the carnage trickled into the divisional area. As soon as they arrived, we pressed them into service to help guard the highway and railroad between Smolensk and Vyazma—

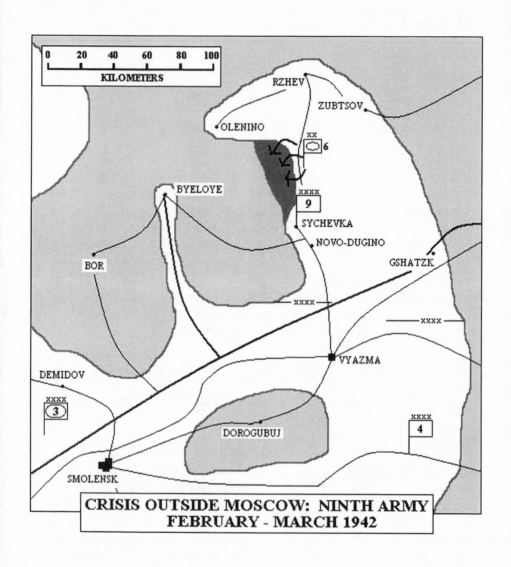

CRISIS OUTSIDE MOSCOW: NINTH ARMY
FEBRUARY - MARCH 1942

the lifelines for both the Fourth and Ninth Armies—against attacks by Russian cavalry, parachute troops, and partisans who had penetrated deep into the rear areas. By mid-February, these returning stragglers and replacements received had brought 6th Panzer Division's total combat strength (*Gefechtstarke*) to about 3,000 men and a handful of operational tanks.

An examination of the general situation at Army Group Center in late January 1942 reveals how complicated the tactical situation had become. In the wake of the December Russian counteroffensive, our front had taken on the appearance of an intricate maze. Each of the armies on Army Group Center's northern flank (Third, Fourth, and Ninth Panzer) commanded several front sectors, the direction of which sometimes varied by as much as 180 degrees. This curious structure developed because we lacked sufficient forces to organize and hold a compact, rigid battle line. Since Hitler had emphatically prohibited any retrograde movements, each unit clung tenaciously to its supply routes, the loss of which in deep winter would have meant the annihilation of the German army just as Napoleon's army had once been destroyed. As a result, our troops never suffered from lack of ammunition and food, despite frequent enemy disruption of supply shipments.

The Russians, on the other hand, had been pouring divisions into nearly impassable and heavily wooded terrain in their attempt to cut our retreating armies to pieces. By mid-January Soviet soldiers found themselves compelled to eat their horses (and ultimately even the skins of their horses) to keep from starving. Russian artillery suffered such a crippling ammunition shortage that batteries were not able to fire more than five to ten shells per day. This state of affairs explains the fact that Army Group Center's front, which due to its unusual irregularity had increased from 500 to 1,800 kilometers (the distance between Vienna and Madrid), could be held for several months by very weak units, composed for the most part of supply and service elements. Moreover, it subsequently proved possible to evacuate exposed positions without suffering any losses.

The Red Army had first driven southward and then turned east toward the highway connecting Vyazma-Rzhev in an attempt to cut off supplies for Ninth Army. The field hospitals and motor pools of several divisions came under attack, and two key airfields near Sychevka were in immediate danger of enemy capture. In the northern sector of this penetration zone we faced a Russian Guards rifle corps, and in the south a cavalry corps. Field Marshal Gunther von Kluge, commanding Army Group Center, did not believe that the overall situation permitted the release of any troops from the reorganizing 6th Panzer Division to serve as the cadre for *Alarmeinheiten* [Alarm Units] that were to be improvised for immediate defensive purposes. By January's end, the situation had become so tense that Stalin felt justified in announcing the impending annihilation of two German armies in the biggest encirclement battle in history.

Events, however, would develop differently.

Because these *Alarmeinheiten* had to be improvised and committed immediately, even though no combat cadres were available, Colonel General Walter Model, commanding Ninth Army, therefore issued orders on 30 January subordinating all the service and supply units in the army rear area, including construction and road-building battalions, to my headquarters. (The reorganizing elements of 6th Panzer Division's own combat troops were attached temporarily to 1st Panzer Division.) By organizing these units for combat and intercepting all stragglers, General Model expected me to build up a defensive front between Sychevka and Vyazma in the most expeditious manner. Even the Luftwaffe units at the Novo-Dugino airfield had been placed under my control for commitment to ground operations.

The initial composition of these units included:

Senior Artillery Commander 307
(staff only)

Assault Gun Battalion 189
(minus two batteries; no vehicles)

Artillery Observation Battalion 618
(minus two batteries; no vehicles)

Engineer Training Battalion 2
(no vehicles)

Senior Construction Staff 17

Construction Staff Commands 9, 42, 104
(staff only)

Road Construction Battalion 532
(no heavy weapons)

Bridge Construction Battalion 7
(minus two companies; no vehicles)

Construction Battalions 91, 208, 408
(no heavy weapons or vehicles)

Bridging Columns 5, 6, 28, 33, 35, 182, 186, 442, 644, 664
(no heavy weapons; vehicles confiscated to transport reinforcements to main front)

Luftwaffe garrison and signals detachment, Novo-Dugino airfield

Improvised platoon of five damaged tanks

Within twenty-four hours the headquarters staffs of all these units had been set to work intercepting every available officer and man in their respective areas, then forming them into *Alarmeinheiten* of varying strength and composition. I ordered that special care be taken to keep men from the same unit together: Depending on their numbers, they formed squads, platoons, or companies under command of familiar officers. Whenever possible, *Alarmeinheiten* of similar composition were organized into battalions and two or more battalions placed under one of the staffs mentioned above. Each element was allowed to keep the weapons and supplies it had salvaged from its original parent unit. I instituted these procedures as a guarantee against the unnecessary splitting up of available manpower and resources. It seemed to me a better policy to commit units of differing strength and composition rather than to destroy unit cohesion by equalizing numbers. Naturally, the strength and composition of individual units had to be taken into account when assigning defensive sectors.

Most of the troops were armed with rifles. Each company had one or two machine guns, and some of the battalions had a few mortars and small-caliber antitank guns that had been procured from ordnance shops in the vicinity. Initially, only one recently repaired artillery piece was available, but the flow of weapons and equipment improved daily as the maintenance and repair shops made a sustained effort to send equipment back to the front. Numerous convalescents and men returning from furlough were employed along the rapidly forming front facing west.

We occupied the most important sectors of our sixty-five-kilometer front on 31 January, gaps were filled the following day, and by 2 February a continuous though thinly held line had been formed. By 6 February my headquarters controlled 35,000 men, and we were able to improvise some platoon-size general reserve units, including one panzer platoon with five damaged tanks that enjoyed at least limited mobility. Frequently our newly formed units underwent their baptism of fire on the very day of their initial organization. Where possible, I had these *Alarmeinheiten* committed in sectors where they could protect their own service and rear installations—a task with which they were only too glad to comply. For the same reason Luftwaffe units were assigned to defensive positions covering their own airfields. *Alarmeinheiten* whose unit assembly areas were farther away from the new front filled in the gaps. The Luftwaffe signal battalion of VIII Fleiger Corps at Novo-Dugino laid the necessary telephone lines and connected them with the airfield switchboard.

To understand the magnitude of this task, it should be recalled that the crisis occurred in midwinter, with temperatures sometimes not rising above −40°F even in daylight hours. The snow had reached a depth of roughly one meter in the open terrain and half that in the woods. We could keep snow shoveled off only the most important supply routes.

The terrain between Vyazma and Sychevka was slightly undulating, and two-thirds of it was covered by forests. In the open areas numerous small villages and homesteads were located, usually grouped around a larger town. All villages—both those in Russian and German hands—were fully occupied by troops, and villages near the front had been prepared for all-around defense. Normally, several villages would be organized to form a defensive system in which the main town constituted the focal point. Defensive constructions consisted of snow barriers (parapets) and ice bunkers in large numbers. While the means available to us made it possible to blast several holes in the solidly frozen ground, it proved impossible to dig trenches or erect earthen parapets. The buildings themselves served as heated shelters and therefore were utilized directly only for defensive purposes in emergencies. It would not have been difficult for either side, particularly for the Germans, to have set fire to villages by means of air attacks or artillery, thus depriving the respective enemy of vital shelter. However, this generally occurred only during heavy fighting: Both sides tended to avoid such destruction because each counted on being able to make use of the villages in the near future. Both sides also feared reprisals.

By 9 February we had improvised a full-strength, completely equipped motorcycle company, utilizing men returned from furloughs and hospitals. Several armored cars were turned over to this tactical mobile reserve, which could then be moved swiftly to any danger point along the *Rollbahn* [main supply route] connecting Sychevka and Vyazma. The men in this company were also well-versed in skiing and carried skis on their motorcycles in order to have cross-country mobility even when the snow was a meter deep. Lieutenant Colonel Martin Unrein, commander of the decimated Motorcycle Battalion 6, assumed personal control of this crack unit and led it in a number of local counterattacks.

The situation remained fluid. During this initial period of organization, several Russian attacks on the Novo-Dugino airfield and the adjacent sector to the north had to be repelled by the *Alarmeinheiten*. In the central sector, opposite Tatarinka, the Soviets managed to occupy several villages before the arrival of the *Alarmeinheiten*, while on the southern wing they held villages only about one kilometer away from the highway, which allowed them to interdict it with mortars. At night enemy ski units infiltrated through our lines, which were not yet continuous, and disrupted Ninth Army's supplies at several points between Vyazma and Rzhev. In view of the extreme cold (with nighttime temperatures sometimes dropping to −60°F) the combined village strongpoints constituted the backbone of our defense. The intermediate terrain could be guarded only by weak outposts, stationed in isolated homesteads, while the roads were only lightly secured by patrols. Despite these difficulties, and under repeated enemy attack, the critical center sector of the front held from the outset.

Thus the improvised front line facing west had served its initial purpose. Within a few days we not only had manned a continuous line but also had established contact with the forces fighting in an arc around Rzhev to the north and with similarly improvised Fourth Army units in the south. Even so, the *Rollbahn* and railroad ran so closely behind our main battle line that continuous disruptions could not be prevented, and the slightest tactical setback on the part of the *Alarmeinheiten* threatened to result in the complete blockage of Ninth Army's only supply artery. The Russian attacks were all the more facilitated by the fact that in this particular sector strips of forest extended as far as the road and railroad bridge across the Osusa River. Both General Model and I agreed that this handicap could be remedied only by advancing our line of outposts farther to the west, in order to gain possession of the forest region, which was roughly ten kilometers wide and just as deep. We realized that this would involve a winter offensive in extreme cold and deep snow, conducted at least in part by improvised units without training in offensive operations. Yet it had to be done. Even though General Model agreed to allow me to utilize the somewhat reorganized *Kampfgruppe* Zollenkopf as the spearhead for the initial attacks, this operation obviously could not be an offensive in the usual sense, let alone a blitzkrieg. The tactics to be used necessarily deviated from the conventional pattern and had to be especially suited to the peculiarities of the prevailing situation and the forces available.

Tatarinka: The First Attack

The immediate objective of our first attack—launched on 16 February—was to seize all villages held by the Russians in the bottom of the valley on both sides of the Vasilevka-Tatarinka road. For this purpose *Kampfgruppe* Zollenkopf assembled for action in the eastern portion of Natchekino and the fringes of the forest adjoining it on both sides. Aside from the three battalions previously mentioned, Colonel Zollenkopf had been reinforced by a few tanks, flak guns, and antitank guns, as well as an infantry battalion that had recently lost its commander. He also received the support of 6th Panzer

Division's twenty-four guns and such air support as VIII Fleiger Corps could provide.

Clearing the enemy out of the western section of Natchekino required bitter fighting at close quarters. Nonetheless, *Kampfgruppe* Zollenkopf succeeded in breaching the strong Russian defensive fortifications and putting the garrison to flight. After removing a variety of mines and other obstacles, the snow was cleared from the narrow stretch of road in the erstwhile no-man's land, thus establishing a connection to the enemy supply route. Only then did it become possible to commit our tanks in small groups—one following the other—in pursuit of the fleeing Russians. The panzers scattered the enemy troops who were falling back along both the road and streambed, then advanced toward Vasilevka, which was the focal point of the enemy defense. The sudden appearance of our panzers prevented the commitment of the Russian reserves prior to our infantry assault on the village. As a result, the enemy positions at Vasilevka were unable to hold out for long against the attacks launched by the two consolidated battalions of Motorized Infantry Regiments 4 and 114: We seized the village that same morning. The two battalions, supported by the panzers, immediately pushed westward and fought their way into Tatarinka against stiff resistance. By these three successive attacks, Colonel Zollenkopf had seized the focal points of the Soviet defenses in the area, and by operating out of Vasilevka and Tatarinka he rapidly mopped up the remaining villages. Even before the short winter day ended, all the captured villages were occupied and the former Red Army defensive positions converted for our use.

Destroying the ice bunkers that had been established everywhere required direct antitank, flak, or tank fire. In order to drive the Russians out of their hedgehog defensive positions and the buildings in the villages, we had to engage in bitter close combat with hand grenades and submachine guns. Our losses nonetheless could be described as only moderate, thanks in large measure to air support from the Luftwaffe and the concentrated fire of the divisional artillery. Only weak remnants of the defeated Russian garrisons fled into the adjacent forests where they began, as best they could, to prepare new positions in the snow. The Russians suffered defeat so quickly because of the absence of air support and the fact that their artillery support had been rendered inadequate due to ammunition shortages. As a result, our attack had driven a wedge fifteen kilometers deep into the Soviet defensive front, and this provided us with the basis for subsequent operations.

Several incidents that occurred during the battle are worthy of note. After the western half of Natchekino had been captured, the Russians launched a counterattack from log bunker positions they had established in the forest south of the village. They intended to strike the flank and rear of our infantry, which had already begun to advance westward toward Vasilevka. However, as soon as the Russian soldiers reached open terrain between the forest rise and the village, our tanks (which had just moved in behind the infantry) caught them with enfilade fire and inflicted heavy casualties. The survivors fell back in an attempt to reach the forest positions they had abandoned, hoping to find refuge there from the devastating fire of our panzers. To their great consternation they were met by hostile machine-gun fire from their own former positions. This fire emanated from Colonel Zollen's southern detachment, which had turned into the forest while the fighting raged in Natchekino and subsequently reached and occupied the abandoned Russian bunkers. This enemy element, caught between two deadly fires, was wiped out.

This disaster suffered by the Russians south of Natchekino resulted from their inadequate combat reconnaissance, which failed to discover in time either the presence of our tanks or the flank detachment advancing through the forest. Otherwise the Soviet commander would have realized the precarious nature of his position and would not have attempted the counterattack. Moreover, the Russian commander had placed undue reliance on his security detachments at the forest edge west of Sereda. These detachments had been long since overrun by our flank unit, but the liaison between the Russian forest bunker position and the security elements apparently functioned so poorly that he had no idea that his position had been compromised. Even disregarding this threat, the Russian commander had executed his counterattack across exposed ground, had taken no steps to protect his troops from any direction, and had pushed large numbers of men across snow-covered fields that provided absolutely no cover. These violations of the basic rules of tactics, namely with regard to reconnaissance, security, and liaison, had resulted in the destruction of his command.

Even though Colonel Zollen's spearhead (which, in open terrain, was supported by all weapons on the march route) quickly succeeded in forcing its way west, the flank detachments moving through the forest found the going progressively more difficult. Although in each stretch of forest these detachments were able to make use of one beaten track the Russians had made, this required the troops to march single file and left both of them, as they were about to exit the forest, unexpectedly confronting enemy positions camouflaged with abatis. They could neither capture these positions by front assault nor bypass them through the thickets on either side of the path due to the deep snow. Moreover, the reinforced infantry company that constituted our northern detachment was suddenly attacked in the center of the so-called Africa forest by numerous snipers in the trees, who held them up for a long time. Both flank detachments failed to capture the Russian positions at the western edges of the forest and thus could not break into the open. At long last units detached from the main body of the *Kampfgruppe* rescued them from these unpleasant situations by attacking the enemy positions from the rear.

The attached infantry battalion, operating under the command of a young captain, had orders to advance south from Tatarinka during the afternoon, so as to create a threat against the next major defensive focal point at Vyasovka. Before this could be accomplished, however, the battalion had to drive the remaining defenders from Potebrenka and the farms immediately south of Tatarinka. Although Colonel Zollenkopf had given the acting battalion commander strict instructions to wait for the arrival of a panzer company and a battery of 88mm flak (both being brought forward from Vasilevka) before undertaking this operation, he attacked without them because he assumed that his companies faced only weak enemy forces. While his troops were crossing a piece of elevated terrain just south of Tatarinka, furious machine-gun fire from several farm buildings caught them in the open and forced them to fall back behind the ridge. The attack could be continued only once the heavy antitank and flak guns arrived and it became possible to demolish the identified Soviet bunkers with direct fire. Due to the young captain's underestimation of enemy strength his battalion took unnecessary losses and the advance toward Potebrenka had to be delayed. Eventually, however, the battalion secured Potebrenka later in the afternoon. Advancing into the forest rim, the troops happened across a log bunker position that was still occupied by Russian troops. This bunker, aside from its obvious defensive mission, also served as heated quarters for the Red Army soldiers in the area. At nightfall the battalion assaulted and captured this position.

Since the bunker's location was not suitable for our defensive purposes, it was demolished. Our destruction of such shelters compelled the enemy to fight and sleep in the open at temperatures lower than −12°F, which considerably impaired his fighting capacity. Consequently, within a short time it would become feasible to have our assault units replaced at such points by improvised *Alarmeinheiten*, which were suitable for defensive purposes. This freed our combat elements for further offensive operations. An even more effective tactic resulted from the seizure of such bunkers, involving a ruse we had earlier learned from the Russians. Just before the enemy troops were expected to arrive at the bunkers for the evening, our patrols evacuated the positions, leaving them intact, but only after emplacing interconnected hand grenades and other demolition charges that the engineers had hidden in the twigs and straw covering the floor. These detonated at the slightest touch, not only destroying the bunkers but also inflicting Russian losses.

In spite of the Russian weaknesses detailed above, we still had no reason to assume that the Soviets would accept defeat with fatalistic resignation, particularly as they still had at their disposal large numbers of armed troops incited by fanatical commissars. As expected, Russian counterattacks began the very next day (17 February). Enemy reserves had been brought up overnight and were now committed, without artillery support, in attacks against our bunker positions in the forward villages that were covered by machine guns, artillery, and tanks. These efforts, which the Russians doggedly repeated during the following days, remained unsuccessful. They only increased their losses without recapturing even a single village. Our forces, on the other hand, even succeeded in improving their positions with local raids against isolated farmsteads.

Vasilevka: A Ski Brigade Defeated

Seen from a tactical point of view, Russian countermeasures thus far had been ineffective. Far more troublesome—in fact, dangerous—were the effects of a pincer attack launched by strong enemy forces from their adjacent defensive sectors against the unguarded communications route from Natchekino to Vasilevka. Along this route the forest extended up to the road on both sides, enabling the Russians to approach the road without being observed. By doing so they cut off Colonel Zollen's spearhead from its rear communications as it rushed westward. Although I had taken this contingency into consideration, it had not appeared very likely in view of what we knew about enemy supply problems and command arrangements. One reinforced Soviet rifle regiment was stationed in each of the two adjacent sectors. These combat groups, I estimated, would not be able to participate in such a pincer attack in large numbers without risking the danger of being smashed. Moreover, these two regiments belonged to different corps headquarters. I knew from experience that in such cases it would be necessary for the army headquarters to which both corps were subordinated to issue positive orders for such an attack and then to coordinate the operation. In addition, the southern rifle regiment would have had to face a long and difficult march, which for ten kilometers would lead through a pathless forest region covered by deep snow. Our security detachments had established a blocking position on the only beaten track through the forest. Therefore the only realistic option that appeared to be left to the Russians was a drive from the north that could be effective only if reinforced by several additional rifle battalions out of the Kholminka sector. In view of the overall situation now prevailing at Rzhev, this seemed doubtful. Should this contingency nonetheless arise, I had stationed our tactical reserve in the Natchekino-Yablonzevo area to deal with it. This reserve, commanded by Lieutenant Colonel Unrein, consisted of the aforementioned motorcycle-ski company, an engineer-ski company from Engineer Training Battalion 2, several assault guns from Assault Gun Battalion 189, and eight armored reconnaissance cars. Fire plans for artillery support from divisional assets had already been created, and liaison arrangements were made to assure coordination between Lieutenant Colonel Unrein's reserve and the defensive sector "Vasilevka" to which the three light howitzer batteries of I/Panzer Artillery Regiment 76 had been moved.

The night of 17–18 February was bright with stars. Calm prevailed in all sectors. For security reasons no movement of vehicles was allowed after dark on the road to Vasilevka, though the route was guarded at irregular intervals by strong patrols. Nevertheless, one Russian ski unit managed to cross the road in small groups between these intervals, then moved south and cut the telephone cable running to the front. The sounds they made were drowned out by the rustling of the trees.

One hour before dawn a German parka-clad infantry-engineer unit equipped with skis advanced down a forest path en route to the village south of Vasilevka, where it had orders to assist in constructing defensive fortifications. Some elements of the Russian ski unit by chance arrived at that spot at the same time. Clad and equipped exactly like the German engineer platoon, the Russians unwittingly joined the staggered march column. Neither the Germans nor the Russians, both of whom had their fur-lined collars turned up while they trudged along without speaking, recognized each other. Not until the combined group reached the fringe of the forest several hundred meters ahead of the village did the Russians come to a halt in order to prepare their attack. The Germans, disturbed by what appeared to them to be an incomprehensible stop, started a dispute that quickly revealed the error committed by both sides. Following a brief hand-to-hand struggle, during which the respective opponents could be recognized only when they spoke, the Russians dispersed and vanished into the forest. Our engineer platoon, which had remained on the road, let off several bursts of submachine fire after them, which immediately aroused the attention of all local security detachments. Complete silence, however, soon reigned again, causing the security elements to think that what had occurred was only a small raid, and they therefore attached no significance to the incident. Only one company, which had settled down in the village located directly opposite the point of the brief firefight, was sufficiently alerted to occupy its defensive positions. Soon thereafter the first engineer troops arrived, all out of breath, and related the strange encounter with the Russian ski unit. Momentarily the entire engineer platoon appeared and reinforced the company in its defenses. Sounds of a brief skirmish coming from one of our forest outposts indicated that the Russian ski unit had passed that way as well.

Just before dawn Russian troops suddenly appeared in front of the northeastern section of Vasilevka. The machine-gun sentries instantly opened a vehement fire, and the alarm spread rapidly to the entire eastern sector as well as the village of Kishenka to the north. Our troops had not as yet had the chance to occupy all the ice bunkers when the leading enemy soldiers jumped into a snow ditch connecting two bunkers. Colonel Zollenkopf was just arriving with an assault detachment, which he led into fierce if brief hand-to-hand fighting that routed the invaders. The Russians also launched an attack from the south, where they encountered I/Panzer Artillery Regiment 76, which direct-fired all the guns in three batteries at a ski battalion advancing in waves. This attack immediately ground to a standstill, and the Russians began floundering about in the snow, trying to take off the skis that hampered their ability to fight. Dawn was already beginning to break, which resulted in a visibility of 300–500 meters and made it possible to train machine-gun fire on the Russians. The attack broke down completely, after suffering heavy losses. However, at practically the same moment, other enemy ski units made a speedy drive against the northern sector, where, heedless of the fire pouring down on them, they succeeded in penetrating at several points. Two reserve assault detachments were still engaged in retaking some of these positions when one German sergeant and his platoon rushed forth from Kishenka, where yet another Russian attack had just been repelled. This veteran NCO had recognized the danger threatening the northern sector and, acting on his own initiative, led his platoon to attack the Russian ski unit in the rear. As this action forced the Soviets to retreat, the first critical phase of the enemy surprise attack had been mastered.

While these actions occurred, the noise of heavy battle could also be heard in the south, where a Russian ski company launched an unsuccessful attack on a small village located on a hill and defended only by a weak German detachment. This turned out to be the ski unit that had become intermingled with our engineer platoon during the night. Because of that incident the Russians had been unable to reach their assembly area for their scheduled attack until daylight.

Another day had now dawned. The snow-covered slope that rose from Vasilevka toward the forest sparkled across its entire 1,000-meter width in the first rays of the rising sun. The edge of the "Africa forest"—so called because of its unique shape—began to be visible, looking as if strewn with diamonds and dipped in gold. Suddenly, four new Russian ski battalions emerged from the southern tip of Africa forest (called "the Cape") and set out over the snow toward Vasilevka. These troops had been charged with achieving with a daytime attack the objective that the night raid had failed to deliver: the capture of Vasilevka and the blocking of our supply route. It was obviously intended that they should carry along in their advance the blood-ied Russian battalions already pinned down in front of the village.

Several hundred skiers presented a spectacle that our troops watched at first as though it were a race meeting. Only as the echeloned lines continued to close (and the leaders had already reached the road) did the German de-fenders seem to realize that they had to prevent the "finish" of these Russian ski troops. Concentrated fire from all weapons hurled the enemy skiers into the snow even before they managed to reach the lines of their comrades. Hundreds of scarcely visible dots denoted the area where the valiant skiers had disappeared with lightning speed as their run ended. Although they gamely attempted to continue on foot, the deep snow made this impossible. The sight of any man-size target was sufficient to attract instantaneous ma-chine-gun fire, which meant certain death.

Ultimately, this great winter sports show had to be concluded in a most unfair manner. Lieutenant Colonel Unrein's motorcycle riflemen and engi-neers arrived from Natchekino on their own skis, accompanied by several StG III assault guns and armored reconnaissance cars, to attack the enemy in the rear. Although the Russians had attempted to protect themselves from such attacks by mining the road (and did in fact succeed in driving back the lead German vehicle), our engineers immediately made their appearance and cleared the road. The assault guns attacked the Soviet flank, driving the enemy back in conjunction with our ski units. In order to escape encir-clement and complete annihilation, the Russian ski brigade found itself forced to withdraw by crawling through the snow under fire from several di-rections, leaving their skis behind. It took the last surviving Russians nearly three hours before they managed to reach the edge of the Africa forest, upon which twenty-four guns were firing and into which they disappeared. For a long while afterward we observed (but did not hinder) Red Army medical troops on skis as the tried to remove numerous severely wounded soldiers. The ski attack had been decisively defeated.

Our troops counted over 350 dead Russian soldiers in the field of snow and captured over 200 prisoners. This amounted to nearly half the original strength of the committed Russian ski forces. Among the dead was the ski brigade's commander, a Soviet general staff officer attached to the head-quarters of the Thirty-ninth Army who had been in charge of training the ski battalions. He had personally led this elite unit, which constituted the army's last available reserve, into battle. During its difficult withdrawal the ex-hausted brigade had also been compelled to leave behind all heavy weapons and any equipment that interfered with crawling. The most valuable capture, however, turned out to be the large map found on the body of the Russian brigade commander. This map detailed the situation of the Russian Thirty-ninth Army up through 17 February, and we immediately put it to good use. As a primary source of intelligence, it considerably facilitated the preparation of subsequent operations.

Despite a fourfold numerical superiority over the single German infantry battalion defending Vasilevka, the Russian ski brigade had been unable to recapture the village. This failure could be primarily explained by the fact that the Russian forces did not attack simultaneously and lacked the support of heavy weapons. During all these battles around Vasilevka on 18 February it was characteristic of the enemy's artillery supply situation that not a single shot was fired by the Russian artillery, even though eight kilometers north of Vasilevka at Bacharevo there were several batteries, including heavy guns. Our defenders, on the other hand, were supported in Vasilevka by an artillery battalion with twelve howitzers, several 88mm flak guns, and a platoon of tanks. In addition, I had earmarked the tactical reserve at Natchekino (which included assault guns and armored reconnaissance cars) for a counterattack in case we should be driven out of the village. Consequently, even if the Russian ski brigade had been committed properly it would most likely have been just as decisively defeated by the preponderance of heavy weapons available to Colonel Zollen.

This conclusion proves the truth of the principle that ski units, without the support of heavy weapons that they are usually unable to take along, cannot prevail against an enemy who, even though numerically far inferior, has heavy weapons at his disposal. The best employment for such troops, therefore, lies in making surprise attacks at night, when the defender will not be able to employ his heavy weapons and tanks with complete effectiveness.

I do not, however, wish to omit special mention of the initiative demonstrated by the NCO rushing from Kishenka to the rescue of his battalion. This is a prime example of the importance of thorough training and preparation before a campaign. At every opportunity, as far back as during the peacetime training of our officers and enlisted men, emphasis was placed on the fact that difficult situations in particular can only be mastered by practicing determination and initiative. To do nothing in situations of this kind was denounced as "shameful" even in training manuals. Making an error in the choice of means was excusable, but never the failure to take action. Every soldier knew that he would be held accountable for his conduct to his superior, who would recognize initiative and condemn inaction. Consequently special importance was attached to training our troops to become self-reliant commanders and determined individual fighters. As a result, as proven again in the battle for Vasilevka, our soldiers were superior to the Russians, who fought en masse, and this was often the reason for victories won against apparently prohibitive odds.

On the other hand, initiative should not be equated with rashness, as the case of the young battalion commander south of Tatarinka demonstrates. He suffered defeat because he underestimated the enemy's strength and attacked without waiting for the arrival of the heavy weapons assigned to him. Worse still, in his overzealousness, he acted against an explicit order and had to take the consequences.

The fact that the Russians could not support their attacks with artillery is reflective of the result of the earlier struggle for supply routes. In spite of all Soviet efforts, we held onto our lines of communications and thus were well supplied, while the Russians suffered. The more troops that the enemy moved into this region (which lacked the necessities of life and was accessible only along one single sled track), the worse their supply difficulties became. Lieutenant General Ivan Maslennikov, commanding the Thirty-ninth Army, found himself caught in the dilemma of having to be sufficiently strong to resist our forces (which, although considerably weaker, were very well supplied) and the supply shortage this created. He attempted to offset this handicap by disrupting our supply lines, but we consistently thwarted this tactic.

Vyasovka: A Combined Arms Attack as a Training Medium

In order to avoid jeopardizing the success attained on 18 February at Vasilevka, and to safeguard all of the supply routes to Rzhev, it now became necessary for us to gain possession of the forest region adjacent in the south, as well as the enemy-occupied strongpoints in the villages grouped around Vyasovka. We knew that we had in large measure succeeded in driving back a superior Russian force in Tatarinka and Vasilevka because the Thirty-ninth Army had to struggle with great supply difficulties. Now I intended to utilize the paralyzing effect of the enemy's ammunition shortage to launch a pincer attack for the specific purpose of annihilating the reinforced rifle regiment at Vyasovka, which was established in typical winter positions. This operation entailed more danger than our attack toward Tatarinka because in order to make a pincer attack (which was the only means of achieving the desired goal) it would be necessary to divide *Kampfgruppe* Zollenkopf (which in reality consisted of only three reinforced battalions) into separate assault groups. Only the following factors enabled me to consider such a hazardous operation: (1) It was impossible for Russian artillery and other heavy

weapons to play any major role in the battle; (2) I was assured the cooperation of strong Luftwaffe forces; (3) our assault battalions were embued with
good fighting spirit and their ranks filled with well-trained soldiers under excellent commanders; and (4) though numerically inferior our attack forces
had been provided with excellent equipment and abundant supplies.

The elevated terrain north of these villages offered good observation
points from which it was possible to view the planned attack like an exercise
on a drill ground. Moreover, the course of the action promised to be interesting and instructive. For this reason I utilized this operation as a "training
medium demonstrating a combined arms attack," which, by General
Model's order, I was to organize and conduct as I saw fit for the instruction
of "officers who had had no combat experience in the east." We contemplated demonstrating to these officers of various ranks, who had been transferred to Russia from other theaters of war or the Zone of the Interior, the
commitment and coordination of combined arms in offensive action against
a network of Russian bunker positions. This strange assignment was super-
ficially reminiscent of peacetime maneuvers but in reality bore not the least
resemblance to such exercises, for it required us to accomplish a mission both
difficult and important: defeating a thoroughly entrenched enemy while
withstanding the effects of a severe winter.

Initially it was necessary to procure battle-tested, fresh troops as well as
all weapons and command facilities that would assure the success of this unusual operation. Due to the reverses suffered before Moscow the entire eastern front was in a critical situation, and the crisis was most acute along the
overextended front of Army Group Center. The 6th Panzer Division had at
its disposal for offensive operations only the same battalions and batteries
that had been committed to the drive on Tatarinka. As before this included
the three consolidated battalions, as well as the few assault guns, tanks, flak
guns, and signal facilities obtained from currently inactive front sectors. All
of our combat units were on foot; some had skis. Supply deliveries were handled by local *panje* sleds driven by 800 Russian volunteer auxiliaries under
our control and supervision (most German supply troops had already been
pressed into ground combat roles with the *Alarmeinheiten*). In view of the
fact that, other than increased support from the Luftwaffe, no additional
forces would be available for the new operation. I decided that it was necessary for the improvised *Alarmeinheiten* to relieve the entire *Kampfgruppe*
Zollenkopf on the very afternoon that the Russians launched their ski attack.
Colonel Zollen's troops immediately shifted to a rest area in the rear. This
maneuver constituted a calculated risk that I accepted because all the Russian counterattacks had so far been decisively repelled. In addition, all artillery, antitank, and flak forces remained temporarily in their old positions

at Vasilevka, and in case of emergency the *Kampfgruppe* could be quickly recalled.

During the rest period we issued the soldiers very wholesome and abundant food, as well as additional butter and 10,000 rations of chocolate and fat. During their ample leisure time, they had the chance to take care of their mail and catch up on newspapers and books. They frequently received visits from their superiors, who looked after the welfare of each individual and concerned themselves with the troubles and complaints of their soldiers. During free and unconstrained conversation, special events and experiences were discussed and complaints and requests taken up. One particularly solemn event was the presentation of decorations, which I always did in person. All officers also considered it their personal duty of honor to visit their wounded troops on days of rest and to care for their welfare.

During this rest period, *Kampfgruppe* Zollenkopf received returning convalescents as replacements for the casualties suffered during the previous operation, along with ample ammunition, some panzers, and numerous signal devices that had been requested to assure the success of our next attack. Improved means of signal communication were essential to control the large area over which comparatively weak forces had to operate and included many kilometers of telephone cable, numerous telephone and radio sets, and the flash-and-sound-ranging equipment needed by the artillery observation platoon.

I decided that the task of conquering the system of Soviet strongpoints extending from Vyasovka to Krisvakovo would require a pincer attack to be launched from the north and east. For this purpose I instructed *Gruppe* North (consisting of the consolidated battalion of Motorized Infantry Regiment 114, six assault guns, one flak battery, and one antitank battery, under the command of Lieutenant Colonel Unrein) to assemble for the attack in the village south of Vasilevka. I placed *Gruppe* East (consisting of the consolidated battalion of Motorized Infantry Regiment 4, the infantry battalion formed by II/Panzer Artillery Regiment 76, one engineer company from Engineer Training Battalion 2, twelve tanks, two flak batteries, and two antitank batteries, under the command of Colonel Zollen) in assembly positions along a line extending from Kosmino to Chochlovka.

For its advance, Lieutenant Colonel Unrein's *Gruppe* North had at its disposal one sled track made by the Russians and one beaten track, while Colonel Zollen's *Gruppe* East was able to use two roads that, as they passed into no-man's land, were completely covered with snow. One ski company, which had been moved between the two assault elements, was to advance from Alexandrovka to Murino using a single snow-covered forest path.

Our artillery remained in its original positions. My instructions called for the I (Light) Battalion at Vasilevka to support *Gruppe* North with three light 105mm howitzer batteries (twelve guns). *Gruppe* East was to be supported by III (Heavy) Battalion at Sereda with two 150mm howitzer batteries (eight guns with an effective range of eighteen kilometers) and one 10mm flat-trajectory battery (four guns with and effective range of twenty-five kilometers). The assault would take place within range of both battalions, and with our signal communications Colonel Grundherr could quickly place the concentrated fire of both battalions in front of either assault element as the situation demanded. To facilitate fire control operations, one liaison officer of the heavy battalion was attached to the light battalion, and vice versa.

In order to ensure uniformity of cooperation between heavy weapons and the attacking infantry, which entailed significant technical difficulties, I ordered all artillery command posts to be established close to those of the infantry commanders. Consequently, at all times every tactical commander would have the commander of his supporting artillery unit at his side. The same principle of local coordination, down through company and platoon level, was also applied to all other heavy supporting weapons (assault guns, tanks, flak, and antitank guns). Often, at the platoon level, a single forward observer or some other direct communication link sufficed.

At the division command post I maintained the followed elements in close proximity:

One special-missions staff officer and several messengers equipped with skis;

One division signals officer who was in charge of telephone and radio equipment and the personnel necessary to operate it;

The commander of Panzer Artillery Regiment 76 (Colonel Grundherr) with his immediate staff, as well as the commander of our artillery observation battalion;

One Luftwaffe liaison officer, who had at his disposal the proper radios to maintain contact with our supporting aircraft units.

Each of the two *Gruppen* also functioned with the aid of a similar but smaller operations staff, which included the respective battalion commander of the supporting artillery. Also at the side of Colonels Unrein and Zollen, or at least close at hand, were the commanders or communication links of their supporting heavy weapons. These heavy weapons commanders also had direct contact with the infantry company commanders and—if the tactical situation so required—assigned messengers directly to the commanders of infantry platoons. Each *Gruppe* also had a Luftwaffe liaison officer present at its command post.

My advanced command post was connected by telephone cable (trunk line), which functioned via Nikite (location of the division central switchboard), with Lieutenant Colonel Unrein at Vasilevka and Colonel Zollenkopf at Chochlovka, which also allowed me easy access to the artillery and heavy weapons commanders. At the two terminal points of the trunk line, as well as at Sereda, we established telephone switchboards for the *Gruppen*, to which their subordinate elements were linked, as well as to the motorcycle-ski company that constituted our tactical reserve. The terminal stations of these subordinate switchboards were located in the immediate vicinity of the front line and were prepared to follow the advance of their respective *Gruppe* in leapfrog fashion. The distance between the telephone stations nearest the front and the forward line of battle was usually about four kilometers, which was spanned by means of infantry or tank radios. We particularly depended on the tank radios whenever our panzers spearheaded the advance of our infantry assault detachments.

In the event of temporary disruption of the wire lines, radio transmitters were available at all times at the respective command posts of division, *Gruppen*, battalions, and the motorcycle company. Thus the tactical operations network in effect extended from me, as division commander, to the foremost attacking spearheads via this series of relay stations. The forward observers of the artillery fire control net—which necessarily functioned independently of the operations net, though it was organized along the same lines—extended as far as the infantry combat zone. Here internal communications were assured by the fact that the tactical commanders simultaneously commanded the artillery fire control. The aviation assets necessary for artillery target reconnaissance and fire direction were also at the disposal of the artillery, and as the fighting progressed our artillery observation platoon stationed at the southern edge of the forest was also employed.

It should also be mentioned that the heavy batteries, even prior to the initial attack, had been placing adjusted fire on all strongpoints in the villages located in the Kholminka-Vasilevka-Vyasovka area by means of a photomap and guidance from aerial reconnaissance flights. As a result, Colonel Grundherr's gunners had already registered the firing data for the most important targets. In view of the settled weather conditions, these factors never changed to any marked degree during the operation. In order to be on the safe side, however, during the attack he required everything to be checked out once more just prior to the advance of our spearheads.

During the decisive phase of the battle numerous artillery observers and the artillery observation platoon established themselves at the forest rims and on the roofs of buildings in captured villages, from which elevated posts they had a clear and direct line of sight to their targets, as far distant as three kilometers. The I (Light) Battalion, Panzer Artillery Regiment 76, had to fire in succession over distances from five to eight kilometers in exactly the direction of *Gruppe* North's attack. The frontage of this battalion and the direction of attack required a gun traverse of 25 degrees. The III (Heavy) Battalion, Panzer Artillery Regiment 76, on the other hand, had to fire in succession over distances from nine to eleven kilometers, partly slantwise to and partly almost parallel to *Gruppe* East's line of advance, which also required a gun traverse of about 25 degrees. The shell bursts of III Battalion in particular were clearly visible to our observers. For that reason, and in view of the fact that the lateral dispersion was smaller than the range dispersion, the heavy guns were able to support the infantry until shortly before it entered the target zone, without endangering our own troops in any way. Moreover, the lateral fire could be shifted quite rapidly because, in most cases, the firing data only had to be changed for lateral fire and not for range. Enfilading artillery fire has a much greater moral effect, particularly in operations with Austrian troops. The drawbacks of the longer wire lines—the installation of which requires more equipment and time and which, owing to the distances traversed, are more frequently subject to disruptions—were more than offset in this instance by the advantages gained by virtue of better visibility and flexibility of fire.

The concentrated fire from both artillery battalions first proved its effectiveness during the attacks on the collective farms (*Kolhkose*) and in the Vyasovka area. Colonel Grundherr directed this fire in person and did not require any greater than normal traverse, as described above. The fire was aimed primarily at the points where the roads entered the villages, at the most important strongpoints already identified through aerial photographs, and at the assembly areas the Luftwaffe had spotted. Any pockets of resistance that could not be conquered by the infantry (even after being subjected to air attacks, artillery fire, and supporting heavy weapons) were identified by the infantry commanders via signal rockets and hit again by the Luftwaffe. During the protracted struggle for Vyasovka, red signal flares indicated the spots where our troops were in any way exposed to danger from friendly fire. In spite of the rising clouds of smoke caused by numerous fires that soon engulfed the village, these signals remained plainly visible. Less hampered by that smoke, our pilots furnished brief orientation reports about the events taking place on either side.

The planning of this attack by no means implied a schematization of the assault procedure or excessive supervision of the front-line tactical commanders by their superiors. My sole purpose was to ensure perfect comprehension with regard to the mission, the contemplated course of action, and the coordination of all weapons. All that remained was to provide support to the *Alarmeinheiten* in case the Russians decided to launch a diversionary attack on any of the villages we had captured in the previous operation. I seriously doubted that this contingency would arise, because it appeared that the Russians had used up their last reserves during their counterthrusts at Vasilevka, and we could discern no indications of enemy attack preparations in the area. There was little possibility of a successful enemy attack against these positions in any case, because we had committed sufficiently large numbers of well-armed troops in improved positions and supported them with antitank and flak guns of all calibers. By all standards I expected these troops (even allowing for the improvised nature of their organizations) to be capable of repelling any attack not support by artillery and heavy infantry weapons, which we already knew that the Thirty-ninth Army's dire ammunition shortage would prevent it from utilizing.

Nevertheless, I took the necessary precautions to be prepared for this bare possibility, for if this contingency did arise it was apt to create a difficult situation for *Gruppe* North and jeopardize the entire operation. These precautionary measures included providing support through additional Luftwaffe units and the available artillery. While supporting the main attack, our batteries had to be prepared to shift fire instantaneously to defend the old positions. It was for this reason that we left intact the tactical communications network installed during the attack on Tatarinka and kept all of the old artillery observation posts manned. This increased requirement for trained artillerymen was met by taking men from the "artillery companies of foot" among our *Alarmeinheiten* in that sector, all of whom were from the same regiment and therefore accustomed to working together. To facilitate the rapid shifting of artillery fire by as much as 90 degrees, our batteries had to be echeloned in such a manner and the individual guns so grouped around the control gun (which remained in one position) that they had a free field of fire before them even after changing their direction of fire. To make this possible the snow had to be removed from the roads leading to the alternate firing positions, and whenever necessary the guns were moved on skis. This shifting to alternate firing emplacements was practiced, and the correct firing data predetermined before the start of the operation, including checkup to ensure the efficiency of the old signal lines and the field of vision from the observation posts.

As will be seen from the narrative of the actual course of action, the Russians did not attack these villages, which eliminated the need to shift artillery fire in the middle of a battle.

The support aviation and bomber wings of the VIII Fleiger Corps, whose assistance had been promised and which could be committed continuously from nearby airfields, constituted a critical asset in conducting this attack.

I personally clarified the plan of attack in all its essential points to the commanding officers and the commanders of all supporting weapons, taking the time to clarify any questions that arose. This briefing was followed by intense discussions between the *Gruppe* and battalion commanders and the chiefs of their attached heavy weapons units. I also attended these meetings, wherein the fine details of coordination were worked out. Such personal discussions were an absolute necessity prior to attacks launched according to an established plan, as they were the only guarantee that frictions and misunderstandings could be kept to a minimum.

My staff issued the written attack order a short while later. It served primarily as a reminder and historical document. Upon the conclusion of the aforementioned discussions, the men who were participating in the training course were separated from the others, apprised of the contemplated operation, and then attached to various units in accordance with their respective branches of service to become acquainted with the details of such preparatory measures.

The three days spent in preparation and recreation passed very quickly, and it was now [22 February] time to carry our plans into effect. The weather continued to be steady and beautiful, and the temperature had fallen a few degrees lower than −12°F, which meant that individual soldiers could move across the snow without skis. The sled tracks and the wider beaten paths had frozen solid and could even be used by tanks. All in all, the weather was ideal for the contemplated "training attack."

One obstacle remained to be eliminated: the deep snow that covered the roads on which the attack was to be launched, especially in *Gruppe* East's sector between the Russian and German outposts. The snow was deep enough to have considerably handicapped the movement of tanks and heavy weapons. It was therefore necessary during the night of 21–22 February to remove the snow from these roads and clear them beyond the outpost area. Since both sides engaged every night in snow removal from their respective roads, the Russians were familiar with these sounds and our actions did not rouse their suspicions. Besides, during moonlit nights that were bright with stars, skirmishes always took place between reconnaissance patrols, and on these occasions the forward security detachments on one side or the other sometimes found themselves pushed back as far as their respective main battle line. Consequently, the Russians attached no special significance to these incidents either.

On the roads leading from Kosmino and Chochlovka toward the enemy lines, small elements of our forces attacked the Russian security detachments as they had so frequently in the past and pushed them back as far as the most advanced bunker positions at Krisvakovo. Engineers followed closely behind, carrying out snow removal operations as close as possible to the Soviet lines. Farther back, we employed armed construction battalions to clear the snow on the approach roads. Now and then a Russian searchlight swept the outpost area but could not detect anything suspicious because the hill sloping toward the brook valley, where the construction battalions were working, could not be observed. The beam of light therefore passed over our work parties without disturbing their activities in any way. In the meantime, all assault units moved into their assembly areas, and the construction troops withdrew while it was still dark.

Both *Gruppen* now stood ready to strike and were waiting for the designated time, with the assault scheduled to be launched simultaneously on both fronts, which were separated by roughly sixteen kilometers. The attacking wings were to meet each other midcourse and join forces at Vyasovka. As far could be calculated, we expected this to happen around noon.

Suddenly, fire flashes blazed up with great intensity from the north, illuminating the waning night sky. A thunderlike rumbling followed, then the droning and roaring of the heavy and light shells—fired in unbroken succession from all guns—as they began battering the ice bunker positions on the eastern outskirts of Krisvakovo to pieces. After ten minutes of intense bombardment, the burst of fire gradually shifted toward the western half of the village. At that moment—0640—all assault columns started forward simultaneously. Shortly thereafter the silhouettes of German infantrymen penetrating into the village from three sides became visible in the glow of burning huts.

Perplexingly, we could also see the shapes of other men, moving in the opposite direction, soon followed by numerous others. This made us wonder whether or not there had been some sort of setback, but we did not remain in doubt for long. Green signal rockets began to appear at the western edge of the village, indicating that the assault battalion had captured Krisvakovo. Soon afterward we also received the initial telephone situation report, which informed us of the capture of eighty Red Army soldiers. Those prisoners, passing toward the rear, were the ones we had earlier observed moving in the wrong direction. By sunrise the remaining length of road up to Krisvakovo had been cleared of snow sufficiently for the tanks to push forward and take their place at the head of the assault column, with each tank followed immediately by an engineer assault detachment. These teams had the mission of penetrating Chmelevka, which was already being subjected to heavy artillery fire, and to clear the Russians out of any ice bunkers still intact with hand grenades and flamethrowers. As the engineers assaulted each bunker in turn, the tanks kept enemy troops in adjacent bunkers and machine-gun nests in check with suppressive fire.

From the forward division command post at the southern edge of the forest, we watched the skillfully coordinated action of the tank-engineer assault teams. Elements of our ski company had snatched the location from the enemy only a short time earlier. The officers "participating in the course" and acting as spectators had also arrived; security was provided by the ski unit and some antitank guns. After a brief disturbance caused by a Russian light tank that burst forth from the forest (but was quickly put out of action by an antitank gun), we continued the "course of instruction" through observation and training. The lesson proved very instructive inasmuch as the relatively short distance from the fighting made it possible, even without field glasses, to follow all particulars of our attack procedures and the Russian defensive measures. The observers also had an excellent opportunity to listen in as reports from the combat units filtered in, and we dispatched additional orders whenever necessary.

The tactics employed by the joint assault detachments and tank-engineer teams proved very successful because smoke blinded and heavy artillery fire pinned down the Russian antitank batteries to the point that they were unable to function. Our tanks recognized them and shot them down when they attempted to change position. On the other hand, the Russian troops in the intact ice bunkers offered desperate resistance and significantly hampered the advance of our infantry. Fortunately, other German infantry troops, who had by then forced their way through nearby gaps, became aware of this problem. Thus some of these elements turned and attacked the tenacious Russian defenders from the rear and quickly mopped them up. In this fashion the southern half of Chmelevka fell to our assault battalion. At the northern outskirts of the village, the Russians still vehemently resisted the consolidated battalion of Motorized Infantry Regiment 4, whose arrival had been delayed by snowdrifts. Only by committing our infantry reserve forces, supported by tanks, to an attack from the southern part of the village was it possible to break this resistance and complete the seizure of Chmelevka.

The two assault battalions, advancing in wedge formation on both sides of the road, now continued their attack, with the consolidated battalion of Motorized Infantry Regiment 4 to the north and that of Panzer Artillery Regiment 76 to the south. Our panzer spearheads, advancing by bounds, soon reached a point halfway to Vyasovka, at which point enemy antitank fire hit their flank. This fire came from fortified positions that the Russians had established in depressions and hollows on a rise in the ground following the southern side of the road. These firing positions had been expertly camouflaged and offered a perfect view of the terrain gradually sloping back toward the forest. The tanks had to pull back from their exposed position to some nearby farmsteads. The infantry companies advancing in loose formation in the wake of our tanks on the north side of the road had been hit to this point only by intermittent artillery fire, which was insufficient to pin them down. Now, however, Russian heavy mortars and machine guns in Vyasovka took them under fire and compelled them to halt their brisk drive and resort to pushing forward small groups in short jumps. The consolidated infantry battalion of Panzer Artillery Regiment 76 to the south also found itself pinned down by the fire coming from the bunkers and ditches located in a rise in the ground and occupied by a large number of Soviet troops.

Only when the Luftwaffe's ground-attack aircraft appeared and forced the Russian antitank crews to take cover could the tank spearheads move up to the troublesome targets and put them out of action. As for the ice bunker positions that had succeeded in halting our infantry advance, they had been located in positions open to full view from my division command post. We therefore employed the 88mm flak battery that had been emplaced as local security for my headquarters to take these positions under direct fire; it quickly silenced several of the weapons that were harassing our troops. The entire Russian position east of Vyasovka, however, became untenable only when hit by the destructive enfilading fire of all batteries from both artillery battalions. Those Red Army soldiers in the demolished ice bunkers suffered the heaviest losses and fled back to the west. But as we observed through field glasses from the division command post, commissars with their pistols in hand instantaneously confronted these shaken troops and drove them back to the fight. At that critical moment, several panzers veered in that direction and covered the wavering Russian line (now completely in the open) with fire from their main guns and machine guns. The effect was devastating. Under the cover of this fire, the consolidated infantry battalion of Panzer Artillery Regiment 76 renewed its assault and seized the entire fortified intermediate terrain in front of Vyasovka, which by then the consolidated battalion of Motorized Infantry Regiment 4 had also penetrated north of the road.

Gruppe North started its advance at the same time as *Gruppe* East, but without benefit of a preliminary artillery bombardment. In two columns, each spearheaded by assault guns and assault detachments, Lieutenant Colonel Unrein's troops moved south. At first the Russians, as we had expected, offered only feeble resistance. At the approach of our assault guns the enemy security detachments immediately withdrew to the forests on both sides of the road in order to harass the German infantry companies that followed with flanking fire. These Russians were taken greatly by surprise, however, when our ski units that had been detached along the forest rims attacked and scattered them. Thus for the first four kilometers the advance continued without difficulty; only when our leading elements had reached the *Kolhkose* and the edge of the woods to the east thereof did they come across well-fortified ice bunker positions, which were supplied with numerous heavy weapons.

Lieutenant Colonel Unrein realized that it was inadvisable to assault these positions head-on. Consequently, he halted the *Gruppe's* advance and requested artillery and air support for a deliberate attack on the *Kolhkose*. Close-support aircraft soon appeared in waves, their fire pinning the Russians down in their bunkers even as the available light howitzer batteries opened fire. Meanwhile, the consolidated battalion of Motorized Infantry Regiment 114 regrouped for its attack. At the decisive moment the artillery bombardment was increased by the addition of the heavy batteries as well, while the 88mm flak battery attached to the *Gruppe* began to target previously identified bunkers with direct fire and to demolish them one by one. Bomber squadrons, which had been held in readiness, subject to call, now arrived exactly on time for their salvo bombing attack on the *Kolhkose* positions to be coordinated with the fire of our artillery and other heavy weapons. This final increase in the intensity of our bombardment was the signal for starting the assault on the fortified strongpoint.

The last bombs and heavy shells had scarcely detonated when the assault guns and forward assault detachments breached the bunker position. Infantrymen quickly followed, mopping up the Russians bunker by bunker. Nothing but a handful of completely exhausted soldiers remained of the two Russian rifle companies charged with holding their positions at all costs in order to deny us entry into Vyasovka. From the division command post we could not see this attack but listened to the tremendous din of battle amid the roaring bomb explosions. Lieutenant Colonel Unrein's staff kept us fully informed of events as they progressed.

Rolling across the ruins, which were all that remained of the *Kolhkose*, our assault guns immediately continued pushing south toward Pribitki. Again the Luftwaffe's close-support aircraft (which the Russians had come to dread) made their appearance. Circling and roaring over the fortified group of farms, they once again pinned down the Soviet defenders just as they also came under the fire of the assault guns. Bypassed on both sides and under concentric attack, this enemy strongpoint—garrisoned by a single rife company—also succumbed to the superior strength of our aircraft and heavy weapons.

Meanwhile, the ski company that had been placed between the two *Gruppen* as a connecting force by then had finally succeeded in fighting its way out of the forest. This company had been repeatedly held up inside the forest since it could not be assisted by heavy weapons. An enemy strongpoint located in a clearing fell only after a frontal assault and bitter close-quarters fighting. This particular battle took place just two kilometers from my command post, and both local security detachments and the spectator/students were alerted for possible action. Fortunately, the victory of the ski company made their commitment unnecessary.

After detouring around the fortified strongpoint in Murino, the ski company attacked the rear of the previously mentioned forest bunker position, in front of which one of Lieutenant Colonel Unrein's infantry companies remained tied down. Through the coordinated action of both units, support by heavy weapons, this tenaciously defended position also fell to an assault. Thus all the outlying strongpoints had been captured or destroyed, with the exception of the one at Murino that had been isolated. For the next step we had to encircle Vyasovka, which now resembled an octopus deprived of its tentacles, and conquer the focal point of the defense by an all-out concentric attack.

All forces of both *Gruppen* and their supporting units had already begun their concentric advance on Vyasovka when suddenly the Luftwaffe reported fresh Red Army troops approaching from the south. The pilots estimated their strength at one rifle regiment consisting of two or three battalions and predicted that the regiment would reach the Vyasovka area within two hours. There they would obviously attempt to eliminate the danger of the town being encircled, either by reinforcing the sorely pressed garrison or by attacking one of the two *Gruppen*.

This abrupt change in the battle situation made it necessary for me to reach a new decision. I did so without delay and put the revised plan into effect by issuing the orders through my staff and assistants. The spectators, who were now situated in an adjacent building, were then apprised of this interesting turn of events. Without telling them what I had decided, I asked each member of the training course to state what his choice would have been had he been in command. Each officer was also expected to write down in keywords the orders necessary for the execution of his preferred plan, which meant that they were all required to solve a real problem in tactics while under fire. I told them, *"Hic Rhodus hic salta!"* (This referred to an incident in one of *Aesop's Fables* dealing with a man boasting about his exploits on the Island of Rhodes, and in the course of the story he is told: *"Hic Rhodus hic salta!"*—"Here's Rhodes, go ahead and jump" [literally translated], meaning, "Show me what you can do!")

The officers in training obviously had difficulties arriving at the proper decision for such an unusual situation. They were not as yet sufficiently familiar with the enemy's mentality, the peculiarities of Russia as a theater of war, and the effects of such an exceptional situation. Consequently their judgment was based on their theoretical knowledge or their experiences gained in other theaters of war, and they thus proposed the following three alternatives for solving the problem:

1. To annihilate these fresh Russian forces by means of the Luftwaffe and to continue the attack;
2. To contain the Russians at Vyasovka with part of our forces and to attack the new Russian regiment with the bulk of our strength;
3. To withdraw our forces to the line extending from the farm buildings across the edge of the forest to Chmelevka and there assume defensive positions.

The officers were thunderstruck when I later informed them of the decision I had made and of the only brief orders I had issued. These orders were worded as follows: "The attack will be halted; the enemy regiment will be allowed to continue its march and is to be annihilated at the same time as the Russian forces occupying Vyasovka." These orders had been immediately transmitted to all units as well to the Luftwaffe, with the notification that the schedule for the execution of the all-out assault had been postponed from noon to 1500.

In keeping with this revised plans, the initial order—"Stop the attack!"—went out by telephone to the two *Gruppen* commanders and the Luftwaffe, while my operations officer briefed the artillery commander and the liaison officers about the situation and objective. A few minutes later I spoke personally with both Colonel Zollenkopf and Lieutenant Colonel Unrein on the telephone, briefed them, and gave the following order:

The line reached so far will be held, and the enemy troops advancing toward Vyasovka from the south will not be hindered in any way. You will strike only if they attack your positions or attempt to bypass them. If, as I expect, they march into Vyasovka, you will close the gap behind them at the sector boundary between the two *Gruppen* and prevent any enemy troops from breaking out of the encirclement. I contemplate the annihilation of the new Russian troops along with the forces currently occupying Vyasovka by means of the original planned concentric attack. The artillery and the Luftwaffe have received similar instructions. The attack will probably start at 1500; wait for specific instructions to that effect.

Under constant observation by the Luftwaffe, the Russian rifle regiment continued to march toward Vyasovka and rejoiced that it had managed to arrive there in time to reinforce the town's battered defenders. We utilized the three-hour delay in the attack schedule to study a series of excellent aerial photographs that had just been received, checking and supplementing them with ground reconnaissance reports. These consolidated findings were then evaluated with reference to the detailed plan of attack.

Our final revised plan outlined the sector boundary between the two *Gruppen*. This boundary followed a north-south direction along a road in the western part of Vyasovka, with the road being explicitly marked on the basis of aerial photographs. The new plan also envisioned the use of the motorcycle company in conjunction with *Gruppe* North to prevent any Russians from escaping into the large forest north of Vyasovka. I held another conference with Colonel Zollenkopf and Lieutenant Colonel Unrein to discuss these details while my operations officer transmitted the necessary orders to the supporting units.

No sooner had the last Russian companies arrived at Vyasovka when the Luftwaffe appeared on the scene in majestic flight and attacked the enemy units that had not yet been committed but were still milling in groups around the buildings. At the same moment all artillery, tanks, assault guns, antitank guns, flak, and infantry heavy weapons commenced a bombardment of the soviet strongpoints and trenches that were situated to most seriously hamper our penetration into the town. The furies of war were raging as if all hell had broken loose, and Vyasovka was soon enveloped by smoke and flames. Our assault columns, advancing from all sides, drew ever closer until the two *Gruppen* joined forces and completed the encirclement.

There was now no escape left for the Russians. Tanks had already demolished or engineers captured the foremost bunkers, and the engineers had started blowing up the antitank obstacles in the main road, as well as clearing the minefields. The way into the town lay open. Assault detachments and tanks in ever-increasing numbers vanished from our sight into the thick mass of smoke pouring out of the burning buildings. Colonel Grundherr shifted his concentrated artillery (as did the Luftwaffe bombers) to target the fortifications in the center of Vyasovka, then slowly walked their fire to the north. From the division command post we could trace their path closely through the violent explosions and huge clumps of earth that were thrown high into the air.

Meanwhile the crackling and rattling of machine-gun and submachine-gun fire became more and more pronounced. Salvoes of hand-grenade explosions repeatedly rent the air, indicating that additional Russian strongpoints had been taken by assault. Gradually the noise of battle shifted north in the wake of the aerial and artillery bombardments, until it ceased as night began to fall. Fighting flared up only once more, far off in the north, when the strongpoint at Murino (which had become the enemy's final refuge) was attacked and captured. Several hundred prisoners were captured and marched off to the rear. At that point one or two battered Russian companies still succeeded in escaping into the woods under cover of darkness; these were the only forces who managed to escape what the prisoners referred to as "the holocaust."

The battle of Vyasovka had cost the Soviet Thirty-ninth Army two regiments, whose destruction had been witnessed by numerous observers. Never before had these spectators attended a class in tactics that was quite so convincing. This was a lesson taken from life and initiated those officers in the realities of winter combat in Russia, for which the pincer attack at Vyasovka may be regarded as a classic example.

The Snail Offensive

Despite the successful outcome of the operations at Tatarinka and Vyasovka, the Russians still maintained a Guards rifle corps of three rifle divisions far too close to the critical Vyazma-Sychevka-Rzhev lines of communication for the safety of Ninth Army. General Model and I both believed that it would be necessary to drive the Soviets back at least another ten to fifteen kilometers on a forty-kilometer front to place the supply lines of Ninth Army beyond their reach. This meant that a line favorable for defense had to be reached that followed the edge of the vast wooded marshes and that all villages and towns in the fertile region immediately to our east had to be taken from the enemy. As a secondary but important objective we intended to deprive the Soviets of valuable shelter and sources of supply while making these villages available to our own troops. This would be a particularly hard blow at General Maslennikov's Thirty-ninth Army since there were only a few small, poor villages within the swampy forests, and the supply difficulties of his divisions were increasing daily. Now that General Model had launched a successful panzer attack at Bely, the Thirty-ninth Army was practically surrounded except for a narrow, pathless strip across the front.

Ninth Army, however, could not spare additional combat units for such an offensive, leaving me with only the three reinforced battalions from 6th Panzer Division and the improvised *Alarmeinheiten* that had been organized for the defense of the *Rollbahn*, airfields, and railway. Driving back an estimated twenty-seven Russian rifle battalions with these forces, and inflicting severe enough losses that the *Alarmeinheiten* would be able to hold the new line thus achieved without risk, would again require thoughtful improvisation.

Immediately after the victory at Vyasovka, I called the sector commanders of the defensive line to a meeting, informed them of the necessity of an
offensive, and began indoctrinating them in the combat methods that would
be used. Although my final objective was to roll back the enemy at least fifteen kilometers, I did not then reveal this to the assembled officers. The mere
thought of starting an offensive with their motley units caused the commanders of all the *Alarmeinheiten* to raise serious objections that can be
fully expressed only by a single word: "impossible." Only a patient, detailed
explanation of the tactics to be employed, for which I had coined the term
"snail offensive," gradually began to dispel the numerous objections that
were admittedly perfectly valid from a conventional military standpoint.

First of all, I pointed out to the commanders that time was not an important factor in this offensive. The speed of a snail would be sufficient. In selecting the place of attack they would proceed like a snail that would move
only to a place where it could find a worthwhile objective without incurring
any danger. The method of advance would therefore resemble that of a snail
slowly groping its way and immediately retracting its feelers or changing its
direction whenever faced by an obstacle. Any setback must be avoided, because it would discourage our improvised combat troops and tie them up for
a long time, just as a snail withdraws into its shell in a dangerous situation
and does not dare to continue on its way for quite a while. Nor were the commanders to forget the shell of the snail, which affords safety and shelter in
case of danger. Despite all precautions, however, *Alarmeinheiten* commanders had to keep in mind the rewarding objective at all times, exactly as a snail
would do in the same situation.

This comparison served to illustrate the basic idea of the combat methods
to be employed in the snail offensive. Fortunately, many of the officers had
enjoyed the opportunity to watch the practical application of this doctrine
during the Vyasovka operation. This provided a framework for discussing the
initial operation, which from a morale standpoint would be of paramount
importance.

The success at Vyasovka had left a deep wedge in our new lines, a salient
that included three villages held by small Russian security detachments.
There I knew that an initial victory should be easy to obtain. As with our
previous operations, the attack would not start until everything had been so
well prepared that success could be expected with certainty. The enemy dispositions remained under our observation because we held high ground that
allowed us to dominate them with cross fire from two angles. The foremost
village was held by the strongest Russian element, the two farther to the rear
by smaller ones. A platoon of volunteers led by an experienced officer was to
sneak up at night on each of the small villages, effect a penetration from the

rear, make a surprise raid at dawn, and annihilate the enemy. Surprise was achieved, the two villages were captured, and the large one in front was cut off. We brought up machine guns and heavy infantry weapons to stop the enemy's attempt to break out of the larger village during the next day. At dusk we reinforced our forces in each of the smaller villages and seized the entire Russian contingent from the large village as it attempted to break out under cover of darkness. As each village passed into our hands, engineers and construction troops immediately prepared them for defense.

A few kilometers to the south another small Russian strongpoint complex was taken by similar tactics. A very strong covering force with heavy weapons always remained in the old main battle line to prevent any potential reverses. The main battle line moved forward only after new defensive positions had been constructed in the frozen ground and the snow cleared from supply and communications routes. As long as the enemy showed any sign of counter-attacking, strong reserves stayed behind the danger points and no further offensive moves were initiated. Similar operations began in other sectors, adapted to local conditions and carried out at irregular intervals. The first week of the snail offensive resulted in the occupation of fourteen villages and the capture of numerous prisoners, while our own losses were negligible. Most important, however, was the confidence that the troops in the *Alarmeinheiten* gained in this combat method, regarding which the Russians themselves coined the expression "the mincing machine," which aptly defined our "attacks with limited objectives" that were conducted with all heavy weapons under firm control.

The first operations had been undertaken in close conjunction with Colonel Zollenkopf's reinforced battalions of the 6th Panzer Division, but gradually the *Alarmeinheiten* themselves became confident enough to undertake more complicated missions. However, it remained essential to attack in the most effective manner and to secure our objectives without becoming involved in a heavy engagement. Even though the Russians in this area were better trained and equipped than our improvised units, their supply of ammunition was limited and they were too weak to organize a continuous line of defense. Only outpost lines secured their individual strongpoints, and my subordinate commanders soon discovered that the best method of overcoming these obstacles was to capture the villages in which the outposts were located in order to isolate each heavily defended strongpoint until it was nearly encircled. Then the Red Army soldiers often abandoned the strongpoints voluntarily rather than risk the conflagration our heavy weapons we were capable of visiting on them.

Bogdanovo, a village situated in dominating terrain on our southern wing, was the linchpin of one of the most important Russian strongpoint systems near our line of communications. From there the Russians frequently launched raids farther south, penetrated to the *Rollbahn*, and stopped all traffic. In order to eliminate these inconvenient supply disruptions, OKH dispatched the *Fuehrer Begleit* [Escort] Battalion, a crack unit that normally served as Hitler's personal bodyguard, reinforced with heavy weapons and artillery as it was moved up to take this defensive anchor by assault. After only a short briefing and hasty preparations the battalion launched a frontal attack in the orthodox manner, forced the weaker village outpost detachments to withdraw, and then advanced almost to the edge of the main strongpoint. There the Russians, counterattacking from all sides and inflicting considerable German losses, pushed the battalion back and even encircled one company. This company was finally rescued after great difficulties, but due to the heavy losses incurred there General Model did not allow the attack to be repeated.

After this failure General Model shifted the boundaries to include Bogdanovo in the 6th Panzer Division and ordered me to capture it. Within a few days the snail offensive procedure scored another success by almost completely isolating the main Soviet strongpoint. When *Kampfgruppe* Zollenkopf attempted to close the ring, the Russian garrison, though continuously raked by heavy artillery fire, hastily evacuated the village in a costly daylight withdrawal. We immediately occupied the village and held it against all later counterattacks.

In one month the snail offensive achieved the capture of eighty villages and advanced the front from eight to thirteen kilometers. The principal success, however, was to put Maslennikov's Thirty-ninth Army on the defensive along the entire Vyazma-Sychevka front, making thrusts against the *Rollbahn*, railroad, and airfields out of the question. More and more battle-hardened soldiers and reconditioned weapons had meanwhile been made available and supplied to the front; the number of tanks and artillery pieces increased significantly. By early March the operations of all units, whether from the 6th Panzer Division or the *Alarmeinheiten*, were well coordinated, and the commanders had full confidence in the new combat tactics. Thorough preparations and careful implementation had prevented even the slightest failure.

I could now grant subordinate commanders much greater freedom in continuing the offensive. Division headquarters no longer interfered with details. Each sector was assigned a weekly phase-line that was to be reached under optimum conditions. This line was not to be crossed without my approval, because safety considerations outweighed those of speed. Whenever the *Alarmeinheiten* ran into particular difficulties, they called upon 6th Panzer Division elements under Colonels Zollenkopf or Unrein, which were supported by tanks, assault guns, heavy weapons, and the Luftwaffe. All Russian attempts failed to halt the slow but steady advance of the improvised front: Where the enemy collected reserves, we paused, and when they had been called away to another danger point, we attacked. Since the Thirty-ninth Army no longer possessed sufficient forces or ammunition to appear in strength in several places simultaneously, Maslennikov lost ground slowly but surely.

By mid-March the Russians had been pushed back into marshy forests and forced to relinquish more than 200 villages. To push farther would have been impossible, primarily because the commands on my flanks had not joined our offensive. Our units on the extreme ends of the new sector had to remain in their initial positions in order to prevent the Russians from opening gaps through which they could infiltrate into our rear.

Improvised Propaganda

Among the many wounded and dead Russians we collected on the battlefield in mid-February was Vera, an eighteen-year-old female sergeant. After a few hours' treatment for shock, she recovered from her horrible experience, which she compared to "the end of the world." Vera had been a medical auxiliary to the battalion holding a major strongpoint that had been completely annihilated except for herself, one officer, and fourteen enlisted men.

During her first days as a prisoner of war Vera was under severe emotional strain. Her interrogation confirmed intelligence on Soviet dispositions gathered from other prisoners. By her admission she was a member of the *Komsomol* [Communist Youth Organization]—in other words, a committed Communist. Before she was evacuated in a transport with other prisoners she innocently requested permission to return to her former regiment. Asked for the reason for this unusual request, she replied in a calm and serious tone, "I want to tell my comrades that it is hopeless to fight against such weapons and that the Germans will treat them well. They should come over to the German side." Asked whether she had any other reasons for returning, she admitted, "Yes, I would like to save the life of my friend who is still over there." To the question of whether this was not a subterfuge to escape from our clutches, she replied, "No, I have already stated that I shall return and bring along my friend."

Since Vera could not possibly give away any of our secrets, and her remarkably self-assured statements seemed trustworthy, I decided to grant her request. Dressed in civilian clothes she crossed our lines at a point opposite the sector still held by her regiment. Our troops escorted her through the deep, snow-covered forest to a spot near the enemy's forward outposts. She promised to return to the same point once her mission was completed.

Several days passed, but the girl did not return. After twelve days most people expressed doubts about her true intentions. But on the fourteenth day the designated front sector reported the arrival of two Red Army deserters, one of whom was a woman. Half-exhausted from the long trek through deep masses of melting snow, Vera and her companion—a Russian sergeant—had finally arrived.

She had an interesting story to tell. After her return to Russian lines, Vera was immediately interrogated by a commissar, who doubted the veracity of her story when she told him that she had been well treated by the Germans and had managed to escape in civilian clothes due to the carelessness of her guards. For five days and nights he had her imprisoned in an ice bunker in the company of criminals and fed only bread and water. When questioned again, Vera stuck to her story. As a result, she was returned to her regiment, given another uniform, and assigned to a front-line battalion as a medical auxiliary. This battalion had been urgently awaiting replacement since it had lost its entire manpower with the exception of one lieutenant and a handful of soldiers. After being initiated in her duties, Vera took the lieutenant's map and compass and went to the front. There she surprised a Red Army sergeant while he was reading one of our propaganda leaflets and persuaded him to desert by telling him about her own experience in our hands. She talked to a few more men and told the same story; they believed her and spread the tale like wildfire.

One hour after Vera's return to our lines the remnants of the sergeant's unit, consisting of six men and one machine gun, appeared at the point where she had crossed and surrendered themselves. Having overheard Vera's conversation with their sergeant, they decided to follow their example. For several days thereafter, groups of two or three deserters arrived daily at various points along the front. This provided the division intelligence officer with surprisingly exact information on enemy intentions and facilitated the planning of further attacks.

With regard to the effect of the propaganda leaflets that the Luftwaffe dropped from the air, Vera told us that they were hardly ever read by Russian soldiers because such an offense was punishable by death. Moreover, the contents were not believed because of the intense counterpropaganda to which the commissars subjected them. But she was certain that her former comrades would believe anything she wrote in personal letters. We accepted this idea, and soon this valuable correspondence was in full swing. Our patrols delivered her handwritten letters at various points in the forest near Russian outposts by attaching them to the branches of trees; their red markings made them easily recognizable. The results were unmistakable, since the number of deserters doubled very quickly. When, in addition, Vera's voice was recorded and transmitted over loudspeakers near the enemy lines, the number of deserters along the entire sector increased so much that it exceeded 400 only three weeks after the start of this improvised propaganda campaign. This figure was much higher than the combined total of deserters on all other sectors of Ninth Army's front. The idea of using Vera as the mainstay of a propaganda campaign had proven quite effective.

Four days later a few bottles of liquor made a powerful propaganda improvisation that eliminated the danger of a local enemy penetration. After one of our limited-objective attacks, the Russians attempted several strong counterthrusts. The situation became very tense when several Soviet tanks penetrated our lines and I had to commit our last tactical reserve. Ultimately we destroyed the offending tanks, but while this took place some Russian infantry infiltrated our lines as well. Not many Russians got through at first, but more and more followed. In this difficult situation the local *Alarmeinheiten* commander sent a civilian with a few bottles of liquor to the Red Army soldiers now behind his lines and invited them to taste these samples. They were told that they could drink to their heart's content if they decided to come over unarmed. Slightly inebriated by the first bottles, they began to arrive hesitantly and in small groups without weapons. As soon as the first wave had convinced itself that the Germans had no intention of killing them, about fifty additional Russians turned up to receive their liquor. They indulged so heavily that they forgot all about their weapons, quite apart from the fact that they were now physically incapable of returning to them. Meanwhile, one of our security detachments picked up the abandoned weapons and stopped all further Soviet infiltration attempts.

Kholminka: The Last Attack

The final attack conducted by 6th Panzer Division prior to being withdrawn from Russia for rehabilitation in France occurred in late March. The objective of the operation was the elimination of a Russian forest salient about eight kilometers deep and the capture of Kholminka, which lay at its base.

Though considerably stronger than it had been in January or early February, 6th Panzer Division in many respects remained a motley organization. It now consisted of the divisional staff, an understrengthed signal battalion, three consolidated infantry battalions, one motorcycle company, one panzer company, one assault gun platoon, one panzer reconnaissance platoon, one medium artillery battalion, one heavy artillery battalion, and one flak battalion. In a positive sense, officers and NCOs not only had considerable combat experience in Russia but had gained specific experience in winter fighting during the attacks on Tatarinka and Vasilevka. Moreover, supplies (including ammunition) remained generally adequate for a limited attack. Finally, we had the continued assurance of Luftwaffe support out of the Vyazma area, which had proven so beneficial during February.

Two Red Army rifle regiments, supported by two artillery battalions, occupied the objective area, with their headquarters in Kholminka. Their six battalions held the area south and east of the town, generally organized in strongpoints along the edge of the woods, so as to block the approaches to Kholminka. Suffering from supply difficulties, the Russians had found themselves unable to launch any further large-scale attacks.

Terrain and weather determined, to a marked degree, both our plan of attack and the eventual course of the operation. A meter of snow covered the ground in the open, restricting all movement. Although frozen on the surface, this snow broke easily under a man's weight. Movement in the forest was even more laborious, for the snow-laden lower limbs of the trees, primarily firs, touched the ground, impeding the attacker while concealing the defender. An almost impenetrable tangle of limbs, stumps, and windfalls formed an additional obstacle to all movement. At the end of March the weather was clear and sunny, with the temperature rising nearly to the freezing point during the day, but falling precipitously again at night.

Under such conditions there could be little thought of deploying troops on a broad front. An advance of any distance had to be carried out in column, along cleared or beaten paths and trails. This applied to tanks and assault guns as well as men. Wheeled vehicles were confined entirely to the cleared road between Tatarinka and Mashchekino, which constituted the jump-off line. Trackless snowfields separated our outposts from those of the Russians except for a single trail that led north into the tip of the wooded salient just west of Mashchekino. On the other side of this no-man's land the Soviets naturally labored under the same handicaps. Luftwaffe photos revealed heavy sled traffic leading out of Kholminka.

With this conditions in mind, I considered three possible routes of attack: westward from Podukhye; northward from Masilyevka; and northwest from Mashchekino through the woods. The first I discarded because it would have entailed a time-consuming regrouping of the division's forces, which had already been concentrated in the Masilyevka-Mashchekino area and, consequently, would have left the southern area vulnerable to a counterattack.

The second alternative offered the shortest route to the objective and led through only a short neck of woods. But this was also the most strongly defended sector and could be most easily reinforced by the enemy. Moreover, the configuration of the forest, the slopes of which were fortified, was such that an attack from the south, necessarily crossing open ground, would immediately have come under heavy fire from the front and both flanks. On both of these routes traversing the open country the snow was especially deep, which would have hampered movement by foot and denied our infantry the support of tanks and assault guns.

The third possibility—attacking through the woods—had the disadvantage inherent to all attacks through forests and, in addition, was the longest route to the objective. Yet this route also followed the only available communications links to Kholminka—a narrow sled road leading north through the forest from Mashchekino, and a trail that ran along the western edge of the woods for several kilometers and then through the narrow neck of woods into Kholminka. I also thought that the Russians would be less likely to expect an attack in this area and that the sector would therefore be less strongly held. Thus having decided on the third route as the line of attack, I discussed on 23 March my proposal in detail with all the subordinate commanders who were to participate in the operation. I gave special attention to the effort to achieve tactical surprise in order to deceive the enemy as to the route of the main attack.

The main effort of the attack I intended to make along the road to the north, while a secondary attack was to follow the trail along the western edge of the woods. The eastern column would consist of two infantry *Kampfgruppen* of battalion strength, commanded by Captain Kueper and Lieutenant Hesse, supported by an engineer company and our available armor (one PzKw IV, three PzKw 38ts, and five StG IIIs). *Kampfgruppe* Schmising, whose mission was diversionary, consisted of roughly an infantry battalion primarily composed of new recruits. In addition, I ordered feints and demonstrations from both Podukhye and Vasilevka. Lieutenant Colonel Unrein's motorcycle company and panzer reconnaissance elements were to remain in reserve. Our artillery (including flak employed in a ground support role) was tasked to support the operation from positions in the Mashchekino area. Aided by aerial observations, Colonel Grundherr's gunners ranged in on all known enemy defensive strongpoints during the days immediately preceding the attack.

With the attack scheduled to begin on 31 March, our troops spent the two preceding nights clearing the snow from the main column's approach road, from the point where it left the main highway just west of Mashchekino to the outpost positions, so that our armor could move up to support the infantry from the outset. Meanwhile, preparations in and around Vasilevka, including demonstrations by armored cars and transport vehicles, occurred openly, while artillery fire fell on the positions defending the approach to Kholminka across the narrow neck of the forest. All of these efforts went forth in the hope of deceiving the Russians as to our true intentions.

The operation got under way as scheduled. Adding a final touch to the deception scheme, *Kampfgruppe* Schmising moved out at 0500, two hours in advance of the main column, so as to make the first contact with the Soviets. The route followed by Schmising's troops, moreover, had been selected to give the impression of preparing the way for a stronger attack across the open country to the west. At dawn the Luftwaffe carried out a bombing raid, spearheaded by twenty-five "Stukas," on Russian defensive positions in the neck of the woods and on the village of Kholminka itself.

At 0700 the main column, proceeding double file, jumped off from positions just west of Mashchekino, led by experienced assault troops and combat engineers equipped to destroy enemy bunkers. Immediately following were the bulk of our tanks and assault guns, accompanied by snow-removal teams, more engineers, and additional infantry from Kueper's battalion. The few remaining AFVs [armored fighting vehicles] were distributed throughout the length of the column to deal with possible flank attacks, while Hesse's battalion brought up the rear.

Schmising's battalion met no resistance initially and made fairly rapid progress. The main force, however, came under fire almost immediately from Soviet bunkers in the southern edge of the woods. Resistance there was overcome fairly rapidly by a combination of tank fire and assault, and these bunkers yielded our first prisoners. Following this initial encounter the advance moved forward slowly. Snow piled up rapidly in front of the tanks and assault guns, whose movement had to be governing entirely by the snow-removal effort. In addition, the narrowness of the road in several spots required that trees be cut before the tracked vehicles could proceed.

Meanwhile, Captain Schmising had pushed forward about three kilometers, half the distance to Kholminka, where he had run up against the first Russian strongpoint astride the trail. A flank assault sufficed to eliminate this resistance without much difficulty, but a much stronger position, protected by wire obstacles and abatis, barred the way about a kilometer later. A front attack on this position failed and revealed that the approaches to the bunker had been mined. This reversal had its effect on the younger recruits, and some reorganization became necessary before the column could get moving again. Captain Schmising decided to bypass the Soviet position and led the battalion east into the forest for a short distance before turning northwest. No longer following the trail, the troops had to proceed step by step through the trackless and nearly impenetrable forest, fighting underbrush and guided only by compasses.

About noon, as the head of Schmising's column neared the northern edge of the forest, the entire battalion suddenly came under rifle and machine-gun fire from both sides. Once more the battalion's situation became critical, as the sudden attack from different directions had a demoralizing effect on the new men. Only the prompt and energetic measures of experienced officers and NCOs allowed a hasty defense to be organized and the attack countered by our own fire. Gradually these leaders organized little islands of resistance, calmed the panic-stricken recruits, and established a strong hedgehog position. Informed by radio of the course of the action, I ordered Schmising's battalion to remain in place until the main column could join it. No artillery or air support could be provided, since it was impossible to determine the exact position of either friend or foe.

In the meantime the main column had inched its way east along the sled road for nearly two kilometers. Tanks and assault teams combined two or three times to overcome strongpoints along the road, and many raids against the flanks of the long column had to be repelled. Casualties among messengers and horse-drawn supply sleds finally necessitated armed escorts for the latter. As the column finally approached the northern edge of the woods at noon, all of the division's artillery concentrated its fire on the final enemy position directly to the front. Russian artillery promptly countered with a heavy fire, inflicting several casualties. Fortunately, the Luftwaffe now responded to my call for support and succeeded in silencing the Soviet batteries, located about three kilometers west of Kholminka. At 1300, the spearhead of Kueper's battalion broke through the final defensive position at the edge of the woods.

A single strongpoint still lay about 1.5 kilometers to the northeast, between the edge of the forest and Podubbye, constituting a potential threat to the main column's rear. An infantry company, supported by several assault guns, was dispatched to remove this threat. Without awaiting the outcome of that action, Captain Kueper resumed his advance to the west, hoping to capture Kholminka before dark, which would mean that he might enjoy air support for his final assault. Advancing through the open terrain, however, proved impossible as long as his left flank remained exposed to fire from the woods. This forced Captain Kueper to order Lieutenant Hesse's battalion to proceed along the edge of the woods—paralleling the road—to remove the threat from that sector. Aided by a slowly rolling artillery barrage, Hesse's men fought their way through the Schmising's embattled battalion during the afternoon.

By that time Kueper's battalion and its supporting armor had reached Kholminka and, in a final assault (preceded by an air attack), fought its way into the eastern half of the town. There the attack ended for the day, just short of completing the mission, with the troops exhausted by the their day-long battle with the enemy and the elements. Mop-up operations and the capture of the western half of Kholminka, which was not strongly held, were carried out on 1 April. More than 300 prisoners were taken, and we counted about 150 Russian dead. The 6th Panzer Division's casualties totaled eighteen dead and forty wounded.

Just before the division was transferred to France for reorganization in April, we encountered yet another example of the Soviet propensity for committing atrocities against our troops. An elderly Russian civilian, a carpenter, appeared at division headquarters and reported that he had encountered a group of about forty German prisoners of war with a Red Army escort in his village a few kilometers behind the enemy front. These prisoners, he continued, had soon afterward been halted at the northern outskirts of the village, where they had dug deep pits. According to eyewitness reports, the prisoners had subsequently been shot and then buried in those pits. A few days later the village was captured in a German attack; the incident was investigated and found to be true.

Chapter 7

OUTSIDE STALINGRAD

Back to Russia

IN THE MIDDLE OF NOVEMBER 1942, after being adequately rehabilitated, provided with a complete reissue of weapons, and thoroughly trained in the West, the 6th Panzer Division—its units again above authorized strength—rolled eastward in seventy-eight trains of approximately fifty cars each. During the 4,000-kilometer journey from France there were unpleasant incidents, since such a large-scale troop movement—which crossed the whole of Europe in scarcely two weeks—could not remain hidden from the enemy. In the extensive marshy forests of the Pripyat region our troops became the targets of several partisan raids, directed especially against the trains carrying tanks and artillery, since these seemed both less dangerous and offering greater rewards. The tarpaulins camouflaging them did not prevent the trained eyes of the partisans lurking in ambush from identifying the big weapons.

Had I allowed the division to adhere to the entraining regulations governing troop movements, these trains would have been defenseless. These regulations, designed to economize in the use of freight cars, provided that troops, weapons, combat equipment, and ammunition were to be loaded as compactly as possible. This process necessarily split up units because the tactical preparation of the troops was not a consideration. (In addition, the trains carrying our panzers had to include compressed forage to facilitate the difficult winter provisioning of horse-drawn units in the East.)

Although fully acknowledging the reasons for these measures, based on my experiences with conditions in Russia I was primarily concerned with the ability of the units being transported to go immediately into combat. I gave priority, therefore, to such preparations over all other considerations, making allowances for other factors and compromises with the civilian railroad authorities only to the extent that they did not interfere with the troops' readiness for action during the movement. Hence, in spite of the fact that it was prohibited by regulations and the protests of the rail transportation authorities, I had the division transported in "combat trains."

This involved a different way of loading men and equipment, as well as a different order and distribution of the various combat elements. Allowances had to be made both for repelling partisan raids and leaving the train to fight regular Red Army forces. Care also had to be taken to ensure that, in the latter case, the men in each train (together with the men in the trains immediately following) would form a combined-arms force capable of fighting independently until reinforcements arrived.

The course of 6th Panzer Division's movement and its arrival at our destination proved the value of these measures. Partisans along our route everywhere encountered a well-prepared, abruptly initiated defensive operation, no matter whether they blasted tracks or placed obstacles on the rails. Defensive countermeasures had been envisaged against all of these possibilities. In particularly dangerous stretches of the rail line, trained sentries with their weapons ready to fire (and with hand grenades also primed) were positioned along both sides and at either end of every car. The men in each car had been placed in the brakeman's boxes; at night searchlights went into action whenever necessary. Their cones of light, shining out of both sides of the train as soon as the first shot was fired, dazzled the partisans and made it possible for our men to see every movement and discern their intentions. Thereupon they were defeated with rapid fire and hand grenades.

The brakes were applied and the train came to a sudden halt. At the same moment, active—aggressive—defensive measures commenced. We had drilled this into the men until the response became automatic. While the machine guns fired from the brakeman's boxes provided protection, our grenadiers would rapidly mop up along the forest edges, and presently the train would be rolling east again.

More time had to be taken when the tracks had been destroyed, but this predominantly occurred at points where it was possible to repair them quickly, since all stations, bridges, and other important objectives were protected by permanent sentries. In order to prevent derailments and to protect the locomotives from being damaged, the engineers drove through partisan-infested areas at a slow pace, pushing two or three empty cars ahead of the engine.

In most cases the technical damage could be eliminated quickly by engineer teams riding in the leading sections of each train. We had provided these engineers with the appropriate tools and equipment. During such halts as were necessary for them to work, the train was secured from all sides and patrols searched the immediate vicinity. At night the crews removed the tarpaulins from their tanks and made them ready to fire; this proved to be a very effective means of defense. We included a large number of emergency ramps throughout the trains, which made it possible to unload the panzers quickly whenever necessary and to commit them against especially strong partisan groups. In order to increase protection for the artillery transports (which the enemy particularly liked to attack), we frequently assigned 20mm flak guns to them, since the partisans had a devout fear of the tracer ammunition they fired.

These precautions yielded good results. Because of them, most of our trains suffered insignificant losses and arrived at their destinations on schedule, despite numerous partisan raids. Only one artillery train suffered the loss of a battalion commander and several men killed in a surprise raid undertaken by an unusually strong partisan group in conjunction with a demolition of the tracks. Even this train, however, arrived at the detraining point with all its guns and without any delay to speak of. The partisans, on the other hand, sustained severe losses as a result of the powerful defensive operations that had been immediately initiated. They were particularly taken aback by sudden and vigorous counterattacks, which forced them either to engage in bloody close combat if their forces were strong, or to flee in haste.

Raid on a Troop Train

The scenes that the soldiers of the 6th Panzer Division had observed on their journey across the European continent were still passing through their minds. The coasts of Brittany, washed by the booming waves of the Atlantic, lay far behind. Far behind also lay the peaceful towns, villages, and hamlets of the West and their homeland, which they had passed through so quickly. The verdure of meadows and fields brightly reflected the autumn sun, and the spires and gables of churches and castles were radiant. Paris and Berlin, the two great cultural centers of Europe, as well as the ruins of Warsaw, left a great impression on everyone who had seen them. All that was now a distant dream.

For days and nights the troops had been rolling through the Eastern countryside, through its extensive forests and marshes, its infinite plains and steppes, its sluggish streams and rivers. By the time the transports had reached Rostov on the Don River—the "gateway" to the Caucasus—after passing through Kharkov and Stalino, traversing the Donets River basin, and passing the Sea of Azov, the soldiers had already forgotten their adventures with the partisans.

Instead of moving on in the direction of the Caucasus, however, the trains veered north; our destination was suddenly uncertain. No one was able to say where the trains were headed. The situation was still obscure when, on the evening of 26 November, the first trains passed Tsimovniki, where the headquarters of Fourth Panzer Army was temporarily situated, itself on its way north. Trains jammed all the stations, and the sidetracks had become clogged with huge Russian locomotives captured during our offensive.

A cold wind blew through the monotonous brown steppe, driving before it innumerable balls of tumbleweed. They resembled a pack of hounds chasing game at top speed, moving forward in great leaps. A few camel riders moved alongside the train on steppe trails, trying to reach their solitary huts before darkness fell. At every halt we inquired of the personnel of the numerous evacuation trains running south which was the last station it was possible to reach. "This morning it was still Kotelnikovo," was the answer. This was the information that Colonel General Hermann Hoth, commander of the Fourth Panzer Army, had given me at a briefing at his temporary headquarters, for which I had been summoned away from the lead train.

The situation, General Hoth then revealed to me, was even worse that the first conference with Field Marshal Erich von Manstein, commander of Army Group Don, had led me to expect when we met as I was en route to Rostov. The Russian IV Cavalry Corps, reinforced by tanks, was advancing along the southern bank of the Don River, and its leading elements had already crossed the southern branch of the Aksay River. The enemy's Fifty-first Army was slowly advancing on both sides of the railroad in the direction of Kotelnikovo. Intelligence had already identified two tank corps assembling behind the northern branch of the Aksay River.

Facing these enemy forces of considerable strength, south of the Don River, were a few Luftwaffe flak batteries that had just moved up from the Caucasus and the VI Rumanian Corps headquarters staff with a headquarters guard totaling thirty men. Far off in the steppe, the remnants of the 5th and 8th Rumanian Cavalry Divisions, with a total combat strength of about 1,200 cavalrymen, were retreating. Thus one could not speak of a German front any longer; in fact, within the entire area there was not a single German unit capable of offering even temporary resistance to the advancing Russians. This situation resulted in part from the fact that all of the German and some of the Rumanian units composing Fourth Panzer Army had been encircled in Stalingrad and that the Rumanian divisions employed on a very broad front south of the city along the edge of the Kalmyck Steppe had been equipped with hopelessly inadequate antitank weapons. Thus the Russian tanks had easily pierced their front and scattered them so effectively that the weak remnants were disintegrating. Even General Hoth's headquarters staff had barely escaped the disaster. I learned that the battle-weary 23rd Panzer Division was about to be moved up, but this was small comfort, since the division had only the combat strength of two weak battalions and, having artillery but no tanks, would first have to undergo emergency rehabilitation behind the Sal River before it could engage in even defensive combat.

The approaching troops of the 6th Panzer Division as yet knew nothing of this highly unpleasant situation, but they realized that they would be entering combat soon and displayed every confidence in their own strength and ability. The trains lunged ahead at full speed, slowly climbing the hills between the river valleys in broad sweeping curves, then plummeting quickly into the next valley. Climbing and descending these grades in a pitch-black night, the lead trains neared their destination. Guards and sentries performed their duty in the usual manner, just as they had done through the partisan-infested regions. All the men in the first train rested on benches, in baggage racks, and on the floors; they were fully clothed and their weapons handy.

It was dawn on 27 November 1942 by the time the train had climbed the last hill between the Sal and Aksay River valleys. The aroma of morning coffee drifted over from the field kitchen as the train entered Semichnoya, the last station before Kotelnikovo, which was our final destination. The long voyage, the endless rolling and grinding of wheels, the rattling and bumping of the cars would soon be over, or so the gradually awakening soldiers thought as they searchingly looked over the dim outlines of the area in which the small town was likely to be situated. After several weeks of rail travel, they expected comfortable quarters to be waiting for them.

Just then, a long evacuation train from Kotelnikovo roared into the station. Two engines had strained to pull it up an ascending stretch of twenty kilometers. With intense curiosity the men asked the personnel in the evacuation train how things were going in Kotelnikovo. "There is complete calm and order," they were told.

Two evacuation trains are waiting for your arrival, an they will be the last to leave the town. Aside from a few planes, we saw no Russians. Except for a few old men constituting the railroad station guard, there are no German soldiers in the town. A few groups of unarmed Rumanians drove herds of sheep past us. That is all we were able to see. The Russian farmers in the surrounding countryside are surprised that we are evacuating the town, and they regret it very much. They were always polite and ready to help, and they will be very glad to see you.

A few short, shrill whistles sounded by the train commander called the troops back into their cars and put a sudden stop to the questioning. Shortly thereafter the train started again with the usual jerk and grinding of buffers.

Quickly it neared its destination. The soldiers on board packed their personal belongings and felt happy at finally being able to leave the train in which they had been tormented for weeks. A nice little town in the valley of the northern arm of the Aksay River was already coming into sight. At the edge of town stood a triumphal arch adorned by withered wreaths of flowers. This arch, which was visible from afar, had been inscribed in large Rumanian letters, "It is good that you have come!" The welcome had been meant for the Rumanian troops who had marched in several months ago and were now encircled in Stalingrad, waiting, along with their German comrades, to be rescued.

No sooner had the men tried to guess the meaning of this strange welcome than the train pulled into the large station. Suddenly the earth shook with a hail of shells. The ground quivered, black earth was thrown up on all sides, the windows were shattered, the brakes screamed, the wheels screeched, and with a sudden jolt, which threw men and equipment into a heap, the train came to a halt. All the troops leaped from the cars, just as they had done on the occasion of the partisan raids that they had so frequently gone through. The Russians, coming from the station building, were already storming the train with cries of "Urrah!" At that instant our machine guns and submachine guns began to fire from the car roofs on the earth-brown figures advancing on the train from both sides.

In the next minute, however, the infernal din caused by detonating shells and yelling Russians was drowned out by ear-splitting cheers from our infantrymen, who, led by Colonel Unrein (commander, Panzergrenadier Regiment 4), rushed forward with bayonets and hand grenades to fall upon their enemies. Although it required ferocious hand-to-hand fighting, in the course of an hour our grenadiers had wrested the station from them, then proceeded to mop up the freight cars, buildings, and other railroad installations in the area.

The Russian artillery, which, during this action, had aimed its fire at the end of the station where the train had entered as well as the western exit from the town, now redirected toward the center of the station, ostensibly for the purpose of incapacitating this part of the installation for any further detrainment of troops and to destroy the fully loaded transport train sitting there. It was not difficult to see that the Russians would soon achieve this objective, since they had obviously employed local observers wearing civilian clothes who, with incredible accuracy, always adjusted the fire toward those points where it could do the most damage. Abruptly, however, this very effective artillery fire—being delivered by at least two or three batteries—ceased. We expected that the guns would resume their bombardment at any moment, once a new target was selected, but nothing of the kind happened.

The guns remained silent. This was especially fortunate for us, as the fire had already done a good deal of damage that had to be quickly repaired by the engineer platoon of Panzergrenadier Regiment 4. Civilian railroad personnel, once they recovered from their initial confusion, assisted them.

The railroad administrator wanted to send all rolling stock still present in the station to the rear as quickly as possible and to stop directing troop trains into Kotelnikovo. I disapproved this idea and, on the contrary, demanded that all movements to the rear be halted and that 6th Panzer Division's following troop trains be driven into this station with the utmost speed. Thus the second train arrived soon after the raid, and it was possible to unload it—and all subsequent trains—without the slightest interference from the enemy. The Russian cavalry unit, which had dismounted at some distance, crept through the flood plains of the river without being noticed, and then carried out its raid, had meanwhile been vigorously pursued and scattered. The Soviet artillery still remained mysteriously silent.

Only much later in the morning did we discover the reason for the puzzling silence of the enemy batteries. In the midst of the crisis, a genius had taken matters into his own hands. Colonel Helmuth von Pannwitz happened to be in a tank repair shop at the eastern edge of Kotelnikovo when the artillery began firing. Realizing the great danger threatening the station and the town, he quickly rallied such tanks as were at all battle-worthy, appointed the maintenance team as tank drivers and gunners, and with six panzers immediately conducted a counterraid against the Soviet artillery. Since he came from the cavalry, a daring enterprise of this sort was natural to him.

Making a quick decision, von Pannwitz had his improvised force advance by bounds behind the hedges of the railroad embankment and through defiles in the terrain in such a skillful manner that he suddenly appeared in the rear of the firing guns. The surprise of the Russian artillerymen was therefore even greater than that of our grenadiers in the arriving transport train. Colonel von Pannwitz's makeshift crews fired every round at extremely close range, scoring a series of direct hits; meanwhile machine-gun fire from the tanks cut down the enemy gun crews before they could turn a single gun on their assailants. As a result, the improvised panzer platoon was able to complete its work of destruction in a few minutes. Piles of wrecked guns, ammunition, and wrecked limbers that the Russians had rushed up to support the raid now surrounded large numbers of dead soldiers, who had paid a high price for their successful surprise barrage.

After rendering an honorary salute, which is every brave enemy's due, the small armored force returned to its repair shop without having suffered any losses. This day, on which they had proven that they not only knew how to hammer, weld, bore, and drive but also how to fight, remained unforgettable to these mechanics. The gallant von Pannwitz and his group of fighters received the decorations that they fully deserved. It goes without saying that they immediately became fast friends with the soldiers of Panzergrenadier Regiment 4, whom, in the true spirit of brotherhood in arms, they had helped to save.

The day that began with such adversity had finally ended in complete success. The Russians had been dealt a stinging defeat, and Kotelnikovo—which was critical to any contemplated offensive action toward Stalingrad—remained firmly in our hands. By evening the town was garrisoned by a *Kampfgruppe* consisting of division headquarters, the headquarters and II Battalion of Panzergrenadier Regiment 4, and one company of Panzer Engineer Battalion 57. In conjunction with the flak batteries still in position and the brave "damaged-panzer platoon," we were well prepared to defend our position against even heavy enemy attacks.

The same measures that had allowed our transport trains to move through partisan-infested territory with relative safety had again proven their value. My insistence on organizing the transports as "combat trains" made it possible to push Fourth Panzer Army's assembly area far forward into the Aksay River valley, thereby making the distance to be covered in an attack toward Stalingrad as short as possible.

The *Cannae* of Pokhlebin

During the following days, the detraining of the remainder of 6th Panzer Division proceeded without further incident. On 28 November the advance elements of Colonel Zollenkopf's Panzergrenadier Regiment 114, including some light artillery, arrived. These elements had detrained the previous day in the Tatskinkaya area on the rail line north of the Don leading toward Stalingrad and then marched overland to Kotelnikovo by way of the Don River bridge at Tsymlyanskaya. The remaining combat echelons followed closely behind, alternatively using the northern and southern routes, and established themselves upon arriving in the assembly area around Kotelnikovo. I could not understand why the Russians discontinued their advance almost as soon as the first German troops appeared, even though they had certainly received orders to reach the southern army of the Aksay and to occupy Kotelnikovo. Instead of attacking while they still had superior numbers, the Russians idly watched for ten days as our strength in the town increased. I have never resolved this enigma, just as it has been impossible for me to understand why neither our detraining troops nor the endless truck convoys (moving along in broad daylight) were never attacked even once by air, although the Luftwaffe had no fighter planes aloft.

Had the Russians been more enterprising, they could have compelled Fourth Panzer Army to locate its assembly areas behind the Sal River—fifty kilometers farther to the rear. This would have substantially reduced the probability of any successful relief attack. As it was, we found ourselves allowed to assemble the 6th Panzer Division in essentially a peacetime fashion, despite the proximity of superior enemy forces. I remained aware throughout this period, however, that Field Marshal von Manstein and General Hoth had run a great risk in virtually sending the troops of the relief force into the lion's mouth.

To forestall a "fatal bite," I grouped 6th Panzer Division's combat units in an unusual defensive pattern that displeased General of Panzer Troops Friedrich Kirchner, commander of LVII Panzer Corps, and even worried General Hoth. Fortunately I was able to muster sound arguments in favor of these dispositions and defended them energetically, with the result that I was not ordered to change them. I rejected General Kirchner's proposal that we establish a defensive line along the Aksay River, with the left flank anchored on the Don, because the area was simply too wide to be held even after our entire force was assembled, and such a deployment would have left us with an open right flank that was impossible to defend. Instead, I ordered a network of local strongpoints established, each occupied by a combined-arms force. This network, in the form of a perimeter defense covering an area ten by twenty kilometers, had Kotelnikovo as a focal point and offensive bridgehead. Behind it, at Semichnoya, a strong mechanized general reserve was assembled, which I could easily shift in all directions across the rolling terrain that makes a broad sweep south of the Aksay River. Every local strongpoint was expected to be able to defend itself and assist its neighbors. Consequently, enemy infiltrations into this defensive network became almost instantly threatened with destruction by cross fire and concentric attacks from several strongpoints. By employing the mechanized general reserve, it was possible to prevent the Russians from forcing their way through the gap to the Don River or from unhinging the entire position by bypassing us to the east.

This unusual form of organization also had the advantage of permitting us to initiate our planned offensive at any given moment by assembling the mechanized general reserve in the bridgehead at night and then forming it into a spearhead. Only weak covering parties screened our flanks. The twenty modern SdKfz 233 eight-wheeled armored cars of the newly organized Panzer Reconnaissance Battalion 6, commanded by Major Friedrich Quentin, were employed to watch the gaps and undertake reconnaissance on the flanks and in the rear.

I had thoroughly discussed these tactical measures and the planned manner of operation with all of my subordinate commanders to ensure the cooperation of all elements in any situation in the interests of the whole. Subsequent events would justify these decisions, despite the fact that peacetime regulations insisted that panzer divisions constitute a well-defined means of attack and were not suited for defensive missions. These regulations also warned that tanks must not be moved at night, since their crews could not see well in the dark and might expose their machines to serious damage. What the writers of these manuals overlooked was the fact that the specific necessities of warfare often make it mandatory to discard the dogmatic peacetime training rules and to replace them by actions that meet the requirements of reality.

Such was the case when the Russians made their first attempt to destroy our assembling units in the Kotelnikovo area by a flanking attack from the northwest. On previous days, the crews of our SdKfz 233s had already observed hostile scout patrols mounted on small steppe horses at various points along the fifteen-kilometer gap to the Don River. These patrols would disappear with the speed of lightning as soon as they saw a German armored vehicle. Their chief interest appeared to be centered on the defile at Pokhlebin and the hilly ranges north of Mayorovo. Dismounted scouts crept up to the defile through the high steppe grass and brush in the Aksay Valley, but vanished as soon as a few rounds from our covering parties whistled toward them, and were therefore unable to penetrate our screens. The Russians were visibly amazed, on the other hand, to discover no Germans on the hilly ranges west of the defile, where our forward artillery observers had occasionally spotted them. This same observation by the enemy must have been made on the morning of 5 December, the day of the first Soviet attack.

That morning a Russian combined-arms team (consisting of dismounted cavalry and tanks) poured out of Verkhniy-Kurmoyarskiy at dawn, attacking the motorcycle company stationed at Topolev on the Don. They quickly pushed the company back as far as Kudino. This enemy advance did not come as a surprise, having been telegraphed by Russian reconnaissance activity over the past several days. The initial engagement at Topolev confirmed that the Soviets, after pushing through the gap, would either lunge west to attack our rear or move directly to the south to hit our flank.

The enemy attack force on the Don River remained in front of the motorcycle company at Kudino, which the company had managed to hold, while the main body of the Russian 81st Cavalry Division veered south toward Pokhlebin, preceded by its attached 65th Tank Brigade. Presently the heavy 150mm batteries of Lieutenant Colonel Graf's III Battalion at Semichnoya took these forces under fire, and they were soon afterward joined by the rest of the guns of Colonel Grundherr's Panzer Artillery Regiment 76. The sixty-four Russian tanks constituting the spearhead element of the attack continued to advance without any apparent concern for the hail of shells pounding down near them. The dismounted cavalry, however, at once disappeared into the flood plains of the Aksay, from which they later reappeared north of Pokhlebin, resuming their attack even though they had failed by this maneuver to evade our artillery fire.

The long column of advancing Russian tanks came to an abrupt halt in front of Pokhlebin when the leading vehicles were destroyed by the 75mm antitank guns belonging to the antitank platoon of Panzergrenadier Regiment 114. At almost the same time, machine-gun fire from First Lieutenant Kelletat's reinforced 3rd Company, Panzergrenadier Regiment 114, holding a blocking position at the town and defile, forced the dismounted cavalrymen to take cover. Despite these checks, more and more Soviet forces came up to reinforce the attackers, who hoped to capture the town by encircling it. Our antitank platoon repulsed several tank attacks against overwhelming enemy numerical superiority, but the platoon's strength decreased as individual guns were, one by one, identified and finally overrun. Eventually, the lead Russian tanks managed to penetrate into the village.

The Soviets obviously believed that they had won out when their two leading tanks reached the center of the town, but the last gunner of the sole surviving antitank gun destroyed them as well. Six tall black columns of smoke indicated the total losses that the enemy had suffered at the hands of three antitank gun crews who had perished to the last man in an unequal fight. A sublime drama had thus drawn to its close.

This exemplary heroism on the part of a small group of staunch and courageous soldiers had made it possible for the enemy's tank brigade to be held up in the defile for nearly two hours. The time thus gained proved sufficient for the main body of Captain Hauschildt's I Battalion, Panzergrenadier Regiment 114, coming from the Mayorovo strongpoint, to attack the Soviet dismounted cavalry in the flank and detain them in the Pokhlebin defile until the afternoon.

Only the enemy tanks—by utilizing a passage through the swampy valley of the Siberachnaya Stream—managed to make headway in the direction of Kotelnikovo. Without regard for the battle raging in their rear, and the tank losses inflicted by the antitank guns of the attacking I/Panzergrenadier Regiment 114, they doggedly crossed the Semichnoya Stream, which was quite difficult to ford just then as the result of a partial melting of the snow that had fallen a short time previously. These tanks were obviously determined to seize the village of Sakharov, three kilometers to the east on a bend in the Aksay. Captain Koch's 6th Company, Panzergrenadier Regiment 4, which had been pushed out of Pokhlebin, stubbornly defended this town with the assistance of a single artillery battery. Several Russian tanks fell victim to armor-piercing, hollow-charge shells during the advance, and when the grenadiers knocked out the first vehicles to enter the village with magnetic antitank hollow charges, the majority of the Soviet armor withdrew. The battered tanks now fell back to the west in a broad sweep, still attempting to reach their ultimate objective: Kotelnikovo. Now the Russian tanks entered the real killing ground, coming under the cross fire of six artillery batteries whose heavy and light shells pounded them on both flanks from ranges of two to four kilometers. This hail of fire proved so formidable that several more tanks were damaged and others sunk into marshy holes while trying to maneuver evasively.

At that moment the main body of the dismounted Turkestani cavalry regiment had succeeded in forcing back I/Panzergrenadier Regiment 114 so far from Pokhlebin that it was able to penetrate into the area between the two streams mentioned above. Before the cavalrymen were able to aid the tanks, however, an unexpected event occurred during the early hours of the afternoon. Colonel Walther von Huenersdorff, commander of Panzer Regiment 11, had brought forward the first two companies of his regiment as far as Kotelnikovo. Despite being heavily outnumbered by the Russian tank brigade, Colonel von Huenersdorff grasped the critical nature of the situation and at once committed his panzers in a counterattack. In bitter fighting, with heavy losses on both sides, our tanks managed to throw the numerically superior Soviet armor back across the Semichnoya. Meanwhile, the attempts of ever-increasing numbers of dismounted Russian cavalry to cross this stream and attack to the east were frustrated by the combined fire of multiple batteries, which hit the enemy simultaneously from strongpoints to the south, east, and west, dampening their spirit of attack.

When darkness fell, the din of battle gradually subsided, though as the day drew to a close it was clear that the outcome of the battle was as yet undecided. Although the Russians had achieved a local penetration into our defensive system, our troops had frustrated his bid to seize Kotelnikovo. The situation of his original attacking force, a dismounted cavalry regiment supported by a tank brigade, was unfavorable: Caught in a defile and squeezed in between marshes and the Aksay River, this force was caught in the cross fire from several of our strongpoints. On the next morning (6 December), however, the enemy commander would be able to commit his 115th Cavalry Division and to have the Fifty-first Army (which had spent the previous day standing idly by) attack from the east. If both the cavalry corps and the infantry army gave each other the proper tactical support, our situation would be grave indeed. The only potential assets with which I could seek a decisive turn of events were the main body of Panzer Regiment 11 and Captain Kueper's II Battalion, Panzergrenadier Regiment 114, with its armored personnel carriers, neither of which [units] had yet arrived. To solve the problem of having these units available in time was my sole concern as the sun went down on 5 December.

As has already been mentioned, Soviet partisans had a special interest in tank trains. Their continual raids had caused such delays that many of our panzer units, which had originally been placed at the head of the division's movement, ended up at the rear of the combat elements upon arrival. Although these trains had priority, it would normally have been physically impossible for them to arrive and be unloaded prior to 6 or 7 December. This would have been too late. Only unusual measures could still make their timely commitment feasible. The first of these measures was to halt all other rail movements in the area concerned and—contrary to the safety provisions of the railroad regulations—permit these trains to move within sight of each other. Since the few stations near enough Kotelnikovo to allow the tanks to arrive in time were insufficient for unloading a large number of armored vehicles, it was necessary for me to order a large number of trains to stop in the open and for the tanks to unload in complete darkness by means of the emergency ramps available on the trains. Furthermore, again contrary to regulations, night marches of several hours' duration had to be undertaken in completely unfamiliar terrain.

Despite these emergency measures, the first tank trains did not arrive at the Semichnoya station to be unloaded until 2000 hours. The tanks that had unloaded in the two preceding stations had already begun their night march toward the hilly ranges surrounding the Semichnoya station. The tanks and APCs that had been forced to detrain in the open followed them. Now the experience gained by the division during the winter fighting outside Moscow and the long hours of training in France (including night movements) paid off: Everything went smoothly. By 0100 hours, 6 December, the last units had arrived in their assembly areas. An hour before, Colonel von Huenersdorff had set out with the leading elements of his regiment, after I had given him a thorough situation briefing, a map orientation, and mission objectives. Led by Major Friedrich Quentin's SdKfz 233s, whose crews were familiar with the terrain in the area, the entire mechanized combat force of tanks and infantry mounted in APCs had arrived at its line of departure by 0400 hours and, despite the darkness, was prepared for the counterattack one hour later near Mayorovo, where the command post of Panzergrenadier Regiment 114 was located.

As soon as there was enough light to permit firing, the noise of battle again rose over the previous day's battlefield. This area was situated in a valley. Our tanks and infantry again attacked the dismounted cavalrymen, who offered stubborn resistance and threw new reserves into the fighting. Unaware of our night-time reinforcements, the enemy meant at all costs to keep open the defile at Pokhlebin, which constituted his route of approach to Kotelnikovo, especially as the Russian commander intended to commit the 115th Cavalry Division to force a decision. In long columns our observers could see the tank, cavalry, and motorized elements of this division advancing toward Pokhlebin along the same road that the enemy had used the previous day.

Substantial elements had already vanished into Pokhlebin and the ravines when—all of a sudden—our panzers appeared in several wedge-shaped formations along the snow-covered hills. Plodding forward through the snow, they slowly advanced on their victims, who as yet were unaware of the imminent disaster. This was in part due to the fact that the Russian IV Cavalry Corps had only recently been transferred into this area on foot from the Afghan border, where it had previously performed border patrol duty without ever seeing combat. Inexperienced as they were, the cavalry commanders failed to observe even the most rudimentary rules of precaution. Not a single cavalryman, infantryman, or tank climbed to the concealed parts of the rugged terrain to reconnoiter or provide protection. If this had been done, the movements of our panzer companies could never have escaped attention. In their inexperience the Russians were not even aware that possession of this hill range was decisively important to their attack on Kotelnikovo, or else they would have occupied it. As it was, the catastrophe quickly overtook them.

Gripped by paralyzing terror, the Soviets suddenly saw more than 200 tanks and armored vehicles descend from the hills and fall on their columns. From close range 200 guns opened fire on tanks, artillery, and vehicles. Flames shot up; columns of black smoke from tanks that had been hit rose into the sky; trucks were overturned and burning. Three hundred machine guns took a terrible toll among riders and horses. Those who escaped this inferno tried to get across the river, but the thin ice broke. Men, tanks, and equipment disappeared into the cold waters. The men at the end of the column thought that they might be able to escape a similar fate by running in the opposite direction, but their attempt to do so was in vain. Twenty SdKfz 233s and the machine guns of II/Panzergrenadier Regiment 114 blocked their path, and the escapees recoiled back into the pocket being rapidly tightened by a concentric attack on Pokhlebin.

By 1000 hours the fate of the IV Cavalry Corps had been sealed. There was no longer any escape, though the encircled enemy continued for hours to offer stubborn resistance. The Russian tanks and antitank guns engaged the companies of Panzer Regiment 11 as they rolled down from the hills in a fire duel to the death. The tracer stream of the armor-piercing shells traveled up and down in quick succession, but soon more and more of the shells came from the hills, while fewer and fewer were the responses that flashed from below. One volley after another from our heavy batteries boomed into Pokhlebin, throwing up columns of black earth; the town began to burn. A sea of fire and smoke veiled the horrible end of the brave garrison, yet fire still flared up occasionally from isolated antitank guns when our panzer spearheads entered Pokhlebin. The panzergrenadiers following the tanks were obliged to use hand grenades to break the last resistance of the enemy's motorized infantrymen, who stubbornly fought on from every house and hole. They lay around their wrecked antitank guns by the dozens, with only a few survivors clinging to the marsh and the brush. By noon, however, Pokhlebin had finally been cleared of the enemy.

In the area between the town and the previous day's front a few enemy tanks still fought to support the breakout attempt of the Russian elements encircled there. Some tried to escape across the Aksay, but only a few managed to do so. Others attempted to break through or infiltrate between our local strongpoints but had to give up after being caught in cross fires and suffering heavy losses. Finally, a larger force thought it had found a gap between two dry riverbeds and tried to escape westward at this point. Our covering parties had not initially spotted it due to the thick smoke, but they eventually reported the approach of something that was neither men, horses, nor tanks. Only when this mysterious unit had surged over the crest of the range and was preparing to storm forward toward Mayorovski was it identified as a camel brigade. This brigade ran headlong into the fully prepared panzers and antitank guns whose mission was to prevent enemy tanks from escaping via this route. First Lieutenant Radzuweit's 8th Company, Panzer Regiment 11, and Captain Neckenauer's Panzerjaeger Battalion 41 received these beasts and their riders with such a burst of fire that the leading elements broke down at once, and those following behind ran back wildly. Our panzers attempted to pursue but could not do so successfully, as much of the ground was too marshy to bear their weight. The fleeing camels proved quicker and better able to move across country and, consequently, won this important race. Many of them regained their freedom since they alone were able to ford the Aksay River.

By early afternoon the pocket had been mopped up and the two-day battle ended. During the next few days, however, stragglers and isolated cavalry troops continued to be discovered in the dried-out riverbeds where they had hidden. The men and puny steppe horses we captured in a half-starved condition and promptly provided for. The local terrain clearly showed the traces of a deadly struggle. The 85th Russian Cavalry Division had been smashed in the Pokhlebin area, the 115th Cavalry Division on its way there. On the highway and scattered throughout the town we counted fifty-six burned-out

Russian tanks of the 65th Tank Brigade, which—blackened by smoke—topped the debris around them. Just a few hours ago these silent machines had been the cavalry corps' proud backbone. Guns, vehicles, ammunition, and military equipment of all kinds had been overturned, smashed, and burned. In between lay piles of dead Red Army soldiers and their horses. Cart roads and meadows had been trampled and plowed up by tank tracks. Smoldering planks and demolished blockhouses choked the town streets and added to the chaos, while a pervasive smell of burning vitiated the atmosphere. Innumerable prisoners and more than 2,000 horses fell into our hands. The two Russian division commanders had been killed, while the corps commander had fled across the Aksay and escaped the shots that our outposts on the opposite bank had fired at him, though his entire escort was captured.

The hotly contested Pokhlebin defile had witnessed immortal deeds of heroism. The antitank platoon that, on 5 December, had halted the initial onrush of Russian tanks did so by sacrificing itself. The guns lay on the ground, smashed by enemy shells, and at their side lay the bodies of the platoon commander, First Lieutenant Freiherr von Plettenberg, and his crews. The counterpart to this "battery of the dead" in the "Thermopylae of Pokhlebin" was to be found in the Russian tanks and antitank guns that had also defended their positions to the last. Brave though inexperienced enemies had found soldiers' graves there. Thus the struggle for Pokhlebin ended with the planned Cannae being inflicted on the Red Army; for the enemy cavalry corps a final defeat, though for the soldiers of the 6th Panzer Division only a victorious prelude to the relieving attack on Stalingrad.

The "Golden Bridge"

"Liberate Stalingrad!"

That was the momentous mission upon the execution of which the fate of 300,000 troops depended. A task of historic magnitude was to be attempted, and the further conduct of the campaign hinged on its successful completion. Officers and men down to the lowest-ranking private were fully aware of this. Conscious of the great task and of their responsibility to their own people, whose eyes had anxiously turned toward the city on the Volga, all ranks were prepared to do their utmost to master this difficult assignment. This attitude and this willingness to sacrifice their lives, when coupled with their extraordinary skills and hard-won Russian combat experience, would lead to exploits bordering on the miraculous.

After Pokhlebin, the troops awaited the order to advance on Stalingrad with impatient good spirits. As yet, however, it remained necessary to wait for the arrival of the most critical supplies. Above all, the remnants of the

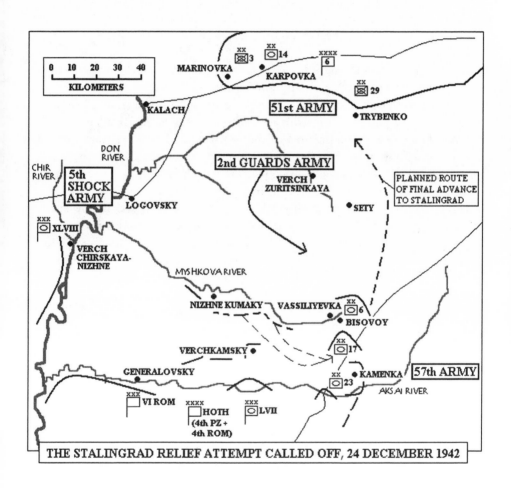

THE STALINGRAD RELIEF ATTEMPT CALLED OFF, 24 DECEMBER 1942

23rd Panzer Division, regrouping behind the Sal River, had to complete their emergency rehabilitation. In the interim, many of the men from the panzer-grenadier regiments who had originally been transferred from the cavalry found entertainment riding the small steppe horses, which had fallen into our hands by the hundreds. With fur caps set atop their heads and sabers dangling from their belts, they galloped all over the area. Their long legs almost touched the ground. These riders actually made the streets look different, since they were now full of horses rather than tanks. One could almost imagine the scene had the Turkestani riders, instead of our panzers, won the battle.

After a few days the signs began to multiply that the enemy was poised to try and throw the 6th Panzer Division off balance by attacking from the opposite flank. On 9 December Luftwaffe reconnaissance flights and Major Quentin's reconnaissance patrols identified a combined-arms column that seemed intent on bypassing the Kotelnikovo area in a broad eastward sweep. This column was led by a cavalry battalion (composed of two or three troops) behind which followed two infantry battalions with some tank support a good distance back. Obviously this represented a strong Russian reconnaissance force whose mission was to develop the situation and discover the strength of the German forces being assembled. I believed it reasonable to assume that this reconnaissance element might well be followed by a strong armored force from the IV Mechanized or XIII Tank Corps with the intent of throwing back Fourth Panzer Army while it was still preparing to relieve Stalingrad.

Major von Kessel, my operations officer, had also anticipated such a design on the part of the Russians from the outset and had ordered the appropriate countermeasures. By 7 December Colonel von Huenersdorff's panzers had again been assembled in the vicinity of the Semichnoya station. Of the sixteen tanks that had been disabled in the battle of Pokhlebin, it had been possible to make quick repairs on a few that had suffered only light damage, while the others could be replaced by vehicles that had recently arrived. Accordingly, Major von Kessel and I placed our panzers twenty kilometers behind the front, on the same dominating, rolling terrain from which they had advanced on the night of 5 December to deal the Russians a decisive blow. Possibilities for shifting troops rapidly across this terrain were excellent, no matter whether the movements had to be carried out by day or night. A thin layer of snow covered the gently rising ground, through which the brown steppe grass protruded; neither the snow nor the dry grass would impede our tactical movements at all. We planned to defeat the enemy force about to attack Kotelnikovo from the southeast in exactly the same manner as we had dispatched the cavalry corps a few days earlier.

The Russians, conversely, in advancing over the same rolling terrain into the valley of Kotelnikovo, would find themselves channeled between two very deep, dried-out riverbeds, which were several kilometers long. These riverbeds constituted an absolute antitank obstacle; nor could men and horses cross them without bridge-building equipment. With these riverbeds on their flanks and the Aksay River squarely across their line of march, the Soviets would have no escape route once our mechanized reserve force of tanks and APCs came out of its assembly area and attacked their rear. A second Cannae would surely have been inflicted upon them.

For this reason, and also because we considered it critical to defeat the greatest possible number of enemy forces before beginning the relief thrust toward Stalingrad, I wanted very badly for the Russians to commit strong tank forces behind their reconnaissance echelon. To induce them to do so, however, required us to construct a "golden bridge" to lure them into the trap. To this end, our dispositions were altered to appear careless, leaving the Russian reconnaissance force an unobstructed path that would tempt them to "pick the seemingly ripe fruit" at Kotelnikovo. As our observers watched, the Soviet lead element actually chose the route leading directly into the lion's den.

By 9 December the Soviet reconnaissance force had advanced through Budarka, and his cavalry spearheads had already reached Pogozhka, but not a single German soldier could be seen far and wide. All of our SdKfz 233s and other elements that had previously been employed there had withdrawn in accordance with their orders, now watching the enemy's movements from well-camouflaged hideouts. The Russians became visibly ill at ease when their leading scout patrols entered the first farms of Kalinin and Lenin, only to find them clear of Germans. Nor did they discover the carefully concealed mechanized reserve in the Semichnoya-Kommissarov area. On the other hand, the enemy cavalrymen saw German railroad trains rolling past them, barely three kilometers distant, as well as considerable truck traffic on the road west of the tracks.

These same movements were observed by the Russian horsemen feeling their way forward to the edge of Negotny, in which Major Quentin's Panzer Reconnaissance Battalion 6 was situated. Soldiers and camouflaged vehicles actually filled the village to capacity. Holding their weapons in their hands and ready to leap up in case the enemy attacked, motorcycle riflemen crouched on the floors of the farm huts. Machine-gun teams lurked in hidden corners, waiting for the appropriate signal to fire on the unsuspecting enemy, whose movements our scouts watched closely from dormer windows. But nothing happened. Only fowl moved about in the village, which otherwise appeared quite dead. Barking dogs indicated the approach of the enemy cavalry and advance scouts, some of whom crept up to within 100 meters of the outermost houses. The two infantry battalions, which had cautiously entrenched in the rolling terrain west of Budarka, now also followed, reaching Pogozhka that afternoon. They dug in again, north of the town, with the handful of supporting tanks protecting their flanks and rear.

For two days now the Luftwaffe had been looking in vain for any strong Russian tank forces following up the reconnaissance effort. Yet even though we had not offered the slightest resistance to their lead element, no such force could be found. I decided to allow the Russian reconnaissance force to keep advancing, to the extreme limit that the situation permitted.

The Russians accepted this offer, pushing their infantry battalions forward another eight kilometers toward Negotny. At the same time, the cavalry in Kalinin received reinforcements, and its scouts went forward almost as far as the Semichnoya station without being disturbed in any way. This, however, represented that extreme limit of what was possible to allow in the way of concessions. Our dispositions had already placed the railroad and the Negotny garrison at substantial risk, and I thus decided to set off the alarm and be satisfied with the small fish already in the net.

Just as I reached that decision, the Russian reconnaissance unit started to withdraw. Apparently their courage failed them, and they were hurrying to pull back before nightfall. No raid was going to be forthcoming, as an unusually tense but completely peaceful day drew to its close. The commanders of the enemy armored elements evidently had no intention of crossing the "golden bridge" we had so carefully built for it. What may have been the reason for this refusal? I could only believe that the "Cannae at Pokhlebin" had paralyzed the Russian commander's initiative, hurting his forces too severely for him to feel any desire to undertake a similar venture so soon.

Not even a "golden bridge" could change his attitude.

Flank Protection by Means of a Sideways Thrust

The order to commence the relief attack toward Stalingrad finally arrived on 10 December. This order provided that 6th Panzer Division would effect a breakthrough at the railroad line on 12 December and reach the northern arm of the Aksay River as quickly as possible. The 23rd Panzer Division, commanded by Lieutenant General Hans Freiherr von Boineburg-Lengsfeld, was to accompany the attackers, echeloned to the right, and provide flank protection for 6th Panzer. For our vulnerable western flank, however, there were no covering units available. This provision in LVII Panzer Corps's attack plan confronted me with a difficult tactical problem.

On the one hand, quickly breaking through the entrenched Russian Fifty-first Army between Pimen-Cherni and the road leading north from Kotelnikovo would require the concentration of all our forces. Yet it was impossible to ignore the remnants of the IV Cavalry Corps, since these remnants had been assembled in the Verkhniy-Yablochniy and Verkhniy-Kurmoyarskiy areas and now forces had moved up to strengthen them. Our best estimate suggested that these reinforced remnants comprised several troops of dismounted cavalry and camel units, supported by fourteen tanks. Although such a motley force was no match for a panzer division, its presence undeniably represented a serious threat to our supplies, which depended completely on the railroad line and the highway running parallel to it. Any disruption of this vital artery might have a fatal effect on the entire relief operation; precautions therefore had to be taken to meet this danger.

The customary way for a unit to protect its flanks is to detach a flank security patrol to accompany the main body. In the present case such a patrol would have to have been at least battalion strength, supported by artillery and armor. This was plainly impossible, for detaching a force of this size permanently from 6th Panzer Division—either during the initial breakthrough or during the course of the attack—would have decreased our striking power to such an extent that the planned rescue operation would be jeopardized. Detachment of a "stationary" flank security screen had the same disadvantages.

As a result, I decided that it was immediately necessary to deal this enemy force a single blow that would eliminate it completely. For this purpose I concentrated the division within a very small area behind the covering parties in the bridgehead, which were in contact with the enemy, and then pushed forward along the hilly range on both sides of the rail line and penetrated the entire depth of the decimated cavalry corps. Thereafter, Colonel von Huenersdorff's Panzer Regiment 11, together with Captain Kreis's II Battalion, Panzergrenadier Regiment 4 (once released from covering the bridgehead), had orders to liquidate the Soviet forces on our western flank in the Verkhniy-Yablochniy area with a powerful blow, so as to render superfluous any further requirement for flank protection. In order to employ a maximum number of troops for both missions it was necessary to execute these missions successively: The large-scale breakout had to be followed as soon as possible by the sideways lunge to crush the remnants of the cavalry corps.

Before dawn on 12 December, 6th Panzer Division, with the 23rd Panzer Division echeloned in depth on our right, was ready to attack. Our combat troops had assembled without incident in the bridgehead north of Kotelnikovo during the final hours of darkness, leaving their old sectors looking the same as ever. A sunny wintry day dawned; the officers checked their watches. Everyone was fully conscious of the significance of the approaching hour.

Suddenly the sounds of explosions disrupted the silence. Every gun in the division commenced firing, and it almost seemed as if the shells were going to land within our own lines. Involuntarily, everyone flinched and stooped, but the first salvo was already screaming over the heads of the men and landing on the Gremyachi station. The earth quivered from the detonation of the heavy shells. Stones, planks, and rails were hurled into the air. The salvo had hit the center of the Russians' chief strongpoint. This was the signal for the "witches' Sabbath" to follow.

While Colonel Grundherr's artillery maintained a rapid rate of fire, Colonel von Huenersdorff's panzer crews started their motors, and the majority of our armored vehicles began to roll forward. Like a spring tide they overran the Soviet position, advancing across the steppe in deep wedge formations, their guns sending death and ruin into the fleeing enemy forces. So abrupt and forceful had been the impact of this catastrophe on the surprised Russians that they were unable to rescue their heavy combat equipment. Light and heavy artillery batteries stood intact in their firing positions, where they had been enveloped and caught from the rear by our panzers before firing even a single accurate round. The limbers that the Russian artillerymen had been moving up as quickly as they could had not reached the guns because our machine-gun fire killed the horse teams drawing them. The few surviving horses nibbled at the frozen steppe grass, still standing in teams together with the bodies of those who had bled to death from their wounds. Blood on the snow marked their paths. The remnants of the Soviet infantry had been scattered, disappearing into the tall steppe grass as if they had been whisked away by a gust of wind.

By early morning we had overrun the command post of the Russian division, followed soon afterward by that of the corps, both of which had been evacuated in great haste. As a result, enemy operations were paralyzed. Major Quentin's Panzer Reconnaissance Battalion 6, which advanced east of the railroad, maintained contact with the 23rd Panzer Division, which had opened its attack at the same hour and had advanced eighteen kilometers from the hilly region on both banks of the Kremoyarski Aksay River as far as Pimen-Cherni. In the beginning, the 23rd Panzer had faced stubborn resistance from a Russian rifle division, but once we had severely defeated the main body of the Fifty-first Army, that resistance quickly began to decrease.

The principal action had thus enjoyed complete tactical success within a few hours. Now the moment had come to eliminate any lingering threat to our flanks. The main body of Panzer Regiment 11, comprising over 100 tanks, pivoted westward according to plan and struck the retreating Soviet units that had not been directly affected by the breakthrough. Everywhere Colonel von Huenersdorff's panzer crews encountered rewarding objectives that held no danger for tanks and could therefore be rapidly liquidated. The tally of captured Russian artillery and other heavy weapons, as well as that of horses and vehicles of all kinds (even including field kitchens), increased by the hour.

A few hours earlier, Captain Kreis had prepared the drama of Verkhniy-Yablochniy. His plan here provided for a feint attack from the south against the elongated village. This attack would simulate the presence of strong German assault forces and, hopefully, induce the Soviets to commit the cavalry corps remnants situated between the Don River and Yablochniy to the defense of the endangered village. This maneuver was also intended to divert enemy attention from the approach of our panzers on their mission of total annihilation.

As the first step in executing this plan, II/Panzergrenadier Regiment 4 undertook a surprise attack on the enemy covering parties situated opposite it, overrunning them easily and scattering their troops in various directions. Stragglers entered the village and spread grossly exaggerated news of the advance of heavy German forces toward Verkhniy-Yablochniy, as a result of which all Russian garrisons in this and surrounding villages along the lower Aksay and Don Rivers were alerted. The Luftwaffe, which was very active that day, soon afterward reported considerable activity in all enemy-occupied villages and a heavy reinforcement of the defensive positions on the southern edge of Verkhniy-Yablochniy.

Captain Kreis's attack made rapid headway. His plan to feign the presence of strong forces, coupled with the necessity of advancing across open terrain covered only by a thin layer of snow, called for broad and deep echelonment of his troops. Occasional weak fire from a light Russian battery in no way impeded the progress of the movement.

Machine-gun fire settling on our grenadiers as they moved closer to the village was much more unpleasant, since it forced them to the ground and made it necessary to commit heavy weapons. Moreover, the method of advancing had to be altered in order to avoid excessive losses. Instead of alternatively rushing forward whole groups, the officers ordered their men to work themselves forward individually, from cover to cover. This practice of creeping up, which had been adopted from the Red Army, was familiar to our veterans, who were well-versed in all Eastern [Front] combat methods. Favored by the steppe grass protruding from the snow, scouts and even a few patrols were able, during the morning, to reach nearly the edge of the village. They reported the enemy to be constantly reinforcing his garrison.

According to Luftwaffe and ground reconnaissance reports, numerous small groups of Soviet forces remained continuously on the move from the Don and Aksay along the Fedorova Stream to Verkhniy-Yablochniy. By noon Captain Kreis's entire battalion had worked its way within a few hundred meters of the village. The chief concern now became the vulnerability of the battalion's left flank, which the enemy could threaten and attack with tanks and infantry. We countered with a deeply echeloned reserve, supported by a panzer platoon.

The remnants of the Russian IV Cavalry Corps had still not quite recovered from the blow dealt them scarcely a week earlier and were by no means ready to contemplate offensive action. Instead, they remained content with hastening to the aid of their comrades in threatened Verkhniy-Yablochniy. Thus they did precisely what we desired them to do and fell into the trap. However, I was still concerned that the enemy might have drawn the correct conclusion from the defeat of the main body of the Fifty-first Army, which had by then occurred, and withdrawn hurriedly to the north or west. Had the Russians done so, Colonel von Huenersdorff's panzers would have pushed into a void, and the division would have found the enemy still on its flank the following day. The result would have been a critical loss of time, because if the Soviets withdrew to the Don River, Captain Kreis's battalion would have had to follow them, while the panzers would have had to rush precipitously for any chance to destroy the enemy force short of the river.

As yet there remained time for the Russians to elude our blow, but their command appeared blind to the threat to his rear—or else had received no orders to withdraw. Accordingly, the Soviets continued a staunch defense of the village against all penetration attempts by our grenadiers. Occasionally one of our combat patrols would capture a house or seize a line of trenches, but the Russians usually recaptured them in counterattacks supported by tanks. Every hour seemed endless, as the men of II/Panzergrenadier Regiment 4 repeatedly had to feign eager attempts to capture the town until Panzer Regiment 11 appeared in the Russian rear. The afternoon was consumed by the panzers bypassing a swamp east of the town and then assembling behind a range of hills for the decisive stroke. Accomplishing their assembly only one hour before sunset, the panzers stormed ahead in a wild chase, with their flanks echeloned forward. Innumerable tank turrets appeared in the steppe grass, and immediately thereafter our panzers rattled down the slope. Muzzle flashes and thundering bursts from numerous guns indicated the extent of the enemy's ruin. His efforts to throw his few tanks and defensive weapons against the new adversary (even long enough to keep open an escape route for the bulk of his troops) proved to be too late and in vain.

Following a short, unequal struggle, ten of the fourteen Russian tanks went up in flames. The columns of their fires and the blazes of Soviet strongpoints situated in burning houses colored the evening sky a deep crimson. A field of debris formed by demolished huts, weapons, and equipment buried the Russian garrison. Having executed their part to perfection, the tanks of Panzer Regiment 11 disappeared as quickly as they had arrived, leaving to continue their march north toward our main objective. Captain Kreis's infantrymen, who had witnessed this unequal battle from their dugouts, encountered scarcely any resistance when mopping up the town and were thus quickly reassembled to be made available for a new assignment. The few surviving Turkestani raiders became prisoners, with only four tanks and a few stragglers managing to fight their way free to the west. On the following morning [13 December], a flak battery disabled the last Soviet tanks from an ambush position on a hill north of the captured town, as they attempted to reach the lines of the defeated Fifty-first Army. Now every threat had been eliminated; the sideways thrust had proven a complete success in clearing 6th Panzer Division's left flank for the main offensive.

The "Revolving Battle"

Panzer Regiment 11 had every right to be proud of its achievements on 12 December. In a single day the panzer crews had won two battles while fighting their way forward nearly seventy kilometers without sustaining losses. This was recognized as a favorable prelude to the Stalingrad operation, but it was still far from a triumph. Our objective remained far distant, and everyone knew that hard battles remained. To Generals Hoth, Kirchner, and me the task of defeating the Soviet tank forces blocking the road to Stalingrad, given their great numerical superiority, seemed almost insoluble.

Behind the northern arm of the Aksay River lurked the Russian IV Mechanized and XIII Tank Corps, both of which were very ably led and stood ready to attack and destroy our relief forces as they crossed the river. These two corps had avoided the dissipation of their striking power by refusing to use the "golden bridge" offered at Kotelnikovo and by standing aloof from the fighting on 12 December. On the other hand, this corps had been dispersed over a large area and thus offered us the opportunity to gain local superiority each time we attacked and to defeat the army detail.

These thoughts gave rise to my decision to push forward throughout the night of 12 December across the northern branch of the Aksay into the hilly region surrounding Verkhniy-Kumskiy, concentrating my entire armored spearhead in order to defeat the enemy tanks wherever they might be found. Such a maneuver greatly exceeded the mission assigned to me by Generals

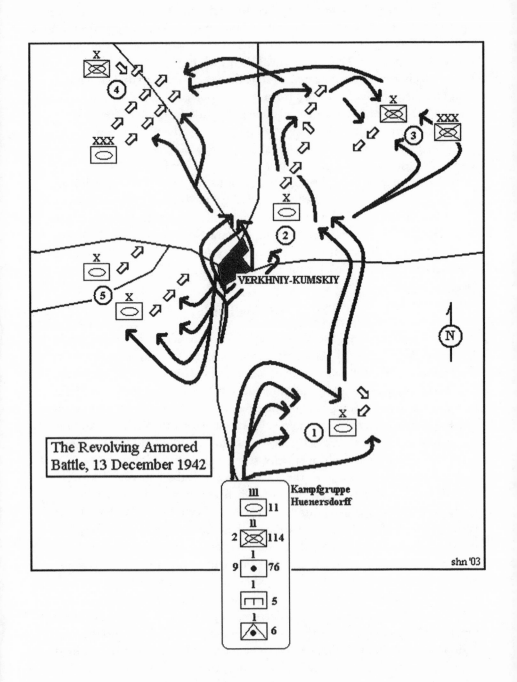

The Revolving Armored
Battle, 13 December 1942

VERKHNIY-KUMSKIY

N

Kampfgruppe
Huenersdorff

III		
	11	
11		
2		114
1		
9		76
1		
		5
1		
		6

shn '03

Hoth and Kirchner, who had ordered only that the 6th Panzer Division pursue the fleeing Russians as far as the Aksay to seize a bridgehead there. Yet the fact that the envisioned operation was dangerous and might lead to an unusual tactical situation was no reason for shrinking from its execution. After all, the objective I assigned Colonel von Huenersdorff was not the capture of a village or the defense of an area. On the contrary, his mission was to weaken the Soviets while keeping our own losses as small as possible and to continue to do this until our tanks outnumbered those of the enemy, making a decisive defeat possible. Accordingly, our tactics consisted of engaging various elements of the IV Mechanized and XIII Tank Corps separately, dispatching each one, eluding a defeat, and maintaining the initiative.

In view of the heavy demands made on our panzer crews during the successive battles of 12 December, I ordered a brief rest immediately after sunset, during which the panzer regiment refueled its tanks and received supplies. Soon afterward, in such complete darkness that only the pale light of the stars made it possible to identify—and then at close range—the dim outlines of tanks and their dark trails through the snow, Panzer Regiment 11 began rolling forward. The rattle of tank tracks suddenly echoed across the silent steppe, arousing the Russians, who were desperately trying to close the gap caused by our breakthrough north of Chilikovo. Since the enemy had lost his antitank weapons in the previous day's fight, our panzers could overrun his positions without any loss of time, leaving it to the panzergrenadier battalions following behind to come to grips with them. By the first light of dawn our panzer spearheads had reached the northern arm of the Aksay and begun seeking a crossing point. Eventually they discovered a ford at Saliyevsky, and crossed the river. Captain Remlinger's I Battalion, Panzergrenadier Regiment 4, followed up immediately and formed a bridgehead, while the engineers commenced construction of a bridge. Major Quentin's Panzer Reconnaissance Battalion 6 threw back the enemy security detachments north of Chilikovo and across the railroad. This action protected our right flank, since movement by Russian tanks and trucks had been observed on the southern bank of the Aksay River. Captain Hauschildt's I Battalion, Panzergrenadier Regiment 114, drove the Soviets from the rolling terrain west of Chilikovo and now occupied this region to ward off any attacks from the west.

As though they had been "fired from a rocket," Colonel von Huenersdorff's panzers spurted north. The thrust "hit the enemy in the heart," completely upsetting all of his plans. This, finally, was the real starting point in the dramatic struggle to relieve Stalingrad. Only by defeating an enemy of twice our strength would we be able to open a relief route to the Sixth Army. The commanders of the armored forces on both sides knew this and brought to bear all their strength, courage, and tactical abilities in a supreme effort to secure the victory. The result of this awareness of the significance of their actions was the armored "revolving battle" around Verkhniy-Kumskiy, in which 500 tanks engaged for ten continuous hours in a bitter struggle.

This "revolving battle" centered around the village of Verkhniy-Kumskiy, which the 6th Panzer Division reached first and held until the end, a factor that allowed *Kampfgruppe* Huenersdorff full freedom of action and the ability to exploit the advantage of always fighting on interior lines. As a result, at all times and in all places our troops and tanks arrived ahead of the enemy, to whom all passages leading through Verkhniy-Kumskiy remained blocked. We further enjoyed the advantage of having a far more flexible command system than the Russians, chiefly due to the fact that the radio equipment in our tanks was far more modern than theirs. On the other hand, the Soviets had at their disposal twice as many tanks, and all were models that were fully a match of our panzers. Moreover, the Russian tanks were followed by numerically superior infantry forces, though those troops arrived on the battlefield relatively late and after much of the issue had been decided.

The composition of *Kampfgruppe* von Huenersdorff included:

Headquarters, Panzer Regiment 11

I Battalion
Major Loewe

II Battalion
Major Dr. Baeke

II Battalion, Panzergrenadier Regiment 114
Captain Kueper

1st Company, Panzerjaeger Battalion 41
First Lieutenant Durban

1st Company, Panzer Engineer Battalion 57
First Lieutenant Roessner

III Battalion, Panzer Artillery Regiment 76
Lieutenant Colonel Graf

6th (Medium) Battery
First Lieutenant Neuhaus

8th (Heavy) Battery
Captain Hoelzer

9th (Heavy) Battery
First Lieutenant Plecher

The actual course of this battle turned out to be just as unusual as the situation from which it took its start. *Kampfgruppe* von Huenersdorff's immediate objective was Verkhniy-Kumskiy. The valley of the Aksay River was still veiled by ground fog, which even the first light of dawn could not penetrate. Tank after tank forded the river and rolled north, a column apparently without end. Fortunately, the country and cart roads between the river and the village were all passable both for track-laying and wheeled vehicles.

The first rays of the sun had finally managed to break through the haze just as the lead element in the column crested the hill immediately south of Verkhniy-Kumskiy. Before the eyes of our troops the steppe spread out in a deceptively peaceful appearance. Verkhniy-Kumskiy, whose outlines could now be clearly discerned, lay in the valley. Our light reconnaissance tanks had already reached the village and radioed back that it was clear of the enemy. At a rise in the ground identified as Point 140, which lay west of the route of advance, covering parties had already been posted and reported no contact with or sign of the enemy.

Suddenly, Colonel von Huenersdorff received an urgent message from armored reconnaissance elements on Hill 147, east of the line of march: "There is a heavy concentration of enemy tanks in a broad depression south of here. More tanks are arriving."

The situation was clear. Roused by the abrupt appearance of German tanks north of the Aksay, the Russians had responded by throwing their nearest available force directly against us. This was a Soviet tank brigade, whose mission was to push into our flank and tie us down while another tank brigade—approaching Verkhniy-Kumskiy from the north—would strike our flanks and rear as we turned to deal with the first threat. Even before the tank brigade near Hill 147 had completed its assembly, it attacked our flank with its available forces.

The Soviets, however, had seriously underestimated the striking power and flexibility of a German panzer regiment. No sooner had the Russian tanks reached the edge of the depression than the guns of the sixty panzers of Major Dr. Baeke's II Battalion, which Colonel von Huenersdorff had swiftly moved into position behind a low range of hills, suddenly opened fire. More than a dozen hostile tanks that had come into full view were set ablaze, and the others retreated back into the depression in order to escape a similar fate.

With Colonel von Huenersdorff riding beside him, Major Dr. Baeke pushed after them, forming his tanks into a wide ring around the depression and initiating a concentric attack. This ended with the complete encirclement of the Russian tank brigade, despite its best efforts to lunge both north and south to regain its freedom. Failing to escape, the enemy tanks

now formed an all-around defense within the extremely tight pocket and offered fierce resistance. Another attempt to break out toward the east proved
fruitless, as II Battalion's shells hit them from all sides and drove them back
into the pocket.

This unequal battle was soon over, with the result that a Russian tank
brigade perished heroically at the precise spot where, not an hour earlier, it
had triumphantly assembled for its attack. More than seventy Soviet tanks
remained on the field, their guns still turned menacingly toward all sides
against our panzers. Thus the first enemy attack had ended in a "tank graveyard," which continued to impress both friend and foe for a long time to
come. It would repeatedly be mistaken by both Soviet and German pilots as
an active tank assembly area and bombed by both sides. Many a soldier—either from the Wehrmacht or the Red Army—was terrified when he suddenly
came on this mass of silent tanks, and then—deeply moved when he realized
his error—raised his hand to salute.

The battle south of Hill 147 still raged when Colonel von Huenersdorff's
final armored elements began entering Verkhniy-Kumskiy, which was successfully occupied before the Russians arrived. Soon afterward, however,
Major Loewe's I Battalion found itself embroiled in combat with Russian
tanks hurrying to the scene in order to rescue the encircled tank brigade,
whose desperate calls for support they had received. As a result of this onslaught of Soviet tanks, Major Loewe had to pull his panzers back into the
northern edge of the village, which could be held against superior numbers
because he received a continual flow of reinforcements as the other elements
of the *Kampfgruppe* arrived in sequence. With I Battalion's tanks providing
cover, Captain Kueper's panzergrenadiers moved up, prepared their positions, and assumed responsibility for the defense of the village.

This meant that the panzer battalion was again available for more flexible
operations. Such operations were critical, as the Russians—in their attempt
to reach the dying tank brigade—had already tried to drive their tanks past
Verkhniy-Kumskiy on both sides. Maneuvering skillfully and constantly re-
distributing his forces, Major Loewe—though outnumbered—managed repeatedly to prevent the Soviets from enveloping them.

Suddenly, however, the situation became even more dangerous, as a third
enemy tank brigade joined the battle, pushing forward on our eastern flank
in an attempt to cut off the forces in Verkhniy-Kumskiy from Major Dr.
Baeke's II Battalion near Hill 147. Abruptly the din of battle near Hill 147
ceased; apparently the fight there had been decided. Yet the Russian tanks
did not withdraw. Was it possible that the enemy had somehow succeeded?

Just then Colonel von Huenersdorff radioed for Major Loewe to hold out:
He was rushing to the rescue with II Battalion. The hearts of the troops

leaped, because to them this message meant victory. Indeed, the familiar outlines of PzKw IIIs and PzKw IVs had already appeared on both sides of Hill 147, their numbers increasing as the soldiers looked on. At top speed four wedge formations of panzers raced down the slopes, even as more and more tanks crested the ridge.

The Russians became visibly uneasy. For quite some time no radio transmissions had arrived from their advance brigade around Hill 147, and now the German panzers suddenly poured down into the valley in large numbers. The Soviet tank crews realized that this meant a first defeat had already occurred, which threatened to be followed by a second one. This situation called for immediate action: No time could be lost. Officers and men—both German and Russian—understood this instantly, and as a result all radio messages were sent in clear. The Soviet tank brigade in front of Verkhniy-Kumskiy sent out repeated calls for help, to which it finally received an answer: "Mechanized brigade on the way. Hold out, hold out!"

Meanwhile the lead panzer wedges had already reached the valley, and from his observation point at Hill 147 Colonel von Huenersdorff could tell that they were following orders precisely. Every officer knew that speed was essential if a decision at Verkhniy-Kumskiy was to be forced before the arrival of the enemy mechanized brigade. Colonel von Huenersdorff's plan behind this attack, which consisted of a double envelopment of the Russian tanks while holding onto the village, began to materialize on the battlefield.

Almost as quickly, the Soviet commander recognized the German plan and tried in vain to increase the length of his front in order to escape the envelopment of his flanks. Again and again heavy fire—either from the panzers rushing down the hill or those in the village—prevented him from doing so. The first panzer wedges had already reached his flanks and began to compress his forces tighter and tighter. Still the enemy commander resisted tenaciously, trying to eliminate the threat to his flanks by bending them back. Our pressure, however, constantly increased, and as his flanks became more and more attenuated, his defensive ability weakened. What was the use of the promised reinforcement unless it arrived in time?

By this point some of Major Dr. Baeke's panzers had already appeared in the enemy's rear to block his last line of retreat, a deep, sunken road. But only a handful of tanks interdicted this road, and a breakthrough to the rear was still possible. The enemy commander knew that soon it would be too late: His losses were already very high, and further resistance might entail the complete destruction of his brigade. These considerations apparently induced him to order a withdrawal. He took advantage of his last chance to escape utter annihilation and broke contact with our forces. Sacrificing the covering parties on his flanks and his rear guard (the latter being overtaken and crushed by our left wing), the defeated remnants of the tank brigade made good their escape to the northeast via the sunken road.

A second tank bridge had been defeated, losing thirty-five to forty tanks, which meant it could no longer be considered a serious adversary. The remaining Russian tanks, however, might still regain a certain importance if they reinforced the mechanized brigade that was on the way. Hence Colonel von Huenersdorff knew that his victory was not a total one, though it did constitute another severe blow to the Soviets.

Soon the *Kampfgruppe* began intercepting a succession of radio messages from both east and west, whose increasing frequency seemed to presage a simultaneous, concentric attack by numerically superior Russian forces. These elements consisted of tank units and motorized infantry, to whom Verkhniy-Kumskiy had repeatedly been assigned as a critical objective to be reached and seized as soon as possible. Having penetrated twenty kilometers north of the Aksay in a single night, compromising the assembly area of a Russian tank corps and thrashing two tank brigades, *Kampfgruppe* von Huenersdorff represented a danger to be eliminated immediately.

Fortunately, Colonel von Huenersdorff was accustomed to thinking calmly in the heat of battle. Receiving aerial reconnaissance reports from the Luftwaffe that the strong Russian force approaching from the west was still nearly two hours' distant, he quickly decided to attack the mechanized brigade as it arrived from the northeast around noon.

First he attacked the armored elements of this brigade on the western flank, and when they had turned to meet his assault he pushed through a depression that shielded our panzers from view, and the main body of Panzer Regiment 11 slashed into the enemy's rear. In the resulting confusion, the motorized Soviet infantry following directly behind its tank vanguard withdrew across country to the northwest and escaped Colonel von Huenersdorff's attempt to "strangle" them. The Russian tanks, on the other hand, suffered heavy losses from the cross fire delivered by our numerically superior tanks, but they retired only after their heroic resistance had covered the withdrawal of their infantry. The other Soviet force, approaching from the northwest to assist the mechanized brigade, made contact with our reconnaissance screen, which delayed them until it was too late to intervene.

Soon afterward the approaching mechanized brigade veered to the northeast in order to attack *Kampfgruppe* von Huenersdorff from the rear. Unexpectedly, it abruptly ran up against a defensive front made up of well-protected panzers, which had been detached from the main body of Panzer Regiment 11 during the pursuit of the other mechanized brigade, ordered to pivot 180 degrees and take position to block any further Russian advances from the northeast. A bitter tank duel now ensued, in the which the Soviet tanks—having moved forward without cover—suffered considerable losses. The commander of this Russian brigade, however, used this sacrifice to swing his motorized infantry and some antitank guns around the panzer detachment's flank, taking our vehicles under fire from the rear. The situation quickly became critical, as there were reports of additional enemy tank forces arriving from the west. Even so, our tank crews bravely held their ground, having been assured by Colonel von Huenersdorff that he would come to their aid as quickly as possible with the majority of the tanks.

The main body of Panzer Regiment 11 now likewise pivoted 180 degrees, driving straight through Verkhniy-Kumskiy, where the lead Soviet tank spearheads had already engaged Captain Kueper's panzergrenadiers holding the village. Now also for the first time in the battle, Russian artillery entered the fight, firing into the village from the west. Lieutenant Plecher's battery of 150mm howitzers, committed to the defense of Verkhniy-Kumskiy, returned fire immediately and soon silenced the enemy guns. Individual Soviet tanks that had rashly ventured too close to the village had already been liquidated by Lieutenant Durban's 75mm antitank guns, even before the panzers arrived.

Colonel von Huenersdorff detached a few tanks from his main body to throw back the Russian advance guard with a quick thrust, while ordering the majority of the panzers to drive straight through the village. These slashed directly into the flank of the second Soviet mechanized brigade so quickly that the latter scarcely had time to form a new defensive front. Attacked on both sides of the road by two strong panzer wedges, while also under attack from our detachment to the north, the enemy found himself compelled to beat a hasty retreat, leaving more than thirty disabled tanks on the battlefield.

In the meantime, strong motorized Soviet forces, with their infantry dismounted, had approached Verkhniy-Kumskiy and taken it under fire with mortars, machine guns, and infantry guns. Under the protective fire of their heavy weapons, the Russian infantry filtered closer and closer to the village, which they soon hemmed in from both the north and east. Worse still, the Soviet tanks had resumed their attacks and were making rapid headway on the road from the west. A few hostile combat patrols had actually entered the village, though these had been destroyed in bitter fighting or driven out of the village.

The situation became critical when some T-34s broke into Vekhniy-Kumskiy and destroyed a number of howitzers and antitank guns before the close-assault antitank teams of Lieutenant Roessner's engineer company managed to liquidate them. This made Captain Kueper's predicament worse; radio messages were arriving from our reconnaissance tanks to the effect that strong enemy tank forces were now advancing on Point 140, southwest of the village. It was clearly the enemy commander's intention to occupy Verkhniy-Kumskiy and the hills to the south in order to cut off the *Kampfgruppe* from its route of retreat and destroy it. This attack represented the Russians' final, desperate attempt to offset the severe defeats they had already suffered with a decisive victory before the day drew to its close.

Kampfgruppe von Huenersdorff, after successfully defeating the second Russian mechanized brigade, now quickly turned 180 degrees yet again and sliced through the enemy's encirclement with a massed panzer assault. Without pausing, both battalions of Panzer Regiment 11 drove straight to Point 140, where they arrived simultaneously with the Soviet armor. Here the heaviest clash of the day occurred, as more and more Russian tanks ran up against the strong German front, but were stopped each time by our concerted fire. Even so, the enemy was unwilling to give up his attacks and now staked everything on a single card. Heavily concentrated and echeloned in depth, all of his tanks rolled forward like a huge wave, threatening to swallow up Panzer Regiment 11 in its entirety. This mass attack also failed, halted in the hail of fire from more than 100 German panzers.

Colonel von Huenersdorff had waited for this moment to play his final trump. Throughout the battle he had maintained an uncommitted armored reserve, which was now committed in a decisive counterattack. This surprise thrust into the Soviet flank caused their lines to waver almost instantly. Seeing this, Colonel von Huenersdorff ordered his main body forward in a general attack. Despite offering fierce resistance, the enemy finally broke and began flooding back. Countless armored wrecks covered the landscape of this climactic engagement, serving as eloquent testimony to the proportions of the Russian defeat.

Captain Kueper and the brave defenders of Verkhniy-Kumskiy had meanwhile been encircled again and were in a distressing situation, with enemy forces attacking from all sides. More heavy weapons had become disabled, and ammunition grew scarce. So far the courageous panzergrenadiers and engineers had still managed to finish off every penetrating Russian tank with magnetic antitank hollow charges, but it seemed that as each tank was destroyed another appeared in its place. Nevertheless, the German troops did not yield a single inch of ground to the motorized Soviet infantry. Captain Kueper's increasingly desperate calls for help did not escape Colonel von Huenersdorff's attention, even though he was engaged in a heavy battle near Point 140. No sooner had the main body of the Russian armor been routed than the tanks of Panzer Regiment 11 reversed course again to rescue their comrades. For the second time that day, massed German tanks broke through the encirclement and saved Verkhniy-Kumskiy.

Afterward, the battered but undefeated garrison was escorted on both sides by the weapons and vehicles of Panzer Regiment 11 as all of *Kampf-gruppe* von Huenersdorff moved together toward the bridgehead at Saliyevsky. On the hills south of the village, remnants of the Russian forces attempted to block the *Kampfgruppe*'s progress, but our panzers quickly opened up an exit toward the south and formed a rear guard to prevent the enemy from harassing the movement any further.

The 6th Panzer Division's unexpected thrust across the Aksay River had induced both sides to dispatch strong elements of combat aircraft to the scene. First, Russian bomber wings and fighters had hastened to the aid of their distressed tank units. These circled over the battlefield at progressively lower altitudes in order to identify their targets clearly. This expedient failed, as the rapidly changing picture of the battle made it practically impossible to distinguish friend from foe. The same thing happened to the Luftwaffe. Both the German and Russian pilots finally found themselves obliged to attack less rewarding targets, of which many were to be found on supply roads and on the open steppe. There the bombs fell in large numbers, causing both Red Army and Wehrmacht officers great concern for their vehicles. Actually, these aerial attacks were not half as destructive as they seemed, because by this point the convoy commanders on both sides had learned to leave great distances between their vehicles, and as a result losses were very limited.

Despite the problem of target identification, the raging armored battle continuously tempted the combat aircraft of both sides to participate directly, but as their respective strengths over the battlefield kept increasing, their attacks on each other became more and more vehement. By noon the fighting had developed into a truly three-dimensional "revolving battle," involving both ground and air forces. Russian bomber wings had superiority of numbers, but the Luftwaffe's fighters repeatedly inflicted severe losses on them and eventually repulsed them completely. On the ground and in the air, the same strength ratio prevailed, and surprisingly similar tactics were employed. As the course of both "revolving battles" reflected each other, so did their results: The Germans were victorious.

Night was already falling as the last planes disappeared and Colonel von Huenersdorff's lead tank was sighted by the garrison of the Saliyevsky bridgehead. This bridgehead had also repulsed two enemy attacks during the course of the day, thus frustrating the Russian attempt to isolate the *Kampf-gruppe* while it was engaged around Verkhniy-Kumskiy. A third attack was just in progress as Panzer Regiment 11 arrived, and for the first few moments the defenders feared that the approaching tanks represented enemy reinforcements. Had such been the case, the bridgehead would have been lost. Instead, our panzers made their final attack of the day, striking the rear of the

Russian tank brigade that was hammering violently at the bridgehead. In the growing darkness, our forces managed not only to thwart the Soviet plan but also to incapacitate several more fleeing Russian tanks.

The unique armored "revolving battle" was finally over, its end as unusual as its beginning. To the Russians' great surprise, 6th Panzer Division's tanks withdrew to the Aksay River despite the successes they had achieved. Heavily battered, the enemy did not dare pursue them or launch a counterattack of his own during the following days, remaining content to occupy the hills south of Verkhniy-Kumskiy with motorized infantry. Later we discovered that the Soviets had lost more than half of their available armor in this heavy struggle, which constituted the reason for their reluctance to attack again. Moreover, Russian commanders could not find a plausible explanation for our voluntary withdrawal to the Aksay and regarded it as a feint designed to lure them into a trap. In reality, the shortage of fuel and ammunition, as well as the situation of the main body of 6th Panzer Division, made it impossible for me to allow Panzer Regiment 11 to remain north of the Aksay. Furthermore, the main purpose of this unusual thrust had already been achieved: The "revolving battle" had broken the enemy's armored backbone and won us—at least temporarily—numerical superiority in tanks.

A Bridgehead as a Tank Trap

In order to shield 6th Panzer Division's long line of communications from the Aksay River back to the Kotelnikovo area, Captain Remlinger's I Battalion, Panzergrenadier Regiment 4, had formed its bridgehead on both banks of the river. The two remaining companies of Major Wolff's Panzer Engineer Battalion 57 (under First Lieutenant Prinz and Captain Andersch) had begun the construction of a bridge that would allow the passage even of tanks, which they completed within a few hours. Upon the bridge's completion, Major Wolff's engineers, with the Panzerjaeger *Lehr* [Training] Battalion (which had been attached to the division by LVI Panzer Corps), assumed the task of securing the northern bridgehead. This freed Captain Remlinger's battalion, reinforced by an antitank platoon, to concentrate its entire force on the southern bank.

As a result of 6th Panzer Division's highly unusual deployment, the southern bridgehead actually represented the most vulnerable sector. North of the Aksay most nearby Russian forces had been tied down in the "revolving battle" around Verkhniy-Kumskiy. To the south, on the other hand, it had become necessary to detach Captain Hauschildt's I Battalion, Panzergrenadier Regiment 114, to support the 23rd Panzer Division, and to disperse the remaining combat units throughout the various sectors. There each element became involved in fighting the remnants of the Soviet Fifty-first Army that had been defeated the previous day. These enemy elements still controlled much of the region south of the Aksay River.

On the morning of 13 December, Russian infantry escorted by a few tanks appeared at the western flank of the southern bridgehead. This unit assembled along the lower course of a deep, dried-out riverbed, which, lined by tall shrubbery, stretched for several kilometers alongside our main supply route, and which we lacked the troops to secure. Since the Soviet tanks were unable to cross the riverbed (which was three to four meters deep and five to ten meters wide), they fired through the gaps in the shrubbery at our truck convoys moving toward Saliyevsky. This situation forced us to detour all supply traffic around to reach the bridgehead from the east.

After the Russians failed to halt the movement of our supplies with this tactic, they attacked the bridgehead directly about noon with two infantry battalions that crossed the dried-out riverbed, supported by the fire of their tanks from the far bank. Lively fire from Captain Remlinger's grenadiers quickly stopped this attack, and a prompt counterattack threw the Russians back across the riverbed. In the afternoon the enemy repeated this effort, this time gaining the eastern bank of the dried-out riverbed. To the immense surprise of the German defenders, eight or ten tanks suddenly advanced out of the riverbed, having been moved across through the use of field expedients. Although these tanks met heavy fire from all weapons and sustained immediate losses, they nonetheless overran the front line of our infantry and pushed over the Aksay bridge into the village. Fortunately, the intense fire from our troops forced the accompanying Russian infantry to take cover, thus separating them from their tanks. Soon afterward the sound of heavy detonations could be heard from Saliyevsky: The tanks fell silent, with six columns of smoke and fire providing clues to their fate. Not a single Russian tank managed to escape; the Panzerjaeger *Lehr* Battalion had done its job.

A third Soviet attempt occurred at twilight, with this assault on Saliyevsky being supported by armor from north of the river. This was the unit that had the misfortune to clash with *Kampfgruppe* von Huenersdorff as it was returning from the "revolving battle" at Verkhniy-Kumskiy. As narrated above, this fight ended with the loss of several more Russian tanks as the remainder fled to avoid destruction.

Regardless of these repulses, the Russians attacked the southern bridgehead three more times with newly arrived tank and infantry forces—twice on 14 December and once on 15 December. Each time, our panzergrenadiers in their narrow trenches and deep dugouts were overrun by the tanks without suffering the slightest injury. As veteran Eastern Front campaigners, they had long since become immune to the shock effect of advancing enemy tanks. As soon as the black monsters trundled past, the heads of the German infantrymen reappeared, directing devastating machine-gun fire across the open battlefield. This suppressive fire threw the Russian troops following in the wake of the tanks back to their line of departure or forced them to remain motionless in shallow depressions in the sand until nightfall. Both courses of action involved heavy enemy casualties. The few Soviet detachments that successfully braved our fire, by following closely behind individual tanks, reached our defensive positions, and even crossed them, but were liquidated in close-quarters fighting or taken prisoner.

Out of nearly a dozen enemy tanks that penetrated into Saliyevsky during each attack, not a single machine survived to return to its line of departure. The village street was blocked by the burned-out wrecks of their predecessors, requiring them to enter the village from the side, through narrow gaps between groups of houses. Wherever such a gap was wide enough to admit tanks, Major Wolff had systematically deployed his tank destruction elements. Hidden in houses or camouflaged in holes over which the Russian tank crews drove unsuspectingly, they awaited the approach of their victims and—at the proper moment—attacked with magnetic anti-tank hollow charges. A thunderous blast, usually followed by a jet of flame, usually signalled the abrupt end of each tank and its crew. Even if one or the other of the tanks managed to escape these tank destruction teams and continue its advance, it was all the more certain to fall into the hands of the next team. As a final precaution, Major Wolff had emplaced a few well-camouflaged antitank and flak guns, as well as laying mines, to provide them with a warm reception. These guns also covered the northern approaches to Saliyevsky and gave a proper sendoff to any vehicle attempting to flee in that direction.

In this manner Major Wolff and Captain Remlinger turned the Saliyevsky bridgehead into an organized tank trap that twenty Soviet tanks entered without a single one surviving to leave. The mysterious tank destruction teams became the terror of all Russian tank crews, who had developed the habit of driving their tanks singly or in small groups through villages, forests, or shrubbery to avoid German antitank guns, flak, and combat aircraft. The measure of the achievements of the men in the tank destruction teams appears alone from the fact that 15 percent of all Soviet tanks incapacitated during 6th Panzer Division's thrust for the liberation of Stalingrad were credited to them. Their most brilliant achievement, however, consisted of the three-day struggle to keep open the division line of communications through Saliyevsky.

Two Panzer Regiments Lunge into the Void

During the struggle for Saliyevsky on 14–15 December, *Kampfgruppe* von Huenersdorff had been deliberately spared. After the heavy panzer battle of 13 December, the tanks of Panzer Regiment 11 required a brief reconditioning, which they underwent in the Klykhov area on the northern bank of the Aksay. I also moved the division command post to that point. By 16 December all minor damage to the tanks had been repaired, returning to service twenty-two of the thirty vehicles incapacitated at Verkhniy-Kumskiy. Forty-two assault guns, under the command of Major Koch, had recently arrived to increase Colonel von Huenersdorff's strength for the impending decisive offensive.

On 16 December I planned a concentrated attack with all available forces against the Russian IV Mechanized Corps, which had now established itself in the rolling hills south of Verkhniy-Kumskiy. Higher headquarters forbid such an attack. Instead, General Hoth issued orders for an armored thrust to be undertaken by the combined panzer regiments of the 6th and 23rd Panzer Divisions. He envisioned a flank attack that started at the southern enemy flank to roll up the length of the Russian forces along a twelve-kilometer range of hills. Once again, therefore, endless columns of tanks, pouring out from Klykhov, climbed the gentle slopes of the Aksay Valley, rumbling toward the scene of such fierce fighting three days earlier. This mission, however, was quite different from the assignment given to Colonel von Huenersdorff that day.

Panzer Regiments 11 and 201 had the mission to sweep away the hostile motorized infantry forces that had established themselves in the hills after the close of the "revolving battle." These elements had so far remained completely inactive, and it seemed an easy task to overrun the Russian infantrymen who had dug in like field mice and drive them off the hills. The second part of the mission, which consisted of seizing and holding this extended range of hills, appeared somewhat more difficult to experienced panzer officers, who knew from the outset that Captain Kueper's II Battalion, Panzergrenadier Regiment 114, was far from sufficient for this task. His grenadiers could, at most, occupy a few strongpoints, leaving the gaps between them to be secured entirely through the flexible deployment of our tanks.

To achieve this end, it would have been necessary for Colonel von Huenersdorff to divide his reinforced *Kampfgruppe* into several subunits and keep these behind each gap in order to have a force immediately available to counterattack enemy penetrations. This represented a daunting assignment, for if the Russians even once succeeded in infiltrating through the tall steppe grass without being observed, it would prove impossible to find them. Hence it was understandable that the tank crews were uneasy, though they held out the hope that their appearance would induce the Soviet tank forces to engage them again in open battle. If that happened, our troops had confidence that they would achieve a great victory.

In reality, the course of events occurred much differently from what either General Hoth or our tank crews anticipated. The well-camouflaged Russian infantry, which was situated in groups of two to four men in a system of deep foxholes and narrow trenches, allowed itself to be overrun by the two panzer regiments. Then, using their innumerable antitank rifles, each of which could be operated by a single soldier, they opened fire at close range against the more lightly armored vehicles of Captain Kueper's battalion, inflicting heavy losses. Over and over again it became necessary for the tanks to wait or even turn back and assist as the panzergrenadiers had to deploy to locate and identify an invisible enemy in combat on foot. The various enemy nests proved so well hidden in the steppe grass (which was brown like Red Army uniforms) that the only way to find them was actually to stumble across them. Usually, some unlucky German soldier had been killed by a bullet before a nest was identified. Even the Luftwaffe proved unable to deal with this "invisible ghost." Never before had our tank crews felt so powerless, although they would have been able to stand their ground against the strongest Russian tank attack. The Soviet armored forces, however, had become far too cautious to run the risk of another defeat.

By early afternoon Colonel von Huenersdorff reported that he had reached his objective but could not eliminate "this invisible enemy," and I ordered him to return to his line of departure. The lunge into the void had brought us losses, but no success. Worse, we had lost a precious day.

Two Infantry Battalions Outdo Two Panzer Regiments

On 17 December I was given a free hand to attack in the manner I had proposed the previous day. Dismounted panzergrenadiers and the motorcycle infantry of Panzer Reconnaissance Battalion 6, not tanks, were to achieve a decision this time. Major Quentin's motorcyclists and Captain Hauschildt's I Battalion, Panzergrenadier Regiment 114, assembled for the attack in extended order in the Saliyevsky bridgehead. In the rear—somewhat to the right—around Klykhov and concealed in a depression, Panzer Regiment 11 [was ordered to] assemble. This reserve force remained at my personal disposal. All of these movements were carried out at night and completed well before dawn.

At sunrise the seasoned combat patrols of Panzer Reconnaissance Battalion 6 advanced through a gully covered by tall grass and worked their way close to the first objective: a Russian artillery observation post on Hill 140, which commanded a view of the entire area. All of Major Quentin's troops had camouflaged themselves and their weapons to such an extent as to be almost indiscernible, even while moving.

I planned initially to paralyze this main observation post (which was situated on a "projecting point" in the hills), then to penetrate the center of the Russian defenses and expand that breach on both sides. Once a broad enough corridor had been opened, the division's main body would advance on Verkhniy-Kumskiy and capture this bastion. Panzer Artillery Regiment 76 received the mission of supporting the infantry's infiltration by concentrating the fire of all guns on the penetration point, then supporting the assault to roll up the Russian position, and—finally—of breaking up hostile counterattacks. Our heavy 150mm howitzers, in cooperation with the Luftwaffe's dive-bombers, were to smash Soviet artillery wherever it could be detected and bombard potential tank concentrations. Engineer assault detachments, as well as flamethrower and mine-clearing teams, had been attached to the attacking infantry companies. The panzers stood by for the opportunity to pursue a defeated enemy or to engage any Soviet tank forces that might appear during the attack. Finally, both battalions of Panzergrenadier Regiment 4 remained in reserve, ready for commitment as needed.

Aerial reconnaissance was active on both sides, but nothing stirred on the ground. The Russian positions appeared virtually unoccupied. No shot was fired. Owing to their excellent camouflage, even the assembling German assault troops revealed no indications of an impending battle.

At 0800, like a thunderstorm from a clear sky, all of Colonel Grundherr's guns suddenly starting firing as fast as they could. A hail of shells targeted the Russian observation post and smashed it to pieces. Smoke from burning steppe grass and reddish clouds of dust deprived the enemy of all visibility as the first assault detachments advanced. A few minutes later, light signals sent by the leading detachments revealed that they had captured the observation post and penetrated the enemy position. Immediately the artillery shifted its fire, and the most difficult job of the assault detachments began. The first German dive-bombers appeared on the horizon and approached their targets with majestic calmness. The lead aircraft turned its nose toward the ground and swooped down on a Russian battery that it had identified, followed by the remaining planes of the squadron. Just as it seemed that the planes must crash into the ground, bombs were released at the very last moment and the aircraft shot up again. Tremendous detonations caused the surroundings to quiver, and huge mushroom clouds of smoke shot into the air. Where enemy guns had been emplaced a minute ago, ten-meter-deep craters now gaped. The dive-bombers assembled, assumed a wedge formation, and flew off again. They had not yet completely disappeared from sight when the next squadron appeared and continued the work of destruction. In sequence additional squadrons followed, until the Soviet artillery fell completely silent.

Balls of smoke, immediately followed by the booming of the flak guns, announced the arrival of a Soviet bombardment wing. Before it reached the battlefield, there was a furious air battle between its fighter escort and the Luftwaffe's Messerschmitts, during which three blazing Russian Ratas were downed so quickly that the column of smoke from the first still hung in the air when the second and third met their fate. Then the six Luftwaffe fighters pounced upon the enemy bombers, downing several of them, which exploded in tall columns of flame immediately after hitting the ground. The others turned around and disappeared, and for some time the air was clear of enemy aircraft. Then similar scenes recurred over and over again.

Unconcerned about the events taking place in the sky, our assault detachments advanced step by step on both sides of the original penetration. Machine-gun crews and snipers kept their eyes on the enemy: Every Red Army soldier who showed himself was hit by a well-aimed shot, every Russian patrol crawling forward found itself hit by rapid bursts of machine-gun or submachine-gun fire. If rounds were fired from a nearby foxhole, a volley of hand grenades was the response. The enemy's weapons began to fall silent.

The flamethrower teams of the engineers smoked out a number of bunkers. Flames and smoke, visible from afar, indicated the location of such activities, and even the most stubborn pockets of resistance could not endure these "infernal fireworks." At some spots the effect of the gunfire was heightened by the burning steppe grass, which drove the Soviets from their hideouts. The snow, however, prevented the steppe fires from attaining larger proportions. Fire for direction from signal pistols pointed out particularly annoying targets to the artillery and mortars. The forward observers immediately directed the fire of their batteries to each spot. The amazing accuracy of our artillery fire greatly assisted the infantry's steady advance.

It was not the fascinating spectacle of a panzer battle that presented itself to the eyes of the spectators, but the laborious and arduous small-scale operations of assault detachments and individual infantrymen. More and more small groups appeared along the crest of the hill, and the din of battle continually moved forward along both sides of it. By noon, Major Quentin's motorcycle troops had cleared the Russians from their assigned sector, and an hour later I Battalion, Panzergrenadier Regiment 114, reported the same from its sector. A three-kilometer-wide breach had been opened through the center of the Soviet defenses.

I gave the order for our reserves to assemble for their attack on Vekhniy-Kumskiy. Scouts reported that the village and the hills immediately to the north of it had been occupied by strong enemy forces. Upon approaching the village these patrols had received fire from all directions. Reconnaissance aircraft identified numerous antitank guns and entrenched tanks on the edge of the village and in camouflaged positions on the hills, as well as groups of Russian tanks moving from the west toward Verkhniy-Kumskiy.

I had no intention of sending two panzer regiments to certain doom. Nor would our panzergrenadiers, descending completely exposed hill slopes devoid of any cover, have been able to survive the destructive enemy fire. Heavy losses without commensurate gain would have been the result, and these would have certainly jeopardized the entire attack toward Stalingrad. For this reason—and despite General Hoth's objections—I ordered the attack halted until after nightfall. Our infantrymen, who had been well trained for night combat, would have to go it alone.

During the course of the afternoon the Russian heavy weapons that could be identified in the village outskirts and surrounding terrain were shelled by Colonel Grundherr's artillery, operating with both air and ground observation reports. I requested additional support from the dive-bombers, which arrived again and pounded Soviet tank concentrations, the entrenched tanks, and the antitank positions until the sun set. Misled by the "tank graveyards" left by the previous battles for Verkhniy-Kumskiy, the first squadrons dropped their heavy bombs on these instead of the well-camouflaged enemy tanks. The following squadrons, alerted to this mistake, attacked the real Soviet tanks. The flames of burning vehicles confirmed the good results achieved during these air attacks.

After nightfall the panzergrenadiers and motorcycle infantry attacked as planned. Preceded by assault detachments, they noiselessly advanced along guiding lines that had been determined by observers during the daylight, with the smoldering ruins of burned houses providing just enough light to facilitate orientation. The movements and the calls of the Russian soldiers showed clearly that they did not expect a night attack. Like specters, the assault detachments crept up to the edge of the village, observing the distribution of rations and the unconcerned activity there. The moment was ripe for a surprise attack, and from three sides our troops stormed forward, cheering as they entered the village. The surprised Russians were gripped by panic and tried to escape. Our assault elements took numerous prisoners and hurled the remainder of the enemy garrison back to the hills. Russian tanks in the village turned north in order to escape the tank destruction teams heading toward them. Several remained stuck in the confusion of fleeing men and vehicles and were blasted. Al the antitank guns and damaged tanks, along with a great deal of heavy equipment, fell into our hands.

The key position of Verkhniy-Kumskiy had been captured, almost without sustaining any losses. Thus the intensive training of our infantry in night combat and tank destruction yielded excellent results. Two infantry battalions had gained the victory that had been denied two panzer regiments on the previous day.

To the Mishkova River

After the capture of Verkhniy-Kumskiy, the main body of 6th Panzer Division, with Panzer Regiment 11 in the lead, received the mission of pursuing the defeated Russian IV Mechanized Corps, pushing through it, and—in a speedy advance—reaching the Sixth Army at Stalingrad. Yet no sooner had our tanks passed through the village on their way north than orders from higher headquarters required me to bring them back and face them eastward in the valley. Our task had abruptly been changed, and 6th Panzer Division was to commit its main force to assist the adjacent 23rd Panzer Division, which was under attack by a newly arrived I Guards Rifle Corps that—with tank support—was pressing it back across the Aksay River.

One after another the combat units of 6th Panzer Division moved rapidly in that direction along good roads. The mission of pursuing the Russian forces defeated at Verkhniy-Kumskiy had to be turned over to Major General Frido von Senger und Etterlin's 17th Panzer Division, which had arrived on the battlefield in weak combat strength on the previous evening. This fatigued division had just completed an overland march of 1,000 kilometers from the Orel area.

Early in the afternoon of 18 December, twelve kilometers east of Verkhniy-Kumskiy, Panzer Regiment 11 encountered an enemy antitank front consisting of approximately twenty antitank guns, which the I Guards Rifle Corps had emplaced on both sides of the approach route to protect its western flank. Without hesitation, Colonel von Huenersdorff ordered his tanks to envelop the Soviet guns from three sides and pour such a hail of shells on them that the entire antitank unit was smashed in a few minutes, with not a single man, horse, gun, or vehicle surviving this storm of steel. Hardly pausing, 6th Panzer Division rolled on. When the lead tanks appeared, the I Guards Rifle Corps instantly discontinued its attack at the Aksay River and retreated east. Supply columns, seized with panic, fled to the rear. Uncoded distress calls telling all units to rally east of the railroad as quickly as possible were transmitted by all the radios in the Soviet corps. The corps commander himself was on the scene, urging his men on.

Freed from its distress, the 23rd Panzer division immediately recrossed the Aksay. Both General Hans von Boineburg-Lengsfeld and I were tempted to initiate a joint attack on the confused enemy corps to inflict a crushing defeat on it, but the overall strategic situation made it mandatory to pass up such a project in order to reach Stalingrad before it was too late. I immediately ordered Panzer Regiment 11 to break off its pursuit and turn north again. Without having sustained any losses, Colonel von Huenersdorff—followed by the main body of the division—drove toward the Mishkova River during the night of 18–19 December. This was the area in which we had originally planned to meet the Sixth Army when it broke out of Stalingrad. En route Panzer Regiment 11 encountered only weak resistance, which it broke very quickly. The problem of navigating across the pitch-black, monotonous steppe proved to be a much greater difficulty. Snow covered the few existing tracks, and only with the aid of compasses and maps was it possible to keep moving toward the objective. At a few points, dried-out riverbeds and isolated marshy sections caused extensive delays, since it became necessary to reconnoiter detours. It was a difficult night march.

Only at dawn on 19 December did our panzer spearhead reach the Mishkova River, which was now protected by strong enemy forces. A daring surprise advance by our lead tanks brought the only bridge and the center of the village of Bolshaya-Vasilevka into our hands. All efforts made by the Russians to eliminate this small bridgehead before the division's main body could reinforce it were futile.

About noon, Panzer Artillery Regiment 76 had moved into position, and I committed both panzergrenadier regiments—supported by artillery and tanks—in an attack to expand the bridgehead. Colonel Unrein's Panzergrenadier Regiment 4 attacked toward the east, while Colonel Zollenkopf's Panzergrenadier Regiment 114 cleared the western half of the village. Our grenadiers captured the entire village (which was two kilometers long) only after bitter house-to-house fighting.

The Soviet command realized the magnitude of the danger threatening the ring around Stalingrad from the south and hurriedly moved all available units to the scene in order to destroy Fourth Panzer Army's spearhead. The Russian tank corps no longer possessed the strength to accomplish such a mission, having suffered so heavily over the past week that it ceased to constitute a serious threat. Hence the Russians resorted to their time-honored practice of trying to smash the Bolshaya-Vasilevka bridgehead by means of concentrated artillery and rocket fire, and then to "wash it away" with massed infantry attacks. The Second Guards Army, which had been detached from the troops besieging Stalingrad, had been reinforced by reserves from the eastern bank of the Volga River and now assembled in the northern hills and in the valley east of Bolshaya-Vasilevka for an all-out assault on 6th Panzer Division.

Thousands of Red Army soldiers filled the snowfields, slopes, and depressions on the endless steppes. No German soldier had ever seen such multitudes advance on him. The leading ranks were thrown to the ground by a hail of high-explosive shells, but more and more waves followed. Every attempt on the part of the Russian masses to reach our lines was thwarted by the fire of machine guns, artillery, and heavy weapons. The frontal assault had been halted in its tracks.

A few hours later, the Russians poured into Bolshaya-Vasilevka from the east, like a stream of lava, pushing Panzergrenadier Regiment 4's flank back some 100 meters. Shortly thereafter they pushed through the gap to the 23rd Panzer Division and rolled forward toward the rear of our troops in the bridgehead. We lost the eastern half of the village and the area around the cemetery, but the main defensive positions of 6th Panzer Division stood unshaken, like a rock in the surging sea. Just when the encirclement appeared about to close, a sudden concentration from all of Colonel Grundherr's guns mowed down the Russian infantry. Even as the shells exploded, the 150 tanks of Panzer Regiment 11 surged out of the village at the same moment that Major Koch's forty-two StG III assault guns hit them in the rear. Overwhelmed, even the strongest nerves of the enemy were unequal to this eruption of fire and steel. Russian soldiers threw down their weapons and tried like madmen to escape the infernal cross fire and the deadly armored envelopment. Then occurred something very rare throughout the course of World War II: In mobs of several hundreds, even while being shelled by their own artillery and rocket launchers, Red Army soldiers ran west toward the only open spot in the vicinity and surrendered to our covering parties stationed there.

The battle raged on, but the climax had passed, the crisis had been weathered. The threatening masses on the flank and in our rear had either been smashed or taken prisoner. Even the Soviet combat method of last resort—the mass attack—which had so often yielded good results, had failed this time. The 6th Panzer Division's defensive battle on the Mishkova River had been crowned by an important victory.

Prepared for the Final Thrust

On 23 December, Colonel Unrein's Panzergrenadier Regiment 4, again with artillery and tank support, undertook a counterattack, recaptured the eastern section of Bolshaya-Vasilevka, and reoccupied the cemetery south of the river that the Russians had previously seized. This last operation completely restored the situation that had existed on 20 December. Much more important, however, was the fact that now both the Soviet tanks and masses of infantry had been overcome, so that no insuperable obstacle remained between the liberators and Stalingrad. The initiative had now passed into German hands, and the troops awaited the long-hoped-for breakout attack by Sixth Army. Such an attack could be facilitated only by the defeat of substantial elements from the encircling forces on the Mishkova River. That the order for the breakout to commence had not been given immediately after our victory at Bolshaya-Vasilevka seemed incomprehensible to everyone.

Orders issued by General Hoth's headquarters on 23 December finally seemed to remove all doubt. These orders provided for a thrust of thirty-three kilometers, to be undertaken by the combined armored elements of all three divisions of LVII Panzer Corps on the morning of Christmas Eve. This column was to approach the encircled city as closely as possible, in order to link up with Sixth Army, which apparently was no longer in condition to fight its way free. The panzer *Kampfgruppe* would provide an armored escort to cover the withdrawal of the Stalingrad troops to the Mishkova River, where the main bodies of the 6th, 17th, and 23rd Panzer Divisions would cover their crossing. This represented an unusual mission, to say the least, but in view of the Soviet defeat on the Mishkova its success appeared possible if not assured. Since the railroad line had long since been extended back up to the Aksay River, and since, in addition, several thousand trucks were available to us, the problem of supplying and evacuating these troops did not seem insoluble. We likewise assumed that the soldiers of Sixth Army, who had been encircled for only a month, would muster the strength necessary for a march behind the Mishkova if their freedom and lives were at stake.

All preparations for this final thrust to decide the fate of Stalingrad were quickly made. The *Kampfgruppe*, which consisted of 120 panzers, forty StG III assault guns, twenty-four SdKfz 233 reconnaissance cars, one panzer-grenadier battalion mounted in APCs, one motorcycle company, one engineer company, and one panzer artillery battalion, was ready for the final lunge on the afternoon of 23 December, when without warning a counterorder called for 6th Panzer Division to be pulled out immediately. We were to cross the Don River bridge at Potemkinskaya during the night of 23 December and reach Morosovskaya if a forced march.

Right down to the most junior soldier it was absolutely clear that this signified defeat at Stalingrad. The remaining two panzer divisions of the LVII Panzer Corps, the 17th and 23rd, were not even sufficient to make a stand against the Russian forces on the Mishkova, let alone repulse them. Although nobody yet knew the reasons behind the order, officers and men had a strong inkling that something ugly must have happened.

By dawn of 24 December the 6th Panzer Division, in a march column 130 kilometers long, rolled over the blood-drenched steppes, on which it had fought so successfully, toward an uncertain future.

Chapter 8

KHARKOV AND KURSK

Defense and Recovery

BY 23 NOVEMBER 1942, THE RED ARMY had closed the ring around Stalingrad and started the most powerful winter offensive of the war. Advancing rapidly, the Russians annihilated in quick succession the Rumanian, Italian, and Hungarian armies along the Chir and Don Rivers, opening a 560-kilometer gap in the German front. This breach equaled the length of the entire Western Front in World War I. Initially, only isolated German divisions, committed in support of the allied and satellite forces, stood in the way of the Russians, like the stays of a corset. The bulk of German reserves—including five fully equipped panzer divisions—remained tied down in Western Europe because of the Allied invasion of North Africa, although some of these divisions later appeared on the Eastern Front. Army Group A, in the Caucasus, found itself in danger of being cut off, forcing an immediate withdrawal. The army group's motorized units (mainly First Panzer Army) redeployed along the Donets River in order to strengthen the southern wing of Army Group Don. North of the gap, Second Army had been forced to evacuate Voronezh and the Don front, with its southern wing being pushed far back to the west. Gradually, two-thirds of the entire Russian front began to sway and crumble. As Soviet pressure mounted constantly, the only solution was to withdraw farther and farther to the west.

In the wake of this impending disaster, the staff of XI Corps, which had been lost at Stalingrad, was reconstituted from an unassigned corps staff that was hastily organized in the beginning of February 1943. Formed in the area north of Kharkov, it originally consisted of Lieutenant General Hans Cramer and several general staff officers who happened to be in this area on an inspection trip. The staff had to assume command over the 168th, 298th, and 320th Infantry Divisions, which had all been committed to cover sectors formerly held by Hungarian and Rumanian forces. These divisions lacked a

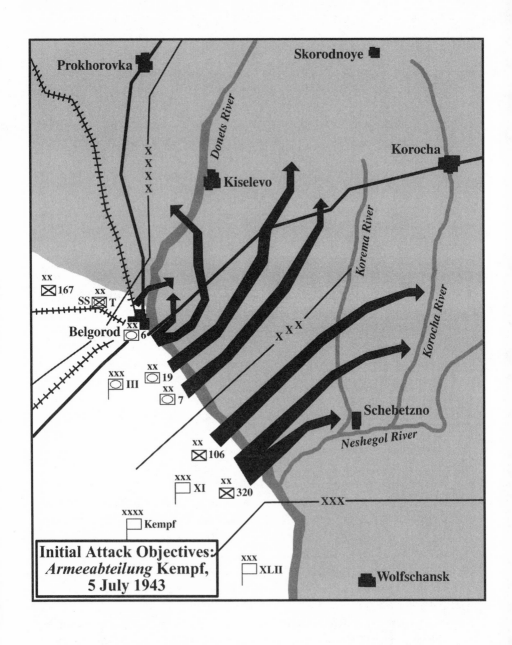

Prokhorovka

Skorodnoye

Donets River

Korocha

X
X
X
X

Kiselevo

Korema River

Korocha River

xx
⊠ 167

xx
SS ⊠ T

xx
Belgorod ⊘ 6

X X X

xxx
⊘ III

xx
⊘ 19

xx
⊘ 7

Schebetzno

Neshegol River

xx
⊠ 106

xxx
☐ XI

xx
⊠ 320

XXX

xxxx
☐ Kempf

Initial Attack Objectives:
Armeeabteilung Kempf,
5 July 1943

xxx
☐ XLII

Wolfschansk

higher headquarters after the collapse of Germany's allies on the Stalingrad front. The lower echelons of the staff were picked from the field units, and a Hungarian signal battalion (later replaced by a small German unit) took care of signal communications. The initial difficulties were being gradually overcome when I took command on 10 February, though it took six months and required numerous reassignments and organizational changes to transform the improvised corps staff into a regular one. Both the XI Corps (known officially as Provisional Corps Raus until midsummer) and II SS Panzer Corps were assigned to another improvised headquarters, *Armeeabteilung* [Army Detachment] Kempf.

Some of the units assigned to XI Corps had been recently transferred from France, but others had been forced to fight their way out of repeated encirclements. For example, the 320th Infantry Division, which had held a sector on the Don Front with Italian divisions on its flanks, suddenly found itself behind Russian lines because of the rapid disintegration of our allied armies. Major General Georg Postel, the division commander, decided to fight his way back to German lines. En route all of the 320th motor vehicles ran out of gasoline and had to be destroyed. The horse-drawn batteries and field trains also lost a tremendous number of animals in battle and from exhaustion. The division's fighting power and mobility were both thus severely impaired. To avoid the fate of so many other divisions at Stalingrad and along the Don, General Postel had to resort to desperate improvisations. What the division needed either had to be wrested from the Russians or taken from the land.

First, the troops procured hundreds of the small peasant *panje* horses for the light vehicles. Oxen pulled the medium artillery, while cattle and oxen served as draft animals for transporting radio and signal equipment. Even General Postel himself decided to use such a team as a sure means of transportation. The loss of many machine guns, antitank guns, and artillery pieces could be offset only by weapons captured from weak Red Army detachments in sporadic raids; the ammunition for these weapons also had to be taken from the enemy. Similar methods were employed to obtain rations. Small radio sets and other sensitive equipment had to be carried on litters. Infantrymen atop the *panje* horses were charged with reconnaissance and security. The difficult retreat of the 320th Infantry consumed several weeks and was an uninterrupted series of marches, combat actions, and improvisations.

As General Postel's division approached Kharkov on 13 February, it suddenly made radio contact with II SS Panzer Corps, defending the city, and asked for assistance in its attempt to break through to friendly lines. *Obergruppenfuehrer* Paul Hausser, commander of the II SS Panzer Corps, coordinated a strong panzer thrust out of his own lines with a simultaneous attack to the west by the 320th Infantry Division. Achieving tactical surprise, this attack pierced the Russian lines at the designated point, and the division was able to slip back into German lines.

The 320th Infantry Division's appearance hardly resembled that of a German army unit: a strange conglomeration of weapons, equipment, vehicles, and litters; small and large shaggy horses, oxen, and cows; all accompanied by soldiers in such a strange variety of winter clothing that the overall impression was that of a traveling circus on parade. Yet what General Postel led into Kharkov was a battle-tested unit with excellent morale that had courageously fought its way through enemy territory, had returned to its own lines, and was to be considered a precious addition to the *Armeeabteilung*'s strength. By 14 February the 320th Infantry once again stood shoulder to shoulder with the *Leibstandarte Adolf Hitler* and *Das Reich* SS Panzergrenadier Divisions, as well as the *Grossdeutschland* Panzergrenadier Division, in the Kharkov defenses, facing east. The strong will to survive and the skillful improvisations demonstrated by General Postel and his soldiers had enabled the division to avoid destruction.

Unfortunately, by 14 February, Kharkov itself had been surrounded by three Russian armies and its defenders ordered to hold out in a hopeless situation. In his last telephone message, *Obergruppenfuehrer* Hausser called attention to the seriousness of the situation and stated emphatically that the only choice was between losing the city alone or losing the city with all the troops in it. The reply was that "Kharkov must be held to the last man." On the following morning a second order came through by teletype stating that "Kharkov must be held to the last man, but the defenders must not allow themselves to be encircled." On the strength of this ambiguous order, the second part of which precluded the first, the encircled II SS Panzer Corps, the *Grossdeutschland* Panzergrenadier Division, and the 320th Infantry Division took immediate steps for a breakout to the rear without the knowledge or approval of the *Armeeabteilung*. After two days of hard fighting, which ended with the loss of several hundred motor vehicles, Hausser rejoined the German lines, having saved five divisions. His decision to evacuate the city would soon be proven correct.

The next Soviet thrust, aimed at Poltava, ground to a halt about fifty kilometers short of that city because the Russian troops had become too exhausted to continue. Now the Soviets placed all their hopes in the Third Tank Army, commanded by their most capable tank expert, Colonel General Markian M. Popov. Throughout mid-February, Popov had advanced practically without resistance in the direction northwest of Dnepropetrovsk with the apparent intention of reaching the Dnepr bend. His objective was to cross the Dnepr before the Germans could build up their defenses along the river. Soon, however, it became obvious that his forces lacked the necessary drive.

During this fighting an incident occurred that proved the fact that it was not at all unusual for women to fight in front-line Red Army units. A Soviet T-34 was apparently rendered immobile by a direct hit, but when German tanks approached, it suddenly reopened fire and attempted to break out. A second direct hit again brought it to a standstill, but in spite of its hopeless position the T-34 defended itself until a tank-killer team advanced on it. Finally it burst into flames from a demolition charge, and only then did the turret hatch open. A woman in a Red Army tanker uniform climbed out. She was the wife and crewmember of the Russian tank company commander who, killed by the first hit, lay beside her in the turret. So far as Russian soldiers were concerned, women in uniform were superiors or comrades to whom respect was paid.

Meanwhile, we were building up strength for a frontal counterattack. Divisions arriving from the west detrained at Poltava behind the defensive screen established by XI Corps. We held this line with our three infantry divisions and the reconnaissance battalion of the *Totenkopf* SS Panzergrenadier Division. *Totenkopf's* other motorized elements, as well as the *Grossdeutschland* Panzergrenadier Division and the *Fuehrer Begleit* Panzergrenadier Battalion, had moved to rest areas west of Poltava but still close to the front. These units formed a mobile reserve to be committed in the event that the Red Army attempted to capture Poltava by an enveloping thrust through the gap to the north. The Russians actually tried to outflank Poltava, but our infantry divisions, supported by the *Totenkopf* battalion and tactical Luftwaffe units, eliminated this danger. During these actions the enemy showed definite signs of weakness and exhaustion, and the time for a major counterattack seemed to be approaching.

Quick action was indicated since the snow was beginning to thaw. Mud formed on the ground, and soon all movements would become impossible. But deep down the soil was still solidly frozen. Cold nights prevented a quick thaw and favored movements during the early morning hours. Meanwhile, *Armeeabteilung* Kempf's battle-weary front-line troops had been granted a short breathing spell and the opportunity to integrate newly arrived replacements and equipment. By 10 March the *Armeeabteilung's* counterattack forces stood ready to jump off; their morale was excellent.

The XI Corps's main effort had been placed on the southern wing of its front, where terrain conditions favored the employment of panzers. There *Grossdeutschland* was assembled and given the mission of attacking toward Valki. Adjacent on the left, 320th Infantry Division attacked after an artillery preparation delivered by all guns in two divisions, supported by corps artillery. The infantry penetrated the Russian positions, mopped up a strong-point on the main Poltava-Kharkov highway, and threw the enemy back beyond a flooded brook on the other side of Valki. This normally insignificant watercourse had suddenly grown into a raging torrent, which brought the attack to a halt after a gain of less than two kilometers. *Grossdeutschland*'s panzers attempted to overcome the swift current farther upstream and finally succeeded in crossing several hours later. More than eighty panzers broke through the second Russian position on the eastern bank of the brook and rolled toward Valki. Soon our engineers threw an improvised bridge across the brook, and the attack regained its momentum.

Farther north, the 167th and 168th Infantry Divisions also penetrated Soviet positions on their front after heavy fighting. These divisions captured a number of villages and attempted to establish contact with LI Corps of Second Army to the far left of the *Armeeabteilung*. The reinforced *Totenkopf* reconnaissance battalion, committed between the 320th and 167th Infantry Divisions, closed in on the Soviet positions situated in the woods and penetrated deeply into the forest. The battalion's light tanks advanced along the railroad tracks running parallel to the woods. By afternoon, XI Corps had made progress along its entire front and kept the crumbling enemy on the move.

On 11 March XI Corps committed all its forces to a concentric attack on Bogodukhov. For this purpose the corps zone had been narrowed to sixteen kilometers (its width had already been reduced from ninety-five to forty kilometers at the end of the first day). The Russians defending Bogodukhov could not resist the onslaught of our ground troops, which were closely supported by the Luftwaffe. Bogodukhov fell after brief house-to-house fighting, and XI Corps then established contact with the spearheads of II SS Panzer Corps, which had just entered Olshany, twenty-four kilometers southeast. After annihilating strong Soviet forces in the Olshany area, *Obergruppenfuehrer* Hausser turned the corps he had saved from encirclement to the east, enveloping Kharkov and cutting off any Russian route of withdrawal to the north.

While XI Corps's main force received orders to advance northward in an attempt to establish contact with LI Corps and thereby isolate the enemy in the Akhtyrka area, I ordered the 320th Infantry Division to screen the pivoting movement of II SS Panzer Corps. Ever increasing mud and floods slowed the advance at every step. Although all bridges across the swollen Vorskla, Udy, and Lopan Rivers had been destroyed, our infantry and panzer units nonetheless continued to reach their daily objectives. Many motor vehicles and horse-drawn artillery pieces, however, bogged down along the way. On the other hand, the considerably lighter artillery of the Russians and their *panje* wagons pulled through everywhere and escaped our pursuit.

Grossdeutschland carried the main effort and reached the upper Vorskla, with the 167th Infantry Division following closely behind. Since LI Corps on the southern wing of Second Army had lagged so far to the west, no contact with it could be established, and the Russians around Akhtyrka escaped encirclement. In order to continue the operation by a thrust on Tomarovka, our panzer elements had to pivot to the east, changing the direction of their attack. I replaced them with elements of the 167th Infantry Division, which formed a line facing north to provide flank cover. The advance on Tomarovka was delayed because territorial gains to the east automatically led to an extension of the open flank, which our limited forces could not easily support.

By the second day of the thrust toward Tomarovka, the strong 167th Infantry Division had been almost entirely immobilized along the flank. I decided that we would have to await the arrival of LI Corps before the eastward thrust could be resumed. Unfortunately, OKH—which was responsible for coordinating the operations of the two army groups—was too far removed from the scene, and its decisions therefore failed to keep abreast of the fast-moving events at the front. When OKH finally ordered LI Corps to relieve the 167th Infantry, we continued our advance and *Grossdeutschland* entered Tomarovka. On its approach to the town, *Grossdeutschland* destroyed a considerable number of Russian tanks, while many undamaged ones that had bogged down in the mud were retrieved and turned against the Red Army.

It was in this action that PzKw VI Tigers engaged the Russian T-34s for the first time, and the results were more than gratifying to us. For example, two Tigers acting as a panzer spearhead destroyed an entire pack of T-34s. Normally the Russian tanks would stand in ambush at the hitherto safe distance of 1,200 meters and wait for the German tanks to expose themselves upon exiting a village. They would then take the tanks under fire while our PzKw IVs were still outranged. Until now this tactic had been foolproof. This time, however, the Russians miscalculated. Instead of leaving the village, our Tigers took up well-camouflaged positions and made full use of the longer range of their 88mm main guns. Within a short time they knocked out sixteen T-34s that were sitting in open ground, and when the others turned about, the Tigers pursued the fleeing Russians and destroyed eighteen more tanks. Our 88mm armor-piercing shells had such a terrific impact that they ripped off the turrets of many T-34s and hurled them several yards. The German soldiers witnessing this event immediately coined the phrase: "The T-34 tips its hat whenever it meets a Tiger." The performance of the new Tigers resulted in a great morale boost.

Farther to the south, Kharkov was recaptured by the *Leibstandarte Adolph Hitler* SS Panzergrenadier Division after four days of street fighting in which Tigers again played a decisive role. The *Das Reich* SS Panzer-grenadier Division turned north, advanced on Belgorod, captured the city, and linked up with *Grossdeutschland*, which had now thrust beyond Tomarovka. Between these two points two German infantry divisions slowly struggled through the mud in their effort to reach the western bank of the river. When our counteroffensive had begun there was still some snow on the ground, but just before the *Armeeabteilung* reached the upper course of the Donets a sudden rise in temperature created a severe muddy condition. All vehicles except those on the only hard-surfaced road in the area, leading from Kharkov to Kursk, became helpless. Our infantry could still slog forward, but heavy weapons and artillery were delayed and finally moved up only with great effort. Even the T-34s of the Russian rear guards had become embedded to such an extent that we could not retrieve them until warm weather.

Entering Zolochev, a small city twenty miles north of Kharkov, our troops had occasion to discover the extent to which the Russians sought to intimidate their own population through atrocities. The inhabitants told the German military police that Russian security troops, before their retreat, had herded and whipped a large number of local boys between the ages of fourteen and seventeen years naked through the streets in intense cold. Afterward, they were said to have disappeared into the firehouse where the NVKD [Soviet secret police] had its headquarters, never to be seen again. During a subsequent search, all of the missing boys were found in a deep cellar of the firehouse, shot through the neck and covered with horse manure. The bodies were identified and claimed by relatives. Nearly all had frostbitten limbs. The reason for this particular atrocity was assumed to have been the alleged aid rendered to German occupation forces.

The Russians also apparently sought to impress German troops and lower their morale by committing numerous atrocities directly against them. One such case occurred in Second Panzer Army's sector several hundred kilometers to the north. During fighting over the village of Zhizdra in early March, a battalion of the 590th Grenadier Regiment, 321st Infantry Division, was assigned the mission of mopping up a sector overgrown with brush. The attack failed. When, on 19 March, the sector again passed into our hands after a counterattack, forty corpses of soldiers were found with their eyes gouged out, or their ears, noses, and genitals cut off. Corpses found in another sector of the battlefield bore signs of similar mutilations.

Despite atrocities like these, such Russian elements as escaped across the Donets were badly mauled, and our reconnaissance units advancing beyond the river met little resistance. Even though our attack divisions appeared fully capable of continuing their drive, the overall situation and the prevailing mud made such a decision inadvisable. Moreover, the objective of the frontal counterattack had been achieved. The breach in the German lines, open for four months, had been closed and the greatest Russian winter offensive fought to a halt. After suffering a defeat of gigantic proportions at Stalingrad, the German army once again held a continuous line anchored on the Donets River.

Situation, 10 April 1943

After Army Group South had concluded its 1943 spring offensive, the enemy in front of *Armeeabteilung* Kempf primarily remained on the defensive. The Russians, though generally quiet, demonstrated greater activity in the northern sector of the front, between Belgorod and the army group boundary. Lively reconnaissance efforts, artillery reinforcements, the arrival of reserve forces, and the improvement of the natural terrain features for defense all suggested that the Soviets intended to strengthen their defenses in this new sector of the front as quickly as possible. In rear areas, lively traffic of all kinds indicated a rapid and intense reorganization of heavily batter units. Although intelligence identified no new Red Army units at the front, it seemed entirely possible that railroad traffic (in excess of normal troop replacement and supply requirements) had delivered at least three new rifle divisions into the Kursk area and two into the area of Valuiki–North Oskol–St. Oskol. Aside from this observation, we received indications that significant forces had shifted from the sector opposite the German Sixth Army, as well as from the sector facing Army Group Center, into the North Oskol–Korocha–St. Oskol area. It proved impossible to determine then whether these units were being concentrated for offensive or defensive purposes.

Armeeabteilung Kempf's main line of resistance and disposition of forces is [described here]. In addition to the 106th, 167th, and 320th Infantry Divisions and the *Totenkopf* SS Panzergrenadier Division already committed at the front, the following units had been assigned to the *Armeeabteilung* at that time for "reorganization and training in local areas": Headquarters, III Panzer Corps; Headquarters, II SS Panzer Corps; 6th and 7th Panzer Divisions; *Grossdeutschland* Panzergrenadier Division; *Das Reich* SS Panzergrenadier Division and *Leibstandarte Adolf Hitler* SS Panzergrenadier Divisions. Beginning in late April, the following units arrived: Headquarters, XLVIII Panzer Corps; 11th Panzer Division; 168th Infantry Division; and Army troops (armored and self-propelled antitank gun units, flak, artillery, engineers, bridge trains, road construction battalions, etc.). The *Armeeabteilung* placed reorganizing units in the vicinity or west of Kharkov. Units committed at the front rotated one-third their strength (one reinforced regimental *Kampfgruppe*) at a time, for purposes of reorganizing near the front.

Since the original attack date had been set for 4 May, maximum efforts were made to move up required personnel and material.

As soon as the *Armeeabteilung* realized that the Red Army had moved additional forces into the area northeast of Belgorod, a panzer *Kampfgruppe*—established by rotating elements of the panzer divisions refitting further to the rear—was placed on alert north of Kharkov. This deployment prepared us to meet any Soviet attempt to launch a surprise attack on Kharkov.

During this period of protracted position warfare, the 106th Infantry Division, south of Belgorod, managed to take a large number of prisoners. These prisoners were taken in midday raids, since it had been ascertained from deserters that the Russians in this sector—which could be readily observed from the western bank of the river—were allowed to move only at night and therefore slept during the day. The prisoners admitted that many of their comrades were dissatisfied and would like to desert; however, they were afraid of being fired upon by our troops and would have difficulties crossing the deep river that separated them from the German lines. Contact with the company of malcontents was soon established and the necessary arrangements made. Unobtrusive light signals on the chosen night informed the Russian company that the necessary ferrying equipment was ready and that German weapons stood ready to cover their crossing. All necessary precautions had been taken in case of a Soviet ruse. Just the same, the company really dribbled down to the banks of the river and, in several trips, was ferried across the Donets in rubber boats. The company commander, an Uzbeki first lieutenant, was the first man to reach our lines. Part of the company, unfortunately, ran into Russian minefields, suffering considerable losses from exploding mines as well as from the fire of the alerted enemy artillery. The result of this undertaking was that, having become unreliable, the 15th Uzbek Rifle Division was immediately withdrawn from the front, disciplined, and committed elsewhere.

Situation, About 30 June 1943

Enemy forces moving into previously identified assembly areas since May had been increasing to such an extent that we had to plan on facing a heavy concentration of Soviet reserves in the area of Korocha–Volokonovka–North Oskol, as well as the Kursk area. Though we observed no general forward movement of Russian units during May, June brought a continuous strengthening of the enemy front, particularly in terms of artillery, heavy weapons, dug-in tanks, etc. We concluded that the Soviets intended to maintain a defensive stance, however, because they were undoubtedly aware of the numerous panzer divisions in the Kharkov area, while the course of our front line strongly suggested the potential for a large-scale attack. On the other hand, the prospect of a pending Russian offensive could not be completely dismissed given the manifestation of increasing enemy strength throughout June.

Large-scale and well-planned construction of field fortifications accompanied the Russian buildup, which the Luftwaffe monitored through aerial photographs taken during daily flights. Opposite Belgorod, where the main weight of the German attack would fall, the Russian defensive system consisted of three successive fortified belts, extending by the end of June to a depth of forty kilometers. We documented in great numbers the following features: positions on reverse slopes; switch positions; dummy installations; alternate artillery positions (up to four per battery); and alternate positions for dug-in tanks. Mines not only covered the approaches but had been laid to an unprecedented depth. Towns located within and behind the Soviet defensive system—to a distance of sixty kilometers—had been evacuated and transformed into what were practically fortresses, coupled with covering detachments. Most positions appeared already occupied, and reserves had bivouacked in dugouts near the forward areas.

No changes had occurred in the *Armeeabteilung*'s main battle line since 10 April. West of Belgorod, Headquarters, Fourth Panzer Army, assumed command of II SS and XLVIII Panzer Corps, while Headquarters, III Panzer Corps; 6th, 7th, and 19th Panzer Divisions; and a number of Army troops had been attached to the *Armeeabteilung*.

After units had been reorganized and refitted, the *Armeeabteilung* concentrated on intensive training for the attack and on the tactical instructions of the subordinate commanders—both in practice and in theory—with particular emphasis placed on the types of missions the troops would be expected to perform. Field exercises with live ammunition, as well as demonstrations in which the Luftwaffe and other elements participated, contributed to the achievement of a high standard of combat readiness. Map exercises and terrain orientation meetings occurred concurrently, while special courses taught military bridge construction and minefield clearing. Simultaneously, in order to deceive the Soviets regarding German intentions, new large-scale defensive positions were constructed at the front and in forward areas.

In connection with this training effort, XI Corps staff made a thorough study of the problem of crossing the extensive minefields on the eastern side of the Donets. The usual procedure of sending engineer detachments to clear narrow lanes for the advance of the infantry spearheads was not considered satisfactory since the terrain offered no cover and the enemy could inflict heavy casualties upon engineers and infantry by concentrating his fire on these lanes. Several improvised methods for overcoming this obstacle were therefore under consideration.

The identification of the mined area was the first prerequisite, since the infantry had to know its exact location prior to the crossings. This was possible because the German-held western bank commanded the Russian positions on the other side of the river. Another prerequisite was that the infantry should be able to spot the location of individual mines at close range with the naked eye. In many places small mounds or depressions, dry grass, differences in the coloring of the ground, or some other external marks facilitated the spotting. The engineers had made a number of experiments in mine detecting. In the early days of the war, the infantry sometimes crossed narrow minefields after individual engineers lay down beside the mines as human markers, taking great care not to set them off by pressure. Although neither engineers nor infantry troops suffered losses during these early experiments, the procedure was risky and could be applied only on a small scale. It was therefore of little consequence in the later stages of the war.

A second, more promising method that fulfilled expectations consisted of marking individual mines by placing small flags or other simple markers next to the mines. This was done by engineers or infantrymen who were trained in the recognition of mines. This procedure was applied repeatedly and showed better results than the first, but its large-scale use presented difficulties. The third and best method was to thoroughly instruct all infantrymen in enemy mine-laying techniques and in spotting mines by using captured enemy minefields as training grounds. This procedure required that all infantrymen be sent to rear areas in rotation and was therefore rather time-consuming.

These requirements could be met in the case of Operation Citadel since the time of the attack had been twice postponed with an ensuing delay of several weeks. The divisions committed in the narrow attack zone had moved two-thirds of their combat forces to the rear, where the daily training schedule featured tanks passing over foxholes and the crossing of Russian-type minefields. This training paid off since it helped the soldiers overcome their fear of tanks and mines.

The Mission of *Armeeabteilung* Kempf

The plan of attack assigned *Armeeabteilung* Kempf the mission of providing an aggressive screen along the eastern flank of Fourth Panzer Army, which was to advance across the line Malino-Oboyan. Specifically, the *Armeeabteilung* had to hold the Donets front from the right boundary of Fourth Panzer Army to the mouth of the Nezhegol River, while advancing to

the Nezhegol-Korocha line to screen its own panzer elements for a push in
the general direction of Skorodnoye. After breaking through the Donets position, III Panzer Corps would take over responsibility for aggressively
screening the flank of the entire operation in the sector Korocha–Seim River.

The *Armeeabteilung* had to calculate on meeting the following Red Army
forces:

Day One: four rifle divisions in the first line between the mouth of the
    Nezhegol River and Belgorod;
Day Two: all other divisions located in forward areas (estimated at four
    rifle divisions);
Day Three and beyond: considerable tank and mechanized forces from the
    Ostrogozhsk region.

That the STAVKA [Soviet High Command] intended to hold the shoulder
of the Kursk salient with all available forces became increasingly apparent
from troop dispositions and the extent of the defensive system in the Belgorod area. We projected that the Soviets had three alternatives from which to
choose in committing their strategic reserves:

1. Piecemeal commitment during a defensive battle (this would have been
    best for us).
2. A concentric counterattack (starting the third or fourth day).
3. A counteroffensive of major proportions.

The following German units were available to the *Armeeabteilung*:

1. For defense along the Donets sector: XLII Corps with 39th, 161st, and
    282nd Infantry Divisions (one division, composed of just two infantry
    regiments, had to be spread over a front line 145 kilometers long);
2. For gaining the Nezhegol-Korocha line: XI Corps (also known as
    "Corps Raus") with 106th and 320th Infantry Divisions;
3. For the panzer attack on Skorodnoye: III Panzer Corps with 6th, 7th,
    and 19th Panzer Divisions, as well as 168th Infantry Division.

Considering Russian dispositions, defenses, and terrain, German strength
could be considered only minimally sufficient for the assigned mission.
Clearly, there could not be any major losses at the outset of the operation.

The offensive would occur in three phases. First, the Donets would be
crossed and the first Russian defensive belt penetrated. Given the weakness
of our force, tactical surprise at least in terms of timing and the choice of

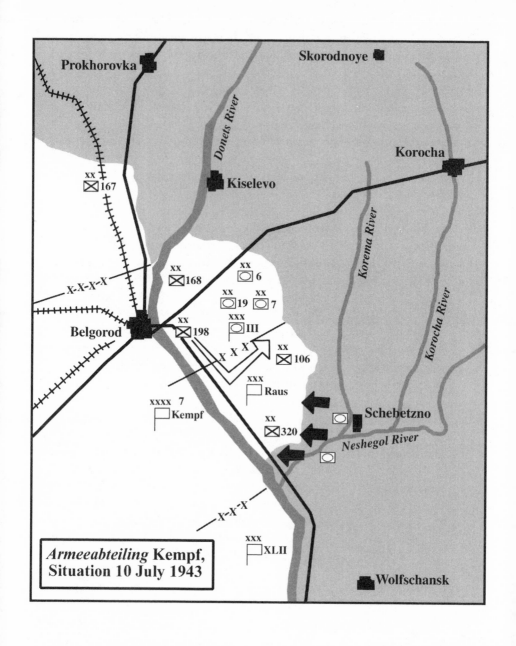

Prokhorovka

Skorodnoye

Donets River

Korocha

XX
⊠ 167

Kiselevo

Korena River

X-X-X-X

XX
⊠ 168

XX
⊡ 6

XX
⊡ 19

XX
⊡ 7

Korocha River

XXX
⊡ III

Belgorod

XX
⊠ 198

X X X

XX
⊠ 106

XXX
⊏ Raus

XXXX 7
⊏ Kempf

XX
⊠ 320

⊡

Schebetzno

⊡

Neshegol River

⊡

X-X-X

XXX
⊏ XLII

Wolfschansk

Armeeabteiling **Kempf,
Situation 10 July 1943**

river crossings would be essential. Next, the *Armeeabteilung* had to break through the enemy's second and third defensive belts as rapidly as possible to avoid giving the Soviets enough time to commit their strategic reserves. Finally, enemy strategic reserves would be engaged on open ground. With the large number of Red Army tank corps standing by, we could reasonably expect major armored battles, during which our panzer divisions would have the opportunity to demonstrate their superior leadership and weapons.

However, long before the panzer divisions could enter what we hoped would be the battle's final, decisive stage, they had to accomplish a mission strictly relegated to infantry divisions in normal operations: attack across a river against a prepared enemy deployed in depth. Flat bridgehead terrain, barely 100 meters in depth, was available only at the western outskirts of Belgorod.

Because the *Armeeabteilung*'s primary mission required safeguarding the eastern flank of Fourth Panzer Army's advance, the closest possible contact between that army and III Panzer Corps had to be maintained. This meant that III Panzer Corps would have to execute an almost immediate thrust to the northeast, disregarding any threats to its own flank. For XI Corps, strung out across a thirty-five-kilometer sector with just two reinforced infantry divisions, there would therefore be no panzer support available. Instead, XI Corps had to establish its screen along the Koremye sector by forming narrow wedges. A diversionary Red Army attack against Kharkov from the Donets bend (on either side of Chuguev and astride the Chuguev-Kharkov highway) remained a threat to the overall success of the operation; we had no reserves available to counter such an attack. Upon repeated requests by the *Armeeabteilung*, Army Group South eventually consented to assemble some of its own reserve forces in the area.

As far as possible, the enemy had to be kept from detecting the movement of German forces into their assembly areas. By spacing the assembly areas far apart and occupying them at staggered intervals, the *Armeeabteilung* attempted to deceive the enemy about the attack's timing and the locations of contemplated crossing sites. Movement forward into the assembly areas by the panzer divisions had to be confined to the hours of darkness. Movement into assembly areas and artillery positions had been completed by 4 July.

In the Chuguev area additional and extensive deception measures attempted to convince the Russians that we contemplated attacking in the Donets bend toward the line Izyum-Kuryansk. Motorized columns advanced toward the front lines in daylight, artillery moved into positions and conducted registration fire, and simulated reserves practiced river crossings.

We had to remain aware of the fact that the Russians made considerable use of the civilian population for intelligence missions. A favorite practice was the employment of boys eight to fourteen years old, who were first trained for this work and then allowed to infiltrate at suitable front sectors. Immediately before the offensive opened, more than a dozen such children were picked up in the Belgorod area alone. They gave detailed reports on the kind of training they received and their modus operandi. The training of these children had been supervised by Russian officers, it had lasted four weeks, and there had been sixty participants. The youths came from communities near the front on both sides of the battle lines and therefore were thoroughly familiar with the locale. Many were staying with relatives or acquaintances in German-occupied localities and therefore not easy to discover and apprehend. Their talent for observation and skill at spying were remarkable. For this reason, civilians in localities near the front (within six to ten kilometers of the front line) had to be evacuated, not only because of the danger from enemy artillery fire but also as a preventative measure against espionage.

Kursk: The Penetration, 5 July

The Russians became aware of the date of the attack, probably because of a venture by the unit on the left in the afternoon of 4 July. From 0200 to 0220 the Soviets laid down a destructive fire on suspected crossing sites around Belgorod, resulting in considerable German casualties. At 0225, following a short artillery concentration, the *Armeeabteilung* commenced the Donets crossing on a wide front. This assault succeeded at all crossing sites in a surprisingly short time, though at some locations only after bitter hand-to-hand fighting. The attack took place without Luftwaffe support, which had been totally committed to Fourth Panzer Army. In addition to organic divisional artillery, the following units were committed to deliver supporting fire (note that flak units had a dual mission of fire support and air defense):

XI Corps sector:

> 153rd Artillery Command
> > 1/77 Artillery Battalion (105mm)
> > 2/54 Artillery Battalion (105mm)
> > 1/213 Artillery Battalion (105mm)
>
> 4th Flak Regiment
>
> 7th Flak Regiment
>
> 48th Flak Regiment
>
> 905th Assault Gun Battalion
>
> 393rd Self-propelled Panzerjaeger Battalion

The three flak regiments, fielding a total of seventy-two 88mm and approximately 900 smaller flak guns, had been attached to XI Corps to serve as a substitute for missing medium artillery. According to Luftwaffe policy, the subordination of flak officers to army unit commanders was forbidden; the corps artillery commander therefore depended on the voluntary cooperation of the senior flak commander. This led to repeated minor frictions but worked out quite well in general.

The flak regiments' first mission was to take part in the artillery preparation under the direction of the corps artillery commander. For this purpose the flak regiments were echeloned in depth and committed in three waves. The first echelon was in position in the main line of resistance and closely behind it; its mission was to place direct fire on enemy heavy weapons and pillboxes. In addition, it had to form flak assault detachments for antitank combat to give close support to the advancing infantry. Together with the corps artillery, the two other regiments were to shatter the first enemy line of defense and paralyze his infantry by delivering sustained concentrations. After that, elements of the first echelon, with the exception of the assault detachments, as well as the entire second echelon, were to support the advancing infantry. The third echelon was to take over the antiaircraft protection of the entire artillery area and was also to participate in counterbattery missions.

III Panzer Corps sector:

3rd Artillery Command
    612th Artillery Regimental Staff
    228th Assault Gun Battalion
    2/71 Artillery Battalion (150mm)
    875th Heavy Artillery Battalion (210mm)
    2/62 Artillery Battalion (105mm)

99th Flak Regiment

153rd Flak Regiment

The 6th Panzer Division, III Panzer Corps sector, supported the attack of the 168th Infantry Division with its heavy weapons and was assigned the mission of crossing the river and pushing beyond the 168th Infantry lines toward St. Gorodische as soon as the 168th succeeded in widening the narrow bridgehead at Belgorod.

For purposes of deceiving the Russians, XLII Corps conducted a feint attack across the Donets along its northern wing, while in reality its combined artillery (which had been concentrated in the area) supported the XI Corps attack.

Soviet intelligence found out that the attack was to start on 5 July at dawn. The Russians laid down intensive harassing fire on the jump-off positions, but this interference ceased as soon as the German artillery concentration started. In XI Corps area these fire concentrations were placed so well and the initial shock so great that the first assault wave was able to cross the enemy minefields, penetrate his main line of resistance without delay, and thrust a few hundred yards beyond it. Thousands of tracers fired by the numerous small flak guns proved particularly effective.

The beginning of the attack had been set for sunrise so that the infantry would be able to detect enemy mines without difficulty. The 106th and 320th Infantry Divisions quickly thrust their spearheads across the minefields and suffered practically no casualties. Only one battalion acted contrary to orders and attacked before daybreak, its commander being afraid that he might otherwise suffer heavy casualties from enemy fire while his men were crossing the extended open terrain in his zone. In the dark, this battalion ran into the previously uncovered minefields, and the two advance companies suffered approximately twenty casualties from mine explosions. When the battalion continued its advance by daylight it had no further losses.

Since the Russians had abandoned their trenches during the artillery concentration and fled into their deep dugouts, the advancing infantry surprised them and had no difficulty in ferreting them out. But when the infantry reached the two- to three-mile-deep zone of battle positions prepared in the preceding months, they had to make extensive use of hand grenades in order to mop up the maze of densely dug-in trenches and bunkers, some of which were a dozen or more feet deep. At the same time, artillery and flak fired counterbattery missions against enemy heavy weapons that had resumed fire from rear positions, on reserves infiltrating through the trench system, as well as against Russian medium artillery. The third echelon of the flak regiments was fully occupied with defense against Soviet bombers, which attacked XI Corps's area incessantly. During the first two hours of the attack they downed more than twenty enemy aircraft.

We encountered strong enemy forces offering stiff and bitter resistance in their deeply echeloned, amply fortified, and heavily mined battlefield. This remained the case throughout the process of widening the initial bridgeheads as well as during the battle for the area between the Donets and the railroad line, which was also located within the first defensive belt. Throughout the morning, Russian artillery, automatic weapons, and aircraft began to participate in the battle with ever-increasing intensity. Both the tactical reserves of the forward units and elements of rifle divisions and independent tank brigades located just behind the front launched counterthrusts against our penetrations. By early afternoon these efforts had become systematic coun-terattacks. Even so, after costly see-saw fighting, XI Corps's main body reached the railroad line by evening, and some elements even crossed it.

Suddenly a fierce Russian counterattack, supported by forty tanks, threw back our covering force from the woods on the southern flank and hit the 320th Infantry Division, which was echeloned in depth on the corps's right wing. Defensive fire of the divisional artillery and a concentration of all medium flak batteries stopped the enemy counterattack at the edge of the forest. Then the medium flak was directed against tank concentrations, which had been recognized in the underbrush, and dispersed them. Repeated Soviet attempts to resume the attack from this area failed without exception; flank protection was soon restored and the threat eliminated.

During this counterattack about 150 men from the 320th Infantry Divi-sion were taken prisoner. Shortly thereafter we monitored a telephone con-versation between Russian lower and higher headquarters (probably regi-ment and division), which went about as follows:

> Regimental commander: "I have 150 *Fritzes* [derogatory term for German soldiers] here. What shall I do with them?"
>
> Division commander: "Keep a few for interrogation, and have the oth-ers liquidated."

That evening, the presumed regimental commander reported the order executed, stating that the majority of the *Fritzes* had been killed immediately, the remainder after they had been interrogated.

In III Panzer Corps sector, 7th Panzer Division crossed the Donets at Solomino and succeeded in effecting a deep penetration of the enemy de-fenses, though only after a bitter tank fight. This penetration extended to the high ground north of Krivoy Log. Forcing the Donets in the southern part of Pushkarnoye, 19th Panzer Division encountered strong resistance and ex-tremely unfavorable terrain (swamps and minefields) in the wooded area southeast of Mikailovka. Nonetheless, after repulsing a strong Russian tank attack, the 19th managed to cross the railroad line. Neither the 168th In-fantry Division nor the 6th Panzer Division succeeded in penetrating the enemy's main defensive belt in the Belgorod area, which meant that the *Armeeabteilung*'s mission for the next few days would involve blasting this stronghold open from the east.

By capitalizing on the element of tactical surprise, the *Armeeabteilung* was fortunate enough to breach the first defensive belt between the Donets and the railroad line; after bitter fighting we were even able partially to roll up this line. Only the 7th Panzer Division achieved a penetration of the second defensive belt; at all other points the enemy stood his ground, employing an offensive-defense in many areas.

Threats to both flanks became apparent as the *Armeeabteilung* pushed northeast. The large wooded area northwest of Shevekino provided a well-concealed jump-off point for Russian counterattacks. Costly fighting in the woods was to be expected in any attempt to break through to the Korenye sector. After the losses on the first day (almost 2,000 men in XI Corps alone) it appeared doubtful that this objective could be attained without the help of additional forces.

The Belgorod bastion, seizure of which was bound to tie down major forces for the next few days, had expanded as a result of the *Armee-abteilung*'s continued advance toward the line Korocha-Skorodnoye, until it formed a deep wedge pointing south and lodged between *Armeeabteilung* Kempf and Fourth Panzer Army. Fresh enemy forces were already pouring into this wedge, which would represent an ever-increasing threat to our left flank.

Higher headquarters had been hoping the troops would encounter an enemy weakened in his power of resistance. This proved to be a delusion. The Russians appeared to be materially prepared (good rations, equipment, and arms) as well as morally inoculated against all symptoms of deterioration (high degree of patriotism; confidence in victory aroused; failure of our efforts to induce enemy troops to desert).

Kursk: Breaking Through the Second and Third Lines, 6–7 July

The initial success of the first day required immediate exploitation of the breach at Krivoy Log, where the 7th Panzer division had punched through. All our forces concentrated to this end, and the *Armeeabteilung* even abandoned the nonessential and costly Bezlydovka bridgehead on the southern flank. On the western bank of the Donets, elements of the 106th Infantry Division assumed the defensive. The 6th Panzer Division redeployed from Stary Gorod for commitment behind the 7th Panzer, in order to reinforce the assault spearhead. After bitter fighting with Russian tanks, the combined armored strength of these two divisions sufficed to break through the deep defense system, gaining the high ground at Myasoyedovo and even pushing on toward Melekhovo. Coordinating its attack with elements of the 7th Panzer Division, XI Corps seized the commanding heights between Korek and the Donets, then established a screen facing east. The *Armeeabteilung* likewise

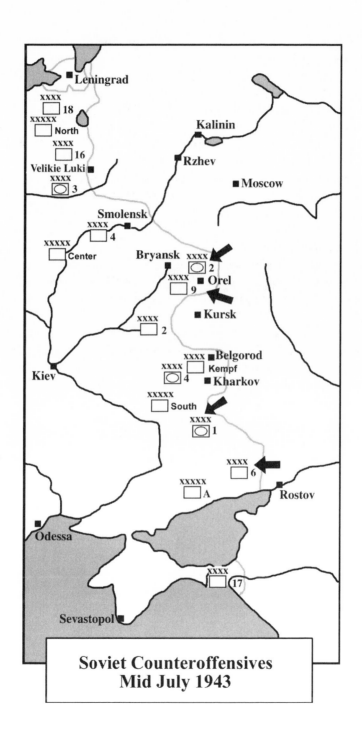

**Soviet Counteroffensives
Mid July 1943**

gained ground with an attack launched from the south and southwest against the area immediately east of Belgorod. Extremely stiff Soviet resistance characterized the fighting in this area, especially around the enemy stronghold of Kreida, which was heavily manned and well supported by automatic weapons and artillery.

The Russians attempted to counter our breakthrough attack by launching numerous thrusts and attacks from the woods west of Koren, where they had assembled three of their front-line rifle divisions, which had been reinforced by two new rifle divisions and two independent tank brigades. Attacking with strong infantry elements and the two tank brigades, the enemy focused his main effort in front of the 106th Infantry Division. In the resulting engagements, XI Corps scored a considerable defensive victory, thanks primarily to the excellent performance of our infantry in permitting the Soviet tanks to roll over them (a procedure that had been especially stressed during training), which succeeded in separating the enemy tanks from their own infantry supports. The tanks pushed up to and beyond the Shevekino-Belgorod road, but the Russian infantry attack broke down in front of our lines, which now held without budging.

The enemy tanks struck the corps's center, behind which several flak assault detachments and numerous medium antitank guns were sited in a mutually supporting formation. As the Russian tanks ran headlong into this dense network of antitank defenses, I personally led the reserves of the 106th Infantry Division, with support from thirty-two assault guns, antitank guns, and flak assault detachments, to envelop and ultimately knock out all sixty tanks that had penetrated the sector. The last Soviet tank that had penetrated to the divisional command post was surprised by an assault detachment carrying gasoline cans and was set on fire. On the whole, while determined, the Russian attacks lacked coordination, and since they were unsuccessful, the enemy moved to concentrate his forces for an offensive main effort between Polyana and the woods east of Shcholokovo. Even here the screen would be held in bitter fighting after the arrival of a continuous flow of reinforced *Kampfgruppen* from the 198th Infantry Division, which had been brought up from Chuguev in motorized columns.

The Soviets attempted to break up the *Armeeabteilung*'s panzer thrust to the northeast by committing two newly arrived rifle divisions and elements of the II Tank Corps against III Panzer Corps. Simultaneously, the Russians pressured the western flank in the area Blis, Igumenka-Hf., Postikov. While repulsing strong attacks from Melekhovo, we managed to encircle the forces opposite the western flank, destroying one rifle division and heavily mauling another; elements of the latter withdrew along the Syev Donets Valley to the northeast after abandoning its heavy equipment.

The enemy position had thus been breached to a depth of thirty kilometers; six Soviet rifle divisions, two tank brigades, and three tank regiments had been battered. Evaluation of aerial photographs revealed one last defensive belt along the line Ushakovo-Sheyno-Sobyshno. In continuing its advance, the *Armeeabteilung* had to expect an encounter with three additional groupings of Russian forces:

1. Five or six mauled rifle divisions and tank brigades opposite the western flank.
2. Three or four rifle divisions of the Sixty-ninth Army. (Both of these groups could potentially receive reinforcements from the St. Oskol area, including two tank corps and one cavalry corps.)
3. One tank corps and elements of three rifle divisions located in the triangle formed by the Syev Donets and Lipovy Donetsm that could operate against either the western flank of the *Armeeabteilung* or the eastern flank of Fourth Panzer Army.

Kursk: The Drive on Prokhorovka, 11–16 July

In order for III Panzer Corps to achieve freedom of movement toward the northeast to cover the right flank of Fourth Panzer Army, we would have to break through the Russian Sixty-ninth Army between Ushakovo and Sobyshno. After breaking through the last enemy position between Razumnoye and Syev Donets, the drive on Skorodnoye would require the concentrated strength of III Panzer Corps. Such a maneuver would be possible only if enemy forces in the Donets triangle (which threatened our own flank) could be thrown back or destroyed. Neither of these maneuvers could be allowed to jeopardize the execution of the other, and it did not appear possible to tackle both enemy groupings simultaneously without Fourth Panzer Army assistance in cleaning out the Donets triangle.

At this time, however, Fourth Panzer Army faced a bitter struggle with Soviet infantry and strong tank forces along the length of its front. Crossing sites on the Psel River could be gained only after costly fighting, and Russian strength in front of the bridgeheads increased by the hour. A breakthrough toward Kursk, upon which the entire operation hinged, seemed doubtful unless Fourth Panzer Army could be reinforced, and diverting any elements to assist in mopping up the Donets triangle might cause the forward attack of II SS Panzer Corps's right wing to cease altogether.

In his concern over Fourth Panzer Army's attack bogging down, Field Marshal von Manstein considered the following course of action: discontinuation of *Armeeabteilung* Kempf's attack, and redeployment of III Panzer Corps on the eastern wing of Fourth Panzer Army. Such a solution became the subject of a conference between von Manstein, Hoth, and Kempf in Dolbino at the *Armeeabteilung*'s headquarters on 11 July. Emphasizing the *Armeeabteilung*'s dwindling combat strength, the mounting threat to the eastern flank, and the absence of all reserves, Kempf favored discontinuing the attack. Field Marshal von Manstein postponed his final decision pending the outcome of a projected visit with General of Panzer Troops Hermann Breith, commander, III Panzer Corps. Presumably due to the tactical successes of the past few days, Breith presented von Manstein with an optimistic view of the situation, and the field marshal ordered III Panzer Corps's attack to continue.

The III Panzer Corps broke through the Russian positions between Ushakovo and Sobyshno, penetrating quickly into the Alexandrovka area. At the same time, the *Armeeabteilung* secured several bridgeheads over the Syev Donets on either side of Rehavel. "Open terrain" beckoned: Freedom of movement for the operation against Skorodnoye had been won, a jump-off position for the drive on Prokhorovka had been gained, and—as a result—coordinated action with Fourth Panzer Army's flank became possible.

The next challenge grew out of the overall situation. The Russians committed additional strong tank forces against Fourth Panzer Army's eastern flank, and heavy defensive battles raged. Now the *Armeeabteilung* received the most important mission within the scope of the overall operation: defeat Soviet tank forces in the area south of Prokhorovka and forcibly clear the road to Kursk. This would still require enemy resistance in the Donets triangle to be eliminated as a prerequisite.

The recently won penetration near Alexandrovka had to be held in order to serve as a jump-off point for the thrust toward Prokhorovka. The XI Corps defensive screen, therefore, had to be lengthened along the Razumnoye toward the northeast, even though we were holding existing positions only with elements whose strength dwindled rapidly. Only the 6th Panzer Division could be made available as a covering force for the screen toward the north, which it managed by aggressive tactics. That the other two panzer divisions of III Panzer Corps were enabled to maintain their attack could be ascribed to the heroic defensive stand of the XI Corps along a dangerously wide sector.

Confronted by strong Russian defenses and counterattacks by the II Guards Tank Corps, the panzer *Kampfgruppen* of the 7th and 19th Panzer Divisions nonetheless attacked Shashovo from their bridgeheads across the Syev Donets [beginning on 12 July]. Elements of four rifle divisions in the Donets triangle attempted to evade the encirclement and break out toward the north. Assisted by the 167th Infantry Division (which had been holding position on the western side of this enemy bastion), III Panzer Corps cleared the wooded section south of Gostishchevo of the enemy—an action yielding over 1,000 prisoners and large amounts of weapons and equipment.

Our continued drive toward the high ground on either side of the line Ivanovka–Maloye Tablonovo collided with strong Soviet tank forces. The German panzers, however, demonstrated their superiority in the course of several heavy armored battles. Suffering heavy losses, the Russians retreated north, and we established contact with the western wing of Fourth Panzer Army north of Teterevino. High tank losses had so thoroughly weakened the Soviets that Army Group South could now undertake the decisive thrust toward Prokhorovka; the appropriate field orders were immediately issued.

In the meantime, however, the Red Army attacked the far southern wing of Army Group South along the Mius River and at Izyum. As a result, the strategic reserve that was to have been allocated to the drive on Kursk— XXIV Panzer Corps with *Wiking* SS Panzergrenadier Division and 17th Panzer Division—never arrived. On the southern wing of Army Group Center, not only had Ninth Army's assault been unsuccessful, but the Russians had launched a major attack against the Orel salient. Simultaneously, XLVIII Panzer Corps (on the western flank of Fourth Panzer Army) had been halted by strong enemy tank forces (at least one tank army). Army Group South intended to respond to this threat by temporarily assuming the defensive on Fourth Panzer Army's eastern flank in order to crush the Soviet tank army and resume a coordinated drive on Kursk. Meanwhile, after 7th Panzer Division had been detached, *Armeeabteilung* Kempf received only the weakened 167th Infantry Division in exchange to assist in covering its long eastern flank (code-named "Roland"). The crisis point of the entire operation had been reached: There were no reserves remaining that could be thrown into the battle.

Ultimately, it was the Red Army attack along the Mius River and at Izyum that kept Fourth Panzer Army's intended attack toward the Psel-Pena area from materializing. Once XXIV Panzer Corps had been committed there, no strategic reserves remained to Army Group South, and the Russians held the initiative. The attack toward Kursk was called off, and as early as 17 July II SS Panzer Corps would be redeployed from the Kursk salient; an additional panzer division would follow a few days later. Army Group South nevertheless intended to leave *Armeeabteilung* Kempf and Fourth Panzer Army in their existing line as long as no serious attacks materialized or new concentrations of enemy forces became noticeable.

The large-scale attack code-named "Operation Citadel" had not attained its strategic objective, even though great tactical success had been achieved.

During the period 5–20 July, Army Group South captured or destroyed 412 tanks, 11,862 prisoners, 132 artillery pieces, 530 antitank guns, and a large number of heavy weapons of all types. The Red Army could certainly have used these troops and weapons in the major offensive that had just opened.

Kursk: Withdrawal to the Enlarged Belgorod Bridgehead, 18–22 July

As a consequence of the recall of the 19th Panzer Division on 18 July, *Armeeabteilung* Kempf's front had to be withdrawn to an intermediate position; the Soviets followed closely behind. On 21 July, in order to meet a threatening attack against Army Group South's west wing, both 6th Panzer Division and 167th Infantry Division had to be transferred to Fourth Panzer Army. The front withdrew again, this time to the enlarged Belgorod bridgehead. This position had twice the frontage as the old Donets position and had to be held solely by the remaining elements of XI Corps. Heavy losses since 5 July had reduced the fighting power of XI Corps to less than half.

Armeeabteilung Kempf made repeated requests to move the front back to the line of departure—which would have shortened the front considerably while allowing us to take advantage of the excellent, strongly fortified positions on the Donets. These requests were all refused, since such a withdrawal was "intended" only in the face of a major Russian attack. Over the coming weeks, this decision embroiled XI Corps in a series of costly see-saw battles for the control of the enlarged Belgorod bridgehead, which were marked by excessively wide defensive sectors; diminishing combat strength; disappearing moral and physical strength of the troops; lack of reserves; enormous superiority of Soviet personnel and materials; and the fact that our position had never been fortified. XI Corps was finally permitted to retire into the heavily fortified defensive system anchored on Belgorod on 22 July.

Operation Citadel had the avowed purpose of gaining the Kursk area, destroying the enemy forces in the salient facing Second Army, and—above all—shortening our lines by about 270 kilometers. In order to conserve German strength, the attack was conceived as a swift follow-up operation and climax to the successful pre-spring battles of *Armeeabteilung* Kempf and Fourth Panzer Army around Kharkov. The recapture of Belgorod had created a favorable jump-off point for this purpose. *Armeeabteilung* Kempf submitted its first proposal for such an operation on 1 April, intending to attack by mid-April or early May at the latest. We reasoned that the four-week pause in the fighting necessitated by the muddy season would allow us to reorganize our troops but would be too brief for the battered Russians to make adequate defensive preparations.

The *Armeeabteilung* repeatedly voiced grave concern over ensuing postponements of the operation. The last time, this concern was evidenced by a particularly urgent manifestation, in the form of a verbal report from General Kempf to Colonel General Kurt Zeitzler, Chief of the Army General Staff. Kempf argued that the enemy would make use of the time not only to regroup his units and fortify his defenses in depth but also to assemble a strategic reserve that could be utilized to repulse our assault, launch diversionary attacks, or even spearhead a planned counteroffensive. Nevertheless, the operation was repeatedly postponed. The reason given for this action was the fact that the new weapons (above all the PzKw V Panther and PzKw VI Tiger battalions) would so reinforce our offensive power as to offset the defensive preparations of the enemy.

Armeeabteilung Kempf received no such weapons or units.

Repeated postponement of the attack is one of the primary reasons that led to the operation's failure. The combat efficiency of our units could be brought up to a very high standard but would not keep up with that of the enemy, who—in the same period of time—was able to make gains in strength greatly exceeding our own, thanks to his considerably greater economic war potential. The Red Army had the time and opportunity to bring its defensive measures to a level heretofore unknown. Behind this protective curtain strategic reserves could be assembled without interference.

Other reasons for the failure of the operation included the adherence to a battle plan that had been formulated in anticipation of other events and conditions. This plan provided for an attack to be launched from the shoulder of the Belgorod sector. Once we learned in May and June that this was precisely the area in which the Russians were prepared to offer their stiffest resistance, we should have modified our plans. Either we should have refrained from attacking at all, or the operation should have been carried out to strike the enemy not at his strongest but his weakest point: in this case the front sector east of Sumy. Our panzer divisions would have achieved freedom of movement much earlier, unlike the actual battle, in which they were hamstrung in fighting through the Soviet defensive system against a numerically superior enemy.

Our plans also suffered from the diverging commitment of the forces in the attacking armies. This led to the breakup of the operation into a series of individual battles and, combined with the disparity of forces, caused our command to forfeit freedom of action. What was to have been a "smooth operation" degenerated into a "slugging match."

That disparity of German and Russian strength was critical in its own right. German numerical inferiority, particularly in infantry, forced our panzer divisions, from the beginning, to expend their strength on tasks that were strange to them before they had the opportunity to engage the enemy in open terrain, making full use of their mobility.

Likewise, the German forces assigned to screen the flanks of the attacking armies (which became longer each day) were clearly insufficient.

The failure of the operation is not to be ascribed to front-line leadership or to the troops. In heavy, continuous fighting against a stubborn, numerically superior enemy, our soldiers suffered heavy losses but proved their superior spirit both in the attack and defense. The difficulty of this struggle can be measured at least in part by the casualty figures of XI Corps divisions from 5 to 20 July:

106th Infantry Division	3,244 (forty-six officers)
320th Infantry Division	2,839 (thirty officers)
168th Infantry Division	2,671 (127 officers)
	8,754 total

It is tragic that these troops were not successful, but it would be a historical error to reproach them for their failure.

Chapter 9

BELGOROD AND KHARKOV

The Soviet Breakthrough at Belgorod, 23 July–8 August

THE HEAT OF SUMMER STILL PARCHED THE blood-drenched fields along the banks of the upper Donets River when the four exhausted divisions of XI Corps (106th, 168th, 198th, and 320th Infantry Divisions) returned on 22 July to their old, well-fortified positions on both sides of Belgorod. During the Citadel offensive these divisions had all seen heavy fighting, which continued for the better part of a month, and in which they had taken heavy losses. Combat strengths had declined to 40–50 percent of that prescribed in the tables of organization, and in the case of some infantry regiments conditions were even worse. Nor could these divisions expect to receive any replacements for a long time to come.

On the other hand, our disengagement from the Russians had proceeded smoothly. Even the bridgehead at Belgorod, which XI Corps held as the last German unit to fight east of the Donets River, was evacuated with ease. The Red Army rifle divisions, which had been beaten shortly before, did not understand why the Germans were withdrawing voluntarily, and therefore remained suspicious. These suspicions were not unjustified, since many a German retirement had been followed by a surprise attack, which had wrought havoc on Soviet forces. This time, however, the withdrawal was genuine, with no trickery intended, having been solely dictated by the desire to intercept the counterattack of the still-intact Russian strategic reserves on a shorter, fortified line.

On 5 August 1943, after Soviet artillery had fired heavily for one hour, the enemy offensive began along the Belgorod-Kursk highway, with the unmistakable aim of pushing through the salient around Belgorod where the boundary between the Fourth Panzer Army and *Armeeabteilung* Kempf was situated and thereby dislocate the entire defensive line. In this the Russians succeeded completely. Their heavy barrage hit the 167th Infantry Division, which had taken up positions in a former Soviet antitank ditch, located a few kilometers in front of the well-fortified line. Within a short time massed Red Army tanks had crossed this ditch; by noon they passed the corps command post and poured into the depth of the German positions, all the while firing on our fleeing trains. On the following morning [6 August], after a nighttime forced march, Russian spearheads had reached the surprised headquarters of the Fourth Panzer Army at Bogodukhov. Since Colonel General Hermann Hoth's army had no reserves available to close the ten-kilometer gap in his front between Tomarovka and Belgorod, or even to stop the flood of enemy tanks that had already broken through to a depth of 100 kilometers, Russian spearheads reached the area northeast of Poltava and Akhtyrka on 7 August. [These and other events illustrate] the dangerous situation into which this development thrust XI Corps, which had been fighting with its front to the east.

On the very first day of the Soviet offensive, XI Corps had been attacked in the rear by enemy tank forces situated thirty kilometers in the depth of our positions. These tank forces simultaneously exerted crushing pressure on our unprotected left flank. At this critical moment, XI Corps had not only been left to its own devices but also had been handicapped by a direct Fuehrer Order, which had arrived at the last minute and insisted that Belgorod was to be held under all circumstances.

The corps front now formed a deep salient into enemy territory, which might have disintegrated with complete encirclement as its final destiny. This would have meant a widening of the existing Belgorod-Tomarovka gap from twenty-five to eighty kilometers and the immediate loss of several divisions. In view of XI Corps's limited strength, it would have been a mistake to attempt to close the gap by widening the corps sector—nor was any such plan feasible, since the Russians had kept up their pressure along the entire front. On the contrary, we had to keep our forces together and form a solid breakwater against numerically superior Soviet forces.

With these considerations determining the conduct of operations, I decided—Hitler's order notwithstanding—to fight a delaying action in successive positions until the withdrawal reached Kharkov and then to hold the city. XI Corps therefore had to build up a front facing north and protect its left flank against an enemy envelopment, while the right flank remained anchored on the Donets. We had to resist the immediate temptation to take forces out of XI Corps's eastern front along the Donets River in order to employ them (with their front reversed) along the Lopan River to protect our rear. The Donets front was not only very long, it was thinly held; removing any forces from it would expose this sector to disaster even if the Russians re-stricted themselves to conducting feints and relief attacks. Since such a weakening would have spelled doom for XI Corps, other measures had to be attempted.

The only units immediately available to me were the remnants of the 167th Infantry Division that had become separated from Fourth Panzer Army during the breakthrough (about 500 battle-weary soldiers without ar-tillery or heavy weapons) and the weak 6th Panzer Division, whose men—al-though they only had ten tanks—possessed good morale. As both divisions had been cut off from their own command, I immediately assumed com-mand over them and utilized them to build a defensive screen along the Lopan River. During the night of 5–6 August, I ordered the 168th Infantry Division (on the corps's left and resisting heavy pressure north of Belgorod) to pivot 180 degrees around Belgorod. We evacuated the city after heavy street fighting and occupied a new defensive line (prepared on the high ground immediately south of Belgorod). This positioned the division to join those elements mentioned above in protecting our rear; I also reinforced the 168th Infantry with one company of PzKw VI Tigers and another of StG III Assault Guns—together comprising a total of twenty-five armored vehicles. Sustained by their antitank guns and this handful of tanks, the two weak di-visions (supported by the *Kampfgruppe* of the 167th Infantry) withstood all attacks by Russian infantry, which were supported by large numbers of ground attack aircraft and at least 150 tanks.

In the long, threatened sector south along the Lopan River, XI Corps rap-idly had to improvise combat forces from Luftwaffe ground installations, as well as the corps combat trains and supply services. With the aid of the Luft-waffe's 88mm flak batteries in the 7th and 48th Flak Regiments, which we employed solely against Russian tanks despite the enemy's continuous air raids, these makeshift units managed to prevent the Soviets from pivoting their troops against the Kharkov-Belgorod *Rollbahn* and slicing into the rear of our Donets River front. On the morning of 8 August, however, Red Army tanks succeeded in breaking through the 168th Infantry Division and gaining an immediate foothold on the eastern bank of the Lopan River. Only an im-mediate counterattack by the 6th Panzer Division threw the enemy back and eliminated the threat. This time, by the narrowest of margins, events had played out in our favor.

Meanwhile, Soviet tank forces lunging farther south had managed to force the Lopan River at another location, from which they pushed immediately toward the critical Belgorod-Kharkov *Rollbahn*. By a fortunate coincidence, Assault Gun Battalion 905 had been rushed up from the Kharkov area, and its forty-two StG IIIs hit the enemy tank groups that had crossed the river, destroying them one by one. After this victory, Assault Gun Battalion 905 became XI Corps's only mobile tactical reserve.

Battles Along the Donets River, 31 July–9 August

The regiments of Major General Georg Postel's 320th Infantry Division were situated approximately thirty kilometers south of Belgorod on the hills on both sides of A—— Brook valley, through which a highway ran westward of the big Belgorod-Kharkov *Rollbahn*, and those of Lieutenant General Werner Forst's 106th Infantry Division held position directly north of them. [When writing this section of the manuscript, Raus apparently lacked the names of several villages and streams; they are referred to herein by the same letter designations he utilized. —S.H.N.] Any Russian advance through this valley would quickly interrupt this vital line of communication, which placed a heavy responsibility on the battalions stationed on both sides of the valley to prevent such incursions.

Our tactical withdrawal to the eastern bank of the Donets on 22 July had so surprised the Soviets in this sector that they only cautiously and hesitantly felt their way forward to the river on 23 July. In the 320th Infantry Division's sector the western bank of the Donets was much higher than the eastern, and—particularly at the junction of A—— Brook with the river—the terrain was swampy and covered with reeds. The Donets was not fordable at any point, and it seemed obvious that the Russians would have a difficult time forcing a breakthrough in this locality. During the day they would probably be able to hide along the eastern bank in the maze of trenches remaining from their battered former positions and in the innumerable shell craters, but they would be unable to move into the open without being identified and brought under fire by the German defenders.

The weapons of the 320th Infantry, from their well-concealed bunker positions, controlled the Donets River valley (which was very level along its entire extent of three to four kilometers) so effectively that it was impossible for the enemy to prepare a daylight attack. Our artillery and heavy weapons we positioned in the hills southwest of village B——, zeroing them in on a former bridge site and preparing them for night firing. Ridge 675, which afforded excellent visibility to the east, had been transformed into a virtually impregnable bastion. Shellproof dugouts, deep shelters, and communications tunnels protected the gun crews there from Russian counterbattery fire. Exits from the tunnels that faced the river had been expertly camouflaged, with machine guns emplaced in these exits to command the river in case the enemy attempted a night crossing. Their fields of fire covered not only the potential bridge site but also concentration areas and approach routes on

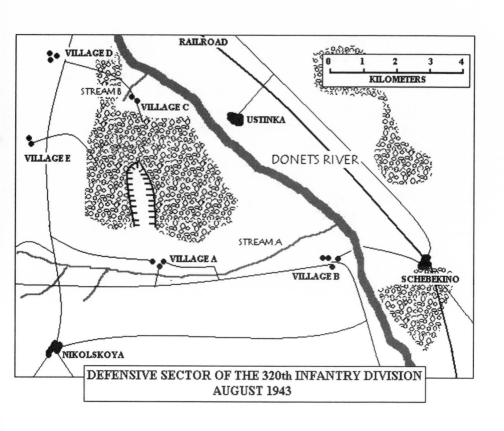

VILLAGE D

RAILROAD

STREAM B

VILLAGE C

USTINKA

0   1   2   3   4
KILOMETERS

VILLAGE E

DONETS RIVER

STREAM A

VILLAGE A

SCHEBEKINO

VILLAGE B

NIKOLSKOYA

DEFENSIVE SECTOR OF THE 320th INFANTRY DIVISION
AUGUST 1943

both banks of the Donets. Firing data for these weapons had been computed and carefully rechecked, while searchlights had been emplaced along the ridge to illuminate the immediate outpost area. The Russians lacked specific knowledge of these meticulous preparations but were fully aware that our troops had enjoyed ample opportunity to improve their defenses. As a result, a dead silence prevailed in the sun-drenched, glittering sand desert on the eastern bank of the Donets throughout the long summer days of late July.

During the brief nights, however, there was lively activity. First, Russian scouts looked for convenient crossing sites along the river bank. Later, small groups of enemy soldiers appeared on the western bank to reconnoiter our defenses and take prisoners. To this end they applied a method that they had already frequently used with success on previous occasions. In the darkness Russian scouts crept up to a German sentry standing in a trench and waited—often for hours at a time—for a suitable moment to overpower him. When they had succeeded in doing so, they immediately gagged the surprised victim, tied his arms and legs with ropes, and made a loop around his ankles, by which he was often dragged over distances of several hundred meters to the nearest Soviet trench. Such abductions were accomplished in complete silence. Only the tracks discovered the following morning indicated the direction in which the victims had been taken.

The only possible method of protecting our troops against this inhumane form of kidnapping consisted of increasing the number of security patrols and sentries, requiring the sentries to maintain constant contact with each other, establishing obstacles with alarm devices, laying minefields, and using trained watchdogs. These dogs, like setters, immediately indicated every movement in the vicinity of a sentry and attacked the Russians as they crept up or lurked in ambush. Despite such precautions, the endurance and ingenuity of the Red Army soldiers proved astonishing. Unable to realize his intention the first night, he continued to stalk our sentries every following night until he successfully acquired a victim. If he became aware of our countermeasures, he avoided them and went off in search of a spot that was better suited to his needs, and he continued to search relentlessly for such a spot until he found one. Often he would be rewarded by the carelessness of a German sentry, which he immediately noticed and exploited. In this strange and brutal manner the Soviets along the Donets managed (as they did on many other occasions) to obtain valuable information concerning the details of our defenses. Thus they determined that the positions of the 320th Infantry Division were particularly attenuated, owing to a shortage of troops, and that this was particularly true of the tree-covered hill sector north of A——Brook.

As a result of this intelligence, the enemy selected this point for his first attempt to cross the river. Fortunately, the men of the battalion positioned here had remained vigilant. They had identified and mined the tracks of the Russian scouting parties and had adjusted their machine guns and mortars on the crossing points used by these parties, so that the weapons were ready for night firing. Thus prepared, they kept a close watch on the river throughout the night of 31 July–1 August. As expected, just before dawn, several companies of Red Army troops appeared and commenced crossing the Donets at three previously reconnoitered points, utilizing improvised equipment. The mines that exploded and killed the first Russian soldiers to land on the western bank took them by complete surprise. The companies near the river on the eastern bank came under heavy, preregistered fire from machine guns and mortars, scattering in panic with heavy losses. Our artillery finished the job by shelling and destroying the river-crossing equipment they abandoned as soon as the sun rose.

General Postel and his troops did not make the mistake of thinking that the Russians would abandon their intention to force a crossing at this location because of a single setback. On the contrary, they repeated the attack on the night of 1–2 August, at the very same crossing sites, employing stronger forces and new equipment. General Postel decided not to interfere immediately but to deliver a decisive blow at the most critical moment. He ordered several batteries to mass their fire on the bridge site to smash the construction work after it had progressed sufficiently. At a prearranged time, just before midnight, all the guns fired upon the bridge site simultaneously and then ceased as abruptly as they had begun. Observers on the ridge made out the silhouette of a bizarre tangle of beams and pillars in the flickering light of burning lumber on the eastern bank of the river. The partially completed bridge was a shambles in the midst of which wounded men were screaming for help as shadows and scurrying figures (presumably medical aid men) moved among them.

Scarcely half an hour had passed when our observers reported that full-scale construction activity had resumed. The sounds of intensive hammering and sawing induced General Postel to order another concentration fired shortly after midnight. The result was equally devastating, though this time silence followed the bursts of our projectiles, a silence interrupted only by explosions from a few ammunition dumps that caught fire after sustaining direct hits. Yet the fires soon died down, and after only a brief interval the Russians again resumed their efforts as if nothing had happened. Obviously, the commander on the opposite shore had positive orders that his bridge had to be complete by dawn.

To frustrate this intention without wasting ammunition, General Postel ordered one 210mm howitzer battery to deliver intermittent harassing fire on the bridge site. Flash observation confirmed that the projectiles had landed on or very close to their targets. After an hour of harassment fire the pattern of Soviet response became clear. When a round did major damage it cause a prolonged work stoppage, but after a near-miss the hammering resumed immediately. General Postel therefore concluded that under these circumstance the Russians might still be able to complete the bridge by dawn, harassing fire notwithstanding.

He therefore decided to employ some of our hidden machine guns to rake the construction site at short intervals with bursts of fire. Judging by the screams of those who were hit, and the immediate suspension of the bridging operation, the rapid precision fire of these weapons had a devastating effect. Even so, the Russians still attempted to continue with the construction, but high losses forced them to slow down and finally quit the work entirely.

At periodic intervals, our heavy howitzers resumed harassing fire to discourage the Soviets from resuming their project and to complete the destruction. Only after daybreak was it possible for our observers to obtain a true picture of the results achieved during the hours of darkness. A horrific sight presented itself. Splintered rafters pointed skyward, and in between hung grotesquely mutilated corpses of the brave mean who had scorned death in the effort to accomplish their mission. Even more mangled bodies were strewn about in a wide circle around the bridge site or lay partially submerged in the mud holes formed by shell craters. Smashed vehicles, dead horses, and all kinds of ammunition and equipment littered the area. Live Russians, on the other hand, seemed to have vanished from the scene of their failure.

Nonetheless, a single small enemy group managed to escape destruction by clinging to the steep slope of the western bank, where our fire could not reach it. During the daylight hours of 2 August, however, combat patrols from the 320th Infantry drove this group into a nearby swamp, though even with mud reaching up to their chests and with the reeds providing scant cover this handful of Red Army soldiers kept fighting and held out until darkness again fell. To the astonishment of the German defenders, at dawn on 3 August not only did this ragged group of Russians still occupy its strip of swamp, it had been reinforced. At its side another one or two "swamp companies" had taken up positions. This was something that German or other European troops would never have done. The swamp was situated on the western bank just in front of the valley position, 300 meters back from the river. General Postel's regiment and battalion commanders had chosen to defend from the valley position because they considered the swamp in their front to be a very good obstacle to any enemy crossing attempt. None of these officers (and no German commander in a similar position) would have thought of placing his men within the swamp just to move them closer to the river.

Conversely, the Russians saw that boggy ground as the chance to gain a foothold on the western bank and so formed a "swamp bridgehead," placing their troops in a situation that the German defenders certainly did not envy. Our infantry frankly considered it impossible that the Russians could remain in the swamp for a long period of time. One observer, stationed in a nearby church tower, had an excellent view of the whole swamp bridgehead and watched incredulously as the helmet-covered heads of the Soviet defenders—their bodies concealed by the reeds—bobbed up and down like corks from the necks of champagne bottles. The Russians rested their rifles in the forks of branches or on boards and remained ready to fire at all times. By their side, the frogs of the swamp frolicked and peacefully croaked their monotonous evening song as an accompaniment to the conduct of the enemy, which seemed senseless to our troops. Yet we knew that the Russians must have taken this step as part of a plan. What could it be? Only subsequent events answered this question.

Apparently thwarted in this crossing attempt, the Russians changed both the scene of action and their method of attack. It seemed plain to our officers that the Soviets felt they had fared badly in the swamp or they would not have abandoned this axis of attack after the second attempt. To change or abandon a plan once it had been adopted was not characteristic of the Russian way of thinking, and when such occurred, we always considered it an indication that the enemy felt himself to have suffered a serious defeat.

The enemy now therefore selected the battalion immediately adjacent to the north as the objective of his next attack on the afternoon of 3 August. This sector covered a group of wooded hills in an area where their elevation varied greatly, affording only a very limited field of view because of dense underbrush. The eastern edge of these hills—thirty to fifty meters high and situated along the western bank of the Donets—provided our defenders with good visibility and the chance to use their weapons effectively. However, the men of the battalion knew from prior experience that once the Soviets gained a foothold in the woods (which were difficult to defend) it would be nearly impossible to dislodge them.

We knew from two years of fighting that the only effective method of driving Red Army soldiers out of a wilderness such as this involved the use of massed troops or resorting to such extremely radical means as flamethrowers, flamethrowing tanks, or by setting the forest on fire. Often it became necessary to encircle and destroy Russians in the woods in close combat, which necessarily resulted in severe losses on both sides. Russian tenacity surpassed anything previously known in other theaters of operation. The danger of becoming embroiled in a fight for these particular woods was all the greater because our line was so thinly manned. The Citadel offensive had left our line companies with scarcely half their assigned combat strength, and no adequate reserves existed in the rear. At best the battalion had to rely on a few well-trained assault patrols and the slender regimental reserve (a company of sixty men) to eliminate any penetrations. To set fire to the young trees with their green leaves would have been impossible. Hence, the officers on the scene regarded the future with grave concern. They knew they would have to collapse the Russian attack in front of the main battle line. Otherwise, we risked the loss of the wooded hill zone, which would make an excellent assembly area for the Soviets to concentrate for a strong thrust into our position. Only the 320th Infantry's divisional artillery (which was strong and still intact) and the Luftwaffe could enable us to thwart the enemy's plan. Both did all they could.

No sooner had the Russians readied their first stream-crossing equipment in the willows and reeds than our observers identified it, allowing us to destroy it by artillery fire despite its excellent concealment. Reconnaissance aircraft also spotted heavily manned trenches in the vicinity of the Donets. A short time afterward, Luftflotte Four's bomber wings arrived on the scene and smashed the enemy's troop concentrations and advanced heavy weapons in wave after wave of attacks. Even the Soviet batteries (which had previously adjusted their fire to target our positions along the edge of the hills) fell silent out of fear not only of German bombers but—even more—from dread of the 210mm howitzer battery from I Battalion, 213th Artillery Regiment, attached to our forward units. This battery had accurately determined the location of the supporting Russian guns by sound-and-flash-ranging and took them under effective and precisely adjusted fire before they were able to change position. This success resulted in a further withdrawal and increased caution (one might say timidity) on the part of the Russian artillery, which served substantially to decrease its effectiveness.

On the other hand, periodic surprise fire from enemy *Stalinorgeln* proved extremely irksome. These rocket launchers changed locations immediately after firing each salvo and hence could never be taken under fire by the 320th Infantry Division artillery. Only after our artillery observers determined that the rocket batteries repeatedly took up position—in irregular succession—at the same three or four crossroads did German artillery manage to silence them. Each of the available batteries from the II, III, and IV Battalions, 320th Artillery Regiment, as well as the attached 210mm howitzer battery, adjusted its fire to one of the known rocket launcher positions so that all the alternate positions could be hit simultaneously by a hail of fire as soon as the launchers fired a salvo. The fire from at least one of the ambush batteries then would certainly hit the target directly, and in fact many a rocket launcher was disabled by use of this method. The crews of the surviving rocket launchers stopped moving their launchers into the open and could no longer fire so freely on our infantry. Thus the rocket launchers ceased to constitute a threat, and this tactical solution once again proved the old saying that "necessity is the mother of invention."

Only after that incident did the troops enjoy a brief period of quiet, which proved to be the pleasant interlude before the storm, as the Russians now decided to capitalize on their proficiency at night operations. General Postel's artillery and heavy infantry weapons attempted in vain to interfere with or break up—by means of harassing fire—the new Soviet preparations for a night crossing of the Donets. This time the Russians intended to try their luck at two points simultaneously. In keeping with the Russian character, the first of these two was where they had suffered defeat the previous day. Yet simultaneously our observers also detected lively movement, the sound of logs dropping, and noise of heavy equipment several kilometers to the south, where a highway bridge had formerly spanned the river. It became quickly obvious that the Soviets intended not just to cross but to bridge the river and that this was where their main effort could be expected. Our troops passed a wearying and tense night, with every man realizing that the Russians planned to throw their full weight of men and equipment into the upcoming battle in order to achieve a quick decision, even if only by sheer weight of numbers.

With the first light of dawn on 4 August, relocated Red Army batteries hurled salvo after salvo across the Donets, devastating the bunker positions of the northern battalion along the edge of the hills. By the time all of the enemy's light batteries and a large number of heavy trench mortars had joined the firefight, it assumed the proportion of a regular witches' Sabbath. Concentrated on a small area, this "infernal" fire demolished all the defense installations and shelters in the position. Uprooted and shattered tree trunks covered the ground, rendering all movement impossible for the surviving German defenders, who could only crouch resignedly in shell craters and await the inevitable assault by Russian infantry.

At length, after the barrage had raged for nearly two hours, the enemy shells began to whistle over the defenders' heads into a position situated in their rear. Our troops had scarcely discerned this shift of fire when the first Soviet infantry appeared, but after the paralyzing wait under nerve-racking fire the chance to fight back came as a welcome relief. Machine guns began to fire their volleys into the attackers, submachine guns started to rattle, and hand grenades burst on every side. All of these sounds were quickly drowned out, however, when the German counterbarrage opened. Concentrated fire from the 320th Artillery Regiment and attached batteries sent mud and columns of water spouting into the air, smashed the enemy's stream-crossing equipment, and inflicted murderous casualties on his forces.

Nevertheless, the Russians somehow succeeded in getting several rifle companies across the river, primarily because our defenses were no longer compact. The devastating Soviet preparatory fire had torn great gaps in the 320th Infantry's defenses, which had been thinly manned to begin with. Soon Red Army assault troops had penetrated through these gaps and enveloped several pockets of resistance—although these isolated posts put up the most desperate resistance. German troops thus fighting on could hear the enemy's cheering troops move farther and farther toward their own rear areas, and their fate appeared to be settled. Yet our encircled soldiers held their ground, even in this apparently hopeless situation, clinging to the chance that detachments from the adjoining units or the regimental reserves would come to their rescue. Until this happened, however, they were on their own; each hour seemed an eternity.

Suddenly German machine-gun fire raged in the forest to their rear, easily recognizable by its very high rate of fire. Soon the distinctive rattle of submachine guns joined in, the bullets whistling past the defenders' hedgehog positions. Volleys of hand grenades exploded, and a rousing "Hurrah!" echoed through the din of brutal fighting in the forest.

"Our reserves are attacking!" the encircled men cried out to each other as their hearts leaped. "They are coming, they are coming!" Soon the first few groups of Russians could be discerned in full flight through the trees, and their numbers kept increasing. Here and there the fighting flared up again at close range but subsided almost as quickly. The forces surrounding our cut-off troops decreased rapidly as they were caught up in the current of the retreat.

Close on their heels followed the rescuers, spearheaded by a heavily armed combat patrol, and by noon the entire position was back in German hands. This time it had still been possible, through the use of the last local reserves, to eliminate the Soviet penetration and thus avert calamity. Yet even though the Russians had suffered severe losses, they nonetheless clung tenaciously to a thin strip of the western riverbank. They held this narrow piece of ground thanks almost entirely to the weight of their artillery, which now threw down a protective curtain of fire. Such an action clearly indicated that the enemy intended to move up reinforcements and renew his attack.

The Russians assaulted the reformed German line that very afternoon, timing their attack to coincide with an attack farther south, which consumed the main efforts of our artillery and air support. To repulse this new attack, no more reserves were available, and the Soviets managed to achieve a deep penetration into the woods. Only the commitment of the divisional reserve (about a dozen assault guns and a 100-man company of combat engineers) succeeded in stopping the Russian thrust at the western edge of a gorge that traversed the forest from north to south. Fortunately, a variety of forest roads and narrow lanes through the woods facilitated the movement of the assault guns, which—in cooperation with the engineer company—provided critical support to the retiring, scattered units of the badly battered infantry battalion. Our retreating soldiers rapidly assembled along the rim of the gorge, which was a few meters in depth and conveniently situated for an improvised defensive line. There the battalion made its stand and, with the help of the assault guns and engineers, frustrated every Russian attempt to cross the gorge. Each time a Soviet machine gun appeared on the opposite rim of the gorge, our observers identified it as soon as it opened fire, and the deadly accurate fire of our assault guns destroyed it. With every passing hour the German battle line grew stronger as men returning from furloughs or the hospital made their way forward, along with soldiers from the division service and supply units, who were usually moved to focal points during a crisis. In addition, the engineers quickly mined the bottom of the gorge, as well as felling tree obstacles and erecting alarm devices. Taken altogether these measures so greatly increased the strength of our resistance that even before sunset the threat of a Russian breakthrough had been eliminated.

In the meantime, however, the situation of the battalion farther south had taken a desperate turn. The northern flank of this battalion had been caught by the enemy push just described and was forced back into a weak oblique defensive line. Instead of pivoting heavy forces southward to expel the battalion from its dominating hill position (which necessarily would have weakened the attack toward the forest gorge), the Russians bypassed the thin German line, hoping to be able to take the defenders in the rear and collapse our entire valley position. Undaunted, this brave battalion frustrated those plans by holding fast in its critical position, despite the risk of encirclement.

All of a sudden a completely unexpected event occurred. In the gap between the battalion defending the gorge and the battalion on the hill, soldiers in German uniforms carrying German equipment appeared and, in good German, reported the arrival of reinforcements, come to aid the threatened sector in the nick of time. Understandably, the troops received this news with great joy, and the story spread through the battalion with lightning speed. Before the battalion commander had time to ascertain the strength and origin of this seemingly providential reinforcement, the Soviets launched an assault along the battalion's entire front. In minutes the situation became critical, and the battalion committed every last man to the front line.

This was the moment when the "German" soldiers from the newly arrived companies poured out of the woods in dense columns and opened a murderous hail of fire against the battalion's flank and rear. Through the confusion that followed, shouts rang out: "Here are Germans!" "Don't fire!" "Cease fire!" "Madness!" "What's going on here?" For precious minutes no one among the defenders comprehended what had happened. Abruptly, all firing ceased as these new "Germans" had become hopelessly intermingled with the defenders. Now they unleashed ear-splitting yells of "Urrah! Urrah! Urrah!" and attacked at close quarters. In this bewildering situation it was impossible to distinguish friend from foe, and everyone in the forest began to fight everyone else. No one seemed to be able to help, or even to disentangle the chaos.

The battalion commander suddenly grasped the purpose of the insidious attack and realized in a flash that only one decision could possibly save his unit and keep the entire valley position from being rolled up. He ordered an immediate retreat toward the northern edge of A——— village, a call that had the effect of a kindling spark. Even in the midst of confused fighting our soldiers recognized their commander's voice and passed on the order; soon every German soldier understood exactly what had to be done. The order would not be easy to execute, but unless it was carried out every man and piece of equipment would soon be lost. Yet the commander held firm in his belief that his officers and his seasoned infantrymen could make it.

The battalion commander hastily gathered together a few officers and all the enlisted troops in his immediate vicinity and formed them into an assault detachment that he led personally. Holding submachine guns or rifles in front, ready to fire, or with daggers and hand grenades in clenched fists, this group killed the masquerading Russians wherever they met them, recognizing the enemy by his Mongolian features regardless of the uniform he wore. In this fashion the commander and his men pushed their way through the fighting soldiers, reaching the forest edge in short bounds where they found the relative safety of the gullies and depressions that led into the village. Imitating their commander, other officers and senior NCOs formed their own detachments and fought their way back toward the village. As each contingent arrived, the commander immediately incorporated them into his improvised defensive positions alongside any soldiers from the rear services who happened to be present in the village already. Absolutely no regard was paid to anyone's unit of assignment—there was no time. In the meantime, regimental headquarters, having learned of the near-disaster, rushed a company of reinforcements to the village on trucks provided by division, along with a handful of assault guns.

Favored by the terrain, which sloped toward the village and afforded cover from both observation and fire, the commander had assembled the remains of his battalion into a coherent defensive position by late afternoon. When the Russians appeared on the edge of the forest soon thereafter, heavy machine-gun fire forced them back to the protection of the trees. Whenever the Soviets repeated their attempt to advance toward the village, artillery and assault-gun fire thwarted them. Time and again the fire of the defenders threw the enemy back into the woods with heavy losses. Gradually, darkness fell, and in the twilight a surprising number of stragglers from the battalion found their way back to the village through various detours. By midnight the battalion had nearly reached the strength at which it started the day; in view of the crisis just past, its losses had been amazingly small. The commander's presence of mind and his ability to assert his will even in a chaotic situation, along with the initiative demonstrated by his officers and NCOs, had been all that saved the entire battalion from certain doom. The Red Army's gross violation of international law, though resulting in the loss of an important defensive bastion, failed to bring about the collapse of the German front along the Donets.

The speed with which this battalion recovered from the blow that it had received at the end of the day is indicated by the fact that the commander was able—that very night—to plan confidently on recapturing the lost position the following morning. In this he demonstrated his confidence in the men who had passed with him through that black day. At dawn on 4 August he intended to strike the enemy (who was certain to try another advance) so hard with a surprise blow that the lost hill position might be recaptured.

At first light the Russian artillery and heavy mortars began shelling the village with a fire that quickly grew in intensity. With a deafening din, echoed over and over again throughout the forest, shells roared and whistled up to burst in the village and on the other side of the road. Under the protection of this wall of fire, wave after wave of Russians broke out of the forest and ran down through the meadow in front of the German positions.

The leading elements of the Russian attack had already come within storming distance when the German counterattack began. Ground-attack and bomber wings appeared over the scene and struck the enemy on a continuous basis. The assault guns (whose number had been greatly increased overnight) moved forward against the Soviet line, all guns blazing. These guns and the machine guns being fired from trenches, foxholes, and houses, as well as the artillery, antitank guns, and flak, spread such havoc in the enemy ranks that the attack literally melted away. Caught in terrain that offered no cover, the Russian soldiers knew that their only chance to survive this hail of fire lay in an immediate retreat to the woods.

At the very moment, however, when the enemy started pulling back, the guns of the 320th Artillery Regiment began firing a deadly barrage into the edge of the forest, inflicting serious losses on the Russians and destroying their cohesion as a fighting force. Men ran in all directions, looking for some way to save themselves, but only battered remnants managed to find refuge in the forest. Even among the trees there was no safety to be found, and no time to reorganize, for the battalion commander now led his men in a spirited counterattack. His thin companies of infantry, still smarting from the enemy's trickery on the previous afternoon, followed the fleeing Russians, tracked them down in the forest, and—by pushing forward rapidly—prevented them from rallying on the original German hill position. Hardly two hours had passed since the beginning of the attack when the leading German infantrymen regained the position held the previous day and secured it in short order.

The treacherous attack on 3 August had indeed created a perilous situation, but the counterattack on 4 August completely nullified any success that the Russians had unfairly gained. Heavy losses in men and equipment were the result of this operation on the Soviet side, including the deaths of the majority of Russian soldiers who had worn German uniforms. Unfortunately, our worn-out and depleted companies lacked the strength to push the enemy back across the Donets, though the 320th Infantry Division still held the critical hill positions in the south and the line of the forest gorge to the north.

Despite the heavy losses repeatedly suffered in bridge-building attempts at the southern bridgehead, the Russians resumed their efforts on the night of 4–5 August. Although we had not expected a resumption of construction at this point, our defensive system remained intact, and our harassing fire was guided by the experience gained earlier. Howitzers and machine guns began firing at the same targets as before. Again, machine guns were by far the most effective antipersonnel weapon, while the artillery fire was directed against vehicles and equipment. As on previous nights, the Russians refused to be discouraged and doggedly continued their bridge construction, until just before midnight they apparently gave up and ceased working. The sound of track-laying vehicles coming from the eastern bank of the Donets gave the impression that prime movers had been moved up to recover disabled vehicles, stores of supplies, and bridging equipment.

In this instance we had arrived at entirely erroneous conclusions. To everyone's great surprise, the sounds of the tracked vehicles did not diminish as dawn approached; on the contrary, the noises came closer and grew louder. When our observers turned on their searchlights, they discovered that what they had taken to be prime movers were in fact tanks that had somehow crossed the river under the cover of darkness. While dawn was breaking, the lead enemy tanks reached the outskirts of village B———, through which they drove with guns firing against our defensive line just to the west. That movement was apparently the prearranged signal for a general attack, as Russian artillery then opened fire on the village from the eastern bank. Shells rained down upon our positions on the ridges and hills surrounding both sides of the valley of A—— Brook, in an obvious bid to neutralize the dominating defenses on the heights.

Our artillery immediately replied with fire aimed at the Russian forces in the valley and east of village A——. This barrage, combined with previously erected obstacles and minefields, delayed the Soviet advance until there was sufficient light to permit more accurate firing. The full morning light revealed that the Russian tanks had cleared the roadblock east of the village and, accompanied by large infantry forces echeloned in depth, had penetrated into the center of the village. Other tanks had followed into the gap and then turned north and south to swing around and begin reducing our defensive positions one strongpoint at a time. Caught off-guard by this attack, the exhausted battalion (minus the assault guns and engineer company, which had been transferred to another sector of the front) had no choice but to fall back rapidly through the valley down which A—— Brook flowed and yielding its defensive positions of the previous day in village A——.

This was a critical moment, for the Russian penetration had reached a position from which it could either turn north—enveloping the defenders of the forest gorge—or plunge forward into the firing positions of the divisional artillery. General Postel immediately ordered the return of the assault guns and engineers to counterattack the enemy spearhead, and despite heavy pressure in the fighting along the Lopan River to the west, I released the II Battalion, 1st Heavy Mortar Regiment (equipped with the *Nebelwerfer* multiple rocket launchers), to support his operations. These forces, assembled by late morning, proved sufficient to halt the enemy's advance and then push him back to the eastern edge of village A——.

During the initial Russian attack that morning, the "swamp battalion" along the riverbank attempted to make its presence felt again. With almost unimaginable tenacity the Soviet defenders in that bog not only had held their position but also had been reinforced by at least several additional rifle companies. When the Russians launched their tank-supported assault down the valley, these troops tried to capture our strongpoint on the hill overlooking the river by a coup de main. To this end they had slipped down the riverbank and attacked the hill from the south. Fortunately, the German detachment posted there was not caught unawares and immediately pinned down these "swamp soldiers" with machine-gun fire. Moreover, an ambush battery from the III Battalion, 320th Artillery Regiment, had been established against just such an eventuality in complete concealment in a forested depression, from which it suddenly opened point-blank fire against the enemy's rear. As a result, the battalion was caught by fire from two sides, which was unbearable even by Russian standards, and which quickly wore out the resistance of even this battle-toughened unit.

By noon the general Soviet attack had been stopped everywhere and the enemy trapped in a deep, but very narrow, pocket in which he could move neither forward nor backward without sustaining heavy losses. His situation became even more unpleasant as all attempts to bring up reserves to force a new breakthrough failed due to formidable German artillery fire from his flank and rear. Only when darkness again fell would the Russians be able to move up sufficient numbers of troops to give their offensive a new impulse. That prospect deeply concerned General Postel and his subordinate commanders, who had already been obliged to employ their last man and their last weapon to stop the original advance. They could not afford to be satisfied with holding the Russians in place but would have to find a way to throw them back across the Donets before night.

Despite the disparity of forces, General Postel determined to employ his nine remaining assault guns and the engineer company in a frontal attack on both sides of the street running through the middle of the village. The combat engineers were stalwart fellows, "prepared to kidnap the Devil from hell," and well versed in working in cooperation with the assault guns. Supporting weapons on the flanks of the Russian penetration (machine guns, antitank guns, and flak) enjoyed a clear field of fire against the enemy positions, quite literally viewing the village in front of them as if it were situated on a raised table. This circumstance allowed for ideal coordination between the assault troops and their supports, to which could be added a few flights of ground-attack aircraft that Luftflotte Four managed to make available. The attack began an hour after noon.

The engineers, it should be noted, were eager above all else to reach the Donets and learn how the Russians had managed to cross such a large number of tanks, in spite of the fact that they had been prevented from building a bridge. This question puzzled everyone, all the way up through corps headquarters, since we had been defending this stretch of the river for months. We had measured its depth along all our defensive sectors and knew it to be an absolute tank obstacle, which during the Citadel offensive even our PzKw VI Tigers and StG III assault guns had been unable to cross until a seventy-ton bridge had been constructed. Yet from the hill to the south (which had been successfully defended against the "swamp battalion"), our observers could plainly see tank tracks leading down to the eastern bank of the river and then emerging again on our side. Many officers on the scene therefore concluded that the tanks that appeared so suddenly must have been amphibious.

As the only officer present who had ever met amphibious Russian tanks, I disagreed. In July 1941, when commanding the 6th Motorized Brigade of the 6th Panzer Division, I had encountered and destroyed six light amphibious tanks on the Szilinia River south of Novoselye, which was located on the large *Rollbahn* to Leningrad. At the time, having only a fleeting glance at these vehicles, I had assumed them to be of U.S. manufacture. The fact that such tanks were never to my knowledge encountered again, and having learned since the war that the United States had no such vehicles in production at the time, I now believe that these six tanks were test models of Soviet origin. Whatever their source, the critical question was one of size. The light amphibious tanks compared to the T-34s that the enemy had employed in this attack were as David compared to Goliath. As a result, I considered it impossible for the Russian tanks that had crossed the Donets without a bridge to have been amphibious.

How then did these T-34s, whose characteristics we knew quite well, manage to make their way across a river whose depth had recently been sounded at three meters? Although the T-34 had the greatest cross-country mobility of any tank on the continent and had often accomplished astonishing feats, it was the unanimous opinion of all the officers on the scene that no T-34 could have been driven across the Donets here. And yet their existence could not be denied.

Many hours of heavy fighting passed before we solved this riddle. First, it was necessary to reach the river, and though completely exposed to heavy flanking fire the Russians offered heavy resistance at every step. Each house had to be wrested away from them in close-in, often hand-to-hand, fighting. Soviet infantry clung even to the ruins of buildings pounded into rubble by our artillery as long as their tanks remained in the vicinity. These T-34s now constituted the backbone of the defense, just as they had provided the momentum for the attack in the morning. Every weapon we could bring to bear was firing from all sides, but this had little effect unless an armor-piercing round chanced to score a direct hit and set one ablaze. Our assault guns, which represented the most dangerous threat to the T-34s, had a difficult mission to fulfill, as the enemy tanks—numerically superior—stubbornly held their ground and forced our StG IIIs to approach at point-blank range. Many of the assault guns suffered direct hits on their reinforced frontal armor before they could manage to incapacitate a single T-34. Once the top plate of the frontal armor on any given StG III was smashed, this vehicle had to be relegated to a secondary place in the rear of those of its fellows whose front armor remained intact.

Despite these difficulties, the assault guns gradually made headway; after an hour five T-34s were burning, whereas only a few of our StG IIIs had sustained light damage, and all remained in operation. Yet by the time our troops reached the center of the village, heavy Soviet losses had ironically created a balance of power. The resistance offered by the enemy infantry trapped in the valley actually stiffened as a result of more and more units being brought under direct fire while being caught in the flank by our advance. Those elements that could do so changed their front to face our assault troops directly. Only after the ground-attack aircraft entered the fight, hitting these units with continual sorties while our artillery fire from the flanks and rear rose to unbearable proportions, did the Russians' will to fight begin to decrease noticeably. The T-34s, however, continued to offer extremely heavy resistance. Their crews realized that any withdrawal would result in certain defeat and ruinous losses. This refusal to yield could not prevent our victory but certainly delayed it; only by late afternoon had the last T-34 fallen victim to our remaining assault guns, whereupon enemy resistance completely collapsed.

Darkness fell as the German assault elements finally passed through the village and our artillery observers could resume their old post in the "eagle's nest" at the top of the church tower that they had been forced to vacate that morning. In the last glow of twilight, assault guns accompanied by engineer patrols following the defeated Russians reached the riverbank where the T-34s had emerged through the morning mist. Even at very close range no sign of a bridge could be detected, and only when the confused engineers sounded the depth of the water could the riddle be solved. At a depth of half a meter, the engineers discovered a submarine bridge. The Russians had built such bridges on other occasions in order to shield river crossings from Luftwaffe aerial observation, and so the existence of such a bridge was less a cause for astonishment than the fact that it had been constructed in an incredibly short time during a devastating artillery fire. Only a closer inspection of the bridge foundations allowed this mystery to be unraveled. We discovered two rows of undamaged T-34s, which had been driven into the water one behind the other, and which served as supports for the improvised submarine bridge. Planking had been hastily thrown on top of them and attached to the tanks with ropes. Thereafter the venture of allowing other tanks to cross the river on top of the submerged T-34s was immediately hazarded. To the Russians the fact that a few tanks overturned and plunged into the water in the process mattered little. The main objective—getting a majority of them across the Donets quickly enough to achieve tactical surprise—had been accomplished. Only our assault guns saved them the necessity of making a return trip over this strange bridge.

The enemy had obviously hoped to retrieve the submerged tanks from the water and utilize them again after a successful breakthrough. As matters stood, however, our combat engineers blasted them in place, sending another dozen T-34s to the same "tank graveyard" that their fellows had found on dry land. These demolitions constituted the last activity at the end of a day of grueling combat. Now the silence of night drew "a veil of peace over the scene."

Once again, an utterly unusual tactic employed by the Red Army had resulted in surprising success and threatened our entire defense with disaster. Only the immediate countermeasures instituted by commanders on the scene and the courageous bearing of General Postel's troops managed to nullify yet another potential Russian success. That such a small counterattack force— nine StG IIIs and about eighty engineers—managed to defeat a numerically superior opponent could in no small measure be attributed to the employment of a large number of automatic weapons, whose fire was coordinated with precision and struck the Russians with annihilating effect. The ultimate result of this small battle underscores what can be achieved by a minimum number of excellently trained men if they are supported by the most effective weapons.

In view of the continuously deteriorating situation on XI Corps's eastern flank, it is understandable that, even after the repulse on 5 August, the Soviets persisted in their attempts to force a breakthrough on the Donets front. By this time the Russians retained only one bridgehead over the river, along the wooded hills and bounded by the forest gorge that our troops nicknamed *Totenschlucht*—"the Gorge of Death." The enemy forces on the eastern rim of the gorge had remained inactive throughout the course of fighting on 5 August, but it seemed certain to everyone that the next Soviet offensive would have to take the form of an assault across the *Totenschlucht* despite all the inherent difficulties in such an attack.

Whether through coincidence or design, the Russians opened their attack on 6 August, at precisely the moment when XI Corps's left wing faced its most critical challenge, with enemy tank and infantry units attacking deep in the rear along the Lopan River. In effect, if the Soviets simultaneously penetrated our rear area there and forced a breakthrough along the Donets, five divisions would be encircled and destroyed. It was imperative that both the 106th and 320th Infantry Divisions hold their positions, even without any prospect whatsoever of additional reinforcements from corps headquarters.

General Postel found himself forced to resort to a desperate expedient in order to concentrate even minimal reserves. He stripped two battalions from thus-far quiet sectors on his far southern flank, replacing these veterans with a thin screen of recruits and replacements from the division's *Feldersatz* [field replacement] battalion. Employing these young troops, inexperienced in battle as they were, side by side on a broad front without any reserve worth mentioning constituted a serious risk, but the events of 6 August, as the redeployment of these units took place, proved that it had been imperative to do so.

After several unsuccessful assaults, the Russians managed to cross the minefields in the gorge by an unsparing and inhuman employment of their men. The method employed was very simple: Company after company was driven forward into the heavily mined gorge in front of the enemy lines until even the last mines had detonated. In the end, "fields of bodies" replaced the minefields. Then the next waves of the attack stepped over the bodies of their fallen comrades to climb the western edge of the gorge.

For hours, the devastating defensive fire of German machine guns thwarted every attempt to break over the edge of the ravine. This fire took such an ever-increasing bloody toll among the Russians that eventually an unbroken line of corpses lay at the rim of the gorge. Many a brave Soviet soldier still held his rifle in fire position, while his head—pierced by bullets—rested on his weapon. Yet the enemy command needed a breakthrough at all costs, and again and again new waves marched into battle across a carpet of the dead, until German resistance finally began to break as a result of the losses suffered and a lack of ammunition.

After the struggle for the *Totenschlucht* had consumed several hours, our infantry finally found itself obliged to withdraw, step by step. We nonetheless managed to maintain possession of the hotly contested western edge of the forest until evening, when reinforcements approached from the rear. Even though the Russians, at horrific cost, had substantially expanded their bridgehead, their efforts to achieve a breakthrough had failed. Not deterred, the Soviets ordered up additional battalions in order to gain a complete success on 7 August.

German reinforcements, however, had also arrived and begun preparing their own attack. The two battalions of the 320th Infantry withdrawn from the south, one battalion from the 106th Infantry, and our few remaining assault guns had the mission of regaining the forest in a concentric attack and throwing the Russians back into the river. A drum-fire barrage delivered by all available artillery, reinforced by the *Nebelwerfer* battalion and several batteries of 88mm flak, would precede the attack. We could not, unfortunately, count on air support, since Luftflotte Four had to commit all its strength to support Fourth Panzer Army against the main Soviet breakthrough, whose masses of tanks had yet to be destroyed. This absence of the Luftwaffe, however, was essentially offset by the fact that the Red Army had also committed the overwhelming majority of its own air assets in trying to bring about a decision against Fourth Panzer Army.

Assembly for the counterattack went smoothly, and at the prescribed hour the *Nebelwerfer* batteries and the concentrated artillery of both infantry divisions opened fire. Causing a terrific din, these shells detonated amid the massed troops that the Russians had concentrated for their own attack, shattering them. Heavy howitzer shells roared down into the *Totenschlucht* itself, landing among the troops and staff that had gathered there. Any danger that the German barrage delivered into the forest might hit our own front line had been eliminated by a systematic withdrawal minutes before the artillery opened fire. This brief retirement had been scheduled precisely according to the clock, went as far as the western edge of the woods, and had been immediately preceded by infantry fire that simulated an attack.

Simultaneously with the surprise concentration of fire that struck the Soviet front line, our real infantry attack commenced. Gradually the artillery concentration moved east, as far as the *Totenschlucht*, which having now been taken under fire from all directions turned into a mass grave for Russian soldiers and Russian hopes. Such a heavy artillery preparation not only lifted the morale of our assault troops but did such damage to the enemy that the attack made rapid progress. With assault guns and strong combat patrols forming the spearhead, General Postel's troops reached the *Totenschlucht* before noon and crossed it a short while afterward. Even to our experienced veterans, the gorge offered a ghastly picture of death and ruin.

The single battalion of the 106th Infantry Division, attacking from the north with the support of a few assault guns, also advanced rapidly and pushed ever more deeply into the Soviet flank. Even the battalion on the southern hills, which had been so battered over the past several days, now joined the fight with gunfire and combat patrols. Everywhere the Russians appeared to be in full retreat. By noon the concentrically attacking battalions had gained direct contact with each other's flanks in all sectors, and the iron ring around the enemy's decimated force drew tighter and tighter. General Postel intended to encircle and destroy the Russians before they could reach the river. By early afternoon the Soviet line had become so constricted that considerable elements of the attacking force, including most of the assault guns, had to be withdrawn from the front for lack of space. Certainly, everyone agreed, in no more than a few hours the entire western bank of the Donets would be back in our hands.

All of a sudden, however, Russian resistance stiffened again. Our spearheads quite unexpectedly encountered heavily mined tree-branch obstacles, tied together with barbed wire, which proved impossible to overcome. Attempts to blast these obstacles show that behind the initial line rows and rows of additional mines had been deployed, which could not be removed because they were covered by heavy enemy defensive fire. For the first time that day the Soviets also opened a lively artillery barrage, reinforced by the fire of heavy trench mortars, which made any further German advance impossible.

Soon it became evident that during the past few days the Russians had established a heavily fortified area on the western bank of the Donets. In the event of a tactical reverse, which the Red Army commanders had to consider as a possibility in light of their experiences over the previous week, they needed an area that could be held under all circumstances. This area represented sort of an "emergency bridgehead" or a "bridgehead within a bridgehead," whose purpose was to save them another costly river crossing if worse came to worst.

Indeed, every German attempt to remove this thorn from our side failed. The assault guns could not keep pace with the other troops in this very uneven and heavily wooded terrain. Nor could our artillery—even the *Nebelwerfers*—effectively "soften up" this small area a few hundred meters in diameter, despite the fact that their hail of fire dislodged many of the tree-branch obstacles, tore gaps in the minefields, and battered the woods. Not even a single combat patrol managed to break into this position. Even employing flamethrowers proved unsuccessful, since the Russians were crouched in small dugouts and bunkers, against which even this terrible weapon proved ineffective. Although a few bunkers were destroyed and a number of dugouts buried under falling earth, enough remained on the other side and in their rear to forestall our advance.

Prisoner interrogations subsequently informed us that a "security garrison" occupied this fortified bridgehead, which had been taken from a choice unit commanded by commissars, and which had not taken part in the preceding battle. These men had been faced with the alternative of holding their positions to the last man or being shot in the back of the neck. Another part of their mission (which they failed to perform) had been to stop any retreating Russian battalions on the western side of the river. These battalions, however, had been so thoroughly battered by the impact of our preparation and the ferocity with which our troops attacked that they eluded the grasp of their commanders. In terrain with such limited visibility, neither the draconian measures of the Russian officers or their commissars nor the fire opened on the troops by the security garrison in the interior bridgehead could stem the tide of the retreat. Instead, they managed only to add to the bewilderment of the panic-stricken rifle companies and increase their losses.

Nevertheless, the Soviets' unusual measure of building a small, heavily fortified "defensive bridgehead" within a large "offensive bridgehead" repaid the effort. Through it the enemy managed to retain one foot on the western bank of the Donets in spite of all the reverses suffered since 3 August. Moreover, this "bridgehead within a bridgehead" remained a thorn in our side while providing a continual ray of hope to the Russians. (It may also have made it easier for many a Red Army commander to transmit the bad news of the final crushing defeat in the woods to higher headquarters.) Eventually, General Postel decided to seal off the bridgehead and cease attacking it in order to avoid unnecessary casualties. Since the Russians also needed time to regroup after the severe losses just suffered, they also refrained from any offensive action, resulting in a brief rest during which both opponents had a chance to recover.

In the meantime, as will be described below, the situation in the rear of the Donets front had greatly deteriorated due to Fourth Panzer Army's rapid withdrawal on our western flank. Red Army tank units along the Lopan River plunged ever deeper in their effort to envelop XI Corps, which caused me to order a phased withdrawal toward Kharkov. This of course necessitated the abandonment of much of the Donets River line. At the last minute, the Russians tried to push forward from their small bridgehead to hit the corps in the rear. Once again they reached the *Totenschlucht*, where so many of their comrades had fallen in vain. But a few hours later, when the Soviets launched their decisive attack across the gorge, they discovered that only German rear guards remained to face them. Having successfully simulated a strong defensive line, these rear guards now pulled out and followed the rest of the 320th Infantry Division that had moved without interference from the river to its newly assigned position. Thus the Red Army's last hope of rupturing the Belgorod-Kharkov *Rollbahn*—XI Corps's vital supply artery— had been shattered.

Retreat to Kharkov, 9–12 August

On the northern front we held position south of Belgorod for one day and abandoned it after the Russians had deployed their forces. Continued resistance in any one position would have led to heavy casualties and the annihilation of the isolated XI Corps. Continuous Soviet attempts to outflank our left wing submitted the command to a severe nervous strain and made extreme demands on the physical endurance of the troops. Yet however great the sacrifices, they had to be made if worse disaster was to be averted. On 9 August the limits of endurance seemed to have been exceeded when, after an all-night evacuation, our troops failed to reach the new phase-line by dawn. Enemy spearheads broke through along the *Rollbahn* and the location of the entire 168th Infantry Division was uncertain. Equally alarming news arrived from the Donets and Lopan sectors. Russian tanks had broken out of the Donets bridgehead, still other Russian forces had crossed the Lopan, and the assault-gun battalion from Kharkov had failed to arrive. Low-flying hostile

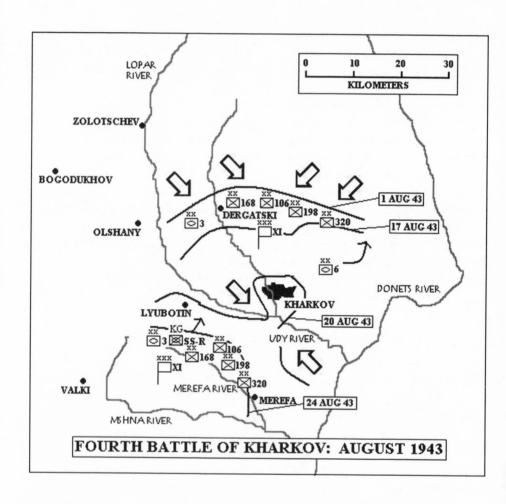

FOURTH BATTLE OF KHARKOV: AUGUST 1943

planes in great numbers dropped fragmentation bombs and machine-gunned troops on the march. Suffering heavy casualties, our soldiers edged toward panic.

A few division commanders came to my corps command post, which by then was situated close to the front line, and requested authorization for an immediate speedy withdrawal to Kharkov in view of the critical situation and the low morale of their forces. Suddenly several trucks loaded with stragglers came tearing down the highway, ignoring all stop signals. When the trucks were finally halted, the stragglers explained that they had become separated from their 168th Infantry Division unit and had been seized by panic when subjected to a tank attack farther up the road. They intended to drive straight through to Kharkov, at that time over sixty kilometers behind our front. They reported that their entire division had been wiped out and added that the 88mm flak batteries detailed to block the highway were no longer in place.

Every experienced combat commander is familiar with this sort of panic, which, in a crisis, may seize an entire body of troops. Mass hysteria of this type can be overcome only by energetic actions and a display of perfect composure. The example set by a true leader can have miraculous results. He must stay with his troops, remain cool, issue precise orders, and inspire confidence by his behavior. Good soldiers never desert such a leader. News of the presence of high-ranking commanders up front travels like wildfire along the entire front line, bolstering everyone's morale. It means a sudden change from gloom to hope, from imminent defeat to victory.

This is exactly what happened. I placed myself at a crucial point along the *Rollbahn*, orienting unit commanders and assigning them a mission in the new defensive system I was attempting to improvise. Some self-propelled antitank guns, fortuitously arriving at this instant, I immediately committed to block the highway against a tank breakthrough, which seemed imminent as the fire from approaching Soviet armor crept ever closer. I then quickly drove out past this newly established line toward the din of battle to find out for myself whether the flak batteries were holding the line. Driving around a curve, I suddenly witnessed the destruction of a Russian tank by the improvised antitank front. I counted eleven more disabled tanks and saw the remaining enemy armor withdraw straight into an extensive minefield where one tank after another was blown up.

Shortly thereafter, Luftwaffe fighters appeared and shot down more than a dozen Soviet aircraft, clearing the air over XI Corps front. When enemy rifle divisions advanced on a broad front, our heavy weapons and artillery pinned them to the ground. Thus the threat of a breakthrough along the *Rollbahn* was eliminated, and our lines held.

Meanwhile, 6th Panzer Division faced a difficult situation on the corps's left flank when, in addition to its own sector, it had to take over the one previously held by the missing 168th Infantry Division. The Russians exerted heavy pressure against the new line, and 6th Panzer Division requested immediate antitank support. I dispatched twelve antitank guns and arranged for an air strike on the Soviet tank column advancing east of the Lopan River. These combined efforts prevented the immediate collapse of XI Corps's flank cover.

Delayed by traffic jams, the long-awaited assault gun battalion did not arrive until noon. After refueling in some gullies covered with underbrush, it was committed in a counterattack against the enemy tanks still threatening the left flank. The mass attack of forty-two assault guns surprised the Russians and hit them hard. The battalion destroyed all enemy tanks and antitank guns on the eastern bank of the Lopan, shattered the Soviet bridgehead, and drove the remaining enemy forces back across the river. By early afternoon the situation was back under control. Reports from the Donets sector indicated that the enemy had been unable to enlarge his bridgehead there in the face of stubborn resistance from the 320th Infantry Division and its supporting assault guns.

Even though the entire 168th Infantry Division was still missing, XI Corps had scored an initial defensive success. The Red Army's intention to annihilate us by a concentric attack from three sides had failed. Heavy Russian losses in personnel and equipment, including sixty disabled tanks, resulted from the day's operations.

During the night of 9–10 August, XI Corps made an unobserved withdrawal to a hastily prepared position about ten kilometers to the south, the salient points of which had already been occupied by advance detachments. Weak rear guards, left behind in the former position, led the Soviets to believe that the line remained fully manned. The next morning, when Russian infantry attacked the position after a heavy artillery bombardment, they found only the rear party maintaining contact. Our troops, who had been thoroughly exhausted by the previous day's fighting and the subsequent night march, were able to recuperate during the morning hours. By noon the first enemy patrols cautiously approached the new position. Its gun emplacements and strongpoints were well camouflaged; Soviet ground and air reconnaissance failed to locate them. The 106th, 198th, and 320th Infantry Divisions held this line, the latter having been pulled back from its positions along the Donets to rejoin the corps.

Russian attacks resumed during the afternoon with increasing violence. The most dangerous Soviet arm by this point was not badly mauled tanks or close air support but powerful artillery. Fortunately, in this particular instance the effect of the heavy artillery concentration was not so devastating as it might have been since the excellent camouflage of potential German targets forced the Russians to deliver flat-trajectory fire. Whenever our machine guns or heavy weapons made the mistake of firing from open terrain, however, they were spotted by hostile observers and quickly neutralized. In order to escape destruction, our gun crews had to employ well-concealed and readily accessible alternate and dummy firing positions.

By the evening of 10 August the Russian attacks had lost some of their sting. Having learned from experience over the past few days, the Soviets made probing attacks after dusk to maintain contact with XI Corps in case of another German night withdrawal. We gave these probes a hot reception and—after all such attacks had been repulsed—withdrew unmolested to the next prepared position. By the time that the infantry arrived to occupy the new line, the bulk of the artillery and antitank guns were already in position and ready to fire. Forming another solid block, XI Corps remained unshaken by renewed enemy onslaughts.

We employed the same delaying tactics during the following days. The withdrawal to successive positions exhausted the troops, but the casualty rate stayed low. The Russians suffered disproportionately high losses, which forced them gradually to relax their pressure on German lines. As the corps front could be shortened and strengthened by units no longer required for flank protection, reserves were formed. The 168th Infantry Division, missing for several days, was found in a well-concealed area when I made a personal reconnaissance trip north of Kharkov. The division commander, Major General Walter Chales de Beaulieu, explained that he had understood his unit was to act as corps reserve and that he had therefore withdrawn to the forests forty kilometers behind the front. Though I recognized that this general had suffered a nervous breakdown, there was no time to be lost. After castigating his conduct in no uncertain terms, I ordered him to commit his division as the covering force in the next position to be occupied. This made it possible to pull out the 6th Panzer Division, designate it as corps reserve, and move it to the forest area for a well-deserved rest.

General Franz Mattenklott's XLII Corps, adjacent to our right, was forced to join the XI Corps withdrawal during the night of 11–12 August because its defensive line along the Donets now formed a deep salient into Russian-held territory. The 282nd Infantry Division on XLII Corps's left wing had not previously been engaged in a tank battle; it offered little resistance to strong Soviet tank forces, which broke through without difficulty and suddenly appeared in our rear outside Kharkov. The situation grew even more critical when the recruits of the newly arrived 848th Grenadier Regiment, overcome by fear of the approaching Red Army tanks, ran for their lives until stopped at the bridges in the suburbs of Kharkov. Strong enemy rifle units poured into the wide gap to exploit the initial breakthrough their tanks had achieved. The 6th Panzer Division had to be immediately alerted, and its spearheads intercepted the Russians in the southeastern outskirts of Kharkov, where they had seized the big tractor plant. Counterattacking, 6th Panzer Division dislodged the Soviets from the factory after fierce fighting, destroyed many tanks, dispersed the Russian infantry, and closed the gap. This action, plus the arrival of 3rd Panzer Division to strengthen our flank, meant that the danger of a breakthrough into Kharkov had been eliminated for the time being.

Tank fright is frequent among newly activated infantry divisions when training in antitank defense has been neglected. Combined arms training with panzer or assault gun units is essential to give each soldier the experience of being overrun by a tank while in his foxhole and to acquaint him with the use of antitank weapons.

The Battle for Kharkov, 13–25 August

Kharkov now constituted a deep German salient to the east, which prevented the Red Army from making use of this vital traffic and supply center. All previous Russian attempts to take the city had failed. Neither tank assaults nor infantry mass attacks had succeeded in bringing about the fall of Kharkov. Boastful reports made by Soviet radio—as well as erroneous ones by some Luftwaffe pilots—announced the entry of Russian troops into the city at a time when XI Corps front stood unwavering, but these did not alter the facts. When the STAVKA perceived its mistake, Marshal Stalin personally ordered the immediate capture of Kharkov.

The rehabilitated Fifth Guards Tank Army received this mission. It was clear that the Russians would not make a frontal assault on the projecting Kharkov salient but would attempt to break through the narrowest part of XI Corps's defensive arc west of the city (the so-called bottleneck) in order to encircle the town. We deployed all available antitank guns on the northern edge of the bottleneck, which rose like a bastion, and emplaced numerous 88mm flak guns in depth on the high ground. This antitank defense alone would not have been sufficient to repulse the expected Soviet mass tank attack, but at the last moment the reinforcements we had so long been requesting—in the form of the *Das Reich* SS Panzergrenadier Division—arrived with a strong panzer component; I immediately dispatched it to the most endangered sector.

The ninety-six PzKw V Panthers, thirty-five PzKw VI Tigers, and twenty-five StG III self-propelled assault guns had hardly taken their assigned positions on 19 August when the first large-scale attack of the Fifth Guards Tank Army got under way. The first hard German blow, however, hit the masses of Russian tanks that had been recognized while they were still assembling in the villages and flood plains of a brook valley. Escorted by Luftwaffe fighters, which cleared the sky of Soviet aircraft within a few minutes, wings of heavily laden Ju 87 "Stukas" came on in wedge formation and unloaded their cargoes of destruction in well-timed dives on the enemy tanks caught in this congested area. Dark fountains of earth erupted skyward and were followed by heavy thunderclaps and shocks that resembled an earthquake. These were the heaviest, two-ton bombs, designed for use against battleships, which were all that Luftflotte Four had left to counter the Russian attack. Wing after wing approached with majestic calm and carried out its work of destruction without interference. Soon all the villages occupied by Soviet tanks lay in flames. A sea of dust and smoke clouds illuminated by the setting sun hung over the brook valley, while dark mushrooms of smoke from burning tanks— the victims of our aerial attacks—stood out in sharp contrast. This gruesome picture bore witness to an undertaking that left death and destruction in its wake, hitting the Russians so hard that they could no longer launch their projected attack that day, regardless of Stalin's imperative order. Such a severe blow inflicted on the Soviets had purchased badly needed time for XI Corps to reorganize.

I sent the following communication to Eighth Army headquarters on 20 August:

The enemy attack has shifted against the left flank of the corps. The enemy attack here, supported by strong artillery fire and tanks, has continued almost without pause. . . . Without a doubt, his objective is to break through the front and encircle Kharkov from the west and northwest. . . .

Under continuous heavy artillery, mortar, rocket, and tank fire, and due to the incessant day and night bombardment of the main line of resistance by enemy aircraft and the bitter defense against enemy attack, the regiments, which have been in continuous combat for the past six weeks, especially those of the 198th, 168th, and 3rd Panzer Divisions, have been bled dry. Not many more enemy attacks can be withstood in the present positions.

If the enemy launches a major attack, the corps will be broken through, the western flank at Kharkov will be torn apart, and the city will be surrounded. . . .

Commander, XI Army Corps
Ia Nr. 440/43 g.Kdos
RAUS.

On 20 August the Russians avoided mass groupings of tanks, crossed the brook valley simultaneously in a number of places, and disappeared into the broad cornfields that were located ahead of our lines, ending at the east-west *Rollbahn* several hundred meters in front of our main battle line. During the night, Soviet motorized infantry had infiltrated through our defense lines in several places and made a surprise penetration near Lyubotin into the artillery position. Since our infantry units were so far understrengthed, this sort of infiltration had become common; our artillery positions therefore had to be fortified and constructed as strongpoints in the depth of our defensive zone. The gunners had to be given advanced infantry training, after which they were issued extra machine guns and hand grenades whenever possible. Nonetheless, after stubborn fighting with the gun crews, twelve howitzers (without breechlocks, which the crews took with them) fell into enemy hands. The spearhead of the infiltrating units then began shooting it out with local security forces in the woods adjoining the XI Corps's command post.

Throughout the morning Soviet tanks worked their way forward in the hollows up to the southern edges of the cornfields, then made a mass dash across the road in full sight. *Das Reich*'s Panthers caught the leading waves of T-34s with fierce defensive fire before they could reach our main battle line. Yet wave after wave followed, until Russian tanks flowed across in the protecting hollows and pushed forward into our battle positions. Here a net of antitank and flak guns, Hornet 88mm tank destroyers, and Wasp self-propelled 105mm field howitzers trapped the T-34s, split them into small groups, and put large numbers out of action. The final waves were still attempting to force a breakthrough in concentrated masses when the Tigers and StG III self-propelled assault guns, which represented our mobile reserves behind the front, attacked the Russian armor and repulsed it with heavy losses. The price paid by the Fifth Guards Tank Army for this mass assault amounted to 184 knocked-out T-34s.

In the meantime, German infantry reserves supported by self-propelled assault guns from the 3rd Panzer Division had recaptured the lost battery positions, together with all twelve howitzers, and bottled up the battalion of infiltrating motorized infantry west of Lyubotin behind our main line. Stubbornly defending themselves, the trapped Russians awaited the help that their radio promised.

Fifth Guards Tank Army changed tactics on 21 August, attacking farther east in a single deep wedge, employing several hundred tanks simultaneously. But even while they moved across the open terrain along the railroad, numerous T-34s were set on fire at a range of over 3,000 meters by the long-range weapons of the Tigers and Hornets. Thus the enemy did not manage to launch his large-scale attack until late in the forenoon, and as the Russian tanks emerged from the cornfields this time they met the concentrated defensive fire of all Tigers, Hornets, Panthers, StG III assault guns, 88mm flak, and antitank guns. The attack collapsed in a short time, with the loss of another 154 Soviet tanks. The weak rifle units following the armored wedge were mowed down by the concentrated fire of our infantry and artillery as they emerged from the cornfields.

Meanwhile, the encircled motorized infantry battalion behind our lines waited in vain for aid. Though it continued the fight with incredible tenacity, by late afternoon its radio announced the unit's defeat and then fell silent forever. After forty-eight hours of heroic defense, this Soviet battalion was killed to the last man—including the radio operators.

Russian losses incurred thus far were enormous, yet Fifth Guards Tank Army still possessed more than 100 tanks, and experience had taught us that further attacks were to be expected, even though such attacks appeared predestined to failure in view of the now vastly superior defense. The few tankers we took prisoner were aware that death or—if they were lucky—capture awaited every one of their comrades.

Contrary to all expectations, however, an eerie calm prevailed throughout 22 August. Several Russian tanks crawled about in the cornfields and towed damaged tanks away in order to reinforce their greatly depleted ranks. Summer heat shimmered over the bloody fields of the past several days of battle. A last glow of sunset brought the peaceful day to a close. Might the Russians have given up their plans, or even refused to obey the imperative order to attack?

Fifth Guards Tank Army in fact resumed the attack and did so on the same day. Before midnight, considerable noise from tanks in the cornfield betrayed a new approach. The enemy intended to achieve during the night what he had failed to gain by daylight attacks.

We were ready for them. Before the Russian tanks had reached the foot of the elevated terrain, numerous flashes from firing tanks had ripped the pitch-black darkness of the night and illuminated a mass attack of the entire Fifth Guards Tank Army on a broad front. Tanks knocked out at close range already were burning like torches and lit up portions of the battlefield. Our antitank guns could not fire properly, since they could hardly distinguish between friend and foe: *Das Reich*'s Panthers and Tigers had entered the fray, ramming Soviet tanks in a counterthrust or piercing them with shells at gun-barrel range in order to block the breakthrough. A steady increase in the flash and thunder of tank, antitank, and flak guns could be perceived after midnight, as our main force of tanks launched a coordinated counterattack. As many tanks and farm buildings went up in flames, the contested plateau was illuminated by their pale light. This finally made it possible to recognize the contours of the T-34s at distances of over 100 meters and to shell them. The thunderous roll turned into a din like the crescendo of kettledrums as the two main tank forces clashed. Gun flashes ripped the darkness from all around throughout an extensive area. For miles, armor-piercing rounds whizzed into the night in all directions. Gradually the pandemonium of the tank battle shifted to the north, even though flashes also appeared farther and farther behind our front, and fiery torches stood out against the night sky. Not until two or three hours later was calm restored in the depth of XI Corps front. The conflict gradually subsided throughout the entire battle position.

After daybreak on 23 August, we could feel the battle had been won, though Russian tanks and motorized infantry still remained in and behind our main battle line, while here and there a small gap needed to be closed. The foremost of the Soviet tanks that had made the forward deep thrust was captured at the western outskirts of Kharkov by a divisional headquarters, and the crew members were taken prisoner. Though the process of mopping up the battlefield required all morning, by noon the position was back in our hands, and XI Corps was again ready for defense.

Only a small patch of woodland close behind our main line was still occupied by a force of Soviet motorized infantry, supported by a few tanks and antitank guns. All attempts to retake this patch of woods failed with heavy losses. Even heavy, concentrated fires by strong artillery units could not force these Russians to yield. Only an attack by flamethrowing tanks finally ended their tenacious resistance by burning the entire strip of woods to the ground.

The Soviet attempt to seize Kharkov by a large-scale night attack of the entire Fifth Guards Tank Army had failed. Their losses totaled more than eighty burned-out tanks, many hundreds of dead, thousands of wounded, and a considerable amount of equipment destroyed in a single night of battle. Fifth Guards Tank Army's effort to recapture Kharkov had cost 420 tanks in three days of fighting; as an effective combat formation it ceased to be a factor for the foreseeable future. Kharkov remained in our hands.

Blunders on the part of Russian leaders were only partially responsible for the fact that every one of the Fifth Guards Tank Army armored attacks failed, though the Red Army troops fought with extraordinary bravery. I was struck by the fact that the enemy had only weak infantry and artillery forces and that his air forces did not participate effectively at any point during these operations. With these deficiencies the tank forces could not be adequately supported, and any tactical successes could not be exploited. I suspect that Fifth Guards Tank Army had been forced into premature action for reasons of prestige by the well-publicized STAVKA orders.

Despite our defensive victory, Kharkov's evacuation became necessary because of unfavorable developments farther south. Our withdrawal was carried out without difficulty on the night of 23–24 August, and XI Corps occupied a previously prepared position a few miles to the west. Situated on high ground and protected by a swampy valley cutting across the approach roads, the new position was considerably shorter than the defense line skirting Kharkov and could therefore be held more efficiently.

During the withdrawal of our rear guard, the only bridge across the marshes that had been left intact collapsed under the weight of some Hornets, cutting off an infantry battalion and eight Hornets on the eastern bank. Russian attempts to annihilate this force were frustrated by our units supporting the bridgehead from the western bank. After holding out for twenty-four hours so that the bridge could be repaired, the rear guard crossed under the cover of darkness on 24–25 August.

Chapter 10

BATTLES FOR THE UKRAINE

Back to the Dnepr

IN ITS NEW DEFENSIVE POSITION west of Kharkov, XI Corps had to ward off some fierce attacks by Russian forces attempting to envelop both flanks. We sealed off several local penetrations with armored counterattacks, but even this strong position had to be evacuated after a short while since it formed a dangerous salient to the east after the adjacent corps of Eighth Army was forced to pull back. The next withdrawal forced the corps into exposed, flat terrain, where we had to extend our flanks until the sector covered the entire sixty-five–kilometer stretch between the Kolomak and Berestova Rivers.

In the meantime the overall situation of Army Group South had deteriorated to the point that Field Marshal von Manstein ordered a general withdrawal west of the Dnepr River. During this retrograde movement, we employed the same delaying tactics that had been so successful during the withdrawal from Belgorod to Kharkov. Again and again, delay on successive positions forced the Soviets to make time-consuming preparations for battle and to suffer heavy casualties, leading to the progressive exhaustion of their corps and divisions. The Russians recognized our intentions and attempted every day to frustrate them by forcing an armored breakthrough. Above all, the enemy wanted to capture major cities commanding the road net needed for speedy maneuvers. In view of the rainy weather, the possession of hard-surface highways became a decisive factor to both sides since the mud prevented any movement off the roads. We took this factor into account and concentrated our antitank defenses in and around important towns. During this phase, therefore, cities became far more important than during the fighting in the area north of Kharkov.

The Red Army achieved its only breakthrough when it blocked our withdrawal across the Orchik River near Karlovka on 22 August. A critical situation developed because of additional delays in the river crossing caused by floods, mud, and the steepness of the western bank. A grave danger existed that the Russian tanks might reach the weakly held western bank before the main bodies of our divisions, which had been forced to take more devious routes. Enemy artillery fire set ablaze the densely populated suburban area of Karlovka near the river, further delaying our crossing. Demolitions of factories, railroad installations, depots, and supplies, ordered by Army Group South in line with Hitler's "scorched-earth" policy, caused additional delays. A major Soviet breakthrough at this point appeared inevitable, when suddenly the Russian tanks themselves began to be mired in the mud, and the danger subsided.

With a change in the weather the ground dried. The infantry divisions were able to move faster, and the daily rate of the withdrawal was increased up to thirty to fifty kilometers. The pursuing Soviet armor did not manage to renew its pressure until XI Corps halted for several days at the Kremenchug bridgehead. Russian striking power had been impaired by several weeks of battering against our delaying actions on successive positions, until the energy of the enemy counteroffensive had finally spent itself.

Kremenchug

Upon the arrival of XI Corps at the Dnepr on 20 September, Army Group South gave my headquarters the mission of organizing and covering the withdrawal of more than a dozen divisions of Eighth Army [west] across the Dnepr at Kremenchug. The river crossing (the Dnepr was 800–1,200 meters wide in this area) was complicated by the small number of bridges available to us. The sectors of First and Fourth Panzer Armies and Eighth Army each contained only a single intact bridge site. A twenty-four-ton-capacity wooden bridge with a five-meter railway and bypass points and a single-track railroad bridge (both at Kremenchug), and motor ferries of twelve-ton capacity at Koloberda, Cherkassy, and Kanev, were the only Dnepr crossing facilities in Eighth Army's sector. The construction of additional bridges would have required at least two months; the motor ferries could provide some assistance but could not possibly solve the problem involving the crossing of entire armies. The long wooden bridge at Kremenchug alone had to serve as a crossing point for elements of six panzer or panzergrenadier divisions (6th, 7th, and 11th Panzer Divisions; 20th, SS *Totenkopf*, and *Grossdeutschland* Panzergrenadier Divisions) and seven infantry divisions (39th, 106th, 167th, 168th, 198th, 282nd, and 320th) whose strength varied considerably. Since some of these sites had already been threatened by the Soviet advance, every possible step had to be taken to delay the enemy advance and simultaneously accelerate the crossing of our divisions over the bridges still in our hands.

Prior to 20 September the crossing facilities at Kremenchug had been used to the limit of their capacity to move all types of supplies to the rear, both by rail and road. Contrary to expectations, these operations had not been completed by the time XI Corps headquarters arrived at the river. Moreover, fleeing remnants of assorted divisions were streaming toward the river in a chaotic effort to reorganize and rehabilitate their shattered ranks in the area west of Kirovograd. Large numbers of vehicles of every description had therefore accumulated on the eastern bank of the river, especially at the approaches of the Kremenchug crossing points.

The tactical situation further complicated matters. Russian parachute troops had landed near Kanev on the other side of the river, and their ground forces had begun to cross the Dnepr upstream of Kremenchug. Only mechanized units were capable of reaching the river's southern bank between the bridges in time to restore the situation. In order to give the panzer divisions precedence over other units, we had to stop all traffic and clear the roads for the tanks and APCs. For several days mixed columns of all arms extending over many kilometers camped in the adjacent fields or—whenever this was impossible because of the many swamps—they kept to the side of the road and waited for the signal that would allow them to continue on their way. Their campfires were close to their foxholes. Alongside these columns—sometimes trapped between them—were streams of refugees and herds of cattle. Only radical measures against traffic violations of all kinds made it possible to put the panzer divisions at the head of the columns.

To coordinate this movement Eighth Army appointed a general officer to act for me as the special traffic commander at the Kremenchug bridge site. He established his central traffic regulation headquarters on the western bank of the Dnepr at Kryukov, a suburb of Kremenchug. Subordinated to this traffic commander were two special staffs and the 10th Flak Division (Flak Regiments 4, 7, 48, 77, 99, 124, 153, and Luftwaffe Signal Battalion 130).

Road Commander East controlled the following elements:

Road Commander East staff	25 men
Bridge commander staff	25 men
Rail transport commander staff	10 men
Two military police detachments totaling	100 men
Emergency platoon (to prevent panic)	50 men
Vehicle recovery platoon	30 men
Maintenance platoon	40 men

Ambulance platoon	40 men
Two engineer companies totaling	300 men
Telephone platoon and radio section	40 men
Total	**660 men**

With these elements the road commander had to sluice columns and regulate movements along the five approach routes leading into the city, while organizing and holding march columns in readiness for the river crossing (with priority to ambulances and other vehicles with special passes that were being filtered through). All side roads had to be blocked. Once the march columns were organized, they had to be directed and guided along the approach routes from their holding areas to the proper bridge site upon call from the central traffic regulation headquarters. Tanks and other tracked vehicles had to be segregated and diverted across the railroad bridge, though scheduled railroad traffic retained priority there. The attached maintenance and recovery units had to repair or immediately evacuate disabled vehicles in order to ensure that there were no interruptions to the traffic flow (ambulances and recovery vehicles were allowed to move in the opposite direction of the withdrawal for periods of ten minutes at two-hour intervals). The bridges had to be maintained and repaired, especially after air attacks; the bridge commander had this responsibility and the authority to organize labor details as necessary. Finally, the military police had to enforce rigorously a maintained speed limit of twenty kilometers per hour at all times.

Road Commander West controlled the following elements:

Road Commander West staff	25 men
Military police detachment	50 men
Emergency platoon (to prevent panic)	50 men
Recovery platoon	30 men
Maintenance platoon	40 men
Ambulance platoon	40 men
Telephone platoon and radio section	40 men
Total	**275 men**

With these elements the road commander had to direct and guide all march elements from east to west into the designated assembly areas on the western bank of the Dnepr. This entailed avoiding all traffic stoppages on exiting the bridge, because the drivers had a tendency to slow down once they had reached safety on the western bank, or to stop altogether to obtain information on the whereabouts of their parent unit. This had a delaying effect and was therefore very harmful. The attempts by mixed convoys to find the right branch of the road and turn off immediately after crossing the bridge also caused major delays. The drivers seemed to forget that many thousands of vehicles behind them were waiting to cross the river. To overcome this difficulty, all units received orders to continue on the highway to the south for thirty to thirty-five kilometers from the bridge without regard for the resulting detours. Drastic steps had to be taken to enforce this order, and many control points—even aircraft—had to supervise the traffic flow. All return traffic (ambulances and recovery vehicles mentioned above) had to be organized and held for their crossing to be coordinated with Road Commander East.

Although the combined strength of these two traffic control units approached 1,000 men, their personnel had to be employed practically without interruption or rest for ten days.

On 20 September all our energies had to be devoted to organization and dealing with the various march columns of supply convoys and straggler elements that lined the approach routes within the holding areas. These columns had to be recalled and reversed in order to clear the roads for the panzer divisions that had priority for the river crossing. By the morning of 21 September two panzer and four infantry divisions, as well as supply columns almost the equivalent of another infantry division, lined the approach routes within the holding areas, up to the final barrier lines established on each road. The estimated crossing time for each divisional march column was calculated at six hours, based on the premise that none of the divisions would be at full strength, though all would inevitably absorb numerous stray nondivisional vehicles along the way. Since the divisions had been organized in close-column formation and some traffic had to move in the opposite direction periodically, the schedule was arranged accordingly. Four of the seven columns crossed the Dnepr on 21 September, with three columns remaining on the eastern bank until the following day.

Meanwhile, at Poltava, our rear guards had held out far longer than the original schedule set by Eighth Army. Even so, twelve freight trains loaded with tanks and other valuable equipment stood ready for demolition because Russian tanks had already cut the railroad connecting the city with Kremenchug. A counterattack by elements of the SS *Totenkopf* Panzergrenadier Division on 21 September cleared the line sufficiently to allow all twelve trains to pass the threatened points and reach Kremenchug in time to cross safely.

By the morning of 22 September eight more divisional march columns (four panzer and four infantry), as well as additional supply columns again equating to a divisional march column, had pulled into the approach routes for the holding areas at the barrier lines. These nine march columns, plus the three remaining from the previous day, brought our total to twelve march columns. The bridges could provide passage only for four of these columns that day, leaving eight march columns still on the eastern bank.

The four march columns crossed the river on 22 September despite the fact that one of the numerous unexpected events that occurred during the operation had to be dealt with summarily in order not to upset the overall schedule of the evacuation. That morning I learned that about twenty-five Pzkw VI Tigers had been abandoned by their crews in the outer Kremenchug defensive line due to technical failures. I immediately ordered some thirty tank transport trailers and prime movers, with engineer support, to recross the river and recover our heavy panzers. The recovery column commander reported directly to the Road Commander West in Kryukov. Since no previous provision had been made to conduct these large and heavy trailers across the bridge in an eastbound direction, westbound traffic had to be temporarily curtailed. The unavoidable delay thus incurred was mostly compensated for during the course of the day. Just as important, the twenty-five Pzkw VI Tigers were successfully retrieved, as our engineers coupled the last few tanks together by cables and towed them across the river with the prime movers.

On 23 September another four march columns crossed the river, followed by the final four on 24 September. The only forces remaining on the eastern bank of the Dnepr were strong rear guards of 320th Infantry, SS *Totenkopf* and *Grossdeutschland* Panzergrenadier Divisions, covering the withdrawal of corps and army supply trains, as well as civilians and livestock. At that point our rear guards still held a defensive line fifteen to twenty-five kilometers out from the city, which kept the Soviets out of effective artillery range. The evacuation of this line and the withdrawal into the final bridgehead position began on the night of 24–25 September.

It had thus required four full days to move the equivalent of sixteen mechanized divisions across the two bridges. The two road commanders worked with perfect coordination and during the first days directed 5,000–7,000 motor vehicles per day across the Dnepr. Later they increased this rate to an average of 8,000–10,000. A total of 70,000 motor vehicles crossed the highway bridge: six panzer and five infantry divisions.

Three infantry divisions, with all their horse-drawn transport, as well as the two large supply columns, crossed the river on the railroad bridge, which had been covered with planks. Alongside this bridge, our engineers built an improvised floating bridge for crossing the 30,000 civilian vehicles that Eighth Army routed through Kremenchug during the same period. The road commanders also regulated the traffic across these two improvised bridges. It proved particularly difficult to designate the approach routes to the bridges in such a manner that the columns would not cut across each other or, where such crossings were unavoidable, to establish tightly controlled intersections at points where cross-traffic would cause the least disturbance.

The two large supply trains had to the cross the Dnepr twenty-five kilometers downstream of Kremenchug at a secondary bridgehead northeast of Uspenskoye, defended by Lieutenant General Werner Forst's 106th Infantry Division. Some of the civilian columns and most of the herds of cattle were diverted to that crossing point. None of the engineer units in the area had any standard military bridging equipment, motorboats, pneumatic pontoons, or civilian shipping facilities. This left the two march columns to resort to whatever expedients they could devise at the time. The last remaining fishing boats were assembled, floats were built from old logs and native wagons without wheels, and some mill boats anchored along the banks were used as ferries.

With these improvised craft the soldiers and civilians were moved across the river with all their equipment and possessions. Wagons unsuitable for use as ferries were disassembled, floated across, and reassembled on the southern bank. Tied to the various makeshift ferries, the horses swam across without resistance. Herd after herd of cattle was driven into the water, but the animals stubbornly shied away from the 800-meter-wide river. Only when lead oxen were willing to precede them did the mass of the cattle follow into the river, accompanied by shouting peasants crossing in boats on both flanks. Slowly, and with deafening roars of protest, the cattle waded across the 200–350-meter-wide shallows. Then they suddenly sank into the navigation channel and, with heads up, swam through the very deep—and at places 350 meters wide—channel until they could set foot on the bottom again, about 100–175 meters before reaching the far bank. Herd after herd, 800–1,000 head of cattle each, was thus driven across the slow-flowing river. Even though some herds had been on the move for a month, and had covered distances of 200–300 kilometers, there were no casualties. A total of 64,000 horses and more than 80,000 head of cattle swam the Dnepr. The young animals followed separately on large, boarded-up ferries. This completely improvised measure contributed greatly to relieving the bridges at Kremenchug and proved very effective.

That XI Corps completed this difficult mission may be attributed to the fact that dual responsibility for the conduct of operations and the technical problems of the river crossing was vested directly in me as the local corps commander. Thus all tactical and technical measures were coordinated under my control. But a considerable element of our success is to be attributed to the efficient special staffs and to the additional crossing facilities—both major organizational improvisations.

Yet all these efforts could have been frustrated had the Russians used strong air forces at the right time, and thus a great deal of the credit for the success of the crossing operation must ironically go to the Red Army. Surprisingly, Soviet combat aircraft were not committed in force until 90 percent of our troops, vehicles, and equipment had completed the crossing. At that point six enemy bombers appeared, and although all were quickly driven off by the intense antiaircraft fire from the batteries of the 10th Flak Division, one bomber scored a direct hit on the detonation device installed on the highway bridge, which had been readied for destruction. The charge was set off and the bridge destroyed. By that time, however, the loss of the bridge was not particularly serious because the rear-guard tanks and assault guns were able to withdraw across the still-intact railroad bridge. Before this attack, enemy air activity had been negligible, and only one light bomber had scored a direct hit on the highway bridge, merely piercing the surface without damaging anything vital to the bridge's structure. Our vehicles bypassed the small hole for the next hour, until the engineers covered it, and the flow of traffic was never even interrupted.

The speed with which the Russians were able to force their own crossings of the Dnepr was a source of amazement to us. Only by calling on all the forces and means at its disposal had Army Group South managed to occupy seven existing bridges in a sector nearly 500 kilometers wide, and even then it succeeded in establishing only one float bridge and one improvised ferry (both in XI Corps sector) because of the scarcity of ferrying material that prevailed at the time. One the other hand, often before our own troops had taken up their new defensive positions on the western bank, the Soviets, in close pursuit, dropped several thousand paratroops over a 320-kilometer-wide part of the sector, established small bridgeheads in several other locations, and soon thereafter began building fifty-seven bridges, nine foot bridges, and numerous other facilities for crossing the river. Thus, while Army Group South held a Dnepr crossing every fifty-five kilometers, the Red Army on average possessed one every six kilometers.

At one ferrying point about forty kilometers downstream from Kremenchug, advance elements of Steppe Front lodged themselves in a small bridgehead and proceeded to ferry tanks across the river on rafts, by day and night. There operations to expand this bridgehead continued regardless of the fact that our artillery soon began shelling them, and without any halt even when some of the tank-laden rafts went to the bottom of the river. At night the Russians even drove ahead of their soldiers large numbers of civilians whom they had gathered up, so that our infantry might expend its scant supply of ammunition. At one point a shallow lake, roughly four kilometers long and 300–500 meters wide, had been used to anchor the flank of our containment force. The western bank of this lake was guarded only by weak security detachments. One night these detachments suddenly came under attack and were driven back by 600–800 Russians. Under cover of darkness these enemy troops had waded across a shallow spot of the marshy lake without wearing a stitch of clothing and—equipped only with small arms and ammunition—had surprised our security elements. Only the quick commitment of mobile reserves allowed us to encircle these Russians and take them prisoner.

The Soviets also made extensive use of raft bridges built by their engineers. These could be used only for crossing waters having a slow current and were constructed of tree trunks, placed side by side and fastened to each other. Depending upon requirements, a second and even a third layer of logs could be added, each layer being laid at right angles to the layer below. Planking, laid across the uppermost layer, served as the roadway, and the load-bearing capacity of these raft bridges could be adapted to meet virtually any requirement by varying the number of layers of logs. At Kiev in early October the Russians built a railroad raft bridge across the Dnepr that possessed greater than a 100-ton load capacity, allowing them to establish rail communications into the city just four days after it had been seized.

The Kiev Salient

The spoiling attack—a surprise thrust into the enemy attack preparations—is a very effective, though rare, operation that aims to disorganize the enemy's assembly and thereby delay and weaken his offensive, or to force him to launch his attack at a less vulnerable point. Such an attack from the defensive can be undertaken only under certain conditions. The enemy assembly area must be easily accessible to a surprise thrust, and there must be strong armored reserves on hand for the attack. The terrain and road net must facilitate quick maneuver under cover of darkness. All attack plans must be concealed from the enemy, or he must be deceived with regard to the real intentions. These prerequisites existed in Russia only on rare occasions, but I was presented with the perfect opportunity to exploit them at the beginning of December, soon after assuming command of Fourth Panzer Army.

The Red Army had broken through north of Kiev, and there were indications of an intention to envelop the entire northern wing of Army Group South, but the forces at the disposal of the First Ukrainian Front turned out to be insufficient for this task. The Soviets did advance seventy-five kilometers to the west, captured the important railroad junction at Fastov, neutralized Zhitomir, and encircled General of Infantry's Kurt von der Chevallerie's LIX Corps in Korosten, but a flank attack by General of Panzer Troops Her-

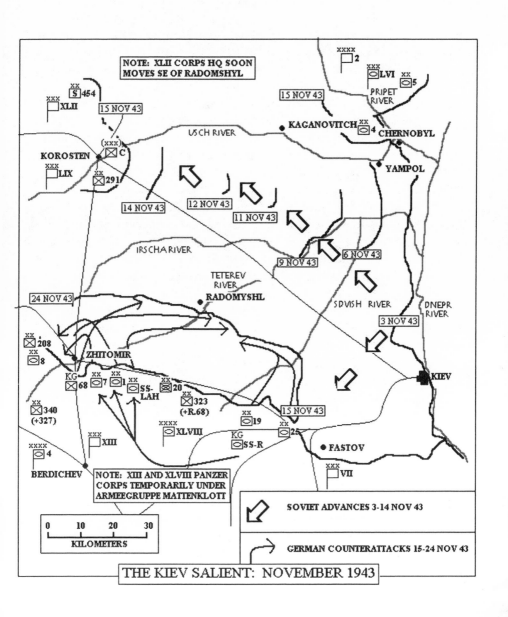

THE KIEV SALIENT: NOVEMBER 1943

mann Balck's reinforced XLVIII Panzer Corps forced them to pull back across the Teterev River. Although Zhitomir had been relieved, Fastov remained in enemy hands, and the siege of Korosten continued. Fourth Panzer Army's front, which had faced east before the recent onslaught, gave way and now faced north, creating an unusual situation in which both the German and Russian flanks were open to the west.

Because of our inability to close this gap, we extended an open invitation to the Soviets to continue their offensive in order to exploit the successes they had hitherto achieved. They obviously believed that they had been handed a unique opportunity to execute a wide envelopment out of First Ukrainian Front's assembly area north of Zhitomir. Troop concentrations and road repairs performed behind the enemy lines forecast an imminent resumption of the Russian offensive, which would first threaten Fourth Panzer Army and subsequently the entire army group.

The situation demanded immediate action, and Field Marshal von Manstein and I decided to avert the threat by striking the flank of the enemy attack preparations with strong panzer forces. General Balck's XLVIII Panzer Corps, with the 1st SS *Leibstandarte Adolph Hitler*, 1st, and 7th Panzer Divisions, was withdrawn from the front and assembled behind the center of Fourth Panzer Army's defensive sector. Meanwhile, the approach routes—some of which led through marshy, wooded terrain—were reconnoitered, bridges repaired, and the partisan units rampant in the woods dispersed by Lieutenant General Alexander Goeschen's 213th Security Division, which was responsible for this area. Immediately thereafter, the combat elements of all three panzer divisions moved out in broad daylight and marched along the main highway toward Zhitomir in order to deceive the Russians into believing that strong forces were being shifted to another sector of the front. We later established that this deception had been completely successful.

In any event, these preliminary steps were actually inevitable, since the movements connected with them had to be executed to enable the XLVIII Panzer Corps to strike deep into the open Russian flank. Without such misdirection, the movements would have required two nights, since the approach and assembly of such a strong panzer corps could not be effected in one night. By carrying out the movements by day, we could time them so that the divisions reached their turn-off points along the main highway shortly after dusk. By that time, half the itinerary had been covered, and the movements continued without interruption. The Russians were deprived of an opportunity to observe this turning maneuver, first to the north, then toward the east.

General Balck conducted the entire movement according to plan without enemy interference. On 6 December, at 0600, all three panzer divisions were poised for attack along the Zhitomir-Korosten highway. Simultaneously, all available army artillery battalions, a *Nebelwerfer* brigade with launchers of different calibers up to 320mm, and an armored train had been moved into position behind the left wing of General of Infantry Arthur Hauffe's XIII Corps on the extreme end of our open flank. These preparations, as well as the concentration of strong reserves behind XIII Corps's wing, were intended to lead the Soviets into assuming that our attack would strike from that sector, exactly where it had bogged down the previous month. The Russians were easily convinced of these intentions because their own reaction in similar situations was identical. When a heavy bombardment hit this sector at dawn, and Major General Hans Piekenbrock's 208th Infantry Division launched a frontal attack immediately afterward, the Soviets felt absolutely sure that their estimates were correct. They shifted strong reserves toward this sector and counterattacked, only to be stopped dead by the concentrated fire of 300 rocket launchers.

The Russians were still completely unaware of the impending flank attack. Only after the First Ukrainian Front had moved all available reserves and heavy weapons close to the front line did two German corps, comprising five divisions, simultaneously assault their right flank. General Balck's three divisions of the XLVIII Panzer Corps executed the main thrust, advancing east toward the Teterev River. Some elements of *Brigadefuehrer* Theodor Wisch's 1st SS Panzer Division were to turn south and attack the Soviets from the rear, while Major General Hasso von Manteuffel's 7th Panzer Division had been assigned to cover the corps's left flank and establish contact with LIX Corps (291st Infantry Division and *Korpsabteilung* [Corps Detachment] C), which was breaking out of the encirclement at Korosten.

Completely surprised by this flank attack, the Russians offered little resistance on 6 December. The minefields they had emplaced to protect their open flank were easily discovered by the Luftwaffe and bypassed. Our panzers crushed and destroyed the entire flank by attacking from the rear. Within a few hours the lead German tanks had penetrated deep into Soviet artillery emplacements, overrunning batteries under the cover of a light ground fog and destroying them. Since the frozen ground had been covered by only a thin layer of snow, the tanks moved quickly and kept on schedule. By the end of 6 December, General Balck's panzer divisions had advanced twenty-five to thirty kilometers into the First Ukrainian Front's flank, taken numerous prisoners, and captured or destroyed large amounts of artillery. General von der Chevallerie's LIX Corps had achieved its breakout and established contact with XLVIII Panzer Corps, and Fourth Panzer Army once again controlled the Zhitomir-Korosten highway and railroad line. The completeness of our tactical surprise had guaranteed the initial success of the operation; only weak remnants of the enemy's forward forces escaped to the rear.

Though the thrust continued on 7 December its momentum was greatly impaired by heavy fog and a breakdown of the 1st SS Panzer Division's supply system. Even though this division dropped out of the attack due to ammunition and fuel shortages, the 1st and 7th Panzer Divisions each advanced nearly another twenty kilometers against negligible resistance. As the attack progressed, elements of General Hauffe's XIII Corps gradually joined General Balck's thrust along the sectors in which the initial attack had swept away all opposition. Farther north, however, LIX Corps found itself heavily engaged and progressed only step by step.

Not until 8 December did we feel the effect of the first Soviet countermeasures, but the handful of tank and rifle units thrown across the lower Teterev River were plainly incapable of withstanding the unified drive of General Balck's three panzer divisions. He quickly overran the Russians' newly established defenses, destroying several tanks in the process; panzer spearheads of Lieutenant General Walter Krueger's 1st Panzer Division reached the Teterev south of the railroad bridge. Lieutenant General Bruno Ortner's 69th Infantry Division, operating on the XIII Corps's right flank, crossed the Teterev at Radomyshl and joined XLVIII Panzer Corps's advance. On the other hand, sizeable Russian forces remaining in the swampy forests along the Irsha River held out so tenaciously that LIX Corp with its two infantry divisions was unable to overcome their resistance. West of the Teterev, we had reduced the enemy to a few bridgeheads, but during the night of 8–9 December the Soviets reinforced them to the point where they nearly burst with troops and equipment. The Russian Sixtieth Army attempted to reverse the tide no matter what the cost.

During 9 December, heavy attacks struck at both XIII and XLVIII Panzer Corps. Most of these attacks were contained, and panzer counterattacks led to some additional territorial gains, but by the end of the day the center of General Hauffe's XIII Corps was in danger of being overrun. I decided that it was now essential to eliminate those Soviet bridgeheads on the Teterev, and on 5 December General Balck utilized the 1st and 1st SS Panzer Divisions as the jaws of a pincer movement intended to annihilate all Russian units remaining west of the river, while the weaker 7th Panzer Division was to protect the northern flank. Desperate Soviet attempts to withstand the onslaught of 200 panzers were in vain, as the powerful drive of the two panzer divisions crushed or reduced one bridgehead after the other. By noon our panzer spearheads had established contact with the fifth and final enemy bridgehead. The XLVIII Panzer Corps blew the bridges, as well as capturing large numbers of prisoners and significant quantities of equipment. The day culminated in an all-out attack with all available tanks and strong elements of XIII Corps against those Red Army units that had dented General

Hauffe's lines during the preceding day. These forces were encircled and annihilated.

The first objective of the operation had thus been achieved: Our surprise thrust from the defensive had penetrated an area seventy-two kilometers in depth, completely destroying one Soviet army and inflicting such casualties on a second that it was at least temporarily rendered ineffective. Russian casualties numbered thousands dead, wounded, or prisoners; over 200 Soviet tanks had been destroyed and approximately 800 artillery pieces captured. Our own losses had been light. The shortened front line again faced to the east and could be held solely by infantry divisions, which meant that XLVIII Panzer Corps was available for a new assignment.

In the second phase of the operation we planned to consolidate our lines. In order to clear the swampy forests along the Irsha River of enemy forces, and to establish direct contact between LIX and XIII Corps, the XLVIII Panzer Corps moved to the Korosten area and launched a pincer attack against the Russian forces in the swamps on 16 December. The 1st and 1st SS Panzer Divisions and Major General Wolfgang Lange's *Korpsabteilung* C (a provisional unit of divisional strength formed by three weakened infantry divisions, each organized into one regiment) attacked from Korosten, north of the Irsha to the southwest, while the 7th Panzer and Lieutenant General Theobald Lieb's 112th Infantry Divisions thrust from positions south of the river toward the northeast. The northern spearhead, advancing in open terrain along the railroad to Kiev, initially made good progress, whereas the southern thrust was slowed down by heavy fighting in wooded terrain. Nevertheless, by 17 December the two panzer spearheads had made contact. Our troops were still combing the marshy forests along the Irsha when strong Soviet tank formations suddenly launched a flank attack from the north. Reconnaissance reported additional Russian armor and motorized rifle forces moving up from Kiev. According to the statements by prisoners, the Russians anticipated a major German offensive to recapture Kiev and had therefore committed all units available in the area.

In view of our limited strength, neither Field Marshal von Manstein nor I had planned such a large-scale operation, quite apart from the difficulties we would have experienced in penetrating the marshy forests extending between the Teterev and the Dnepr. Actually, the objective of the spoiling attack had already been achieved, and the intended creation of a continuous infantry front was well under way. In spite of the reckless expenditure of newly arrived tank and infantry forces, the Soviet counterattack failed to gain ground. We repelled every enemy attack, albeit after stubborn fighting. On 17 December the Russians lost more than eighty tanks, and during the following two days the enemy attack bogged down with the loss of an additional 150 tanks. Minor thrusts, supported by tanks, had been delivered against XIII Corps as well but proved equally futile.

The consolidation phase of the operation accentuated the effects of the initial surprise attack. Two additional Russian armies had been so badly mauled that they became incapable of offensive action, thus eliminating the acute threat in the area north of Zhitomir. A few weeks later, the Russian Christmas offensive was initiated against a less vulnerable sector of the front, a clear indicator that we had forced the Soviets to change their plans.

Blunting the Christmas Offensive

Even during the fighting in the Teterev-Irsha triangle, the Luftwaffe had reported increasing rail traffic from the northwest in the direction of Kiev. Day and night, Soviet troop transports—including hundreds of tanks—moved across the Dnepr bridges and headed west. Doubtless the STAVKA had transferred strong tank and rifle units into the Kiev area, and we could be sure that they either intended to commit them in an effort to regain the terrain lost northeast of Zhitomir or else planned a new operation. Since no new units were identified along the Teterev front, everything pointed to ongoing preparations for a new offensive. During the week before Christmas the Soviets initiated probing attacks along and to the south of the Kiev-Zhitomir highway in order to locate weak points in our dispositions and to acquire advantageous jump-off positions. Daily aerial photographs indicated a steady increase in the number of Russian artillery emplacements, though these appeared unoccupied at first. Then new batteries moved into position and adjusted their fire, a clear indication of an impending offensive. Enemy tank movements, conducted simultaneously on Fourth Panzer Army's right wing near Kanev along the Dnepr, did not fit into the general picture and were executed so clumsily that we immediately recognized them as feints. Even though radio interceptions indicated no change, the heavy truck traffic that began rolling forward every night after 20 December left no doubt that a Soviet attack was imminent. Luftwaffe reconnaissance flights sighted between 2,000 and 3,000 loaded trucks rolling from Kiev to the front during several successive nights, with just as many returning empty, which was the best indication that the enemy would soon launch his assault. The sudden calm that descended over the front on 23 December deceived nobody. On the contrary, it signaled the fact that the Russian offensive could start at any moment, especially since the Red Army liked to begin large-scale operations on Christmas Eve, believing that our troops could be caught off-guard during this important religious holiday.

We took a number of precautionary steps to absorb the initial shock of the first Soviet assaults and to add to the depth of our defenses. Major General Karl Thoholte's fully motorized 18th Artillery Division, which had arrived just two weeks earlier and had been committed to a quiet sector in accordance with specific orders from Hitler, now moved to Zhitomir. This division, which had been formed from the staff of the disbanded 18th Panzer Division, included Artillery Regiments 88, 288, and 388 (totaling nine artillery battalions and one infantry battalion) and was equipped with sixty light and forty medium artillery pieces, as well as twenty-four assault guns; it was thus particularly capable of shattering mass attacks. In addition, General Balck's XLVIII Panzer Corps was pulled out of the line and assembled near Korosten, while Lieutenant General August Schmidt's depleted 10th Panzergrenadier Division—undergoing rehabilitation west of Berdichev—received orders to form a regimental *Kampfgruppe* with all combat-ready elements. This *Kampfgruppe* actually consisted of two motorized infantry battalions, one light artillery battalion, and one signal company. We also managed to reinforce the weak local reserves near the Kiev-Zhitomir highway with about forty tanks and assault guns. Waffen SS trainees at the Zhitomir camp (3,000–4,000 men) were organized into companies and held in readiness for local defense. Although the formation of such reserves was of vital importance, Fourth Panzer Army's front was so overextended that we could not relieve any other units. Since Army Group South could not provide any additional help at this time, we had to face the expected Russian onslaught with very meager reserves.

I ordered an antitank ditch dug approximately fifteen kilometers behind the main battle line; its eastern segment lay behind an unfordable stream. The important railroad junctions at Zhitomir, Berdichev, and Kazatin we protected by fortifications, but only *Alarmeinheiten* composed of service troops were available to garrison them. All nonessential rolling stock and supplies had been evacuated to the west.

As expected, the First Ukrainian Front's offensive opened on Christmas Eve south of the Kiev-Zhitomir highway. After a heavy one-hour artillery preparation, the Russians breached the positions held by the understrength 8th and 19th Panzer Divisions of General of Panzer Troops Walter Nehring's XXIV Panzer Corps, but these divisions continued to defend their main battle line even though completely encircled. By noon this Russian force reached the antitank ditch, crossing it at several points. A second, powerful enemy tank force also penetrated the overextended front of General of Artillery Ernst-Eberhard Hell's VII Corps that morning in the 25th Panzer Division's sector. Only slightly delayed by local resistance, several hundred Soviet tanks rolled in an endless stream toward Berdichev. Here, too, the antitank ditch caused little delay because we lacked sufficient manpower for its effective defense. By the end of 24 December the Russian main effort had reached the Kiev-Zhitomir railroad line.

Another enemy thrust, carried out farther north in the direction of Zhitomir proper, initially made slow progress in the swampy forests south of the highway due to strong antitank fronts formed by General of Infantry Anton Dostler's XLII Corps. During the night of 24–25 December, Major General Gottfried Froelich's 8th Panzer Division and Major General Hans Kaellner's 19th Panzer Division, ordered to break out to the west, attacked the Russians in the rear and disorganized them so thoroughly that they were incapable of continuing the attack on 25 December.

Because the Russians on our northern flank had not yet recovered from previous battles and were therefore condemned to inactivity, the XLVIII Panzer Corps was withdrawn from the Korosten area and committed in a counterattack south of the Teterev. General Balck had orders to block the Russian advance behind the undulating hills between Kazatin and Berdichev, delaying it for as long as possible. To this point we had identified approximately 600 enemy tanks operating in this area. When the XLVIII Panzer Corps arrived south of the Teterev at dawn on 25 December, Soviet tanks columns—many miles long—suddenly came into view. General Balck could not resist the temptation and, instead of following his instructions, decided to make an immediate surprise attack against the open enemy flank. Unfortunately, this flank attack had no chance of succeeding, because 150 German panzers could neither combat nor even deflect the mass of Russian armor that had meanwhile grown to nearly 1,000 tanks. As expected, the Soviets quickly recovered from their initial surprise and held off XLVIII Panzer Corps's attack with about one-fourth of their armor and some antitank guns. Although General Balck's attack disabled seventy-eight Red Army tanks, he could not overcome this obstacle.

The bulk of the Russian First Tank and Third Guards Tank Armies rolled on toward the area north of Kazatin, which was defended only by a regimental *Kampfgruppe* of Lieutenant General Mortimer von Kessel's 20th Panzer Division, the twenty-four assault guns of the 18th Artillery Division, and the *Alarmeinheiten* stationed within the city limits. If this unforeseen threat was to be met, and a breakthrough in depth prevented, the other elements of the 18th Artillery Division that had just been moved toward Zhitomir would have to be pulled out immediately and returned to Kazatin. Traffic bottlenecks, created by the simultaneous use of the Zhitomir-Kazatin road by XLVIII Panzer Corps traveling in the same direction, were unavoidable. Fortunately, the excellent condition of the asphalt road and the adroit leadership of General Thoholte made it possible to pour enough reinforcements into Kazatin (principally the 18th Artillery Division) at the last moment to enable us to withstand the impact of the Russian onslaught.

Our troops also managed to bring the other enemy thrusts in the Berdichev area and east of Zhitomir to a halt, affording XLVIII Panzer Corps sufficient time to comply with its original orders and take up position between Kazatin and Berdichev. General Balck arrived on 26 December, just in time to witness the Russians streaming into Kazatin. Their next objective was obviously to cut the Zhitomir-Vinnitsa highway. General Balck's panzers repelled the Soviet armored spearheads and retook the ridge east of the highway. The Russians responded by splitting their attack forces in an attempt to locate a weak point for a breakthrough attack to the west, but the 1st, 7th, and 1st SS Panzer Divisions took full advantage of the good road net and always reached the critical points in time to block the advance of the Soviet armor. Well concealed by terrain and brush, our panzers allowed the Russian tanks to approach and scored direct hits before they were discovered. On 26 December alone, more than 200 enemy tanks succumbed to these tactics. By the end of that day, the breakthrough area of the First Tank and Third Guards Tank Armies had been completely blocked by XLVIII Panzer Corps, which now began steadily receiving infantry reinforcements. From 26–31 December the Russians attempted to break through General Balck's lines, but the only visible results they achieved could be calculated by their mounting tank losses.

When the First Ukrainian Front eventually realized the futility of its efforts in the Berdichev-Kazatin area, it changed the direction of its main thrust and attempted to unhinge both flanks of our blocking force by outflanking Zhitomir to the north with the Thirty-eighth Army and bypassing Kazatin to the south in the vicinity of Vinnitsa with the First Tank Army and parts of the Third Guards Tank Army. To counteract this move, I withdrew General von der Chevallerie's LIX Corps from Korosten to Novgorod-Volynskiy, and General Hauffe's XIII Corps evacuated Zhitomir to take up new positions south of the swampy forests along the Teterev. In addition, all available elements of two more divisions (the 25th Panzer and 168th Infantry Divisions of the XLII Corps) were moved closer to Kazatin to extend the blocking force's front. To ensure the best possible leadership in the tank battles around Kazatin, the staff of the XLII Corps (which had little training along those lines) was exchanged for the staff of the XXIV Panzer Corps, which had heretofore been employed on the quiet front near Kanev on the Dnepr. A local withdrawal by XLVIII Panzer Corps completed these measures and helped build up a new, integrated defensive system.

Hitler, on the other hand, refused to permit the withdrawal of Fourth Panzer Army's two right-wing corps in position along the Dnepr bend, even though these forces were in imminent danger of being cut off. Only a light screening force maintained contact between the VII and XLII (former XXIV Panzer) Corps and the rest of our heavily engaged army. For the moment the Russians appeared content to probe this screening force without realizing their opportunity, but before long the pressure on VII Corps increased, the salient was overextended, and the front line breached. The Soviets then poured more and more troops into the gap north of Uman without meeting any opposition. The possibility of extricating these two corps from the tightening noose still existed, although they were seriously threatened from the rear. Had they been allowed to use detours or break through, they would have been able to reestablish contact with Fourth Panzer Army and could thereby have been integrated into our second blocking line. But despite increasingly emphatic requests, Hitler ordered the VII and XLII Corps to remain in position. By the time he fully realized the danger of the situation, the Russians had assembled one army north of Uman with a second one following close behind. The staff of General of Panzer Troops Hans Hube's First Panzer Army—along with III Panzer Corps and the battle-weary 16th and 17th Panzer Divisions—was quickly relieved in another sector, shifted to Uman, and placed in command of the two corps cut off along the Dnepr.

In the meantime, the grim struggle continued for weeks along the Fourth Panzer Army's front. In the center, XIII Corps had been weakened by the heavy losses of equipment it had suffered during its withdrawal across the swampy woods south of Zhitomir. Realizing this weakness, the Russians concentrated their tanks opposite General Hauffe's line, anticipating that the breakthrough they had hitherto been denied could be achieved in this sector. During this phase of the fighting they attained several small penetrations that were quickly eliminated with the assistance of XLVIII Panzer Corps, but the divisions of XIII Corps (68th, 208th, and 340th Infantry Divisions, 213th Security Division, 7th Panzer Division, and Cavalry Regiment *Sud*) were gradually reduced and crushed. Their remnants held out among the panzer units, and to unify the command, they were formally subordinated to XLVIII Panzer Corps and the staff of XIII Corps was withdrawn. In a last, desperate attempt to break through, the Soviets massed all available tanks and penetrated our lines. In the subsequent melee, however, all seventy tanks that had gone through were put out of action, thus ending the attacks along this sector during the last days of January.

The Russian armored thrust toward Vinnitsa failed at about the same time, after enemy spearheads had come within reach of Zhmerinka, the important railroad junction from which the double-track lines branch off to Odessa. The III Panzer Corps and XLVI Panzer Corps launched a powerful counterattack with the 16th Panzer Division and three strong infantry divisions, repelled the First Tank Army, and cut off those elements that had advanced as far as Zhmerinka. At one point the bulk of the First Tank Army became encircled southeast of Vinnitsa, but it broke out during the very first night.

To our astonishment, the entire First Tank Army then disappeared. In spite of deep snow and clear weather, we could not even determine in which direction the enemy forces had escaped. From the overall tactical situation, we assumed that they had hidden in the immediate vicinity in a group of numerous, rather large villages with extensive, adjoining orchards. Since our own panzer units had recently driven through those villages, however, the presence of tank tracks gave no reliable evidence that the Russians were hiding there. For two days and nights the Luftwaffe scouted for the whereabouts of the First Tank Army and in this connection took excellent aerial photographs of the entire region in which the villages were located. Yet neither aerial observation nor the study of the reconnaissance photographs provided any clue. Not until the third day, when a strong panzer force pushed into this group of villages, did we establish that the entire Soviet tank army had hidden in the area. All tanks and other vehicles had been excellently camouflaged in barns, under sheds, straw piles, haystacks, and piles of branches, while movement during the day had been strictly forbidden, so that nothing gave away the enemy's presence.

The last major Soviet thrust against the extreme western flank of Fourth Panzer Army was directed against the Shepetovka railroad station. Only the weak 112th Infantry Division held Shepetovka against vastly superior enemy forces, but this attack failed as well. A subsequent attempt to cut off LIX Corps from XLVIII Panzer Corps by an enveloping thrust via Polonnoye proved equally unsuccessful. An infantry division just transferred from Army Group North detrained in Shepetovka in time to launch a counterattack. This division recaptured Polonnoye, sealed the gap, and reestablished contact with General Balck's corps.

This action brought the Russian Christmas offensive to its end. After five weeks of hard struggle, Fourth Panzer Army, with four corps and no more than 200 panzers, had scored a major defensive success against six Soviet armies deploying 1,200 tanks. Although the Russians had forced our front line back by nearly 100 kilometers, they failed to achieve a strategic breakthrough toward far-reaching objectives. Their plan had been to crush Fourth Panzer Army, unhinge both Army Groups South and A, and then annihilate them against the Black Sea or push them into Rumania. This operation failed, and in view of its proportions, the territorial gains obtained by the Russians were really insignificant. Fourth Panzer Army remained intact and held a continuous front line and was even able to furnish two panzer divisions to the First Panzer Army in the Uman area, where another disaster loomed.

This defensive success had been achieved because, after the third day of the offensive [26 December], General Balck's strong XLVIII Panzer Corps was employed as a blocking force. At that time the center of our sector had been broken through, and gaps up to nearly 150 kilometers in width extended on both flanks. But General Balck's blocking force formed the steel clamp that held together the isolated infantry corps and preserved the army from disintegration: The Soviets could not split open this solid army front of twelve divisions. By fighting three successive delaying actions, General Balck had prevented a strategic breakthrough and stabilized the situation sufficiently to permit the formation of a continuous front.

The Struggle for Galicia

Other sectors of Army Group South did not fare as well against the Russian Christmas offensive, which continued until the thaw started in March. The successes gained by the Red Army during this period included the annihilation of two German corps in the Cherkassy pocket, the encirclement of Ternopol and of First Panzer Army, and the general retrograde correction of our front between the Pripyat Marshes and the Black Sea along a line east of Stanislaw-Lvov-Kovel. In February a yawning gap opened on the Pripyat River at the boundary between Army Group South and Army Group Center, and the Russians crossed this extensive marshy region during the muddy period with fourteen divisions, pushing toward Kovel. Several of these divisions turned south through Rowne to attack Lvov. Stopped near Dubno on the Ikwa River by Fourth Panzer Army, they vainly tried to take the few strongly manned crossings over the extensive swamps on both sides of the river. Despite these repeated failures, a Russian battalion abruptly appeared one morning in the rear of Dubno. It was surrounded by our panzers and captured. Interrogation of the prisoners revealed that during the night the Soviet riflemen had crawled on their bellies across the slightly frozen marsh, which was up to 600 meters wide and could not be crossed on foot, arriving at the far side exhausted and covered with muck. This incident served as a pointed reminder that swamps and lakes presented no real obstacles to the Red Army.

In March, Hitler initiated the first of what would become frequent attempts to reverse the tide of the war by the arbitrary designation of "fortified places." In the face of an imminent Soviet attack, many towns suddenly became improvised fortresses and had to suffer encirclement and siege as if they were well-equipped strongholds that had been systematically constructed and provisioned over a number of years. A commander was appointed for each fortress, given absolute powers, and put under a special oath. He thereby received authority of life and death over all persons within his jurisdiction and could employ them as he saw fit, even though most of them were merely passing through his territory. These men and their equipment were frequently the only resources at the disposal of a fortress commander, who actually found himself forced to pick them off the streets.

The location of some of these fortresses was so unfavorable that their defense seemed hopeless from the outset. Despite all remonstrances, even these places had to be held at all costs. For example, Brody, a small town in eastern Galicia completely surrounded by woods, was located in a valley without observation facilities. Dominated by a nearby plateau in Soviet hands, the town was under complete enemy observation and at the mercy of his artillery. At one point the woods even reached up to the edge of the town. Because of the lack of space, there was not even a suitable area for XIII Corps to locate artillery emplacements in case of a siege. In order to avoid an imminent disaster, I circumvented Hitler's order (as described below) and adopted tactics that prevented a siege of the town. Several months later we would not be so fortunate.

The situation at Ternopol was similar. There the garrison, under command of Major General Egon von Neindorff, held out bravely for one month, only to succumb for lack of rations and ammunition after an attempt to break the siege had bogged down in the mud.

At the beginning of April, Fourth Panzer Army launched a flank attack that proved very effective in remedying a precarious situation. Following the heavy winter fighting in eastern Galicia and Podolia, our three corps (XLII, XIII, and XLVIII Panzer) held a line extending from Kovel in the north, through Brody, to Derezhany in the south. The Russian encirclement of Brody was imminent: A gap existed between that town and the army's left wing. Our right wing was completely exposed. The so-called Fortress Ternopol, twenty-nine kilometers to the front of our southern wing, had been encircled for ten days. General Hube's First Panzer Army, forming a roving pocket, was moving north of the Dnestr River toward the gap on Fourth Panzer Army's southern flank, while strong Russian forces drove westward past the pocket on both sides of the river.

Although the overall situation was far from satisfactory, Fourth Panzer Army had at least halted its retrograde movement. The army remained intact after many critical battles and had inflicted heavy losses on the enemy during the winter. Despite evident battle-weariness, the Red Army continued its attempts to take Brody in order to gain a route to Lvov. They did succeed in encircling the city on several occasions, but the encirclements were broken each time by the provisional panzer *Kampfgruppe* Friebe, made up of one battalion of Pzkw VI Tigers and one of Pzkw V Panthers. This *Kampf-gruppe*, augmented by a *Nebelwerfer* brigade equipped with 900 late-type launchers, struck the enemy while he was still in his assembly area preparing for the final, all-out attack.

This mass concentration of fire resulted in the creation of a mass grave. As far as the eye could see, men, guns, smoldering stumps of trees, and blocks of earth lay in the ghastliest confusion. The margin of the forest had vanished to the roots. Such were the remains of an entire army devoured by the fury of war. The Red Army then did what had never been done either before or after: abandoned the siege of Brody and used its newly arrived forces to form a continuous front line opposite Fourth Panzer Army's center. General Hauffe's XIII Corps followed suit, linking up with General of Infantry Franz Mattenklott's XLII Corps to the north, thus at least temporarily closing the gap north of Brody. This allowed *Kampfgruppe* Friebe to be released for other missions.

Fourth Panzer Army's exposed right flank remained under light attack. The Soviets captured a few villages, but local reserves with the support of a Tiger battalion that had moved freely along the flank promptly recaptured them. Thus the army front remained intact, and the southern flank—though exposed—was relatively secure.

Still, the Russian forces that had bypassed General Hube's roving pocket continued their westward drive. Enemy tank spearheads south of the Dnestr River entered Stanislav, and those to the north of the river approached the "fortified area" around the Galich bridgehead. Quickly assembled German infantry, together with advance elements of the Hungarian First Army (which was assembling in the Stanislav-Nadvornaya area) drove the Russians out of Stanislav after heavy street fighting. North of the river, where Russian movements were hampered only by muddy terrain, they reached the Zlota Lipa Valley on an axis of advance pointed toward the Drohobycz oil fields.

The forward elements of First Panzer Army's forces in the pocket had by now reached the Chortkuv area, and Fourth Panzer Army received the mission of relieving them by a flank attack. Strong reinforcements were brought up for the execution of this task. The flank attack was to be launched to the southeast from Berezhany, while a secondary thrust to the Dnestr was intended to pinch off and destroy the Russian rifle divisions that had penetrated as far as the Galich area.

As a preliminary step, the first elements of Lieutenant General Willibald Utz's 100th Jaeger Division, detraining in the army rear area, were ordered to capture the terrain south of Berezhany. Elements of Major General Georg Zwade's 367th Infantry Division were to take the area south of Rogatin, with both of these operations designed to secure the unloading of *Obergruppen-*

fuehrer Paul Hausser's II SS Panzer Corps, whose 9th SS *Hohenstaufen* (*Brigadefuehrer* Willi Bittrich) and 10th SS *Frundsberg* (*Gruppenfuehrer* Karl Truenfeld) Panzer Divisions had just been transferred from Italy. Within a few days after detraining, the corps was ready to jump off. Aware of this new threat, the Russians utilized all available airpower to harass our assembly area, which was restricted to the only two usable roads in the area. This enemy interference, however, was negligible compared to the difficulties presented by the muddy terrain.

The 100th Jaeger Division was to clear the way for the decisive thrust, with the 9th and 10th SS Panzer Divisions following closely behind. The only available all-weather road permitting major mechanized movements led via Podgaytse to Buczacz. The infantry had the mission of capturing heavily defended Podgaytse on 5 April to open the road for *Obergruppenfuehrer* Hausser's panzer thrust. Hardly had the Russian screening force been dislodged from the wooded heights south of Berezhany when General Utz's infantry ran into huge snowdrifts that covered the entire road to a depth of at least a meter along 200–500-meter stretches. Bypassing these obstacles was rendered impossible by the rugged, snow-covered terrain on either side of the road. Security guards had to be posted while the combat troops, equipped only with entrenching tools and a few locally procured shovels, began clearing the snow. After several hours of backbreaking work a single lane was opened, and around noon it became possible to move up the artillery and tanks essential for the impending assault on Podgaytse.

Despite this delay, the 100th Jaeger Division took the strong organized defenses on the high ground in front of Podgaytse the same day. The Tiger battalion attached to the division knocked out the T-34s and antitank gun positions defending the entrance to the town but, in so doing, actually blocked its own advance. The main entrance alone was clogged by sixteen disabled Soviet tanks, and as the infantrymen edged forward in the house-to-house fighting, each wreck had to be towed off, pushed aside, or blown up. By late evening the Tigers had thrust into the town, knocking out thirty-six additional tanks in their advance. The infantry mopped up during the night by the glaring light of burning houses and destroyed tanks and, on the morning of 6 April, turned east toward the Strypa River to secure II SS Panzer Corps's left flank and to make way for the tanks to advance.

The 10th SS *Frundsberg* Panzer Division now took the lead, spearheaded by SS Panzer Regiment 10 with forty-nine Panthers and forty-four StG III assault guns. At the southern edge of Podgaytse, the division ran into strong resistance from skillfully concealed antitank guns, which were too well entrenched to be attacked frontally and could not be bypassed because of the deep, water-filled ditches, ravines, and swamps on both sides of the road.

After close reconnaissance, the guns were finally knocked out, one by one, with concentrated panzer and artillery fire. The way cleared, the tanks rolled forward. To avoid further delay, *Gruppenfuehrer* Truenfeld decided to drive cross-country to Buczacz, but the route chosen for a short cut proved to be a quagmire. Only *Gruppenfuehrer* Truenfeld himself with the five lead tanks got through. Although he was able to establish contact there with the spearheads of First Panzer Army, this achievement served no practical purpose as long as the Soviets still held the highway between Podgaytse and Buczacz. *Gruppenfuehrer* Truenfeld's hasty decision to leave the highway delayed the operation and cut him off from his troops. Their tanks bogged down, the panzer crews, fighting as infantry, undertook the clearance of the highway under the personal leadership of *Obergruppenfuehrer* Hausser. Hostile antitank fire interfered with their advance, and the Russians offered strong resistance in every village along the road. Nonetheless, subjected to increasing pressure from the two SS panzer divisions and the 367th Infantry Division approaching from the Galich area, their efforts proved futile. That evening, near the bend of the road west of Buczacz, the Red Army rifle divisions fleeing east along the Dnestr were blocked off, hurled against the river, and destroyed with the assistance of General Zwade's division. *Brigadefuehrer* Bittrich reorganized his attack units and turned eastward, reaching Buczacz late on 6 April to clear a withdrawal route for General Hube's beleaguered army. The Russians did not readily yield this prize, which was literally being wrung from their grasp. In fierce pursuit they tried to cross the swollen Strypa to cut the escape artery, but they proved to be no match for the liberating forces. Whenever enemy troops got across the river, *Obergruppenfuehrer* Hausser's men threw them back immediately.

By mid-April the right wing of the Fourth Panzer Army had deployed behind the Strypa River, and the front—anchored on the Dnestr to the south—included a bridgehead across the Strypa opposite Buczacz. On this line fixed positions were organized. The objective of the flank attack—the stabilization of the front in eastern Galicia—was attained with the liberation of the First Panzer Army from encirclement and its reintegration into the defense front of Army Group North Ukraine (Army Group South having been so redesignated on 5 April).

Unfortunately, the garrison at Ternopol was lost soon thereafter because the XLVIII Panzer Corps relief effort, spearheaded by *Kampfgruppe* Friebe and the 9th SS *Hohenstaufen* Panzer Division, was prevented by mud from reaching the beleaguered city. Our forces were able to cross the Strypa River and knock out strong antitank defenses but had covered only half of the twenty kilometers to Ternopol when forced by the mud to give up. Thousands of hours of labor were necessary to restore roads and small bridges sufficiently to retrieve our stranded panzers.

A short time thereafter, General von Neindorff was killed, and after four weeks of stubborn defense the Russians took Ternopol. With this "fortified area" a garrison of 6,000 men and considerable stocks of equipment fell into the enemy's hands. Once again the tragic destiny of a "fortified area" had been fulfilled, without having exercised any great influence on the conduct of the war.

Chapter 11

THE BATTLE FOR LVOV

Changing Russian Tactics

THE PAST YEAR HAD BROUGHT definite refinements to the Red Army's methods of attack. Concentrated artillery fires were employed more frequently and supplemented by mass mortar attacks. The Russians attempted to infiltrate through known German weak points. For this purpose they preferred forest areas or hollows previously designated by the tactical command. If they succeeded in infiltrating by this system, they immediately entrenched themselves and laid mines. Subsequently, a period of vulnerability set in, because the artillery and heavy weapons came up very slowly, and cooperation between these weapons and the spearhead units ceased abruptly for a brief time.

The Russian breakthrough attacks themselves were accomplished by the same methods that had been employed successfully by the czar's army in World War I. These methods had little in common with modern tactical doctrines but were based on great superiority of manpower and equipment. After weeks of logistical buildup and moving up the enormous quantities of ammunition required, our front would be breached after several hours of concentrated artillery, mortar, and rocket fire. This was followed by the breakthrough of massed infantry forces and deep thrusts of tank units attempting to gain freedom of maneuver. In 1944 the employment of massed armor somewhat altered this sequence of events, as large numbers of tanks led off the assault, followed by infantry in deep wedges. While Soviet artillery gave good support at the outset of such attacks, communications between the gunners and the spearhead units frequently broke down during any further advance. To the very end of the war it was difficult for the Russians to coordinate fire and movement. The armored penetrations were deep and invariably made in a straight line. Then a halt would be called to bring up the greatest possible infantry strength during the night, which would dig in as soon as the main points of the advance had been reached. Other heavy weapons and support units then closed up in echelons behind the tanks.

This system was absolutely foolproof as long as we did not interfere with the sequence of events. An essential prerequisite for such an attack was that the German defenders would rigidly hold the threatened sector of the front until the deadly blow fell. In the East during 1943–1945, German armies reluctantly complied with this prerequisite since their commanders had strict orders from Hitler not to relinquish a single inch of ground voluntarily. Such rigid tactics were enforced on commanders from division to army group almost without exception through the end of the war. Being of aware of the Wehrmacht's numerical inferiority and our loss of combat efficiency due to extreme casualties, Hitler perhaps doubted its capability of conducting a flexible, active defense and therefore insisted that our troops cling rigidly to prepared positions.

Such tactics could never prevent Soviet breakthroughs, let alone lead to victory. Despite the fact that the Red Army invariably suffered heavier casualties than those they inflicted on our troops, or the reality that the fighting qualities of the individual Russian soldier were vastly inferior to those of their opponents, we could never overcome the critical problem of the Soviet superiority in men and equipment. Aside from the greater individual fighting capabilities of the German soldier, we had no other means of offsetting our numerical inferiority than by employing more flexible and superior tactics. If our highest military leaders lost their faith in the superiority of the Wehrmacht in these two areas, or if our shortages of equipment became so acute that qualitative and tactical advantages could not be exploited, then a favorable outcome of this war was no more to be expected than in World War I.

It was the responsibility of the Supreme Commander, Adolph Hitler, to recognize these facts and draw the necessary conclusions. Until that time, it was the duty of commanders in the field to do their utmost to prevent a collapse of the front lines, where—by mid-1944—the greatest imminent threats to the fighting front were Russian massed attacks with subsequent breakthroughs. Since adequate reserves for a successful defense were rarely available, it became all the more necessary to prevent the annihilation of the front-line units by Soviet fire concentrations, bombing attacks, and massed armored thrusts. In no other way could we hope to preserve the combat efficiency of our depleted divisions.

Zone Defense Tactics

At First Panzer Army during the spring and summer of 1944, my chief of staff, Colonel Karl Wagener, my operations officer, Colonel Adrian Graf von

Puechler, and I introduced zone defense tactics as an improvisation for this purpose. We derived this system from a through analysis of the reasons for the success of most Russian breakthroughs, considering the following as the principal factors:

The annihilation of our front-line troops by mass concentration on points along the main battle line;

The neutralization or destruction of our artillery by heavy counterbattery fire and continuous air attacks;

The elimination of our command staffs by air attack and surprise fire on forward command posts up to army level;

The harassing of reserves by artillery fire and air attacks on their assembly areas;

The disruption of routes of communication to the front, which delayed the movement of reserves and cut off the flow of supplies;

The massed armored thrusts in depth, which enabled the Russians to obtain freedom of maneuver.

For obvious reasons it was our task to neutralize those enemy tactics, or at least to reduce them to tolerable proportions.

There were two ways to prevent the annihilation of our front-line troops: either by constructing bombproof and shellproof positions, or by withdrawing the forward units in time to evade the devastating barrages. Since the construction of shellproof positions required an expenditure of time and materials beyond our capabilities, the adoption of evasive tactics was the only solution. Such evasive tactics had already been employed during the last stages of World War I. The forward positions were evacuated shortly before an imminent attack, and the defending troops moved far enough to the rear into a new an even stronger line to force the enemy to regroup his assault forces, always a time-consuming maneuver. The difficulties encountered by the enemy before he was able to resume the attack were to be enhanced by demolitions of the intermediate terrain. These evasive tactics were pioneered in 1918 in the West when the German armies withdrew to the Hindenburg Line in France and in the South on the Italian front along the Piae River. The loss of some ground that was necessarily involved in the application of these tactics was a well-considered sacrifice, but achieving any permanent gain required that the new positions be held without fail. Another method of evading fire concentration and a subsequent breakthrough was the adoption of elastic defense measures in a deeply echeloned system of machine-gun strongpoints that, however, often lacked the necessary resiliency to halt a major enemy attack.

Another form of tactical evasion that we envisioned can best be compared with saber-fencing tactics. A cut is warded off by sudden retirement with appropriate guard, followed by an immediate counterthrust that permits the fencer to regain his former position. Like the fencer, the forces holding the threatened sector of the front execute a surprise withdrawal at the last moment, moving far enough to the rear that the blow misses, the pursuing enemy can be repelled, and the initial position regained through a prompt counterattack. In order to satisfy these requirements, the terrain in which the enemy pursuit is to be intercepted must be well chosen and systematically prepared so that the withdrawing force can resume the defense within a few hours. It is therefore neither possible nor essential to withdraw the front-line units so far to the rear as to be out of the reach of the enemy's artillery.

Past experience indicated to us that the Russians fired their concentrations only on the main battle line and against preselected strongpoints in the zone of resistance. These areas, therefore, absolutely had to be evacuated, yet depending on the terrain and local fortifications, it was usually sufficient to withdraw the most forward troops only 900–2,200 meters. Here was where we would organize the real forward defense line, taking advantage of all favorable terrain features. Numerous strongpoints and sizable local reserves were distributed throughout these positions, which extended back to the artillery emplacements and even beyond. In a camouflaged area behind the artillery lay the general reserves of corps and army. By following this procedure, targets became so well dispersed that even fire from as many as 1,000 guns had to be directed at such a large area that only local damage could be inflicted, while entire units could not be wiped out.

If, at the same time, our artillery was to avoid neutralization and escape destruction, the batteries had to switch to alternate emplacements in the battle position at the decisive moment (this included provisions for alternate observation posts). These alternate positions had to be prepared well in advance, provided with ammunition, and equipped with a smoothly functioning wire and radio communications system. Additional battery positions and observation posts had to be reconnoitered and organized in depth so that they would be ready for immediate occupancy and utilization in case of emergency. This procedure intended to guarantee continuous support for the infantry even in the event of a tactical reverse, since only the flexible employment of artillery units that remained intact promised a successful defense. Furthermore, each battery had to establish two or three alternate positions and one or two dummy positions, firing from them with at least one registration gun to determine firing data for every emplacement. Altogether this required between five and eight positions to be prepared for each battery, but normally the length of a Russian buildup prior to a major offensive provided sufficient time for such extensive preliminary work.

All necessary precautions had to be taken to protect the command staffs and their communications from destruction by Soviet artillery preparations and the ensuing general attack. For that reason no command staff, from battalion to army, was permitted to stay at the command post it occupied before the start of the Russian attack. Each staff had to prepare a well-camouflaged, shellproof command post away from inhabited communities and was required to install a telephone switchboard in a separate bunker. Communications between the command post and its subordinate units was to be assured by wire, radio, visual signals, dispatch riders, or runners, and in an emergency by a combination of any or all of the above. Telephone wires had to be laid in such manner that they could not easily be cut by fire or tracked vehicles. Wherever possible, our signal troops laid them along ditches and swampy depressions or strung them on trees. We dug radio trucks into the ground in inconspicuous places, protected against shell fragments and well camouflaged before the attack began. From the moment that these trucks were first positioned, until the Russians attacked, strict radio silence was enforced.

Before the general attack, all reserves had to leave their billeting areas and move into their battle-position quarters, which had to be well camouflaged, outside inhabited communities, and ready for immediate use. These quarters had to have telephones, radios, and other communications media readily available.

Routes of communication to the front were of vital importance and therefore had to be kept open under all circumstances. Bottlenecks had to be avoided, defective stretches of the road made serviceable even in inclement weather, and strict controls imposed for two-way traffic. Alternate bridges had to be constructed in suitable places away from the existing ones and provided with approach roads. At least two alternative routes had to be determined through each town or village, so that convoys could detour narrow streets whenever air attacks appeared likely.

One of our greatest problems was to intercept Soviet massed tank attacks and prevent breakthroughs. Given our marked numerical inferiority, this involved extensive countermeasures that could only gradually be enforced and slowly integrated into the defensive system.

First of all, any terrain particularly suited for an armored breakthrough had to be mined to a quite unusual extent. Selecting such areas and mining them with due consideration for Red Army tactical doctrines presented few difficulties to experienced panzer officers. The minefields had to be laid in depth and width in a checkerboard pattern in such a manner that our own panzer divisions could detour around them on the basis of information received. All signs designating minefields were removed prior to the Russian attack. We laid no mines at all in front of our forward units, because the enemy could remove them and even use them for his own purposes before the attack opened. The main battle position was mined in depth up to twenty-five kilometers to the rear. Prior to the First Ukrainian Front's major offensive in the Lvov area that summer, First Panzer Army mined the sector in which we expected the main attack with 160,000 antipersonnel and 200,000 antitank mines within the zone defense. This was the first time that any German army had applied such zone defense tactics.

The most forward divisional antitank guns had to take up positions approximately 1.5 kilometers behind the main battle line. The bulk of the artillery, as well as numerous medium antitank and flak guns, we utilized to form centers of gravity behind the forward guns up to nearly twenty kilometers in depth. All roads suitable for sudden tank thrusts in depth were blocked by tank obstacles, captured immobile antitank guns, and flak guns to a depth of forty kilometers. In case of critical developments, self-propelled antitank guns were to reinforce the defense at key points. To camouflage these guns, tanks ditches had to be dug and approach roads built in suitable terrain.

Army reserves had to be sufficiently strong to support the front and stop the Russians in case they abruptly shifted the main effort and turned their tanks into an adjacent sector that had not been prepared according to zone defense principles. In anticipation of the Soviet offensive against Lvov, under the control of General of Panzer Troops Hermann Breith's III Panzer Corps, the 1st and 8th Panzer Divisions, 20th Panzergrenadier Division, and Tiger Battalion 531 constituted our reserve. The 1st and 8th Panzer Divisions were to support the front in the center of gravity, while the 20th Panzergrenadier Division and Tiger Battalion 531 were to be committed instantly to stop any armored thrust elsewhere, in case the Soviets shifted their point of main effort. The two divisions assigned to the center of gravity were expected to redeploy as necessary and provide them assistance in due course. General Breith also formed mobile *Kampfgruppen* and equipped them with as many antitank and assault guns as possible in order to enable them to provide immediate support to front-line sectors threatened by sudden disintegration. In most cases these *Kampfgruppen* consisted of reconnaissance battalions reinforced by antitank or assault-gun battalions, which were held in instant readiness and formed the advance detachments of their respective divisions.

The task of indoctrinating our unit commanders in all the essential zone defense measures was far from easy. After detailed briefings, map exercises, and tactical walks, they not only grasped the idea but became thoroughly convinced of the expediency and feasibility of the plan and therefore lent their enthusiastic support to its execution. Discussions and training exercises continued down the line to the smallest units.

The next step was to put these measures to their practical test and examine them in the light of experience. Starting with individual arms, these tests eventually extended to larger units. Finally, zone defense tactics were adopted and enforced throughout all corps and divisions in First Panzer Army. The tremendous effort entailed in these preparations was to pay high dividends.

The fencer derives an advantage from cutting into his opponent's sequence when the latter intends to strike, because the attacker usually exposes himself on that occasion. This intercepting blow was also included as a component of our zone defense tactics. Since the Russians moved their forces close to their most advanced positions and massed them before jumping off for the assault, they exposed themselves to concentrated surprise fire from all of our artillery and rocket launchers. Two basic loads of every type of ammunition had been set aside for just that purpose.

The most difficult and critical problem facing First Panzer Army at Lvov was to determine the correct time for withdrawing the front-line units into the battle position. If we chose to move too late, the safety measures against the annihilation of our limited combat forces by the Soviet artillery preparation would have been rendered ineffective. The front-line corps and divisions did not possess the facilities to gather sufficient clues regarding Russian plans to enable army headquarters to draw the correct conclusions about the timing of the Red Army's assault. This can easily be understood, since their observation of enemy activities was restricted to the most advanced areas of the front. Instead, Colonel Wagener and I personally coordinated combat intelligence, aerial reconnaissance, and radio intercepts, which provided so much information on Soviet preparations and covered the First Ukrainian Front's rear areas so completely that we were able to determine the location of the enemy's main effort and the projected starting date for its attack with great accuracy. The most reliable information we secured through radio interception, which provided as much as 70 percent of our best intelligence.

Order of Battle, First Panzer Army

XIII Corps
General of Infantry Arthur Hauffe

  361st Infantry Division
    Major General Gerhard Lindemann

  Korpsabteilung C
    Lieutenant General Wolfgang Lange

454th Security Division
Major General Johannes Nedtwig

14th SS Grenadier Division (Galician)
Brigadefuehrer Fritz Freitag

XLVIII Panzer Corps
General of Panzer Troops Hermann Balck

96th Infantry Division
Lieutenant General Richard Wirtz

349th Infantry Division
Lieutenant General Otto Lasch

357th Infantry Division
Lieutenant General Wolfgang von Kluge

359th Infantry Division
Lieutenant General Karl Arndt

XXIV Panzer Corps
General of Panzer Troops Walter Nehring

75th Infantry Division
Lieutenant General Helmuth Beukemann

254th Infantry Division
Lieutenant General Alfred Thielmann

371st Infantry Division
Lieutenant General Hermann Niehoff

100th Jaeger Division
Lieutenant General Willibald Utz

LIX Corps
Lieutenant General Edgar Roehricht

208th Infantry Division
Lieutenant General Hans Piekenbrock

20th Hungarian Infantry Division

XLVI Panzer Corps
General of Infantry Friedrich Schulz

1st Infantry Division
Lieutenant General Ernst-Anton von Krosigk

168th Infantry Division
Lieutenant General Werner Schmidt-Hammer

III Panzer Corps (army reserve)
General of Panzer Troops Hermann Breith

    1st Panzer Division
       Major General Werner Marcks

    8th Panzer Division
       Major General Gottfried Froelich

    20th Panzergrenadier Division
       Lieutenant General Georg Jauer

    First Hungarian Army (attached)
       Lieutenant General Karoly Beregfy

VII Hungarian Corps
Major General Istvan Kiss

    68th Infantry Division
       Major General Paul Scheuerpflug

    16th Hungarian Infantry Division

XI Hungarian Corps

    101st Jaeger Division
       Colonel Walter Assmann

    18th Hungarian Reserve Division

    24th Hungarian Infantry Division

    25th Hungarian Infantry Division

VI Hungarian Corps
Lieutenant General Ferenc Farkas

    1st Hungarian Infantry Division

    27th Hungarian Light Division

Army reserves
    7th Hungarian Infantry Division
    19th Hungarian Reserve Division
    2nd Hungarian Panzer Division

The Battle for Lvov

The Russians did not disappoint us with regard to the location of the main attack but began their offensive on 14 July, two days later than expected. Interrogation of prisoners confirmed that the attack had been postponed by forty-eight hours at the last moment. As a result of this delay, the evasive maneuver had to be repeated on three successive nights. On the night of 11–12 July the Russians either did not notice the withdrawal because our rear guards left in the forward positions successfully simulated weak harassing fire, or they lacked the time and tactical flexibility to react to this sudden change. On the night of 12–13 July they attacked several evacuated positions with combat teams up to regimental strength and pushed back our rear guards.

Even this turn of events, however, had been anticipated. Strong counterthrusts, supported by massed artillery fire from the regular firing positions, sealed off these Soviet penetrations, and at dusk on the night of 13–14 July our infantry once again occupied the front lines. As expected, the Russians resumed their attacks during the night to determine whether or not we would continue to occupy the positions. When these night attacks had been repulsed along the entire line, and the Soviets had convinced themselves that the positions were being held in strength, the fighting broke off and the front calmed down. After midnight our advanced positions were evacuated for the third time, and when First Ukrainian Front unleashed its main fire concentration at dawn it struck empty positions. The divisions that had retired into their battle positions suffered hardly any losses and—supported by assault guns and Tiger Battalion 531—were able to drive back nearly all Russian forces that had advanced beyond the empty positions. Our artillery preserved its entire firepower because the shelling and aerial bombardments hit the empty battery positions that had assumed the role of dummies. Not a single gun, not a single command post, was hit. Telephone communications from army headquarters down to regimental levels suffered no disruption. The former positions that had been evacuated, on the contrary, were in poor shape, the towns badly damaged by air attacks, and the debris of bombed buildings blocked main roads through several villages. Nevertheless, traffic continued to move along the previously designated alternate routes and halted only intermittently when Soviet aircraft scored direct hits on individual convoys.

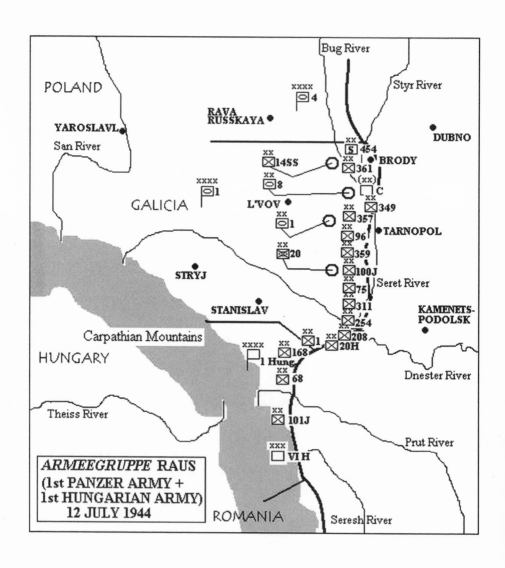

ARMEEGRUPPE RAUS
(1st PANZER ARMY +
1st HUNGARIAN ARMY)
12 JULY 1944

Our reserves had not been touched by Russian air attacks, since they had used the darkness to move into locations unknown to the enemy. On the other hand, advancing Soviet infantry was hit by the defensive fire of artillery and rocket launchers that were fully intact and well supplied with ammunition. Reeling from this concentration, the Red Army infantry attempted to disperse and take cover but walked straight into the minefields we had positioned behind the front-line battle positions. This took the initial momentum out of the attack and prevented the Russian infantry from concentrating its effort in a single direction. First Ukrainian Front's advance slowed down and became hesitant, and practically all its territorial gains had to be abandoned when our troops, having evaded the destructive effect of the initial barrage, started to counterattack that afternoon.

Distress signals from the beleaguered Russian infantry brought their tanks to the scene. Like a cataract released by the sudden opening of a dam, the massed tanks poured across the Seret River into the historic battleground of Yaroslavichi, where exactly thirty years before, during the summer of 1914, Austro-Hungarian and imperial Russian cavalry divisions had clashed head-on in the last major cavalry charge in history. History now repeated itself, as once again the Russians enjoyed numerical superiority, and once again the battle ended in a draw. In 1914 the defenders achieved this result by the use of new machine-gun and artillery tactics, whereas in 1944 we introduced zone defense tactics to overcome our inferiority. On 14 July alone, First Ukrainian Front lost eighty-five tanks to our minefields. The number of disabled tanks increased rapidly, and the entire Soviet armored advance broke down when it came within reach of our carefully deployed antitank and flak guns. The losses assumed truly disastrous proportions when General Breith proceeded on 15 July to counterattack with the 1st and 8th Panzer Divisions.

In 1944, as in 1914, the battle for Lvov was not decided by the cavalry charge or the tank thrust near Yaroslavichi but by a major Russian breakthrough north of Lvov, in the adjacent army sector to which the enemy shifted his main effort. Unfortunately for us in 1944, when this shifted attack concentration hit the right flank of Fourth Panzer Army around Brody, II SS Panzer Corps, with its two strong panzer divisions, had been transferred to the Western Front because the Allies had meanwhile landed at Normandy. For this reason, Army Group North Ukraine no longer possessed sufficient forces to stop the Russian tank drive in the new area of penetration. An unending stream of tank and motorized columns passed Zhelkva, rushing headlong toward the Vistula, which they not only reached without encountering any resistance worth mentioning but also crossed at Baranov.

A tank corps withdrawn from that mass of Russian armor attacked the sector of General Lasch's 349th Infantry Division, which had been left in a quiet part of the line in the trackless forest northeast of Lvov and therefore did not have adequate antitank guns at its disposal. That Russian tank corps forced a narrow gap in the front around Koltov, although it came under attack from both flanks and was heavily bombarded by artillery and *Nebelwerfer* multiple rocket launchers. The Soviets used their heavy KV-1 and KV-2 tanks as battering rams to crush the medium-growth timber. The attacked engineers overcame some of the attendant difficulties by laying corduroy roads across the swamps, which allowed infantry and artillery units to follow the tanks much more quickly than usual. Shortly before this operation, the commanders of both the 1st and 8th Panzer Divisions had assured me that this forest was impenetrable even for Russian armor. The Red Army's advance across this hastily improvised road, constructed with the aid of the most primitive facilities, was, for a time, even accompanied by the strains of band music!

When the Soviets reached the main highway to Lvov, General Breith committed both of his panzer divisions in a pincer attack, which managed to narrow the penetration to four kilometers, but not to close it. The 1st and 8th Panzer Divisions did piece together a second front between Lvov and Koltov, which at first halted the advance of the enemy tank corps, but the Russians were able, by degrees, despite difficult ground conditions, to bypass the exposed flank of this second, improvised front (which rested against a steep bank), to occupy Przemyzl, and thus to block one of First Panzer Army's critical supply routes. Leaving behind a detachment to garrison Przemyzl, the Soviet tank corps then resumed its advance on Lvov via Bobkra, quickly occupying the airfield and fighting its way into the southern part of the city.

The commandant of Lvov, however, held the greater part of the city (including the railroad station and the commanding heights near the city center) with a grenadier regiment of the 68th Infantry Division, local defense battalions, and some service units. In the meantime, a mixed *Kampfgruppe* with assault guns and artillery, under the command of officers from my staff, retook both Przemyzl and Bobkra, severing the supply route of the Russian tank corps. The consequence of this action was that all offensive capabilities of this tank corps rapidly became paralyzed. Peace and quiet returned to Lvov, and life in the northern part of the city resumed its normal course. The local defense and service troops who had been called upon to oppose the enemy now indulged themselves in sunbathing, for the Russians now had ammunition only for self-defense.

The Soviet tank army commander, we discovered through radio intercepts, frequently and emphatically bullied the tank corps commander for his lack of activity and threatened him with "a sore throat" (death by hanging). These menacing words could not change the fact that the isolated tank corps lay for about a fortnight nearly seventy kilometers to the rear of the front, adjacent to the supply center of First Panzer Army, condemned to complete inactivity. Even when First Panzer Army later retreated through the city, the tank corps was unable materially to interfere with the movement through and around Lvov to the upper course of the Dnestr. Owing to a lack of forces with which to wipe out this enemy incursion, we had contented ourselves with paralyzing the corps by cutting off its supply route.

While this penetration was being contained, and the infantry battle raged on the main front, First Panzer Army's northern flank (XLVI Panzer Corps) near Zhelkva ran the risk of being caught up and swept away in the torrent of Russian armored vehicles rushing past the shattered flank of Fourth Panzer Army. There was nothing for it but to bend back General Schulz's flank several kilometers. Well anchored in its new position in the terrain southwest of Zhelkva, the corps succeeded in repulsing all enemy attempts to envelop it and in holding its ground. Unfortunately, an attempt by the strong 20th Panzergrenadier Division, smartly led by General Georg Jauer, to block the crossings of the Bug River by means of a flank attack on Karionka-Strumilova was not successful. The division's 100 assault guns certainly wreaked havoc among the Soviet tanks, but General Jauer's troops soon found themselves encircled by the Russian tank masses. The assault guns immediately changed fronts and burst through the Soviet tank ring, allowing the division to regain its former lines on 20 July. This instance bore out our previous experience that strong armored formations almost always succeeded in breaking out of a pocket or in getting the better of other difficult situations, as long as they acted quickly and resolutely.

Disaster at Brody

The position of General Hauffe's XIII Corps in the Brody area (under control of Fourth Panzer Army) deteriorated daily. Its five divisions (178th and 349th Infantry Divisions; *Korpsabteilung* C; 14th SS Grenadier Division; 454th Security Division; and a weak police formation) were enveloped by a Soviet rifle corps brought up to reinforce the enemy tank formations. The tanks, thrusting out around Brody, had felt their way through the woods beyond Busk, as well as through the gap to the north of Koltov around the corps's other flank. Gradually herded together in a restricted area on the high ground north of Koltov, XIII Corps again passed under command of First Panzer Army. I immediately issued instructions to General Hauffe to work his way as far as possible toward the south and to assemble by 23 July west of Koltov for a breakthrough toward the main road, where XLVIII Panzer Corps's 8th Panzer Division would push forward to meet it from the south. Following a successful breakout, XIII Corps was to reassemble in a certain area to the rear of XLVIII Panzer Corps. Weapons, equipment, and vehicles that were unable to make the grade south of the highway were to be destroyed, especially heavy equipment such as artillery and motor vehicles.

During these days First Panzer Army found itself under fierce attack along its entire front. General Edgar Roehricht's LIX Corps, fighting on the northern bank of the Dnestr, with the 208th Infantry Division and 20th Hungarian Infantry Division, was forced into taking evasive action, withdrawing step by step. This mean that the adjacent XXIV and XLVIII Panzer Corps, still fighting in the main battle zone, had to be moved back to avoid being trapped in a pocket. Because of General Hauffe's critical situation around Brody, however, I had to halt the XLVIII Panzer Corps for another day southeast of Koltov and—in spite of the difficult struggle—ordered General Balck to extricate the 8th Panzer Division from his front line for the liberating thrust against the highway to the west. Everyone realized that this meant the entire army was running a great risk in the interest of saving the XIII Corps. On 18 July I personally explained the situation of the army as a whole to General Hauffe in a telephone conversation and ordered him to launch his breakthrough attack toward the highway under any circumstances, as XLVIII Panzer Corps, which had halted solely to create a protective barrier, could not remain standing any longer without itself collapsing and being devoured with other victims. When General Hauffe objected that he needed an additional day, or else he would lose all of his equipment, I issued the final order: "Then just see that the men are saved." At that juncture the telephone conversation was lost; Russian aircraft had just bombed the decimeter apparatus that was the last means of communication with the XIII Corps.

With the first streaks of dawn on the following day [19 July], General Froelich's 8th Panzer Division set out in accordance with its orders to extricate the XIII Corps. Against powerful Russian resistance, the division drove the enemy back and, just before noon, actually reached the highway west of Koltov, where it mopped up Soviet positions on both sides in considerable width. General Hauffe's divisions lay barely four kilometers opposite and observed this action but did not form up. General Lange and the troops of his *Korpsabteilung* C, as we later learned, had heard nothing about the orders I gave General Hauffe. Only the two foremost battalions, who saw the Tigers supporting the 8th Panzer Division rolling along and fighting on the big road until the afternoon, fell in without having received any orders. These fortunate units reached the highway, arriving with all the weapons they could carry, and gained the safety of the rear area of XLVIII Panzer Corps, suffering only slight losses.

In the meantime, the Russians were bringing up reinforcements from all sides and, that evening, pushed both the 8th Panzer Division and the bulk of the XLVIII Panzer Corps, which had already been forced outside the main battle zone, several kilometers to the rear. General Hauffe had not profited from the hour of deliverance but lined up only on the following morning [20 July], bristling with arms and ready to attack following a burst of fire from all of his artillery. In concentrated masses the thousands of troops in his divisions went over the top with a blood-curdling battle cry—"Forward! Hurrah!"—and overran the Soviet infantry that had been shaken by the Germans' roars. This attack quickly reached the highway, where on the previous day the 8th Panzer Divisions had stood with its Panthers and Tigers. The Red Army rapidly recovered from the paralytic terror that had seized its front ranks, grasped the situation, and fired with artillery, tanks, antitank guns, mortars, and machine guns from all sides into that turbulent flood of humanity with whatever rounds their barrels contained. The men under attack had but a single objective: to reach the life-saving heights and woods on the highway. At the head of those columns, which stretched as far as the eye could see, the generals and staff officers stormed ahead, sharing the lot of the faithful men, whose corpses covered the battlefield in their thousands. On the railroad embankment lay the bodies of General Hauffe and his chief of staff, in the midst of their men, torn by enemy shells, having found there the same death as their comrades. The attack formations farther to the rear were, for the most part, taken prisoner.

Only 6,000 men escaped from that hell and, by exerting their last remaining strength, were able to scale the wooded heights to the south of the Lvov highway. They believed themselves safely to the rear of the battle line of their own adjacent corps but, after only a brief breathing space, were routed out and attacked by a hastily assembled Soviet rifle corps. Instantly their illusions gave place to the sobering realization that they were still in the rear of the Russian front, which was also confirmed by the prisoners taken in the counterattack. On they went, split up into small groups, with neither maps nor compasses, four days over mountains and valleys, through marshland and forests, past Soviet reserves and transport vehicles, in a quest for their own front line. Only on the fifth day did the nearing sounds of rolling cannon thunder show that the German lines were near at hand. Already on the evening of the same day, and in the course of the following night, most of the men managed to reach the safe western bank of the Gnila-Lipa River, where First Panzer Army's front line—moved back in the interim—came to an end. Barefooted, but still equipped with their steel helmets and weapons, the gallant remnants were assembled and reorganized. They were the eyewitnesses to the destruction of the entire XIII Corps, which had missed its last chance for salvation. Forming up just twenty-four hours too late had sealed the fate of General Hauffe's five divisions.

Withdrawal from Lvov

After the XIII Corps had dropped out, the situation of First Panzer Army certainly became more difficult, but it was as yet by no means menacing. Direct contact had been successfully established between the XLVIII Panzer Corps and the right flank of the III Panzer Corps, which had been in the second line before Lvov, thus forming a closed front formed by five corps with considerable defensive power. Nonetheless, the general situation had changed for the worse, as the Soviets were already on and across the Vistula River to the army's north. Strong enemy elements now wheeled around in the direction of the Carpathian Mountains and stood with the heads of their columns before Sambor and to the south of Przemyzl. To the south the front line of the First Hungarian Army was crumbling, and a Russian thrust from Kolomea made it begin to totter. By continuing to hold on to the front line jutting so far out to the east, First Panzer Army risked being enveloped in the Carpathian foothills. In consideration of that risk and of the general situation, I proposed that the battle should be broken off and the front line moved back to the rear of the marshes on the upper course of the Dnestr, which were easily defensible, and which had already played such a role in World War I. As an inducement to accept this proposal, I offered to release five panzer divisions once we had reached the new line. Hitler himself first turned down this proposal but some days later—when the situation had grown considerably more critical—approved it in the form of an order.

This new directive resulted in the abandonment of Lvov and a backward turning movement of First Panzer Army around its right flank. The encirclement of our left flank corps, rainy weather, and the impracticability of the nearly impassable forested and mountainous terrain southwest of Lvov all hampered this movement considerably. Because the isolated Russian tank corps still held its position south of Lvov, and due to the adjacent mountain chain, the army had to be split into two elements during the initial part of the movement. To make matters worse, the Soviets had already blocked the main retreat route about twenty kilometers south of Lvov, which had to be fought clear. In spite of all handicaps, however, First Panzer Army effected the movement in two rushes.

The marsh position on the Dnestr had barely been occupied when the Red Army took Sambor, which was defended only by a motley collection of weak units under the control of the commandant of Lvov. The enemy had thus lodged himself in the deep flank of our new position and could it attack it from the rear at will, with the potential to work havoc with it. Only by immediately recapturing the town could that danger be averted. Therefore, General Marcks's 1st Panzer Division, which had been marching off on a different assignment, had to be diverted back into that direction. A dashing attack made by the panzers and panzergrenadiers of that division broke the Russians' stubborn resistance and led to Sambor passing back into our hands the same day.

Now the road seemed clear to enable me to surrender the III Panzer Corps (1st, 7th, and 16th Panzer Divisions, and 20th Panzergrenadier Division) to the west for other employment. These were to be dispatched along the last line remaining to us north of the ridge of the wooded Carpathians, leading by way of Sanok into the Krakow area, but the Russians anticipated that plan, blocking the direct connection (and our lateral communications) on either side of Sanok with strong forces. General Breith's III Panzer Corps could only proceed by leapfrogging its divisions after first clearing the road by force of arms, at the cost of both casualties and valuable time. Thus Hitler's delay in allowing the First Panzer Army to break away from Lvov (accomplished on 26 July instead of 24 July) now made itself felt.

Battle for the Carpathians

In early August a new danger arose on the army's southern flank. The First Hungarian Army proved unable to hold its ground in the Stanislau-Navorna area against a superior enemy and crumbled into pieces. General Beregfy's southern flank elements fell back through the upper Pruth Valley in the Jablonica Pass, while the northern flank was routed and two divisions—including the German 1st Infantry Division—were enveloped west of Stanislau. In a continued thrust to the west, the Russians were already threatening a rear attack on First Panzer Army to cut off our line of supply. Only by immediately liberating strong forces, together with a disengagement of the front line from the Dnestr to the northern border of the Carpathians, could the danger be averted. The Russian spearheads had already penetrated fifteen kilometers past my headquarters and blocked the road from Dolina to the Vyskov ridge, when the first two divisions changing fronts arrived and isolated the most advanced Soviet elements and wiped them out. We regained Dolina, but to the south of the town the enemy still occupied the road and continued to press toward the west. Cut off from their route of retreat, the Hungarian formations streamed via Bolekhovo in the direction of Struj to escape to their native country via the Verecky Pass. These fleeing remnants congested our roads, thus hampering operations by German troops, who had orders to prevent a Russian penetration to the railroad and main highway leading to the Verecky Pass, as well as to liberate the divisions enveloped at Stanislau. Only energetic intervention by German commanders on the spot and the initiative of our troops, which halted the Hungarian retreat in its tracks and then swept them back along in the opposite direction, prevented a serious disaster. The discouraged *Honved* [Hungarian army] soldiers, wedged in between German formations, had no choice but to keep fighting, and their artillery, as well as the weak remnants of the 2nd Hungarian Panzer Division, stood up gallantly against the Soviets. The attack by General of Infantry Rudolf von Buenau's XI Corps via Bolshevo toward the east carried everything along with it and beat back the enemy. After three days of fighting, the Russians, caught in the pincers created by the troops in the Stanislau pocket attacking to the west and the liberators advancing to the east, were crushed. The two enveloped divisions were able to rejoin the army, and their remaining strength was allotted as valuable drafts to the regiments of stronger units.

Now it became a question of eliminating the final danger, the forward thrust by the Russians in the direction of our supply lines at Skole. In this case it was particularly difficult to reestablish contact with the Red Army spearheads, as the majority of them had disappeared into the thick mountain forests and ravines of the Carpathians. In order to track down the outlying elements of the Soviet penetration and to create an improvised line that would hold up long enough for First Panzer Army to muster the strength for a strong blow, the remnants of the XIII Corps that had escaped from the Brody pocket had to be thrown into a containment line pending the arrival of one of the divisions from the front line. Formed into six battalions, this force advanced out of the Skole area, with tank support from Tuchla, into the difficult forest country. After having moved forward only a few kilometers, these battalions collided with the Russians, became embroiled in heavy forest fighting, and found themselves forced back by stages. The first reinforcements arrived just in time to hold up the Soviets and prevent them from leaving the forest. In the meantime, the main thrust north from Bolshevo made itself felt in the enemy's flank and rear. In front of Skole the Russians began retreating, but they had waited too long. Attacked by one division in the front and three in the rear, the Soviets found themselves crowded together in an increasingly constricted area, despite the fiercest defense their artillery and antitank guns could muster. Grimly they fought to hold open the last road over which their troops and equipment might retreat, but this resistance also proved futile. The 8th Panzer Division broke through into the pocket, blocking the last escape route, their attached Tigers smashing any further resistance. Thousands of prisoners were left in our hands. A chaos of innumerable corpses (both of men and horses), of guns shot to pieces, overturned motor vehicles, and burning supplies was the end of the Red Army's thrust toward Skole. Those who escaped with their lives fought their way through to the partisan bands infesting the woods in large numbers.

This action rang the curtain down on operations between the Dnestr and the wooded Carpathians. First Panzer Army had overcome every kind of friction, dangers, and difficulties. The oil-field district of Brokobycz and Boryslav, which remained in action until the very last moment despite American bombing raids, was evacuated with all stores. Long railroad trains with filled fuel tank cars were lined up, pushed close together, from Skole up to the Hungarian frontier, creating one single long black serpent thirty-five kilometers in length. The heavy German locomotives were certainly able to pull all the trains quickly to the upper Stryj Valley but could not cross the weak bridge on the other side of the Hungarian border. The trains therefore had to be split up and conveyed to their destinations by lighter Hungarian locomotives.

Considering the difficult tactical situation of the First Hungarian Army at Vorochta and Jablonica, together with that of the Slovakians at Dukla, both of which predicted future dangers for First Panzer Army, I proposed a further withdrawal of the front line closer to the ridges of the Carpathians. Such a movement would facilitate support by our allies as it echeloned them farther to the rear and make it possible to release additional forces to fight in Poland and East Prussia. Permission was received to conduct the withdrawal, and it was carried out without incident, the Russians following very slowly and cautiously. Troops now freed from the front line were assembled in the Munkacz-Ungvar area and entrained there. General Balck's XLVIII Panzer Corps went to Poland, and the 1st Infantry Division returned to its menaced homeland of East Prussia.

The First Hungarian and Slovakian Armies, placed under command of First Panzer Army, were consolidated into *Armeegruppe* Raus. The front line of First Panzer Army still lay beyond the Carpathian ridge in Galicia, where on our left-flank XXIV Panzer Corps had repulsed heavy Russian attacks at Dukla. Once the 4th Mountain Division reached the Hungarian right flank at Jablonica, that position also appeared to be secure. These and later attempts by the Russians to invade Hungary through the mountain passes were defeated.

Quiet descended on 15 August along the 350-kilometer front of *Armeegruppe* Raus. Two days later I suddenly received a telephone call and, an hour later, was in a plane on my way to take immediate operational command of the Third Panzer Army in Lithuania and East Prussia.

Chapter 12

EAST PRUSSIA

Desperate Situation in the Baltic

DURING THE COURSE OF THE 1944 Soviet summer offensive, Army Group North found itself pushed back to the Baltic Sea and enveloped at Riga. Third Panzer Army (in the south) was placed under the army group's control and received orders to liberate the pocket with strong panzer formations brought up for the task (4th, 5th, 7th, 12th, and 14th Panzer Divisions, *Grossdeutschland* Panzergrenadier Division, and *Panzerverbande* von Strachwitz). To achieve this objective, I was to take over command of Third Panzer Army and advance from the area west of Schaulen-Auce on the Mitau River, split the enveloping Soviet ring, and reestablish an overland connection to Army Group North.

The route of this intended thrust (130 kilometers in depth) led first through a marshy, wooded district, then across a slightly undulating open plain intersected by several rivers, and finally again had a marshy wooded area before it. Only in the area immediately to the north, surrounding Doblen and Tukum, did more advantageous terrain for an armored attack exist. In that region there were also better and shorter routes to Army Group North (roughly forty kilometers). Nevertheless, the panzer divisions approaching there were assembled south of it for the attack. The reasons given for this inflexible insistence on the southern attack route were situation and objective. There were grounds for apprehending that the forces on the northern flank, composed of a covering division (the army group's training division) and Baltic formations (*Schutzmannschaftt*), would not stand any further advance to the west by the Russians. In the southern area, on the other hand, there were newly arrived volksgrenadier divisions (548th, 549th, and 551st), which presumably had greater defensive power. In addition, the railroad lines and the Koenigsberg-Riga highway entered that area, thus guaranteeing the attacking formations a quicker approach march. Finally,

OKH entertained hopes of quickly overrunning the Red Army's front along its western edge and therefore detailed forces piecemeal for the attack just as quickly as they could be released from the front lines.

The result of all these factors was a dispersed operational employment. General of Panzer Troops Otto von Knobelsdorff's XL Panzer Corps (7th and 14th Panzer Divisions; *Grossdeutschland* Panzergrenadier Division) attacked on the southern flank. The XXXIX Panzer corps (General of Panzer Troops Dietrich von Saucken) made its assault in the center with the 5th Panzer Division, and to the north with the 4th and 12th Panzer Divisions. On the far northern flank of the attack, in the Frauenberg area, Major General Hyacinth Graf von Strachwitz's improvised *Panzerverbande* (composed of the 101st Panzer Brigade and SS Brigade *Gross*, with a strength of about eighty AFVs) had orders to break through the Russian corridor at the right moment via Tukum and place itself in Riga at the disposal of Army Group North as reinforcements. Thus the attack was launched with four spearheads spread over 100 kilometers without any discernable *Schwerpunkt* [point of focus]. To frustrate that plan the Soviet Third Belorussian and First Baltic Fronts had nearby and to their immediate rear of the enveloping front strong reserves, which were so close at hand that they could attack alongside their frontline units in a matter of hours. Under such conditions our attack had little chance of attaining its objectives.

Such was the situation that confronted me, having been recalled from Hungary for the express purpose of leading the relief attack, when I arrived in East Prussia on 17 August. It was not even possible for me to bring any influence to bear on the planning and course of the attack already in progress. Predictably, the thrust stalled after only a few days. The XL Panzer Corps's 7th Panzer Division (Major General Karl Mauss) took the small town of Kelmi after hard fighting on the main highway and advanced across the Dubissa bridge. There the 7th Panzer was covered by the right flank of Lieutenant General Hasso von Manteuffel's *Grossdeutschland* Panzergrenadier Division, whose panzer regiment had advanced as far as the borders of the forest immediately south of Schaulen before stalling at the marshy ground in front of the town. General Mauss had his left flank covered by Lieutenant General Martin Unrein's 14th Panzer Division, which had also become embroiled in hard fighting in the forests. General von Knobelsdorff's attack, thereafter, had completely stalled after gaining about forty kilometers. Lieutenant General Karl Decker's 5th Panzer Division, in the center, started with a smart advance of twenty kilometers across sandy ground, followed by a deep penetration into the forest. The division's spearhead became encircled by the Russians, but with the aid of the main body it was extracted and fought its way back to our lines. Nonetheless, 5th Panzer

Division's advance had been stymied. The remaining units of General von Saucken's XXXIX Panzer Corps—4th Panzer Division (Major General Clemens Betzel) and 12th Panzer Division (Major General Erpo Freiherr von Bodenhausen)—encountered the Soviets in strength and faced an even more difficult time. These two divisions managed to advance only between six and ten kilometers before being halted.

The overall operation, after minor initial successes, had failed owing to the great elongation of the line to the extent that partial successes could have no effect on other actions, let alone combine to create a total victory. The operation had, however, drawn against itself such strong Russian forces that *Panzerverbande* von Strachwitz, which arrived late, managed with the assistance of the cruiser *Prinz Eugen* to take Tukum and push through the undermanned northern end of the Soviet corridor to reach Riga. That action, of course, by no means ensured the liberation of Army Group North.

The poor results of this advance with multiple spearheads did not satisfy Third Panzer Army's chief of staff (Colonel Otto Heidkaemper) or its operations officer (Lieutenant Colonel Hans-Joachim Ludendorff), who had also had a hand in planning the thrust. Their attempt to rejuvenate the northern attack by XXXIX Panzer Corps by withdrawing *Grossdeutschland* from the south and redeploying the division to reinforce 12th Panzer Division also failed to alter the situation in any positive manner. Even though General von Manteuffel's panzergrenadiers pushed several kilometers into the forest, they were ultimately unable to help XXXIX Panzer Corps proceed. Moreover, *Grossdeutschland*'s long southern flank was repeatedly attacked and pinned by the Russian I Tank Corps brought up for the purpose.

The Russians had now reinforced their entire line in strength, and the enterprise appeared doomed to failure. At this juncture Hitler himself intervened in person and expressed the wish that the renewed thrust be directed from Rossenie against Mitau, with the necessary forces withdrawn from other sectors of Third Panzer Army's front. This demand was completely illogical, as the distance to be covered to Mitau from Rossenie was three times as long, and the terrain far more difficult, than on the northern flank where we had already achieved some success. In addition, we realized that there were strong Russian tank reserves in the Schaulen area, which would be well positioned to halt such a drive very quickly.

I therefore decided not to embark on such a venture. Instead, unnoticed by the Russians, I assembled all the available panzer divisions in the woods to the north of Auce, so as to drive with concentrated force against Doblen. The possession of the commanding heights of Doblen was also bound to have a decisive bearing of the possession of the Soviet corridor. Taking the key point vastly increased the chances of effecting the liberation of Army Group

North. In order to deceive the enemy with regard to our objective and generate tactical surprise, the area recently gained by *Grossdeutschland* (some six kilometers in depth) was abruptly abandoned. We pulled the front line back to its initial position prior to the attack, behind which *Grossdeutschland* and the rest of the panzer divisions earmarked for the offensive against Doblen were assembled. The Red Army reoccupied the area only with infantry, withdrawing the tank and mechanized corps that had been employed there in order to shift them farther south.

This deception proved so successful that the Russians completely missed the new strategic concentration. Shortly after the front had been pulled back, five panzer divisions launched an attack into the previously evacuated territory that took the enemy completely by surprise. Our tanks broke through the Russian forest position rapidly, storming the Doblen heights on the second day. Never did the enemy suspect that he might be attacked at the same point that we had voluntarily evacuated a short time before. The tactical surprise achieved was so great that the Russians, despite their great danger, were incapable on the first day of the attack of sending a single fighter aircraft into action. The right flank element of Army Group North, Provisional Corps Kleffel of the Sixteenth Army, wheeled out to the south, made contact with Third Panzer Army, and was placed under my orders. Evacuation of the pocket around Riga began according to plan; the crisis had been successfully mastered.

Retreat from Lithuania

After the relief corridor to Army Group North had been opened, OKH withdrew Third Panzer Army from Army Group Center and subordinated us to Army Group North. The army group commander, Colonel General Ferdinand Schoerner, immediately withdrew XXXIX Panzer Corps and all of the panzer divisions from my control. All that remained to Third Panzer Army in early September were the 548th, 549th, and 551st Volksgrenadier Divisions, the army group's training division, and several Estonian *Schutzmannschaftt* battalions. I did not have a single tank at my disposal. With these inadequate forces, General Schoerner expected me to defend a sector 160 kilometers wide, the northern half of which was heavily wooded. Nothing was done about these disproportionate conditions as regarded strength and area, even when we presented the army group with compelling evidence that the First Baltic Front was contemplating a major attack in the Schaulen area.

General Schoerner, still obviously considerably affected by the earlier envelopment against the Baltic coast, anticipated instead that the Russians would make their assault farther to the north, via Tukum, so as to halt his movement out of the Riga pocket and again encircle the remnants of Army Group North. At odds with that estimate was the fact that the Russians' main concentration of force was too far to the south, and that the Soviet command realized the northern zone of attack was both too narrow and too heavily occupied by German armor to promise decisive results. Above all, the overall strategic situation in the Baltic area argued against Schoerner's opinion. The First Baltic Front faced an extended German flank that offered the prospect of a far more advantageous thrust to the west on the Kurisches Haff, which could be reached from Schaulen just as quickly as the Baltic could be attained north of Tukum. The distance to either coast was about 120 kilometers, but a western offensive would strike only the extended front of untried volksgrenadier divisions, with neither tanks nor other reserves to their rear. To achieve a breakthrough there would not be difficult for the Russians, and a swift intervention in the direction of Memel held out the promise of a colossal success, as it might isolate the entire army group, including the main body of Third Panzer Army, from East Prussia. In that manner four armies (Third Panzer, Sixteenth and Eighteenth Armies, as well as *Armeeabteilung* Narva) would be enveloped in Kurland, cut off from the chief events of the war. First Baltic Front's preparations for a thrust to the west became more clearly recognizable day by day. My staff and I (Colonel Heidkaemper had been replaced as chief of staff by Colonel Burkhardt Mueller-Hillebrand on 1 September) expected the attack at the end of September, believing that the earliest possible date for the Soviet assault was 5 September and the latest would be 10 October.

Only on 4 October did General Schoerner become convinced on the subject of a Russian attack to the west, at least to the extent of ordering the 5th Panzer Division to Third Panzer Army, which had been requesting armored reinforcement for weeks. Moving on a narrow march route during a rainy night, General Decker's division had not even been able to cover the 100 kilometers to Third Panzer Army's rear area when, on the morning of 5 October, First Baltic Front's offensive broke loose after a fierce artillery concentration. (The Russians, on 4 October, had already utilized a reinforced rifle regiment to attack the training division on our left flank, achieving a significant penetration that they extended the following day.) The main assault was delivered exactly where Colonel Mueller-Hillebrand and I had anticipated it, on and to the north of the Schaulen-Tilsit highway in the direction of the Kurisches Haff. This attack hit with full force at Major General Karl Jank's 549th Volksgrenadier Division (XXVIII Corps) and the left flank of Major General Erich Sudau's 548th Volksgrenadier Division (IX Corps), shattering their front lines in several places. These inexperienced divisions suffered very heavily from the hurricane-type artillery bombardment and from attacks by masses of Russian tanks. Already the enemy was threatening to break through toward Tauroggen on the highway, where the resistance put up by the gallant left-flank regiment of the 548th Volksgrenadier Division against heavy armored attacks was gradually weakening. Fortunately, the 5th Panzer Division arrived in the nick of time, and General Decker's attack threw them back, averting the most acute crisis.

On the northern flank, Lieutenant General Johann Pflugbeil's Field Training Division *Nord* was pressed back into the Sixteenth Army's sector. The Soviet thrust to the west, however, was delayed by the arrival of part of the 7th Panzer division, and again a breakthrough was avoided.

In the center of XXVIII Corps, however, things looked very bad. There the First Baltic Front had placed the *Schwerpunkt* of its attack toward Memel. General Jank's 549th Volksgrenadier Division was torn to pieces, and the *Grossdeutschland* Panzergrenadier Division (now commanded by Major General Karl Lorenz), which had been dispatched to our aid by Army Group North, had arrived with only a few of its leading tanks. These tanks—like the entire division—were stranded, however, owing to lack of fuel. What remained of the 549th rallied around General Janks and his commanders, their artillery, and their antitank guns and, by garrisoning villages and blocking roads, attempted to restore a makeshift front line that would at least retard the Russian advance. Soon those *Grossdeutschland* tanks left immobile through lack of fuel were surrounded by the enemy, leaving them in imminent danger of destruction. The volksgrenadiers, however, quickly realized the danger to their only possible armored support and changed over—despite their weakened condition—to the counterattack and, primarily by dint of extreme self-sacrifice, succeeded in rescuing the tanks. Standing firm beside the tank crews, they repulsed the further attacks of the enemy until fuel had been siphoned from motor vehicles of less importance and the panzers were able to move again.

This defense of village strongpoints was unable, certainly, to close the front permanently or halt the Russian onslaught, but it did at least provide a loose kind of connecting line that kept the enemy under control, made his advance more difficult, and inflicted casualties on his troops. As Army Group North could neither create nor transfer fresh reserves to Third Panzer Army, we pressed the Army Weapons School, the Submarine School at Memel, a variety of special staffs, all available transport and service troops, as well as any other auxiliary organizations into the defense. These improvised units consolidated and reinforced the defenses of local strongpoints, especially at important defiles and points of penetration. In this manner a close-nested network of defense was woven that could be broken through or bypassed only by strong Russian forces expending a considerable amount of time. More strongly manned localities usually kept the Soviets at bay during the daytime, but with nightfall such positions were circumvented or attacked concentrically. These therefore had to be withdrawn at night to avoid envelopment and destruction. On predetermined lines, however, a new line of resistance would be organized. By dawn the new line was manned, the connecting link once more established, and the fighting continued on similar lines. By employing every possible tactic of delay, defense, and local counterattack, the First Baltic Front required a fortnight to reach the Kurisches Haff and the Memel River. Even in the sector that could only be defended by strongpoints, where the Russians had placed their *Schwerpunkt*, we were able to restrain their advance to between six to ten kilometers per day, while avoiding an armored breakthrough or unrepairable ruptures of the front line. Either eventuality would have brought them to their objective in two to three days. On the Memel River the same forces, reinforced only by such improvised units as already described, halted the Soviet offensive and successfully repelled every attempt to capture the city of Memel or to cross the river.

During this fighting, Army Group North had been hardly attacked and had extended its right flank in proportion to the evasive actions taken by Third Panzer Army. In this manner a front line was formed toward the south that was getting longer and longer, and finally—between Libau and Memel—resting its wings against the Baltic Sea. The situation thus arose that the enemy desired, with General Schoerner's armies standing with their backs to the sea and again enveloped. His thirty-two divisions, numbering among Germany's best, were no longer in position to interfere with the main Soviet strategic offensive directed against the heart of the Reich. These tactics were championed by Hitler in person and enforced with all the authoritative powers at his disposal. In the end they obstructed all freedom and devoured the very substance of the German Army until there was no army left.

The same fate would have overtaken Third Panzer Army had I accepted General Schoerner's original orders to retreat to the northwest, rather than falling back to the southwest. Had I followed those instructions, East Prussia would have been left almost completely without protection and the road to Berlin via Koenigsberg left open to the Red Army. By fighting as it did, Third Panzer Army was able to keep in contact with Army Group Center and push the bolt against the Soviet advance on the Memel and in the area around the city of Memel, thus averting the greater disaster.

Memel

After the fighting in Lithuania had wound down, Army Group North (now redesignated Army Group Kurland) by the end of October was pressed between the Baltic Sea and the Gulf of Riga to the south of Windau against the sea, with its western wing to the south of Libau. Separated from it by 112 kilometers was Army Group Center (now renamed Army Group North) with its northern flank at the mouth of the Memel (Third Panzer Army had been once again subordinated to this army group). The remainder of the front spread out in a wide curve around East Prussia. Between the inner flanks of the two army groups lay the city of Memel, defended by General of Infantry Hans Gollnick's XXVIII Corps of Third Panzer Army. My other three corps—General of Infantry Gerhard Matzky's XXVI Corps, General of Artillery Rolf Wuthmann's IX Corps, and Lieutenant General Maximilian Felzmann's IX Corps—stood on the left flank of Army Group North's Fourth Army and had to defend the eastern frontier of Prussia.

Already in connection with the battle of Lithuania, the Russians had attempted, when committing their tank corps in pursuit, to cross the Memel River in order to invade East Prussia. This was repeatedly proven by the markings made on maps found on the bodies of dead and wounded Soviet tank officers. That this design was frustrated could be attributed particularly to the smart and skillful defense put up by the 5th Panzer Division. With every means at his disposal and a limited number of tanks, General Decker placed his division on the eastern bank of the Memel as a barrier against enemy tank columns, inflicting heavy casualties. Not content with standing on the defensive, General Decker time and again attacked the enemy with the concentrated tanks and assault guns of Panzer Regiment 31, tearing Soviet formations apart or routing them and wiping out the individual elements that proved unable to save themselves by quick flight. Later, reinforced by Lieutenant General Wilhelm Schmalz's *Hermann Goering* Parachute-Panzer Corps, the 5th Panzer Division attacked the enemy infantry and armored forces concentrated for an assault on Tilsit, throwing them back as well. That success eliminated the immediate risk of an invasion of East Prussia and enabled Third Panzer Army to conduct a withdrawal in good order of all units remaining on the northern bank of the Memel. It soon became clearly evident that the First Baltic Front had abandoned its project of crossing the Memel and had in fact gone over to the defensive.

Only a month later, toward the end of November, did the enemy commence new preparations for crossing the Memel. Intelligence reports suggested that the Russians intended to force a crossing at Pagnit. We identified an engineer brigade sent forward to prepare bridge-building equipment and all other necessary preliminaries for such a crossing. Third Panzer Army, having been previously ordered to surrender all panzer formations, its assault-gun brigade, its heavy antitank guns, and many other heavy weapons, again held a wide front with improvised formations and special units. The potential risk of a breakthrough was great indeed. To cite but one example, a key sector of the front line was held only by a battalion of men suffering from ear infections (including several epileptics), a battalion of soldiers with dental ailments, a *Volkssturmm* [militia] battalion, a local defense battalion, and a Latvian battalion, with no artillery in their rear. Nearly all transfers (including our only reserve units) had been allocated to Fourth Army, which suspected large Soviet concentrations on the Rominter Heide. With Third Panzer Army in such a reduced state, the Russians would no doubt have been successful in making the thrust across the Memel to Koenigsberg. Despite repeated attempts to draw attention to that risk, neither Third Panzer Army nor Army Group North received any supplementary forces.

Nothing having been achieved through military channels despite the efforts of the army group commander, Colonel General Hans-Georg Reinhardt, there remained as a last resort for obtaining information only the exceptional channel, to which no recourse had yet been made, via Erich Koch, the *Gauleiter* [regional party leader] of East Prussia. It was possible for him to see Hitler in person at any time, and the problem could not but be of interest to him, since the fate of his state trembled in the balance. Koch was deeply impressed by the gravity of the situation as I demonstrated it to him with the help of a map in a strictly private discussion held in his Koenigsberg office in early December. The very next day he went to Hitler's headquarters to report accordingly. Hitler was quick also to appreciate the danger of the situation and shared our anxiety concerning the fate of East Prussia. He was initially inclined to take the desired reinforcements from Army Group Kurland and have them transferred to Third Panzer Army on the Memel front. Before doing so, however, he wished to have a consultation with General Schoerner at Army Group Kurland. That consultation changed Hitler's mind; he again became optimistic and asserted that the strong forces under Schoerner's command, in the event of a Soviet offensive aimed at crossing the Memel, would attack the First Baltic Front in the rear and wipe it out. With that news, and the promise of an artillery regiment for the support of the Memel front, *Gauleiter* Koch arrived in Liebenfelde, headquarters of Third Panzer Army.

Scraping up some sort of reinforcement out of the rear area of Army Group North was even less than a vague hope; it was a utopian dream. The forces behind General Reinhardt's front, as the preceding battles had revealed and later events would show, were not adequate for the purpose. All that remained was the poor comfort of the support by an artillery regiment. That comfort proved even less than poor, indeed, when the battered regiment arrived with but two batteries of one gun per battery.

Fortunately, the tenseness of the situation on the Memel unexpectedly relaxed, as the enemy withdrew first his assault forces and then even the engineer brigade. All the more serious, however, became the position of the XXVI Corps on the right flank of the army in the Gumbinnen area, where very strong Russian units were already forming into line, considerably reinforcing the armies already in the area. Innumerable artillery and mortar positions, the numbers of which increased every day, together with the concentration of Soviet airpower, left no room for doubt that the First Baltic Front was preparing a second attempt to invade East Prussia across the same very favorable terrain in which we had frustrated it before. Russian preparations had so far advanced by the middle of December that a Christmas offensive, so popular a feature with the Red Army, had to be expected in that sector. It was certainly not any tactical consideration for our high holiday that made the Soviets promise through their front-line propaganda, just before the feast days, that they would let us celebrate this Christmas in peace. A more likely reason for that apparently chivalrous gesture was that the weather was still far too mild for a Russian winter offensive. Not until January were sustained low temperatures to be expected, which would cause a thick enough covering of ice to form on the rivers, lakes, and marshes—as well as the two bays by Koenigsberg—upon which the Red Army depended to allow it to push forward rapidly into East Prussia. Even though, as with all Russian promises, caution was advisable, for that reason we felt reasonably certain that this time the Soviets would be as good as their word.

At this point Third Panzer Army had three of its best divisions in Fortress Koenigsberg, two in Fortress Memel, and only the two weakest at my disposal for operations in the field. Given the mandated dispersal of Third Panzer Army's divisions, it was necessary to prevent a Russian landing on the west side of the Kurisches Haff. Neither Colonel Mueller-Hillebrand nor I expected a large-scale landing because the Red Army did not possess the prerequisites for such an operation, but it seemed quite likely that the Soviets might attempt to land sabotage or raiding parties, spies, agents, or commandos along the coast under cover of darkness. The coastal defenses, composed of service units, volunteer organizations, and *Volkssturmm* [see below] supported by weak reserve elements from Koenigsberg, were thought to be sufficient throughout the fall to thwart any such operation.

We knew that the Haff froze over in winter, however, and that the ice cover would carry men and vehicles. This might encourage Russian attempts to envelop the exposed wing of Third Panzer Army, cut off our only supply route to Memel, or undertake some other major operation. For that reason we drew up plans to block the Kurisches Haff in its entire width of more than fifteen kilometers.

During the late autumn a number of wooden bunkers with heating facilities were constructed for this purpose. These stood not quite two meters high and each held a crew of three to five men with their weapons. The bunkers were placed on rafts with sled runners in order to give them mobility on ice and simultaneously to protect them from sinking into the water in case the ice suddenly broke. This possibility had to be considered because of the sudden changes of temperature that occur in East Prussia. By the end of December the first groups of bunkers were towed out onto the freezing Haff, the edges of which were by then sufficiently strong to carry them. The bunker positions were spread progressively across the ice as the freezing process continued. Approximately 150 bunkers were laid out in two parallel lines in checkerboard formation, giving each other fire support. The bunkers were reinforced with blocks of ice on the outside and camouflaged with snow. A continuous line of entanglements with alarm signals was to prevent the Russians from infiltrating between the bunkers, and reserves were held in readiness behind both lines of bunkers. When the ice boats and motor sleighs needed by the reserves to give them mobility did not arrive in time, our plans for organizing a combined ice-boat and motor-sleigh brigade had to be abandoned. Artillery support was provided from both shores.

Since the Russians lacked fast means of transportation on ice, they could advance over the long distances on the Haff only on foot. This was probably the reason that they failed to attack throughout December and most of January. At the end of January, however, the Soviets did attempt to unhinge our flank by moving across the ice. Three times they penetrated Third Panzer Army's front as far as the town of Labiau, but each time we threw them back after hard fighting in which we received support from the improvised bunker positions.

Continuous air attacks during 1944–1945 drained Germany's fuel reserves and reduced our means of transportation, forcing us to apply strict conservation measures. Railroads had to carry all supplies as close as possible to the front and were even used for minor local troop movements. In the Tilsit area ration and ammunition trains moved as close as 500 meters behind the front lines. On the lower Memel front, Third Panzer Army engineers built a narrow-gauge lateral-supply railroad only 500 meters behind the main battle line. Every truck had to take a second empty in tow, and with the exception of certain staff cars no passenger vehicles were allowed to undertake individual trips. Passenger vehicles had to be towed by trucks even during troop movements. These and other similar measures became standard operating procedure, and their enforcement was strictly supervised. They did not, of course, alleviate the overall gasoline and oil shortage, but it was only by their introduction that it was at all possible to maintain even the most essential motor traffic.

Heavy losses among railroad tank cars had created a shortage of vehicles capable of transporting fuel by rail. Seventy tanks cars that had been immobilized in Memel were therefore urgently needed to support operations in East Prussia. Unfortunately it was no longer possible to move them out of Memel by rail because the Red Army had the city surrounded, and there were not any suitable naval vessels on hand to transport them across the sea. Colonel Mueller-Hillebrand and I considered a variety of expedients in an effort to resolve this dilemma, but none promised success. Finally, one of Third Panzer Army's engineer officers calculated that the empty tank cars could float on the sea if they were sealed airtight. On-the-spot experiments immediately confirmed this theory, and local naval units instantly received orders to tow all the tank cars from Memel across the Baltic Sea to the nearest port with railroad facilities. Despite considerable doubts on the part of the Kriegsmarine, I insisted on the execution of this order.

The first vessel, with five tank cars in tow, arrived in Pillau (west of Koenigsberg) in late autumn after a night journey of 175 kilometers across the sea. The cars were undamaged upon arrival and could be put back into service without delay. Thereafter the phantom voyages continued in the same manner, night after night, with the number of cars in tow varying between eight to ten per convoy. Everything went according to plan. Only toward the end of these curious railroad-sea voyages was it found that several cars had broken loose because of heavy seas and floated away from the towing vessel. These bobbing tank cars created considerable excitement in coastal shipping, because when they were first discovered the captains reported them as Russian submarines. Naval aircraft and patrol boats immediately put to sea in order to observe this unusual Soviet threat from close range. To everyone's relief, the dangerous submarines turned out to be the turretlike superstructures of the tank cars that had been lost the previous night and were now rocking on the high seas. These runaways were soon caught and towed into port.

East Prussia Braces for the Soviet Assault

As the danger of a Soviet invasion of Germany loomed ever greater toward the end of the year, military authorities and the Nazi party mobilized thousands of civilians to construct a number of continuous defensive lines in East Prussia. Everywhere people could be seen digging trenches and defense positions. Altogether, twelve main defense lines and switch positions were constructed by civilian labor, many of which were well equipped. Perhaps their most outstanding feature was the construction of improvised machine-gun emplacements, which were very practical and consisted of two large concrete pipes. One pipe stood upright in the ground and served as the gun emplacement proper, whereas the horizontal pipe was connected to the base of the upright one and employed as a personnel shelter. This improvisation offered shelter against Soviet tanks, could be constructed in a minimum of time, was easy to transport, and was highly effective.

In addition to these defensive positions, continuous antitank ditches were excavated that cut across all roads. Temporary bridges, ready for immediate demolition in case of emergency, spanned each ditch where it cut through a road. Some 18,000 laborers were diverted to the construction of this antitank ditch alone, although they were also badly needed to build fortified defensive zones. In order that such zones could be prepared at least in the most essential areas, every man belonging to reserve, service, supply, or headquarters units was assigned his daily quota of obligatory digging (measured in cubic meters). Of necessity, the troops had to finish their work at night. To get these positions ready for immediate winter occupancy, the rear-echelon units as well as *Volkssturm* battalions moved into the positions to make the quarters livable. Slit trenches were dug along the roads, and antitank or machine-gun nests were prepared at all important points. Perimeter defenses were established around every village and hamlet.

The combined effect of these numerous, fully integrated defense installations was to transform the most vulnerable northeastern part of Germany—East Prussia—into one great fortress area, imminently suitable for the utilization of zone defense tactics. Although some of these defensive positions never played any part in the subsequent fighting, others proved useful, even critical, during the battle for East Prussia. If they failed to change the fate of that doomed province, it was due to the entirely insufficient number of troops and to the inadequacy of the weapons that could be mustered for its defense.

Concurrently, the Nazi party had begun its most ambitious military project: the mobilization of *Volkssturm*. The original idea was to call on the last forces of resistance the German population was capable of mustering. Here a misunderstood and misinterpreted tradition built on memories of 1813 may also have played a part in the minds of some party officials.

The *Volkssturm* included all men up to the highest age groups as long as they were capable of bearing arms and were not already in the service. This might have provided a broad basis for successfully mobilizing whatever fighting strength had not yet been tapped if there had not been a complete lack of weapons, clothing, and equipment. As the Wehrmacht could spare nothing, the whole project of staging an armed levee en masse was doomed from the very outset.

In East Prussia, however, the *Volkssturm* did a better job than anywhere else, possibly because it was there that the idea of the *Volkssturm* levy had originated because that province was the first threatened by the Russians. There the organization and training of the *Volkssturm* made the greatest progress, as thirty-two battalions were raised. All of these remained in East Prussia even when, in November, the civilian population from the northern districts had to be evacuated. After that, most *Volkssturm* units were utilized to prepare reserve battle positions in the rear areas for a possible withdrawal of the combat troops (who in turn provided instructors for the *Volkssturm* battalions). Months of continuous instruction raised their standard of training to such a degree that a number of *Volkssturm* battalions actually managed to carry out limited combat missions.

A few of these so-called special employment units received modern weapons, such as the most recent 75mm antitank guns, the latest-model machine guns, and some older-type small-caliber flak guns. Some of them even had adequate motor transportation. These units were composed of a small percentage of World War I veterans with the remainder about equally divided between sixteen- and seventeen-year-old teenagers, and elderly men between sixty-five and seventy. Former staff officers who had distinguished themselves in the previous war, but were now afflicted with various physical disabilities, commanded some of the battalions. The majority of the *Volkssturm* battalions, on the other hand, were short of weapons, equipment, and training, and their employment in actual combat operations was out of the question. We planned to integrate them into the field forces only in the case of a general withdrawal of the lines.

From the outset I recognized this state of affairs to be a serious handicap, but it could not be corrected since Third Panzer Army had no jurisdiction over these formations. Time and again we requested that the battalions be immediately disbanded and all *Volkssturm* men fit for combat be transferred into our divisions. Party officials flatly rejected every such request. Thus, during the latter part of January, when the front began to give way, most of the *Volkssturm* battalions employed in East Prussia proved absolutely useless to the armies defending the province. Wherever they did not disintegrate entirely, they suffered heavy casualties. It should be noted that, contrary to standing orders, a few of these battalions had been moved up into combat beside seasoned units during the preceding weeks, and these battalions gave a good account of themselves. Special mention is due to *Volkssturm* Battalion *Labiau*, which fought under Special Division Staff 607, a division improvised from service troops. Three times the battalion was dislodged, but in every instance it succeeded in recapturing its original position from the Russians by launching counterattacks. In this bitter struggle the battalion commander and most of his troops died on the field of battle.

On another occasion the *Volkssturm* performed less well. Showing much zeal in military matters, Nazi party headquarters in East Prussia produced its own 75mm antitank guns with iron-wheeled gun mounts and conducted short training courses to familiarize members of the *Volkssturm* with the weapon. By the end of January the situation near Tapiau, east of Koenigsberg, was obscure. There, the personnel of an army weapons school had been engaged in heavy fighting against advancing Soviet tanks. The commanding officer of the weapons school had been killed, and Tapiau changed hands several times, though at the moment it was held by German troops. Rumor held that Russian tanks had broken through and were advancing on Koenigsberg. Thereupon party headquarters improvised an antitank battalion with twenty new 75mm antitank guns from its training school and dispatched it to the area east of Koenigsberg (without notice to army headquarters) to take up positions for the protection of the city. At sundown strong armored formations suddenly came into sight opposite the antitank position. This impressive spectacle caused such a state of terror among the inexperienced gun crews that they left their guns and ran for cover in all directions. Their leader, a young first lieutenant, tried in vain to halt this flight. Assisted by a few instructors, he succeeded in getting some of the guns ready for action and was just about to open fire when he realized—much to his surprise—that he was facing German panzers. The 5th Panzer Division, which after heavy tank fighting east of Tapiau had succeeded in breaking through Russian lines, was now assembling in this area in compliance with its orders. For once, the failure of an improvisation proved to be a distinct advantage.

Zone Defense in East Prussia

What particularly exercised me as December ended were grave anxieties over the fact that Army Group North did not share my views about the area in which the Red Army would probably deliver its main offensive thrust. Both General Reinhardt and his chief of staff, Lieutenant General Otto Heidkaemper (my former chief at Third Panzer Army) held the opinion that General of Infantry Friedrich Hossbach's Fourth Army, on our southern flank, was the most seriously threatened. Even a personal discussion between

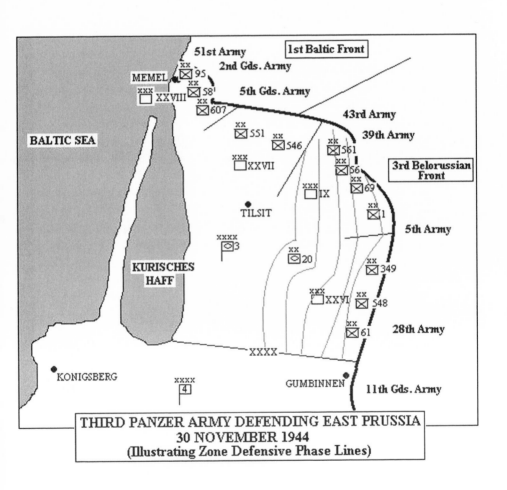

THIRD PANZER ARMY DEFENDING EAST PRUSSIA
30 NOVEMBER 1944
(Illustrating Zone Defensive Phase Lines)

General Reinhardt and myself at Ortelsburg, early in January 1945, did nothing to obviate this strategic difference of opinion. The result was that Third Panzer Army received nothing in return for its numerous transfers of divisions to neighboring armies and—on the contrary—had to surrender to Hungary its one and only reserve, Major General Hermann von Oppeln-Bronikowski's 20th Panzer Division. In its place, just three days prior to the Soviet offensive, we received back the 5th Panzer Division (now under Major General Guenther von Hoffmann-Schoenborn), an excellent unit to be sure but, due to offensive operations while subordinated to Fourth Army, reduced from 100 to fifty tanks and as yet not initiated in the zone defense tactics Third Panzer Army had by then introduced. General Reinhardt had, moreover, made it unmistakably clear to me that, in the event of an attack, I could count on no reinforcements whatever but would have to make do with my own forces and weapons, which were quite meager. After the previous heavy fighting, most of my divisions had only been half reorganized and reequipped. Behind them as reinforcements were only a handful of battalions of *Volkssturm* or raw recruits. General Gollnick's XXVIII Corps, in Memel, was very remote from the main battle zone, and—owing to its exposed position—I could not justify any reduction in strength to its two relatively strong divisions. I therefore resolved to shoulder every risk in order to strengthen the sector most threatened by the impending Soviet offensive. This sector I assigned to the four divisions of General Matzky's XXVI Corps, which had proven their mettle in repulsing the first Russian invasion of East Prussia. Across a front-line sector of only twenty kilometers, I placed under General Matzky's orders all of the army's assault guns (save for a single company retained in support of IX Corps), attaching to it the entire army artillery, a flak regiment, and a mortar brigade. In addition, I placed the 5th Panzer Division in army reserve directly behind this sector. Across the other 140 kilometers of Third Panzer Army's front this left the IX (and later the XXVII) Corps with only four weak divisions, unsupported by army troops or reserves.

The zone defense tactics that had been successfully introduced by First Panzer Army at Lvov had not been emulated by other commands, since the prerequisites for their successful application rarely existed, and most army commanders frankly doubted their practicality and utility. Besides, the overall strategic situation had deteriorated so rapidly that there was a general reluctance to introduce experiments. By the second half of 1944 we rarely had sufficient time for the construction of numerous positions or for the thorough indoctrination and training of troops. Only the most ardent faith in these tactics could overcome all these handicaps and achieve final success. Yet both times that armies under my command—at Lvov and in East

Prussia—were able to employ improvised zone defense tactics, they helped keep intact the combat strength of my divisions, even though subjected to terrific artillery concentrations, and they prevented the Russians from breaking through. On both occasions the Soviets suffered heavy casualties and were forced to shift their main effort to other sectors.

In East Prussia in January 1945 the Third Panzer Army deployed only fifty tanks and 400 artillery pieces, virtually without air support:

Memel area:

XXVIII Corps
    General of Infantry Hans Gollnick
58th Infantry Division
    Lieutenant General Curt Siewert
95th Infantry Division
    Major General Joachim-Friedrich Lang

Kurisches Haff:

Special Division Staff 607
    Lieutenant General Max Horn

Between Kurisches Haff and Inster River:

IX Corps
    General of Artillery Rolf Wuthmann
286th Security Division
    Lieutenant General Wilhelm Thomas
548th Volksgrenadier Division
    Major General Erich Sudau
551st Volksgrenadier Division
    Major General Siegfried Verhein
561st Volksgrenadier Division
    Major General Walter Gorn

Between Inster River and Gumbinnen (main axis of attack):

XXVI Corps
    General of Infantry Gerhard Matzky
56th Infantry Division
    Major General Edmund Blaurock
69th Infantry Division
    Lieutenant General Siegfried Rein

349th Volksgrenadier Division
Major General Karl Koetz
549th Volksgrenadier Division
Lieutenant General Karl Jank

Army reserve:

5th Panzer Division
Major General Guenther von Hoffmann-Schoenborn

Facing us were forty-four Red Army rifle divisions, 800 tanks, 3,000 guns, and strong air forces of the Third Belorussian Front. During December special training in zone defense had been introduced, with the active participation of both the command and troops of the XXVI Corps. Officers and enlisted soldiers alike were inspired with enthusiasm for the idea and put heart and soul into its execution. Our engineer and construction units supervised the home units of Wehrkreis I (East Prussia), twenty-four *Volkssturm* battalions, 18,000 civilian laborers, and the entire headquarters staff of the army's service troops in building position after position. Antitank obstacles, minefields, and a system of local strongpoints and nests of resistance, eighty kilometers in depth, were built. The foremost twenty-five-kilometer belt was fortified on the basis of lessons learned at Lvov. Everyone, from General Matzky down to his lowest-ranking soldiers, made strenuous efforts to improve the defenses. While strongpoints and pillboxes afforded maximum protection and defensive power for our perimeter defenses, precautions had to be taken to prevent them from becoming deathtraps for their defenders. In fact, as all of East Prussia became one giant fortress with the zone defense area around Instersburg and Gumbinnen as its strongest outpost, tactical details and technical improvisations were carefully planned to preclude such disagreeable surprises. The troops realized this, and as a result their morale was excellent: They faced the coming attack with confidence.

Christmas, even New Year's Day, were spent for the first time in peace and quiet. The Soviets had more than kept their word, but soon after the Russians initiated a war of nerves by announcing the start of their offensive three different times and by telegraphing their punches in advance. We did not take these announcements too seriously and refused to be intimidated by the show of tanks along the Soviet front lines.

I was frankly more concerned about Russian preparations along a railroad embankment, a few hundred meters in front of our lines west of Ebenrode, where the Red Army bought up antitank guns and dug eight passages through a dam that Russian tanks had been unable to surmount. These preparations took place too close to the front line of the XXVI Corps to pass unobserved, though the enemy made every attempt to cover the noise of the nightly demolitions by heavy mortar fire and camouflaged the passages with boards and foliage. This was the line on which the Third Belorussian Front emplaced its most forward heavy weapons, which had the mission of eliminating any German interference by direct fire in order to cover the tanks advancing through gaps in the embankment. Other indications that the main effort would be made in this sector included sap trenches dug by the Russians to facilitate the approach of infantry spearheads and the construction of positions connected by communications trenches to provide the cover in which to assemble the first assault wave. Changes in the daily aerial photographs provided by the Luftwaffe provided information on newly constructed emplacements and revealed fresh tracks in the snow leading to ammunition dumps and battery positions. Reports from our agents gave information concerning the arrival of new divisions, and a few radio signals (intercepted despite an unusually strict Russian enforcement of radio silence) uncovered the locations of many forward command posts. These indications made it clear where the Third Belorussian Front intended to place its main effort, at what time, and with what forces it planned to start the attack. These Soviet assault preparations were ponderously methodical: Red Army artillery observers occupied newly constructed observation posts; medium guns registered cautiously; Soviet fighters suddenly swept the sky to stop the Luftwaffe's reconnaissance; and dive-bombers plastered approach routes, command posts, and towns behind our front with machine-gun fire and bombs.

Together with heavy Russian troop movements toward the front—particularly during the nights of 8–9 and 9–10 January—these indications combined to provide me with sufficient military intelligence to issue the code word for the withdrawal to the main battle position at precisely the right moment. I had learned at Lvov that it would require steady nerves and expert evaluation of combat intelligence not to exhaust our outnumbered troops by repeated premature withdrawals or to suffer heavy casualties from the Russian artillery preparation because we waited too long. On 11 January there was a noticeable reduction in Soviet combat activity and movements. The troops of the Third Panzer Army nervously awaited the orders that would spare them from receiving the brunt of the enemy's concentration, but no such order reached the front line. Instead, the graduating class of the Luftwaffe Academy conducted a tour of the army's sector, the young officer candidates watching demonstrations by the newly arrived 5th Panzer Division and inspecting the fortifications of the battle position. Since the front remained calm, it had been possible to fulfill their request to visit some outposts in order to observe the enemy's positions and movements firsthand. Here and there a Russian machine gun fired a few rounds, breaking the silence of a sunny afternoon. Suddenly, some projectiles whizzed through the air and dug up the earth near a crossroads. Several mortar shells exploded near the outposts, and the platoon leader shouted, "Take cover!" Detected by the Soviets, the visitors quickly sought shelter in a deep dugout. After a few more rounds registered in the vicinity, two of our own artillery salvos hit back at the enemy observation posts, restoring the silence. Proud of their "front-line" experience, the officer candidates returned unharmed to the rear.

The following day [12 January] was even more peaceful. No new clues regarding the probable time of the Red Army's attack were observed by our outposts. On the other hand, radio intercepts and the latest observations of our remaining night reconnaissance aircraft left no doubt that strong Russian columns continued to move into the assembly areas, that artillery emplacements had been fully occupied, and that tank units had move up into the depth of the concentration area. I therefore determined to give the code word *Wintersonnenwende* (winter solstice) for withdrawal at 2200 on 12 January. The evacuation of the two forward lines went smoothly, and our divisions moved into the battle position. Three hours later General Matzky advised me that the movement had been completed, the new command posts occupied, and signal communications had resumed normal function.

As usual before a major Red Army offensive, several deserters arrived at our outposts; their statements agreed: A heavy artillery concentration at 0600 was to precede the launching of the attack on 13 January. I immediately issued orders for Third Panzer Army's artillery to deliver a concentration at 0530, targeting the two basic loads reserved for that purpose on the Russian infantry assembly areas. Thus, a heavy German preparation led off the second battle for East Prussia. At 0600 the Third Belorussian Front unleashed a hail of fire from more than 3,000 guns, pouring shells of all calibers on the two forward positions we had evacuated a few hours earlier. By then our infantry and artillery occupied the battle position, which had its forward boundary in our third fortified line. The Russian area fire was scattered over five kilometers in depth and hit only obvious targets—evacuated towns and former command posts. Our reserves, hidden in the woods, remained unscathed. By 0800, after pulverizing the first, empty positions, Russian fire walked forward to hit the second one, though with noticeably diminished intensity. Around 0830 the enemy shells began scattering in the depth of the battle position but gradually fell off to area or harassing fire without definite targets.

Following the initial artillery salvos, masses of Russian infantry had gone into action, carefully advancing through the thick fog that covered the terrain until 1100. Only slightly delayed by the fire of our rear guards in the first position, the Soviets soon rushed beyond this obstacle. Even before they reached the second evacuated position, however, the infantry was pinned down by artillery and *Nebelwerfer* fire. The reports from the assault units back to Third Belorussian Front had announced the capture of the first and second positions but failed to mention that they had taken no prisoners or booty. It was not until 1000 that the lead enemy assault units reached the main battle position. Pinned down by the fire from all of General Matzky's guns supported by the ladder fire of a *Nebelwerfer* brigade, the Soviet advance quickly ground to a halt. Russian infantry commanders sent out distress signals for immediately tank support; their coded cries for "boxes" became louder and louder. Poor visibility continued to prevent the enemy from taking advantage of his superiority in firepower and combat aircraft. Nevertheless, the Russian infantry did succeed in penetrating between XXVI Corps's individual strongpoints. When the fog lifted, these strongpoints were isolated and annihilated.

The Russians directed their main effort against the only elevated terrain in this area, near Kattenau, which they captured about noon after a strong tank attack. Major General Karl Jank's 549th Volksgrenadier Division repelled the Soviet infantry along the forward line of the main battle position as it attempted to follow the tanks. The Russian tanks, however, continued to push ahead from the Kattenau area because our antitank guns were overwhelmed by such masses of armor. The threat was all the more serious since Soviet combat aircraft, initially unopposed, had now made their first appearance in great numbers. They bombed towns, roads, evacuated command posts, and artillery emplacements, as well as attacking anything that moved on the ground. The Luftwaffe, called to the rescue, attacked the low-flying Russian formations despite the odds against our pilots, shooting down several planes and dispersing the rest.

This was the cue for our counterattack. Major General Guenther von Hoffmann-Schoenborn's 5th Panzer Division emerged from the protective cover of the forests to lead the attack, launching simultaneous thrusts against the flanks and rear of the Soviet armor in the Kattenau area. This clash, in which the panzer division was supported by Assault Gun Battalion 190 and rocket-firing planes, raged for several hours. After the combined forces of the 5th Panzer and 549th Volksgrenadier Divisions recaptured Kattenau, Russian tank reserves made a counterattack, but the assault guns and fighter planes repulsed them.

General Jank's infantry, supported by the assault guns, tore huge gaps in Red Army assault columns that had already been weakened by heavy artillery and *Nebelwerfer* fire. Before long, the entire Russian attack force wavered and fell back in confusion. During the evening, the entire XXVI Corps reoccupied the former main battle line. The booty taken by General Matzky's troops was rich, completely aside from 122 burned-out tanks piled up on the slopes near Kattenau. The Russian dead lay in heaps, particularly thick on the slopes of the heights among the destroyed and burned-out Soviet tanks. An improvised zone defense had saved Third Panzer Army's front-line forces from being annihilated and had stopped all of the Third Belorussian Front's breakthrough attempts.

The Soviets continued their assaults during the following days, feeding them with a constant flow of men and equipment. The Russians were unable, however, to repeat the deadly artillery preparation of 13 January, because they lacked the necessary ammunition. Despite a tenfold numerical superiority and heroic sacrifices from Red Army soldiers, these attacks made little headway and failed to overcome the zone defense belt. The high ground near Kattenau changed hands several times, and an additional 200 Russian tanks met with destruction in that area. Only when the Soviets succeeded in penetrating the wooded marshland on the southern flank (which allowed them to outflank the 549th Volksgrenadier Division) did the situation become grave. Two bicycle battalions, sent into action in cold weather and during a fearful blizzard, managed to contain this penetration but could not restore the original position. Meanwhile, the Red Army also pushed forward on the border between Third Panzer and Fourth Armies around Insterburg.

Though still fighting in the main battle zone through 19 January, the withdrawal of XXVI Corps eventually became unavoidable. By degrees and in perfect order General Matzky pulled his troops back, as the Soviets repeatedly attempted to effect a breakthrough at Schlossberg, which would have separated the corps from the army's main body. Every time, however, our combat engineers and assault guns retook the contested little town, and the Russians were thrown back to their initial positions. Flak batteries and a rapid change of front by General Rein's 69th Infantry Division repulsed an enemy tank thrust against Breitenstein on 18 January but left a portion of our front line jutting far out to the east. During the evening of the same day, the Russians approached the flooded Inster River near Insterwalde with a fresh tank corps and managed to scale the steep bank before troops being transferred there from the eastern sector of the Memel front could arrive. The Soviet tanks crossed the antitank ditch leading over the heights, drove the *Volkssturmm* from the well-consolidated position behind it, and advanced as far as the Breitenstein-Hohensalzburg road. During this operation General Rein, who had hastened in advance of his troops to the new position, was killed. Nonetheless, his troops rallied, halting the enemy at Schillen with a concentric attack by several battalions supported with assault guns and thus averted a potentially fatal penetration of the front.

Nonetheless, by the evening of 19 January the strong forest position, already organized some days earlier for the *Volkssturm* battalions, had to be abandoned by the southern elements of XXVI Corps, and as a result General Matzky had to move his entire line back. The Soviets attacking Fourth Army had also captured the Insterburg railroad junction with strong tank forces, and the very next morning (20 January) those tanks pushed forward on the main highway to Kreuzingen in an attempt to strike Third Panzer Army's rear and cut it off from Koenigsberg. Recognizing this danger, I shifted the 5th Panzer Division in a night march in such a fashion that it would be able to fall upon the flank of the Russian tank corps and utilize its tanks to form a barrier at Kreuzingen to protect the army's main body. The Memel front line, still manned between Pagnit and the Kurisches Haff, ran the risk at the same time of being attacked in the rear and isolated. Contrary to the instruction issued by OKH, I gave the order for Third Panzer Army's divisions to leave weak covering parties behind and execute an immediate right-about-turn to attack in conjunction with 5th Panzer Division and beat the Russians decisively in the Kreuzingen area. In this battle with a reversed front, the strong Red Army forces, including large numbers of tanks, were attacked concentrically and thrown back. Kreuzingen itself was retaken by a panzer assault following a hard struggle. Thus the two paved roads leading from the Tilsit area to Koenigsberg remained in our possession, and the danger that IX Corps might be cut off was averted. The subsequent withdrawal of Third Panzer Army toward Koenigsberg went according to plan.

Never would Third Panzer Army have been able to give battle to forty-four Russian rifle divisions, 3,000 guns, and 800 tanks with its nine weak divisions, 400 guns, and 50 tanks (almost completely unsupported by the Luftwaffe), and to hold out for a month in difficult weather conditions, even in the Koenigsberg fortified area, if zone defense tactics had not preserved the troops from annihilation and enabled them to intercept and deflect the heaviest bludgeoning impacts of the Soviet masses.

Chapter 13

POMERANIA

First Meeting with Himmler

TOWARD THE END OF THE DIFFICULT operations in East Prussia, the staff of Third Panzer Army and I were relieved from that assignment and—during 8–10 February—transferred by boat and rail to Rummelsburg in Pomerania. There our headquarters was attached to Army Group Vistula, commanded by *Reichsfuehrer* Heinrich Himmler, but not yet committed. I immediately established personal contact with the Provisional Corps von Tettau on the left flank of *Obergruppenfuehrer* Felix Steiner's improvised Eleventh SS Panzer Army and the X SS Corps on the right wing of Colonel General Walter Weiss's Second Army. Both of these armies were engaged in bitter defensive fighting to the south of my headquarters. It was intended at the time for these two corps to be subordinated to Third Panzer Army as a new army sector.

Shortly after arriving in Rummelsburg I requested to be presented to *Reichsfuehrer* Himmler and be permitted to make my formal report to him. My appointment was scheduled for 13 February. Late that afternoon, several staff officers and I arrived at Himmler's headquarters in a camp in the woods southwest of Prenzlau. There I received a thorough report on the situation and plans by the army group's operations officer, and then by orders from Himmler I was invited to have dinner with him and his closest assistants at 2000. Himmler appeared promptly, received me, and introduced me to his associates. He was obviously in good spirits and carried on a lively conversation that avoided official matters. As he talked, he evinced a marked interest in the arts and sciences. The meal was simple but well prepared and served perfectly. Since guests were present, he made an exception to his normal rule, and everyone at the table was served one glass of red wine, although Himmler himself drank only mineral water.

An hour later, Himmler rose from the table and arranged to meet me for a discussion at 2230 in the office at his quarters. I was with Himmler at the appointed hour, and there I met Army Group Vistula's chief of staff, *Gruppenfuehrer* Heinz Lammerding. The conference, originally planned for only half an hour, was prolonged by Himmler to 0300 because of my lengthy report. Lammerding remained only until about midnight, and then because of the heavy Allied air raid on Dresden he received Himmler's permission to leave and visit his family residing in that city. Consequently, from approximately midnight to the end of the discussion, I was alone with Himmler.

To this very day I remember this conversation in detail, and I am still able to repeat, word for word, Himmler's main remarks and questions as well as my own replies. The conversation became even more thoroughly graven in memory because, on returning to Rummelsburg, I immediately recounted it to my own chief of staff, Major General Mueller-Hillebrand, and also discussed its outcome with others on many occasions.

Himmler began by saying, "As you have been informed by my operations officer, the Eleventh SS Panzer Army, together with other SS panzer divisions and SS panzergrenadier divisions that have been brought up, will break through to the south from the area southwest of Stargard the day after tomorrow. They will attack the Soviet armies flanking Kuestrin from the rear and annihilate them. The *Fuehrer* expects decisive results for the outcome of the war from this attack. Originally I had planned to place you, an experienced panzer commander, in charge of this mission. Unfortunately, it was not possible to obtain your release from East Prussia in time. My suggestion of postponing the attack so that the assembly of forces could be completed, and that you and your staff might still be integrated prior to the attack, was rejected by the *Fuehrer*. Give me your honest opinion as to the course of action and the chances of success in this offensive."

I replied, "A comparison of the strength of both sides (our *one* reinforced panzer army as opposed to the three Russian tank armies and three to four infantry armies) is sufficient to conclude that the attack can lead only to failure. By achieving better coordination of our own units and selecting a shorter route for the attack by your panzer divisions, perhaps some ground my be gained at one point or another, but then they will come to a standstill. Under no circumstances, however, can a decisive result be expected."

Visibly affected by this adverse opinion, Himmler asked me to be just as frank in telling him what I would do in his place.

I said, "Do not attack, but hold the panzer units that have been moved up in readiness to definitively repulse the impending Russian attack. After that attack has been successfully warded off, I would improve the contour of our line through a counterattack, so that we would be able to hold our positions against all future Soviet attacks." After I cited additional reasons for this opinion, we held a lengthy discussion about this point.

Himmler eventually responded, "That is out of the question. The *Fuehrer* had given orders for the attack and will not change his mind. For that reason the attack will be launched under any circumstances. I intend to discuss your proposals as to a more efficient execution of the attack with Guderian." Himmler then summoned Colonel General Heinz Guderian, Chief of the Army General Staff, by telephone to come to him from Zossen immediately.

After I had reiterated the reasons for reaching my conclusions, and very firmly suggested that the attack should not be carried out, I said, "I am convinced that the attack will have come to a standstill by the second day. In that event, I recommend that you no longer fight uselessly, but halt the operation immediately, and withdraw strong reserves for defense against the Soviet counterattack that we must definitely expect. However, under no circumstances can you allow these reserves to be transferred to another theater before the defense against the counterattack has succeeded, since that would bring about the collapse of Army Group Vistula."

A detailed dialogue on this point ensued, ending with Himmler completely convinced by my evaluation. Then, apparently to arouse my enthusiasm, the *Reichsfuehrer* told me confidentially that at approximately the same time Army Group South (employing Sixth SS Panzer Army and other forces flanking Lake Balaton) would launch a large-scale attack against the Russian armies in Hungary that were currently poised for an assault on Vienna. This attack was intended to recapture Budapest.

Judging from my own experience, I did not encourage him in any expectations of success even in that assault, because our forces were again too weak and the Sixth SS Panzer Army would be exposed to the danger of being cut off and annihilated at Lake Balaton. I also recommended that the same procedure be followed in this case that I had advised for Pomerania and added that success could be gained only if it were possible to weld the Sixth and Eleventh SS Panzer Armies (as well as all other available units) into one force and employ it in one of the two sectors. Over the course of another lengthy interchange, Himmler pointed out that the overall strategic and logistical situation would not permit such a concentration of forces and clung to his belief that these two offensives would decide the outcome of the war.

When the conversation turned to the subject of the larger strategic picture, I seized the opportunity of speaking about the serious miscalculations made by the Supreme Command and their consequences. About this time

POMERANIA   321

there was a short pause while Lammerding left for Dresden. The discussion continued now only between Himmler and me.

I said, "*Herr Reichsfuehrer*, permit me to make use of this first opportunity of being able to speak to you, the most influential man in the nation next to the *Fuehrer*, in order to tell you in all frankness what I think about the manner in which the war has been conducted during the last few years and the situation that has resulted from that conduct. I know that my statements could take me to the Moabit Prison and perhaps even to the gallows, but I shall not be able to vindicate myself before God and the German people if I remain silent on the subject."

Gravely, Himmler said only, "Proceed."

"Since Stalingrad our conduct of operation has created serious doubts in the minds of commanders of all grades. During the past few months they have not been comprehensible at all.

"From the standpoint of space alone, it is clear that the advance of the German Army as far as the Volga River and the Caucasus Mountains, with the resulting defensive operations along a 3,000-kilometer-long front, exceeded the capacity of the Wehrmacht and our allies. The bow was strained to the utmost and had to break. The strength-consuming fighting around Stalingrad and on the Don, and the ramifications of these battles, led to a military defeat of gigantic proportions. Two-thirds of the Eastern Front began to totter, our allies were crushed and swept away, and a complete collapse of the front became apparent. The catastrophe was prevented only by the miraculous courage and tenacity of our officers and their troops and through the exertion of every ounce of strength.

"The Supreme Command did not deduce the inevitable inferences from these facts but issued orders with increasing obstinacy and stubbornness, which led to the elimination and destruction of numerous large and very large units. This unsystematic robbery gnawed at the very marrow of our combat strength and has ultimately brought us to the edge of the abyss into which we are in danger of being hurled—unless those miracles occur that our people have been led to expect. The Supreme Command has lost all concept for time and space, and their relationship with military strength, and is leading the subordinate army group and army commanders by the nose in such a fashion that they are able to issue orders only with hands tied and a rope dangling above their heads. They have to carry out impossible orders under penalty of death and in return are driven away in shame and condemned as traitors to their country if the result of the battle is unfavorable."

Here I paused in expectation of some contradictory utterance from Himmler, or orders for my immediate arrest. Neither took place, and the

Reichsfuehrer, unmoved, looked me squarely in the eyes and said, "Continue."

I then began to substantiate my views with specific examples:

"Instead of organizing an aggressive strategic defense in suited sectors selected well in advance, the Supreme Command has been unwilling to surrender as much as a single kilometer of space. Every reserve that has become available has been immediately committed in local offensive operations, which fail because they are carried out with inadequate resources. As a result, in addition to the loss of ground, the employment of these forces ends up with casualties lost for no gain." Here I made specific, detailed reference to the pincer attack against Kursk in July 1943, to the counterattack against Kiev that fall, and to the current plans in Pomerania and Hungary.

"Construction of rear positions has been prohibited for a long time, since allegedly our units look toward the rear and consequently do not present strong enough resistance. The result has been exactly the opposite. For example, during the withdrawal to the Dnepr River, even hastily prepared positions had enormous value, yet along the length of the river almost no such preparations had been made. Consequently, the Russians reached the opposite bank within a short period and completely neutralized this water barrier. The troops felt bitter disappointment, and their misgivings about the Supreme Command grew. To be sure, there were considerable defensive preparations made in East Prussia, but the badly debilitated armies there no longer had enough strength to occupy and hold them.

"Local strongpoints and so-called centers of resistance were introduced as emergency measures that led to stubborn resistance in hopeless situations. This entailed not only the loss of the locality but also the loss of the defending unit itself and a continuing erosion of the army's confidence in the Supreme Command. In the same manner, improperly integrated or encircled and strength-consuming sectors of the front have had to be held at any cost, eating up troop units through attrition or leading to their wholesale destruction. In the Caucasus, the Crimea, Courland, and East Prussia, entire armies and army groups have been left to the defense of such areas until they became encircled and ceased to play any rational role in the main theater of war. The same catastrophic situation threatens both Pomerania and Hungary if the planned operation is carried out.

"Meanwhile, new units, constantly coming from the Zone of the Interior, lack the training and equipment necessary to mold themselves into effective combat teams. Of necessity we throw them into gaps, or into large-scale defensive fighting. Unaccustomed to such stresses, they melt away like snow in the heat of the sun.

"Enemy air action is inflicting such enormous damage at home that very important war materiel either does not reach the front or appears in extremely inadequate amounts." Here I referred to the repeated difficulties in being supplied with ammunition, machine guns, rifles, antitank guns, tanks, assault guns, spare parts, and fuel for our vehicles.

I concluded my analysis by once more calling attention to the fact that in conducting the war in such a manner troops, equipment, and terrain had been lost to such an extent that Germany's very survival was in doubt. Yet with inadequate resources and this threatening situation on all fronts, the nation's government continued to expect "decisive results."

Having finished, I remained silent as we looked at one another for several minutes without uttering a word.

Himmler then moved closed to me, bent over, and spoke slowly in a subdued voice, enunciating every word: "I agree with you."

He then fell silent again.

Astounded by this reply, I drew a long breath and asked, "Then why have you not informed the *Fuehrer*?"

After a brief pause, Himmler said, "I expected that question." After a second pause, he continued: "I have already told the *Fuehrer* all of these things."

"And what did the *Fuehrer* say?"

Pointing his finger, Himmler replied after a short time in a raised voice: "The *Fuehrer* replied most violently, 'You are a defeatist, too!' and in a fit of rage showed me the door." (Later Major General Eberhard Kinzel, the last military expert detailed to Himmler by OKH, and who had been present during the discussion between Himmler and Hitler, confirmed this account.)

Himmler then began describing the difficulties along Army Group Vistula's front and the bitter fighting for the "centers of resistance" at Marienburg and Schneidemuehl. He was particularly worried about the latter, since the loss of Schneidemuehl, though fiercely contested by our troops, was imminent. He knew the local commander, Colonel Heinz Remlinger, personally, and realized that the garrison only had a few hundred combat troops left, who had scarcely any ammunition. Hitler had not even replied to Remlinger's request to break out of the pocket with the remainder of his garrison.

I once more brought the conversation back to the subject of the great danger currently threatening Army Group Vistula and brought out a map on which I traced the Russians' probable intentions on the Pomeranian front:

"At the outset the Soviets will probably break through the front at its weakest point, the Second Army's flank near Koeslin. They will attempt to isolate General Weiss's army from the rest of the army group. Then strong breakthrough attacks on one flank toward Danzig and on the other flank toward Stettin via Stargard have to be taken into account. Both attacks will attempt to split up and annihilate the armies in these areas."

These statements were interrupted by an urgent telephone call from the army group's operations officer. A radio message from Colonel Heinz Remlinger to Himmler was relayed, concerning a successful breakout to the north by Remlinger and the remnants of his garrison. The breakout had been made on Remlinger's own initiative, since up to the last moment he had waited in vain for the requested permission. Himmler listened intently, then replaced the receiver, jumped up, and with joyful enthusiasm paced back and forth as he repeatedly shouted to me: "Did you hear that? Remlinger made it! Remlinger made it! He did exactly right! I say he did exactly right!"

I naturally agreed with Remlinger's independent decision and voiced the hope that a large number of these courageous men—favored by densely wooded terrain—would be able to regain our lines. While we were still talking at length regarding the possibilities of adding this unit to our defenses, the telephone rang again. I listened in on the order from Hitler, transmitted through OKH, requiring Remlinger and his garrison to return to Schneidemuehl immediately and continue its defense.

"No," Himmler said to me. "You are absolutely right. I shall not forward this order."

It was this incident that finally confirmed my belief that Himmler was not tricking me but that he was serious when he said that he agreed with my contentions.

The Situation in East Pomerania

A short time after my first discussion with *Reichsfuehrer* Himmler, the Eleventh SS Panzer Army launched the offensive as ordered by the *Fuehrer*. After achieving insignificant initial success, the operation came to a standstill on the second day with the loss of many panzers. In spite of my emphatic warnings, all of the SS panzer and panzergrenadier divisions that had been moved up for this offensive were drawn out of the front line and transferred to the Silesia-Saxony area of operations, regardless of the fact that far superior Soviet forces were ready to launch a counteroffensive. Just as the front had been unjustifiably weakened by this measure, I received orders from Army Group Vistula to relieve *Obergruppenfuehrer* Steiner's Eleventh SS Panzer Army headquarters. Third Panzer Army was to take over the remaining weak forces for the defense of this wide sector.

On 22 February—twenty-four hours after I had assumed command—the Second Belorussian Front, in overpowering strength, launched its expected counteroffensive. From the orientation given me by *Obergruppenfuehrer* Steiner about the enemy when I assumed command, and from observations during the last twenty-four hours, I had been certain that the Russian attack was imminent. For that reason I had no opportunity to make any kind of decisive changes in *Obergruppenfuehrer* Steiner's inadequate defensive scheme. I was even more handicapped because there were no reserves whatsoever at my disposal. At the time Third Panzer Army assumed control of the troops formerly belonging to Eleventh SS Panzer Army, the units in my sector consisted of:

III SS Panzer Corps
Lieutenant General Karl Decker

23rd SS *Nederland* Panzergrenadier Division
Standartenfuehrer Helmut Raithel

27th SS *Langemarck* Panzergrenadier Division
Commander unknown

28th SS *Wallonien* Panzergrenadier Division
Brigadefuehrer Leon Degrelle

(These divisions had all been considerably weakened a short time earlier in the unsuccessful attack.)

X SS Corps
Lieutenant General Guenther Krappe

163rd Infantry Division
Major General Karl Ruebel

402nd Infantry Division
Lieutenant General Siegfried Freiherr von Schleinitz

Provisional Corps Hoernlein
General of Infantry Walter Hoernlein

9th Parachute Division
Major General Bruno Brauer
Replacement units from Wehrkreis II (Stettin)

Provisional Corps von Tettau
Lieutenant General Hans von Tettau

Reserve Division *Baerwalde*
Commander unknown; this division had been formed from the school units at the Grossborn and Hammerstein training centers.

Reserve Division *Pomerania*

Commander unknown; this division was composed of Volks-grenadier battalions and improvised units that were hastily organized from construction and survey battalions, as well as supply units of all three components of the Wehrmacht. The division contained neither a signal battalion nor artillery nor antitank weapons. Several recently formed regiments and battalions, in fact, lacked commanders. I assigned officers to these positions who were returning from leave to Army Group Courland as they passed by me on the highway. I immediately sent them, in my car, to the units already engaged in fighting as their commanders. Reserve Division *Pomerania* occupied a switch position that extended along the left boundary of the army perpendicular to the front (the old Pomerania position against the Poles in 1939).

Under direct army control:

5th Jaeger Division
Lieutenant General Friedrich Sixt

In army group reserve:

Panzer Division *Holstein*
Colonel Joachim Hesse

Altogether these ten divisions, with seventy tanks, occupied a defensive front of 240 kilometers. Division front lines averaged between twenty-six and thirty kilometers in length. For every kilometer of front, we deployed one artillery piece, one heavy machine gun, two light machine guns, and forty men. We deployed one antitank gun for every 2.5 kilometers, one panzer for every four kilometers, and each battalion was stretched across roughly six kilometers. Facing this line the Second Belorussian Front had concentrated five armies consisting of fifteen rifle corps and one cavalry corps, as well as three tank armies consisting of eight tank or mechanized corps.

During my initial few hours I managed to regroup the 5th Jaeger Division (the unit with the highest degree of offensive capability in the army) along a narrow front, disposed in depth in the sector east of Stargard where we could expect major actions to be fought. I intended to employ the division in depth, in such a manner that with the support of panzers, antitank defenses, and the bulk of our army artillery it would be able to hold its ground at least temporarily even in the face of a powerful Russian attack.

Even before I formally took command, I had issued orders for the construction of a dense network of tank obstacles in the army rear area, which abounded in wooded areas and bodies of water, thus lending itself well to such a purpose. In a few days, with the energetic cooperation of party members and local inhabitants, these obstacles sprang up on all bridges, village entrances, and bypasses, as well as highway and road entrances leading into woods or swampy terrain. Stout-hearted members of the *Volkssturm*, who had been trained in the use of the *Panzerfaust* [antitank weapons], guarded these barriers. Moreover, men equipped with antitank weapons were held in readiness with bicycles and motorcycles for mobile employment and the rapid establishment of strongpoints. The entire civilian telephone network was put into service for the purpose of issuing tank warnings and to maintain communications between the blocked zones and the military authorities. Never before had an area been transformed into such a tightly meshed antitank obstacle within so short a period of time as we had accomplished in Pomerania. The aim of this measure was to prevent Russian tanks that had broken through the front from carrying out a surprise advance, or at least to delay such an advance. Though precautions worked quite well, they represented only a fraction of the precautionary actions that would have been necessary to offer successful resistance against the large-scale attack of the Second Belorussian Front.

Course of the Battle

Initially, Russian attack preparations were observed in two places: on our boundary with Second Army, and in the area east of Stargard. Particularly extensive concentrations of tanks and rifle units were detected east of Stargard. During the past few days, southeast of Neustettin (close to the boundary with Second Army) the Soviets had been conducting aggressive reconnaissances in force, which then abruptly halted. During these actions we took several prisoners from the First Polish Army (serving under Russian command). The presence of this army, together with the comparative calm, led me to the conclusion that the large-scale attack was not to be expected at this point. General Weiss's Second Army also failed to observe any disturbing activity in front of its right wing.

By noon on 22 February, however, I suddenly received a message from Provisional Corps von Tettau that the Russians had broken through in the area of the adjoining division of Second Army, 33rd SS *Charlemagne* Grenadier Division, and that enemy tanks were driving toward the northwest by way of Stegers. During the afternoon, approximately fifteen Russian tanks coming out of the Second Army area actually appeared at the outskirts of Baldenburg, thirty-five kilometers in the rear of Third Panzer Army's left wing. These tanks were stopped at the tank barriers by elements of Reserve

Division *Pomerania* after three tanks were knocked out. Considerably reinforced during the night, the Russians again attacked Baldenburg on the morning of 23 February with approximately thirty-five to forty tanks and one or two battalions of motorized infantry. This enemy force quickly overpowered the garrison of sixty construction engineers and naval surveying personnel, broke through the switch position, and pushed cautiously forward in the direction of Bublitz. The weak local garrison there (service troops of Reserve Division *Pomerania*), which had been assigned to man the tank barriers, combined with our mobile tank destroyer elements, moved up from the surrounding woods, and successfully attacked the Russians. Consequently, the Soviet commander thereafter confined himself to keeping the railway station under fire, without attempting to attack the town. Not until the following day [24 February] did he force his way into the north section of Bublitz and occupy the railroad station after heavy fighting. In the course of this action our *Panzerfausts* destroyed sixteen Soviet tanks.

In the meantime, powerful reinforcements had been moved up in support of the Russian spearhead and had forced the remnants of Second Army's crumpled left wing (15th SS Latvian Grenadier Division and 33rd SS *Charlemagne* Grenadier Division) into Third Panzer Army's sector. There they caused unrest among my improvised units, especially in Reserve Division *Pomerania*, which already suffered from low morale. Moreover, Russian troops following the track of the German refugees had penetrated into Neustettin, occupying the railroad station (approximately twenty kilometers behind our front line). They could be dislodged from Neustettin after only severe street fighting.

Since Second Army, together with the forces that Army Group Vistula had moved up via Rummelsburg (VII Panzer Corps, consisting of 7th Panzer Division, 4th SS *Polizei* Panzergrenadier Division, and the remnants of the 32nd Infantry Division), had failed to block off the Soviet penetration at Stegers, more and more Russian units poured through the gap, deep into the flanks of Third Panzer Army. My own flank thus became enveloped and was pushed back toward Neustettin. Russian pressure constantly increased in the area between Neustettin and Bublitz. The Soviet tank spearheads pushing forward from Bublitz toward the heights east of Koeslin completely cut off our contact with Second Army. This is when we were ordered to use Colonel Joachim Hesse's Panzer Division *Holstein* in an attempted to reestablish contact with General Weiss's army. The division was drawn out of the line south of Stargard, moved into reserve, and then committed in an attack from the area south of Bublitz toward Rummelsburg. After some initial tactical success the division was forced back by far superior enemy forces and the difficulties due to the heavy vegetation along the axis of attack. This encounter, while completely unsuccessful in achieving its objective, nonetheless tied down Panzergrenadier Division *Holstein* in my eastern flank; having previously been the army's only reserve unit, this meant the division was not available later in the defense against Second Belorussian Front's main attack, launched against Stargard about 1 March.

At that point, after a terrific artillery concentration, a sizeable Russian tank force penetrated the front of the 5th Jaeger Division on a line four kilometers wide and six kilometers deep. Lieutenant General Friedrich Sixt's courageous division, deployed in depth, nonetheless managed to block the drive for the time being with its own strength without breaking contact to the right or left. But on 2 March Soviet tanks attacked in such great strength that they penetrated 5th Jaeger Division's front between Falkenburg and Drammburg, causing the left flank of the III SS Panzer Corps and the right flank of XX SS Corps (adjoining General Sixt's division on either side) to be rolled back, cracking the front wide open. Russian tanks almost immediately gained freedom of movement and pushed ahead, By 3 March enemy tank spearheads had already appeared at Regenswalde, eight kilometers east of my command post, which nonetheless remained in position. Strong rifle units followed the Russian armor and widened the gap, while the enemy also gained ground daily in the direction of Bad Polzin and captured Neustettin. Only on our western flank was it possible to repulse all Soviet attacks against Greifenhagen and Pyritz, and even so the latter was encircled on several occasions. In the north, the Russian tide continued relentlessly forward, seizing Koeslin after several days of fighting, and their tank spearheads were threatening Kolberg. Tanks from the south also attempted to reach Kolberg, which had been designated a "center of resistance." Enemy pressure increased daily on the extended flanks of the corps whose sectors had been penetrated.

At the beginning of March Hitler declared the city of Kolberg a fortress. The small city was overcrowded with wounded, the railroad station filled with hospital trains. Columns of refugee carts blocked the roads, and Russian tanks were only forty kilometers distant. Precisely at that moment the newly appointed fortress commander, Colonel Fritz Fullriede, who was entirely unfamiliar with the situation, was flown in by a Fieseler "Storch." He was not acquainted with the duties of a fortress commander and had to be briefed in detail. The "fortress" was absolutely defenseless. Hitler's attention was called to this fact, but he nonetheless insisted that Kolberg be held as a fortress under all circumstances. In his reply to my protests, Hitler assured me that the Spandau depot would receive instructions immediately to dispatch twelve new antitank guns to Kolberg by rail. This was at a time when the single-track railroad line to Kolberg was completely blocked and Soviet tanks were expected to appear in the proximity of the city within a few hours. Obviously, the antitank guns never arrived. Colonel Fullriede was forced to pick his defense force and weapons from the streets. Indiscriminately everybody and everything moving through the city was stopped, whether they belonged to the Luftwaffe, Kriegsmarine, damaged tanks, flak, antitank, or artillery guns, and integrated into the fortress defense.

It was difficult to imagine why Hitler decided that this former small coastal fort should be defended, unless for historical reasons. In modern times, however, the events that occurred in Napoleon's day could not possibly be repeated. Nonetheless, the Russians appeared to be impressed by the glorious past of the city, because their approach was slow and hesitant. The first Soviet attack was delayed for two days, until 14 March, but the defensive tactics employed by the garrison soon revealed their weakness, and after only a few days, on 18 March, the enemy captured the city. Most of the entirely improvised garrison had to be rescued by the Kriegsmarine.

With Himmler Again

The Second Belorussian Front's attack had sealed the fate of Pomerania. After the crumbled line had been reestablished on the Oder River, despite very heavy losses and thanks to the unequalled courage of the troops, I was again summoned to a conference with Himmler on 7 March. This meeting took place in the Hohenlychen Sanatorium northeast of Berlin, where the *Reichsfuehrer* lay ill with angina. Accompanied by his aide, I arrived there at approximately 1500. On my entering, Himmler raised up partially in bed, greeted me in a friendly manner, and offered me a chair near his bed. His aide left the room and we were alone. The ensuing conversation lasted for more than an hour.

Himmler began by congratulating me, saying, "You have passed through some very difficult days, but in spite of all obstacles you have again stabilized the front!"

In reporting on the course of the fighting, I constantly referred to the fact that, in the face of my recommendations to the contrary, all reserves had been withdrawn and transferred to another front. Consequently, the Pomeranian front, thus weakened to the utmost, had been attacked and smashed by the Red Army's counteroffensive as predicted. "Moreover," I told the *Reichsfuehrer*, "during the enemy offensive you repeatedly issued orders that prevented me from acting along lines demanded by the tactical situation. For example, you forbade the withdrawal of protruding sectors to favorably located and well-prepared positions along shorter lines at the lakes. Had I been allowed to do so, unnecessary losses would have been avoided, and forces could have been released for the creation of reserves. These forces would have been adequate to seal off the initial Russian penetrations at Puritz, Stargard, and Neustettin. Instead, the Soviets achieved deep penetrations at Neustettin and in the area east of Stargard where we found ourselves short of troops to contain the pressure.

"The single reserve division—Panzer Division *Holstein*—which I made available by weakening even front-line sectors under direct attack, had to be committed in accordance with your orders toward Rummelsburg via Bublitz with the hopeless task of reestablishing contact with Second Army. In so doing, this division was needlessly exhausted and unavailable at the point of main effort east of Stargard, where General Sixt's 5th Jaeger Division was overpowered and split into pieces after waging an extremely courageous defensive battle against Soviet tanks attacking at a ratio of twenty-to-one. The bulk of the X SS Corps and Provisional Corps Tettau, which were fighting in the area between the two points of penetration, thus came in danger of being encircled and eliminated.

"With respect to the increasing probability of losing those two corps, I requested permission over a period of five days, each day more urgently—finally imploring you—to allow me to pull the forces out of the threatened area during the night to prevent their encirclement, since they would otherwise be sacrificed to no purpose. Even then you did not agree to the withdrawal but instead added special emphasis to your disapproval by threatening a court-martial action against all key officers. As a result, both corps (with the exception of a few elements of Provisional Corps Tettau that may still be able to fight their way back) were captured on the fifth day. These staggering events led to the rapid loss of Pomerania as far west as the Oder, where the remnants of Third Panzer Army have again been able to organize into a unit and occupy positions for successful defense. It has even been possible, thanks to the effective support provided by Kriegsmarine and Luftwaffe units fighting on the ground, to hold onto a series of important bridgeheads on the Oder's eastern bank.

"Even after the two corps had been encircled, impossible orders from your headquarters did not stop. The 10th SS *Frundsberg* Panzer Division, ordered back to us from Silesia, abruptly received orders to reestablish contact with Second Army (squeezed into a small area around Danzig and Gotenhafen) by attacking across Pomerania through territory already occupied by several Russian armies. This altogether impossible mission served to demonstrate the extent to which you and the Supreme Command had misjudged the existing situation. Even the fact that your headquarters neglected to have someone establish personal contact with Third Panzer Army as we struggled through a desperate situation does not explain why you consistently crippled my conduct of operations with rigidly binding orders, threats, and demands with which we could not possibly comply."

Himmler listened to these remarks in a serious and attentive manner, then replied, "I know that you understood the actual danger on the Pomeranian Front and predicted these events in advance."

"It was not a question of prediction. I am thoroughly convinced that any other experienced army commander would have evaluated the situation in precisely the same manner and would have made the same recommendations."

Himmler said, "I have supported your proposals every time and have forwarded them to OKH because the *Fuehrer* has reserved the right to make every decision himself. The *Fuehrer*, however, has always rejected these proposals very emphatically and has reproved me severely."

"As you admitted yourself during our first discussion, such action is really contrary to the interests of our people, for which we are all fighting, and to whom the *Fuehrer*, too, is responsible."

"You are right," Himmler admitted, "but the *Fuehrer* is convinced that he is doing the right thing and for that reason demands the execution of his orders with unremitting harshness. He tolerates no opposition and as a result rejects every recommendation that does not conform to his way of thinking."

Raising my voice, I answered: "But you should not accept a refusal if your convictions differ. Otherwise such actions will lead to a disastrous end."

Himmler said, "Calm down. There will be a turning point soon. We shall win this war."

"That does not make sense to me. I do not follow you," I insisted, but Himmler suddenly ended the conversation and ordered two cups of tea and rolls. Then he asked me to describe such actions to him that could show that our divisions had fought courageously and carried out their orders to the letter. He explained that both he and the *Fuehrer* placed extremely high value on such points and that tactical reports were too cut-and-dried to reveal these facts to any useful degree. I obliged by describing a number of incidents, most from personal experience in the Pomeranian operation, that demonstrated conclusively the courage and self-sacrifice displayed by the troops of Third Panzer Army.

The *Reichsfuehrer* listened with rapt attention and showed great excitement. After I had finished my description of the fighting, Himmler sat up in bed, pressed my hand, and enthusiastically exclaimed, "That was excellent! You should report that to the *Fuehrer* personally! Are you prepared to do so?"

"Very much so. In fact, I had already intended to ask you permission to report personally to the *Fuehrer* on the fateful battle for Pomerania."

Himmler immediately called the *Fuehrer's* headquarters and asked to be connected with him. After only two or three minutes Hitler answered; his voice sounded monotonous and weary, but I could hear it plainly.

Himmler said, "*Mein Fuehrer*, the commander of the Third Panzer Army is here beside me and has just now reported in detail on the Pomeranian battle. The report is very interesting—you ought to hear it yourself. May I send General Raus to you?"

Hitler responded, "Yes, have him come tomorrow. I am having a conference tomorrow afternoon, which will also be attended by all my principal staff members. They can listen to him at the same time."

"Very good. When shall he come?"

Hitler said, "He is to be here at the bunker tomorrow afternoon at four o'clock. He will deliver his report after the conference."

"Good. General Raus will be there punctually."

With that, the conversation between Hitler and Himmler ended, as well as my own discussion with Himmler.

At Hitler's Bunker

I arrived from my command post in Stettin at the Artillery Barracks at 1600, 8 March, to deliver my report on the battle of Pomerania. The report was made in Hitler's bunker, located in a small garden on the grounds of the Reich Chancellery. After repeatedly checking my identification, an SS officer escorted me down a long stairway into the spacious hall—deep underground—of the bunker. On both sides of the hall doors opened into the various conference and work rooms. All the rooms were tiled in white and olive-green, well lit, and simply furnished. At the moment a number of generals who had arrived for the conference were gathering in front of the *Fuehrer's* door. I was speaking with several of the men with whom I was acquainted when an SS *Standartenfuehrer* [colonel] stepped up to me and asked me to come with him for a moment. He led me into an adjoining room and courteously informed me that he would have to search me thoroughly. He did not accept my objection that I was the commanding general of the Third Panzer Army, who had been ordered here by the *Fuehrer* and that I had already established my identity several times. He searched my pockets and clothing thoroughly. I was then permitted to return to the hall and rejoin the other general officers who had come for the conference.

As the officers of Hitler's staff were invited into the adjoining room for the conference soon afterward, I joined other officers who were not participating as an observer. The conference revolved around the events of the past several days, which were reported with the aid of maps by the respective

chiefs of staff: Colonel General Heinz Guderian for the Eastern Front and
Colonel General Alfred Jodl for the Western front. The *Fuehrer* sat at a table,
bent over the maps as he followed the review of operations. Most of the others present remained standing as they listened to the reports. Hitler raised
brief objections only sporadically and did not enlarge technical details until
later. However, to my knowledge no deliberations were conducted, no recommendations were made, and no decisions reached in spite of the grave tactical situation. In the west the Allies had crossed the Rhine, and in the east
the Red Army was advancing into Silesia and Hungary.

Following this conference, Hitler, together with the chiefs of the various
components of the Wehrmacht and his inner circle, remained in the conference room. All the others left. A short time later I was summoned back to the
chamber for my report to the *Fuehrer*. Aside from Hitler, those present
included *Reichsmarshal* Hermann Goering, Field Marshal Wilhelm Keitel,
Admiral Karl Doenitz, Colonel General Jodl, Colonel General Guderian,
Reichsleiter Martin Bormann, General of Infantry Wilhelm Burgdorff, and
their respective chiefs of staff. They sat around a long table covered with
maps. I stepped up to the *Fuehrer*, greeted him, and handed him two situation maps. The first one, from 13 February, displayed the dispositions of the
Eleventh SS Panzer Army and indicated my estimate of Soviet intentions as
reported during my first discussion with Himmler. The second detailed the
actual development of the Second Belorussian Front's offensive against the
sector, for which Third Panzer Army had assumed responsibility.

Hitler glanced distrustfully at me over his glasses, muttering something to
himself that sounded like, "That should not have happened." He then took
the maps into his very trembling hands and compared them. As he contemplated them he realized that each depicted essentially the same information.
I found myself facing a physically broken-down, embittered, and suspicious
man that I scarcely recognized. The knowledge that Adolph Hitler—now
only a human wreck—held the fate of the German people in his hands alone
was a deep shock to me. Without returning my greeting, and visibly angry, he
said only, "Proceed!"

The only interruption to my report occurred when I established the weight
of Soviet numerical superiority against the Third Panzer Army. There the
Fuehrer stopped me in a reproachful voice, saying, "The enemy did not have
1,600 tanks, but only 1,400." I pointed out that aside from the eight newly
constituted Russian tank or mechanized corps, there were also separate
armored units operating in conjunction with the II Guards Cavalry Corps.
Hitler acknowledged by a nod of his head that he would not dispute my
objection.

When my narration reached the events of early March, the *Fuehrer*, who until now had followed my report on a map, suddenly looked up and interrupted me in a hesitant but calm voice, saying, "We have been acquainted with the further course of the operation form the tactical reports submitted by you and the army group. Now tell us how the commanders and the troops behaved in battle."

Hitler, as well as the invited listeners, apparently were well aware that I was about to touch upon the encirclement and annihilation of the X SS Corps and elements of Provisional Corps von Tettau and would give the reasons for these developments. Since this disaster could be traced only to Hitler's orders, forwarded by Himmler, and were contrary to all proposals emanating from my headquarters, the *Fuehrer*, with this interruption, prevented me from speaking freely on the subject or offering his own orders as evidence. This assumption is sustained by the fact that my report up to this point had dealt with tactical aspects of the Pomeranian battle, which would have been just as familiar to him from army reports as that portion that would clearly show the dramatic effects of his personal orders.

After this unexpected change in my report, I described a number of small combat events that well illustrated the behavior of troops and commanders. They seemed the most appropriate reply to Hitler's concern with "how the commanders and troops behaved in battle."

Examples of Valor

After the breakthrough south of Stegers on 22 February, Soviet tanks suddenly appeared on the outskirts of Baldenburg. The antitank barriers on both ends of the town, which extended over a considerable distance, were kept open for the normal through traffic. Suddenly, the guard at the barrier at the southern exit of town saw a Russian tank approaching at full speed. He quickly attempted to place one of the heavy wooden horizontal bars into position. He did not succeed, however, and the leading enemy tank crashed through, firing at the roadblock and pushing into the city. A second and third T-34 followed closely behind and also attempted to pass the barrier. At the last moment, the alerted guards (only three men) still managed to get the crossbar into place despite the tank fire. Nevertheless, the first of these two T-34s continued to try to force the barrier and consequently was destroyed by a *Panzerfaust* while attempting to ram the antitank obstacle. A rifleman firing a second *Panzerfaust* fired a second shot, hitting the third tank and disabling it as well. In the meantime, another soldier from a construction unit also used a *Panzerfaust* to destroy the lead T-34, which had already entered the town. When the Soviet tank brigade to which these vehicles belonged became aware of their fate, it stopped, scattered widely, and halted its advance for the day in a small patch of woods nearby. Thus a few fifty-year-old soldiers through calm, courageous action were able to bring the initial penetration of fifteen tanks to a halt and thus enabled the weak local holding forces to defend Baldenburg, unaided, until the next day. These successful *Panzerfaust* men had seen Russian tanks for the first time in their lives and had put them out of action in short order. For their valor each received the Iron Cross, Second Class.

The Soviet tank brigade, after having been substantially reinforced near Baldenburg, broke through the switch position. The extremely weak holding force of Reserve Division *Pomerania* maintained its position against all the attacks of the Russian motorized rifle units, and thus only tanks were able to open a very narrow gap in the front. Repeatedly the defenders closed this gap behind the enemy armor. As a result, the momentum of the tank attack aimed at Bublitz had been crippled. This was one of the main reasons for the lack of aggressiveness displayed by the tank unit on reaching the gates of the city, where it remained—essentially inactive—for two days. The only reason was that the unit's position in the woods was rendered insecure by our continually prowling tank destroyer detachments. These detachments, armed with *Panzerfausts* and magnetic antitank mines, destroyed or disabled sixteen tanks in the woods on 23 February, and another dozen the following day. In this manner the tank assault against Koeslin was delayed, and we profited immensely from the discovery of maps illustrating the future plans of the tank unit in one of the wrecked tanks.

In order to widen the gap and protect the southern flank of the tank brigade near Baldenburg, a Soviet rifle unit supported by three T-34s turned off toward the southwest, seizing the village of Bischofthum and advancing toward Kasimiroff. This town was defended by a detachment of approximately twenty construction troops under the command of a line NCO who, having been badly wounded, had temporarily been placed in charge of a detachment of highway construction workers. Besides rifles, the detachment had only a single machine gun, and the NCO himself was armed with two *Panzerfausts*. When he noticed the enemy approaching, he deliberately and very calmly issued the order: "Everyone take cover in the foxholes here on the outskirts of the village and permit the leading three tanks to roll by without firing on them. I will take care of these. Fire on the infantry following them, at a range of 500 meters, and prevented their entrance into the village. I shall station myself behind this house on the main street of the village and wait for the tanks."

A few minutes later one by one, and carefully maintaining intervals, the Soviet tanks rolled into the village. The NCO knocked out the last tank with one *Panzerfaust*, whereupon the second tank turned toward the group of houses, firing as it moved toward the spot from which the tank commander presumed the resistance had come from. But using bushes as cover, the NCO had already crept up close to the tank and from only a short distance knocked it out as well, using his second and last *Panzerfaust*. When the lead tank saw the other two go up in flames, it pulled out of this sinister town by a side street and started a hasty retreat. In so doing, the tank pulled the Russian infantry, pinned down by defensive fire, along with it. Immediately the courageous NCO and his men took up the pursuit and during their counterattack recaptured Bischofthum as well. The NCO was again badly wounded in this action.

This action was related to me personally by the battalion commander, with whom I spoke at the main aid station in the presence of the wounded participants in the fighting.

On 25 February the Luftwaffe reported another unit of twenty-two Russian tanks located twenty-five kilometers southeast of Koeslin. A detachment of about sixty antitank fighters, which had immediately started out in that direction, stalked through the woods near the village. At night a strong reconnaissance patrol was dispatched to the village under cover of darkness and managed to locate the enemy tanks. During their reconnaissance, the patrol noticed a light in a house, and Russian officers were observed sitting down to their evening meal. The window was ripped open in one quick movement and at the same moment a hand grenade was thrown into the room. At this signal the antitank fighters rushed into the village, firing rapidly as they came and throwing the surprised tank unit into utter turmoil. In a brief fight they knocked out and set ablaze a number of tanks. In the ensuing confusion, the rest of the Soviet tanks quickly evacuated the village, which remained in our possession for another two days. Shortly thereafter I was able to contact the courageous antitank fighters myself over the telephone from Koeslin.

For three days SS Panzer Reconnaissance Battalion 10 of the 10th SS *Frundsberg* Panzer Division, having been moved up recently, brought strong Russian tank columns to a halt with their assault guns at Regenswalde and Plathe, thus rendering the westward evacuation of long columns of civilian vehicles and carts from Kolberg possible. Subsequently, in action at Greiffenberg, the battalion prevented a Soviet turning maneuver and the further advance of enemy tanks aiming at Stettiner Haff. The battalion continued to offer stubborn resistance until it became completely encircled.

Then, through the exertion of its last ounce of strength, the reconnaissance battalion blasted its way free of the tank encirclement and broke through to our lines.

During early March a Soviet tank unit suddenly appeared at one end of the *Autobahn* running from Stettin to the east, with the obvious intention of advancing rapidly toward Stettin on the best possible road. This was prevented by setting up a barrier at that point, guarded by a weak covering force. This small detachment of valiant soldiers was surrounded and fired upon from all sides by Russian tanks. Using *Panzerfausts* and an antitank gun (which was later knocked out), the detachment prevented the enemy tanks from entering the *Autobahn*. In making this stand, the detachment dwindled down to only a few men. Finally, after two or three hours of this unbalanced struggle, the Russians abandoned their plan of attack when some of our own Pzkw VI Tiger tanks approached. Six enemy tanks set ablaze were the price that the Russians paid for this effort; the *Autobahn* remained in our hands.

In order to prevent the establishment of a bridgehead east of Altdamm, Russian tanks attempted to strike from the north via Gollnow into the rear of III SS Panzer Corps, which was then engaged in bitter fighting along both sides of the Stargard-Stettin highway and railroad line. This disaster was prevented by a reinforced panzergrenadier regiment, located east of Gollnow, which bitterly contested control of the town and railroad station. For more than a day the struggle surged back and forth. Numerous Soviet tanks were destroyed, but our own forces also suffered heavy casualties. Enemy tanks, initially focusing their efforts on the railroad station, drove into our artillery emplacements, where our gunners fought to the last round before being subdued. Two entire batteries were destroyed in the course of this heroic struggle, but their sacrifice saved the entire corps from a much worse fate.

Encircled by the enemy, elements of Provisional Corps von Tettau continued fighting in the Soviet rear near Regenswalde and greatly harassed Second Belorussian Front's operations. On 6 March we reestablished radio contact with this force and ordered it to turn north and attempt to reach the coast west of Kolberg, so that it might fight its way forward along the coast to the Divenow bridgehead. The unit successfully reached the coast on 7 March. Instructions as well as orders had to be transmitted to this force via a Fieseler "Storch" liaison plane, which had to detour far out over the Baltic in order to survive. (As a matter of fact, *Gruppe* von Tettau arrived at the Divenow bridgehead on 12 March, four days after my report to the *Fuehrer*. General von Tettau brought with him about 20,000 soldiers of various units and approximately 30,000 refugees who, with their vehicles and carts, had attached themselves to this movement.)

On 7 March thirty-four Soviet tanks broke into the Divenow bridgehead in an attempt to seize the large bridge, defended primarily by Kriegsmarine personnel. These navy troops, well-trained in the use of the *Panzerfaust* and under command of Third Panzer Army's antitank officer, had neither anti-tank guns nor artillery but were solely equipped (aside from their *Panzerfausts*) with rifles and a few machine guns. Armed only with these inadequate weapons, they took up a fierce pursuit and knocked out thirty-three of the thirty-four tanks that had broken through. One Soviet tank, which had already reached the bridge across the tributary, was blown up together with the bridge.

Just prior to arriving at the *Fuehrer*'s bunker, General Mueller-Hillebrand, my chief of staff, reported that early on 8 March these same naval troops repulsed another attack against the bridgehead. The Russians never reached our positions, however, because the young sailors—greatly inspired by the previous day's victory—did not wait for the attack of the thirty-six advancing Soviet tanks, which were echeloned in width and depth. On the contrary, the Kriegsmarine troops jumped off and in disorganized though effective fashion attacked the rapidly firing armor from all sides. Regardless of their own losses, the sailors forged ahead until they were within *Panzerfaust* range. In a short time all thirty-six tanks were ablaze. Their death-defying courage and reliance on the *Panzerfaust* brought about another complete victory.

Some day, I have hoped, these episodes of unsurpassed heroism would go down in the annals of German history.

Conclusion of a Report . . . and a Career

I finished my narration with the words, "*Mein Fuehrer*, this report should clearly indicate that the commanders of both large and small units, as well as the troops—down to the individual soldier—have done everything in their power to withstand vastly superior Russian forces. They lacked neither ability, willingness, nor courage, but they did not possess superhuman strength. They all fought bravely and tenaciously, even when the situation was hopeless, for no one wanted to be guilty for the loss of German soil. In spite of being outnumbered from six to twenty times in manpower and equipment, the command and troops endured the utmost hardships in trying to avert a complete collapse of the front.

"It can be explained only in this way: that despite all the existing deficiencies, the front has now been firmly reestablished east of the Oder River, even to the extent of being able to launch a successful counterattack yesterday on the southern wing, where eighty-six Soviet tanks were knocked out, and we gained ground suitable for further stabilization of the defensive front.

"As a peculiarity of the Pomeranian battle, I can also report that of the 580 Russian tanks that have been knocked out to this moment, 380—or two-thirds—were destroyed by the *Panzerfaust*, that is, by the courage of the individual soldier. Never before has an army achieved so much success with the *Panzerfaust*.

"Therefore I can only express my complete appreciation to my commanders and all the troops of Third Panzer Army for the great courage and self-denial shown in the unbalanced struggle for Pomerania."

The *Fuehrer* and the others present were obviously impressed by my remarks but did not utter a word. I was dismissed by a trembling nod of Hitler's head. General of Panzer Troops Hasso von Manteuffel arrived the next day [9 March] at my headquarters in Stettin with a *Fuehrer* order requiring me to hand over command to him and transferring me to the officers' reserve pool.

That was the end of my forty-year military career.

A few days later, *Reichsfuehrer* Himmler was also relieved of command of Army Group Vistula.

Chapter 14

FINAL THOUGHTS OF A SOLDIER

Combat Orders

DIFFICULT COMBAT MISSIONS IN unusual situations can be carried out only by units imbued with exceptional courage and under the leadership of commanders and subordinate commanders who have been trained to take the initiative in keeping with the task assigned. Often, neither the commander of a combined-arms *Kampfgruppe* nor any of his subordinate officers may ever receive or issue even a single written order, because constant surprises and the fluctuations of battle make it impossible to follow the customary procedures for issuing commands. There may be neither the time to draw up written orders nor the possibility of delivering them safely to subordinates through all the turmoil of battle. Thus the principle of encouraging "all levels of command to act on their own initiative" and of issuing orders by word of mouth is an absolute necessity, particularly when conducting orders with mechanized units.

At this point I wish to offer some basic rules concerning oral commands and describe the manner in which they should be handled:

The smaller the unit, the more frequently its orders will be issued orally; as a general practice, from the platoon level down I never gave written orders. There were some exceptions in the case of isolated small groups with independent missions, but as the war progressed the practice of issuing oral commands was adopted even by medium and large units in ever-increasing measure. Almost always such orders consisted of a brief summary of the conclusions reached during a conference held with the subordinate commanders in the terrain adjoining the front, or in exceptional cases concerned the outcome of a conference held at high command level with the aid of maps. Such an order was binding and made it possible for the subordinate units to take all necessary measures for its execution without delay. The conference itself, for purposes of expediency, was attended only by those who were to execute the order, their technical assistants, and arms specialists and offered the opportunity to clarify details in connection with the order's execution, as well as to make it possible to consider special requests and resolve misunderstandings. The subsequently issued written order briefly summarized the most important points. It served primarily as a reminder and in most cases ended up as a supplement to the unit war diary. This procedure proved quite successful wherever time allowed and the responsible commander approved the use of it, which was usually the case. Consequently this practice of oral tactical orders became the established rule and corresponded to the principle that command must adapt to ever-changing conditions at the front. What mattered most was not the proximity of headquarters, with its frequently large staff, numerous vehicles, and abundant equipment, but the presence of a commander as the single mind to give orders, make decisions, and take full responsibility.

Tactical orders, as a rule, were not transmitted by telephone or radio, with the exception of operational orders to panzer and other mobile units in the march or in combat, when the rapidly changing situation made it unlikely that Russian interception of our radio messages would have any detrimental effect. By placing radio trucks at least at the head, center, and end of each column it was possible constantly to control the movement of troops and effect changes of direction during the march. In this way it became possible, as during 6th Panzer Division's march through the swampy forests toward the Luga River, to determine quickly the exact point and cause of any road jams and to take corrective action immediately. Without such an expedient the column would have been scattered, would not have arrived at its destination in time (if at all), and certainly would not have arrived at full fighting strength.

I also wish to add a few words with regard to the specific technique of issuing verbal commands. Every order, including the ones given orally, should be brief and explicit. It should convey only essential information and be comprehensible to everyone. Verbosity should be avoided, just as much as speaking too briefly. Furthermore, it is necessary to discriminate and take into account whether the order is being given to an intelligent, well-spoken individual or an inexperienced, plain soldier. As a matter of principle, every verbal order, or at least the gist of it, should be repeated back by the person to whom it is given. Important oral orders should afterward also be set down in writing and subsequently transmitted to the one to whom it has been given by word of mouth. The person issuing the order must know exactly what he intends to say and whether or not his order can in fact be carried out.

Map entries or simple sketches are valuable aids in conjunction with both written and verbal orders. They quickly enable the person receiving the order to understand the situation, help him visualize his task, and make it unnecessary to use too many words. This method proved particularly effective whenever we were called upon to commit a newly arrived unit immediately (and this was frequently the case, especially as far as panzer and other mobile units were concerned).

Tactical Lessons from Winter Warfare

Even during severe winter weather it will be possible for a unit equipped with warm clothing to conduct decisive operations. These troops are, however, as they are during every other season, dependent for their success upon the cooperation of heavy weapons (tanks, assault guns, artillery, antitank and flak guns, etc.) as well as the support of combat aircraft. Nevertheless, winter campaigns are exceptionally difficult and require particularly thorough preparations and a firm conduct of operations. In this connection the coordination of all weapons and tactical commanders assumes decisive importance, and the secure functioning of communications facilities of every description between tactical commanders and the fire controllers of heavy weapons and air support is just as essential as the reliable liaison between the fire controllers and the attacking spearheads.

In view of the fact that the heavy weapons are indispensable, but at the same time necessarily confined to roads, the choice of the direction of the assault and points of main effort will generally be determined by these roads. It is critical to establish a roadway through the snow-covered and mined no-man's land just as soon as that terrain has been crossed by the attacking infantry. Should this not occur, the infantry troops, being separated from their supporting weapons too long, run the risk of being stranded.

Enemy troops handicapped by ammunition shortages can be conquered even by numerically weak forces who are equipped with heavy weapons and sufficient ammunition.

Commanders and troops who are to be committed for operations under difficult conditions—especially in the winter—in a theater of war with which they are not familiar should be retrained promptly on arrival in the area of operations in order to prevent tactical failures and heavy losses.

Maintaining Combat Efficiency

Delays in the arrival of replacements occurred very early in the Russian campaign, and the combat strength of some infantry companies often dropped to unbearably low levels. The first stopgap measure to be introduced was to screen all service and supply units for men who were fit for front-line duty. When these units were no longer in a position to provide suitable men, commanders had to call upon others with little or no training. They were transferred to the infantry as long as they could somehow meet the physical requirements. Since proper training facilities were rarely available, the combat efficiency of front-line units suffered considerably when such replacements were employed. Another expedient was to form rifle companies with surplus personnel from artillery, antitank, or panzer units that had lost their equipment and to commit them as infantry.

Many artillery and signal units were forced to release officers and NCOs to the infantry, and these branches soon became short of technicians and leaders. Any further transfers were therefore out of the question. In such instances the infantry units short of the minimum number of leaders had to be merged. The personnel and training situation of the field forces improved only after each division was assigned its own *Feldersatz* [field replacement and training] battalion, which guaranteed a satisfactory flow of replacements. During position warfare the divisions in the field were able to raise their training standards by organizing a variety of courses, but the shortage of combat units frequently forced commanders to commit these *Feldersatz* battalions as temporary combat units. During the last stages of the war, training and replacement divisions of the various armies, as well as army service schools, were often called into action in emergencies. As a result, training organizations that had been built up under great difficulties were repeatedly torn apart and destroyed.

Maintaining the combat efficiency of the infantry divisions despite their continuous commitment and the impossibility of relieving entire divisions presented a special problem. When the fighting raged with full fury for several consecutive weeks, it proved impossible to relieve the front-line units by reserves because the situation usually was too critical. Only too often our troops were forced to keep fighting until completely exhausted. In order to have at least some small, but well-rested, assault detachments available, the line units alternated in withdrawing a small number of soldiers from the thick of the fighting to give them two or three days' rest behind the lines. For the same purpose, headquarters and higher echelon supply personnel up to and including army staffs were committed at the front in rotation.

Since transportation to and from the Zone of the Interior was often disrupted, leaves and furloughs had to be frozen for long periods. Whenever the tactical situation permitted, armies, corps, and divisions established rest camps for the men who were due furloughs. These camps proved invaluable in maintaining the combat efficiency and morale of the troops. Another improvisation was the introduction of so-called sponsorships at higher head-quarters. Certain staff officers maintained constant personal contact with specific combat units and took them under their wings. Moreover, up to 10 percent of the personnel assigned to headquarters staffs rotated with their comrades at the front to allow them to go on leave or to a rest camp. These measures were of benefit to the troops and improved the relationship between headquarters staffs and combat units.

Rehabilitation units also proved to be a very successful improvisation. Soldiers who had been sentenced to serve extended prison terms, but who showed promise of reforming, were not relieved of front-line duty but put on parole and transferred to improvised rehabilitation platoons, companies, or battalions. These were committed at critical points of the front. The reha-bilitation units had particularly efficient officers and NCOs and usually gave a good account of themselves. This very effective improvisation soon became a permanent institution, which received unanimous approval and was ac-cepted as a good solution not only by the prisoners but also by the officers to whose units they were assigned. In 1944 Rehabilitation Battalion 500 fought exceptionally well at Ternopol in eastern Galicia. When the town fell, a number of NCOs and men from this battalion fought their way back to their own lines under great hazards and hardships.

The organization of indigenous units was another improvisation designed to strengthen German fighting power. Such units were organized in occupied territories and friendly countries, especially by the Waffen SS. They relieved German units of minor duties and were also frequently committed as com-bat units. Their performance at the front was far below the standards of our own troops. For this reason the front-line troops usually objected to the employment of indigenous units in their sectors. On the other hand, many volunteers from POW camps were employed as auxiliaries to replace soldiers transferred from supply and service units, and in general they proved to be both dependable and useful.

Late in the war, when few or no replacements were available, all divisions in the field had to use some of their service troops to form *Alarmeinheiten* (emergency alert units). These were originally intended for the defense of strongpoints in towns in the rear areas or as security detachments for rear positions; but frequently the *Alarmeinheiten* had to be committed in the front lines to close a gap and sometimes even for the purpose of local coun-terattacks.

As another emergency measure, convalescent furloughs granted to sick or wounded soldiers were severely curtailed in order to shorten all periods of absence from the front. But since it was obvious that combat units could use only fully recovered men, most local military authorities failed to comply with such regulations. They also showed great reluctance in carrying out another order that pertained to the induction of men in advanced age groups who were also affected by the draft because the age limit had been raised. It was universally felt that these older men ought to remain in their civilian occupations, where they would be able to serve the nation much better than as soldiers.

Why Was the Russian Campaign Lost?

Despite Russia and the Russian soldier, despite cold and mud, despite inadequate equipment and a virtually ridiculous numerical inferiority, the German soldier actually had a victory over the Soviet Union within his grasp.

Why then did Germany lose the war?

The dynamic offensives executed by the German army during the first two years of the Russian campaign ground to a halt in front of Moscow and at Stalingrad. During the following months of bitter struggle against a tenacious enemy who cleverly exploited the vast space and climatic conditions of his homeland, our strength declined so far that the subsequent Russian counteroffensive could no longer be repulsed. It was Hitler's worst mistake not to have recognized the impending disaster in time or—if he did recognize it—to have dismissed it in his peremptory manner. This obstinate denial of the obvious forced the German army to fight a series of defensive actions against breakthroughs along overextended front lines during the final years of the campaign. Each time our troops succeeded, after extreme sacrifices, in closing one gap, the line gave way at another point. The disintegration of our forces then speeded up as individual corps, and even entire armies, under orders to hold critical cities and areas, were cut off from the main front. The perfection of defensive tactics and the superhuman efforts of the field forces were insufficient to turn the tide as long as we were unable to restore the balance of strength essential for an eventual victory over the Red Army. Under the prevailing circumstances an equilibrium in the fields of manpower and equipment was beyond expectation, but it was within the realm of possibility that our overall military performance would first equal and then outdistance that of the Russians. As a prerequisite, German potential should have been brought into the proper relationship with the elements of time and space to compensate for the Soviet superiority in manpower and equipment, allowing victory to be achieved through the application of superior strategy. At no time should the German army have expended its strength as recklessly as Hitler required it to do in front of Moscow and at Stalingrad. Contrary to Hitler's concepts, a timely halt in the offensive or a temporary withdrawal would not have undermined the confidence of the field forces but would have led to additional successes, the sum total of which might have brought the war against the Soviet Union to a favorable conclusion.

After Stalingrad, we fought delaying actions along a 1,600-kilometer front for four months. Even then, under the leadership of Field Marshal von Manstein, we succeeded in sealing off the wide gaps and stabilizing the front enough to achieve a major defensive victory by March 1943. The enemy had broken through the German front, but eleven panzer divisions assembled in the Kharkov-Poltava area were able to frustrate Soviet intentions by a determined counterattack. Even so, the time had not come to seize the initiative. The Red Army still had to suffer heavier casualties—if necessary we should have abandoned more terrain and shortened our lines to establish a balance of strength to prevent other breakthroughs. Only then could a decisive counteroffensive have ensured a victory in Russia before the Allies landed in France. Defeat of the Western powers was contingent upon the Soviet Union being driven out of the war.

Thus in 1943 the German army in Russia almost succeeded in putting an end to Soviet breakthroughs by adroitly combining various defensive tactics. Victory was once again in the offing, but it turned out to be a Russian one. Our eleven panzer divisions—reconstituted during a lull lasting three months—could not come to grips with the Red Army's reserves to annihilate them because Hitler threw all of the German armor into Operation Citadel in July 1943 and bled it white upon running into a fortified system of hitherto unknown strength and depth. Hitler thereby fulfilled Stalin's keenest hopes and presented him with the palm of victory. The subsequent Soviet counteroffensive, conducted with powerful reserves that were fully intact, broke through our lines. The enemy breakthroughs occurred not only in Army Group South's sector but also in others, where there were likewise no adequate reserves available.

At best, skillful defensive tactics and supreme personal sacrifices were instrumental in producing local, temporary relief. The magnitude of our losses prohibited the possibility of stabilizing the front along a line that by then had been forcibly shortened in the course of events. Finally, a suggestion to shift all German forces from the West to the East in order to stop the Red Army's invasion of Germany and prevent the territorial expansion of communism was turned down by Hitler. While he believed his principal enemies to be in the West, Germany's military leaders, for all their antagonism toward the Western powers, considered Russia their irreconcilable enemy.

APPENDIX: THE LIFE AND CAREER OF ERHARD RAUS

8 January 1889: Born in Wolframitz, Moravia, to Hubert and Josefa Raus; baptized in the Roman Catholic faith on 12 January.

1 October 1905: Enters Austro-Hungarian Army's Infantry Cadet School at Koenigsfeld.

18 August 1909: Commissioned as officer aspirant in Infantry Regiment 1 in Troppau; serves as platoon commander in various units from 1909 to 1914.

1 May 1912: Promoted to lieutenant.

6 August 1914: Enters World War I as platoon commander in Bicycle Light-Infantry Battalion 1; during 1914 fights at Lublin and Beskiden.

1 January 1915: Promoted to first lieutenant; during 1915 fights at Limanova, Gorlice, the Isonzo River, and Mt. Piano.

6 February 1915: Awarded Bronze Military Defense Medal of the Military Defense Cross with War Decoration and Swords.

5 October 1915: Awarded Military Defense Cross, 3rd Class, with War Decoration and Swords.

1 February 1916: Appointed battalion adjutant, Bicycle Light-Infantry Battalion 1; during 1916 fights at Val Sugano, Col de Lana, Mt. Adamello, and in the offensive into southern Tyrolia.

15 March 1917: Awarded Charles Troop Cross; during 1917 fights at Fleimstal, Asticotal, Mt. Meletta, and Col del Rosso.

2 July 1917: Awarded Silver Defense Medal of the Military Defense Cross with War Decoration and Swords.

15 September 1917: Appointed acting commander, Bicycle Company, Light-Infantry Battalion 20.

20 November 1917: Confirmed as permanent commander, Bicycle Company, Light-Infantry Battalion 20.

1 February 1918: Promoted to captain; during 1918 fights at Piave River.

16 March 1918: Awarded Iron Crown, 3rd Class, with War Decoration and Swords.

19 June 1918: Appointed acting commander, Bicycle Light-Infantry Battalion 1.

17 August 1918: Marries Anna Morsani, the twenty-five-year-old Roman Catholic daughter of a school principal in Trieste.

18 January 1919: Selected for retention in the Austrian Army; appointed deputy to the commander of bicycle-troop reserves.

6 May 1920: Attached as adjutant, Bicycle Light-Infantry Battalion 2; appointment becomes permanent on 1 May 1921.

8 July 1921: Brevetted major.

1 October 1922: Attached as infantry-training specialist to Detachment 4 (bicycle and machine-gun troops), Austrian Army Ministry.

1 March 1923: Appointed staff captain.

1 May 1924–15 September 1932: Beginning with appointment as instructor, Infantry Course at Bruckneudorf, holds a series of training posts and attends General Staff training.

19 November 1924: Anna Raus gives birth to Isa Raus.

1 January 1927: Promoted to major.

9 March 1931: Awarded Hungarian War Service Medal.

15 September 1932: Appointed to the General Staff; attached to Infantry School.

2 December 1932: Attached for three months to Detachment 2 (Training) in the Austrian War Ministry.

15 May 1933: Awarded Austrian War Service Medal with Swords.

10 June 1933: Promoted to lieutenant colonel (note that this date of rank will be modified in the *Anschluss* in 1938; see below).

1 September 1933: Tactical instructor, Infantry School, Vienna.

21 April 1934: Awarded Silver Honors Badge for actions during the "February Uprising" in Vienna.

1 September 1934: Commander, Infantry School, Bruck.

8 October 1934: Awarded Military Service Badge, 2nd Class.

19 December 1936: Promoted to colonel (note that this date of rank will be modified in the *Anschluss* in 1938; see below).

1 November 1937: Appointed to post in Austrian Defense Ministry.

25 January 1938: Appointed military attaché for Italy and Albania, with office in Rome.

13 March 1938: *Anschluss* of Austria and Germany.

21 March 1938: Takes military oath to join Wehrmacht.

25 March 1938: Appointed as Austrian liaison officer to German Eighth Army.

1 April 1938: Attached to the staff of Army Group Command 5 (Vienna).

25 May–28 June 1938: Acting commander, Infantry Training Regiment (which later becomes Infantry Regiment 50).

27 July 1938: Assigned rank as lieutenant colonel with seniority from 1 August 1936 (67C) in German army.

1 August 1938: Appointed to the staff of Army Group Command 5 (Vienna).

15 August 1938: Assigned rank as colonel with seniority from 19 December 1936 in Germany army (but this is modified in 1939; see below).

10 November 1938: Appointed as officer on special assignment to General of Infantry Wilhelm von List, Commander, Army Group Command 5 (Vienna).

20 April 1939: Seniority as colonel in German army reduced from 19 December 1936 to 1 August 1937 (26B).

20 April 1939: Appointed chief of staff to Wehrkreis XVII and XVII Corps.

1 December 1939: Awarded Honors Decorations, 4th through 1st Classes, dated to 1 January 1939.

26 June 1940: Appointed commander, Infantry Regiment 243, 60th Infantry Division.

25 July 1940: Appointed commander, Motorized Infantry Regiment 4, 6th Panzer Division.

30 November 1940: Awarded War Service Cross, 2nd Class.

11 March 1941: Declared "fit for duty in the tropics" by Army Personnel Office.

1 May 1941: Appointed commander, 6th Motorized Brigade, 6th Panzer Division.

29 June 1941: Awarded Iron Cross, 2nd Class, for actions at Raseinai and in early advance of 6th Panzer Division into the Baltic states.

6 July 1941: Awarded Iron Cross, 1st Class, for actions in the piercing of the "Stalin Line."

14 August 1941: Promoted major general with seniority from 1 September 1941 (17).

1 September 1941: Awarded Armored Combat Badge.

7 September 1941: Appointed acting commander, 6th Panzer Division. Note that even though Major General Franz Landgraf technically remained the commander of the division until 15 April 1942, Raus is functionally in command throughout most of the next seven and a half months. Landgraf appears to have served as deputy commander and/or officer on special assignment to XLI Panzer Corps during this period.

11 October 1941: Awarded Knight's Cross for defense of the Luga River bridgehead.

29 April 1942: Appointed commander, 6th Panzer Division.

1 August 1942: Awarded Eastern Campaign Medal.

21 January 1943: Promoted to lieutenant general with seniority from 1 January 1943 (18).

14 February 1943: Awarded German Cross in Gold.

7 February 1943: Attached on special assignment to Army Group Don.

10 February 1943: Appointed acting commander of Provisional Corps Cramer (which is redesignated Provisional Corps Raus on 30 March 1943).

20 April 1943: Promoted to general of panzer troops with seniority from 1 May 1943 (5).

10 May 1943: Appointed acting commander of XI Corps, which is the new designation of Provisional Corps Raus.

20 July 1943: Appointed commander, XI Corps.

22 August 1943: Awarded Oak Leaves to the Knight's Cross for defensive fighting from Belgorod to Kharkov during August.

5 November–30 November 1943: Appointed commander, XLVII Panzer Corps.

26 November 1943: Attached on special assignment to Fourth Panzer Army.

30 November 1943: Appointed deputy commander, Fourth Panzer Army.

10 December 1943: Appointed acting commander, Fourth Panzer Army.

14 March 1944: Appointed commander, Fourth Panzer Army.

21 April 1944: Appointed acting commander, First Panzer Army, in the absence of Colonel General Hans Hube; General of Panzer Troops Walter Nehring assumes acting command of Fourth Panzer Army.

18 May 1944: Appointed commander, First Panzer Army.

July–August 1944: Appointed commander, *Armeegruppe* Raus (First Panzer Army with First Hungarian Army and Slovakian Army subordinated).

16 August 1944: Appointed commander, 3rd Panzer Army.

20 September 1944: Promoted colonel general (with seniority from 15 August 1944).

10 March 1945: Relieved of command of Third Panzer Army and placed in reserve status.

14 May 1945–30 June 1947: Allied prisoner of war.

3 April 1956: Died in Vienna General Hospital.

Erhard Raus spoke Italian with fluency, spoke Czech and Slovenian well, and had some command of French.

INDEX